Ensuring Safe Foods and Medical Products Through Stronger Regulatory Systems Abroad

Committee on Strengthening Core Elements of Regulatory Systems in Developing Countries

Board on Global Health and the Board on Health Science Policy

Jim E. Riviere and Gillian J. Buckley, *Editors*

INSTITUTE OF MEDICINE
OF THE NATIONAL ACADEMIES

THE NATIONAL ACADEMIES PRESS
Washington, D.C.
www.nap.edu

PREPUBLICATION COPY: UNCORRECTED PROOFS

THE NATIONAL ACADEMIES PRESS 500 Fifth Street, NW Washington, DC 20001

NOTICE: The project that is the subject of this report was approved by the Governing Board of the National Research Council, whose members are drawn from the councils of the National Academy of Sciences, the National Academy of Engineering, and the Institute of Medicine. The members of the committee responsible for the report were chosen for their special competences and with regard for appropriate balance.

This study was supported by Contract No. HHSF22301015T, TO #18 between the National Academy of Sciences and the U.S. Food and Drug Administration. Any opinions, findings, conclusions, or recommendations expressed in this publication are those of the author(s) and do not necessarily reflect the view of the organizations or agencies that provided support for this project.

International Standard Book Number 0-309-XXXXX-X (Book)
International Standard Book Number 0-309-XXXXX-X (PDF)

Additional copies of this report are available from the National Academies Press, 500 Fifth Street, NW, Keck 360, Washington, DC 20001; (800) 624-6242 or (202) 334-3313; http://www.nap.edu.

For more information about the Institute of Medicine, visit the IOM home page at: **www.iom.edu.**

Printed in the United States of America

The serpent has been a symbol of long life, healing, and knowledge among almost all cultures and religions since the beginning of recorded history. The serpent adopted as a logotype by the Institute of Medicine is a relief carving from ancient Greece, now held by the Staatliche Museen in Berlin.

Suggested citation: IOM (Institute of Medicine). 2012. *Ensuring Safe Foods and Medical Products Through Stronger Regulatory Systems Abroad.* Washington, DC: The National Academies Press.

Photo credits:
Front cover
©2007 Natalie Moraru, Courtesy of Photoshare
Back cover, from top to bottom
© 2009 Joydeep Mukherjee, Courtesy of Photoshare
© 2006 Morgan Rog, Courtesy of Photoshare
© 2009 Wendy Leonard, Courtesy of Photoshare

"Knowing is not enough; we must apply.
Willing is not enough; we must do."
—Goethe

INSTITUTE OF MEDICINE
OF THE NATIONAL ACADEMIES

Advising the Nation. Improving Health.

THE NATIONAL ACADEMIES

Advisers to the Nation on Science, Engineering, and Medicine

The **National Academy of Sciences** is a private, nonprofit, self-perpetuating society of distinguished scholars engaged in scientific and engineering research, dedicated to the furtherance of science and technology and to their use for the general welfare. Upon the authority of the charter granted to it by the Congress in 1863, the Academy has a mandate that requires it to advise the federal government on scientific and technical matters. Dr. Ralph J. Cicerone is president of the National Academy of Sciences.

The **National Academy of Engineering** was established in 1964, under the charter of the National Academy of Sciences, as a parallel organization of outstanding engineers. It is autonomous in its administration and in the selection of its members, sharing with the National Academy of Sciences the responsibility for advising the federal government. The National Academy of Engineering also sponsors engineering programs aimed at meeting national needs, encourages education and research, and recognizes the superior achievements of engineers. Dr. Charles M. Vest is president of the National Academy of Engineering.

The **Institute of Medicine** was established in 1970 by the National Academy of Sciences to secure the services of eminent members of appropriate professions in the examination of policy matters pertaining to the health of the public. The Institute acts under the responsibility given to the National Academy of Sciences by its congressional charter to be an adviser to the federal government and, upon its own initiative, to identify issues of medical care, research, and education. Dr. Harvey V. Fineberg is president of the Institute of Medicine.

The **National Research Council** was organized by the National Academy of Sciences in 1916 to associate the broad community of science and technology with the Academy's purposes of furthering knowledge and advising the federal government. Functioning in accordance with general policies determined by the Academy, the Council has become the principal operating agency of both the National Academy of Sciences and the National Academy of Engineering in providing services to the government, the public, and the scientific and engineering communities. The Council is administered jointly by both Academies and the Institute of Medicine. Dr. Ralph J. Cicerone and Dr. Charles M. Vest are chair and vice chair, respectively, of the National Research Council.

www.national-academies.org

COMMITTEE ON STRENGTHENING CORE ELEMENTS OF REGULATORY SYSTEMS IN DEVELOPING COUNTRIES

JIM E. RIVIERE (*Chair*), Burroughs Wellcome Fund Distinguished Professor of Pharmacology; Director, Center for Chemical Toxicology Research and Pharmacokinetics, College of Veterinary Medicine, North Carolina State University, Raleigh, NC
THOMAS BOLLYKY, Senior Fellow, Global Health, Economics, and Development, Council on Foreign Relations, Washington, DC
CORRIE BROWN, Josiah Meigs Distinguished Teaching Professor, Department of Veterinary Pathology, College of Veterinary Medicine, University of Georgia, Athens
MARTHA BRUMFIELD, President, Martha A. Brumfield, LLC, New York, NY
ROBERT BUCHANAN, Professor and Director, Center for Food Safety and Security Systems, University of Maryland, College Park
JAKE YUE CHEN, Director, Indiana Center for Systems Biology and Personalized Medicine; Associate Professor, IUPUI School of Informatics, Indianapolis
JUNSHI CHEN, Senior Research Professor, Chinese Center for Disease Control and Prevention, Beijing
JANE HENNEY, Professor of Medicine, University of Cincinnati, Ohio
CARLOS M. MOREL, Director, Center for Technological Development in Health, Oswaldo Cruz Foundation (Fiocruz), Rio de Janeiro, Brazil
CLARE NARROD, Research Scientist and Risk Analysis Program Manager, University of Maryland, Joint Institute for Food Safety and Applied Nutrition, College Park, MD
ANDY STERGACHIS, Professor, Departments of Epidemiology and Global Health; Adjunct Professor, Departments of Pharmacy and Health Sciences; Director, Global Medicines Program, School of Public Health, University of Washington, Seattle
PRASHANT YADAV, Director, Healthcare Research, William Davidson Institute, University of Michigan, Ann Arbor

Consultants

HOWARD A. ZUCKER, Pediatric Cardiac Anesthesiologist, Albert Einstein College of Medicine; Senior Advisor, Division of Global Health and Human Rights, Massachusetts General Hospital
NOEL GREIS, Director, Center for Logistics and Digital Strategy; Co-Director, UNC-Tsinghua Center for Logistics and Enterprise Development, Kenan Institute of Private Enterprise, Kenan-Flagler Business School, University of North Carolina at Chapel Hill

Staff

GILLIAN BUCKLEY, Program Officer, Study Director
PATRICIA CUFF, Senior Program Officer
ANNE CLAIBORNE, Senior Program Officer
KENISHA PETERS, Research Associate
RACHEL TAYLOR, Research Associate
MEGAN GINIVAN, Research Assistant
KATHLEEN BURNS, Intern (January-February 2012)
GAELAN RITTER, Intern (January-May 2011)
ELIZABETH WELLS, Intern (June-August 2011)
YING ZHANG, Intern (December 2010-December 2011)
JULIE WILTSHIRE, Financial Associate
PATRICK W. KELLEY, Director, Boards on Global Health and African Science Academy Development

REVIEWERS

This report has been reviewed in draft form by individuals chosen for their diverse perspectives and technical expertise, in accordance with procedures approved by the National Research Council's Report Review Committee. The purpose of this independent review is to provide candid and critical comments that will assist the institution in making its published report as sound as possible and to ensure that the report meets institutional standards for objectivity, evidence, and responsiveness to the study charge. The review comments and draft manuscript remain confidential to protect the integrity of the deliberative process. We wish to thank the following individuals for their review of this report:

Bonnie Buntain, University of Calgary, Faculty of Veterinary Medicine
Stephen R. Byrn, Purdue University, Department of Industrial and Physical Pharmacy
Chi-Wan Chen, Pfizer Inc., Global CMC
Cyprian Devine-Perez, New York University, Langone Medical Center
Linda Dimitropoulos, RTI International
David Fidler, Indiana University Maurer School of Law
Katherine A. High, University of Pennsylvania School of Medicine, Howard Hughes Medical Institute; Center for Cellular and Molecular Therapeutics, The Children's Hospital of Philadelphia
Ann Marie Kimball, Bill & Melinda Gates Foundation
John E. Lamb, Abt Associates Inc., International Economic Growth Division
Glenn Morris, University of Florida, Emerging Pathogens Institute
Donald W. Schaffner, Rutgers, the State University of New Jersey, Department of Food Science
Christine L. Taylor, National Institutes of Health, Office of Dietary Supplements
Liz Wagstrom, National Pork Producers Council
Richard Whiting, Exponent, Inc., Chemical Regulation and Food Safety Center

Although the reviewers listed above have provided many constructive comments and suggestions, they were not asked to endorse the conclusions or recommendations, nor did they see the final draft of the report before its release. The review of this report was overseen by **Marla E. Salmon,** Dean and Professor, School of Nursing, University of Washington; and **Johanna T. Dwyer,** Professor, School of Medicine and Friedman school of Nutrition Science & Policy, Tufts University. Appointed by the National Research Council and the Institute of Medicine, they were responsible for making certain that an independent examination of this report was carried out in accordance with institutional procedures and that all review comments were carefully considered. Responsibility for the final content of this report rests entirely with the authoring committee and the institution.

Foreword

A very high proportion of the seafood we eat comes from abroad, mainly from China and southeast Asia. Most of the active ingredients in medicines we take originate in other countries. A substantial share of the produce we consume is grown in Latin America. Many low- and middle-income countries have lower labor costs and fewer and less stringent environmental regulations than the U.S., making them attractive places to produce food and chemical ingredients for export. The diversity and scale of imports makes it impractical for FDA border inspections to be sufficient to ensure product purity and safety, and incidents such as American deaths due to adulterated heparin imported from China propelled the problem to public awareness. Beyond manufacturing shortcuts, substitutes, and errors, the American food and drug supply can be a potential means for intentional harm, and the risk of terrorism intensifies the need for high levels of interagency collaboration across the FDA, Centers for Disease Control and Prevention, Department of Agriculture, and Department of Homeland Security.

Domestic programs, however, regardless of how well they are coordinated, will not be sufficient for the task. The integrated global economy demands cooperation across borders—to thwart terrorists, reduce environmental hazards, and ensure that our food and medical products are safe and effective. This requires coordination across both industrialized trading partners and emerging economies that have not had the benefit of decades of legal and technical development to ensure the safety of food and medical products.

The IOM *Committee on Strengthening Core Elements of Regulatory Systems in Developing Countries* took up the vital task of helping the FDA to cope with the reality that so much of the food, drugs, biologics, and medical products consumed in the United States originate in countries with less robust regulatory systems. This report describes ways the U.S. can help strengthen regulatory systems in low- and middle-income countries and promote cross-border partnerships—including government, industry and academia—to foster regulatory science and build a core of regulatory professionals. The committee's report emphasizes an array of practical approaches to ensure sound regulatory practices in today's inter-connected world.

I am very grateful to the committee and to the staff who developed this report and hope that the insights, ideas, and recommendations offered here will enable residents in the U.S. and in other countries to benefit from safer food and medicine.

Harvey V. Fineberg, M.D., Ph.D.
President, Institute of Medicine

Acknowledgments

This report is a product of the cooperation and contributions of many people. The committee and staff are especially grateful to Anton Bandy, Jim Banihashemi, Laura DeStefano, Sarah Ziegenhorn, Vilija Teel, and Joel Wu of the Institute of Medicine (IOM). We also thank Linda Meyers and Maria Oria of the IOM Food and Nutrition Board for their advice. We also appreciate the contributions of Bill McLeod of the National Academies and Elisabeth Reese of the National Research Council made to this report.

The committee's overseas workshops went smoothly thanks to the warm hospitality of the Chinese Academy of Engineering, especially Yuan Min; the University of São Paulo School of Public Health, especially Viviane Jaremcrusk, Helena Ribeiro, and Carolina Cavanha de Azeredo Santos; the Academy of Science of South Africa, especially Roseanne Diab, Lebo Makgae, Phakamile Truth Mngadi, and Nthabiseng Toale; and the Public Health Foundation of India, especially Ramanan Laxminarayan, Srinath Reddy, Geetha Ramesh, Sunita Ramesh, and Susmita Roy.

Hongtao Ren of the Chinese Embassy and Debapriya Dutta of the Indian Embassy helped the committee and staff plan their travel in China and India respectively. The following Food and Drug Administation (FDA) foreign staff also worked tirelessly to help the committee and IOM staff prepare for their overseas workshops: Beverly Corey, Dennis Doupnik, Zimei (Mandy) Fu, Christopher Hickey, WeiHua (Evid) Liu, Ana Maria Osorio, Bruce Ross Brenda Uratani, and Lixia Wang.

Many people kindly introduced the IOM staff to key speakers. They are particularly grateful to Bob Baker, Dai Ellis, Michael Gropp, Mat Heyman, Paul Young, and Chen Zu.

The committee thanks all the speakers and moderators who participated in committee meetings, as well as others who provided information, input, and assistance. They include: Elaine Alexander, Claudio Poblete Amaro, Deborah Autor, Vani Bhambri Arora, Sunil Bahl, K.A. Balaji, Shabir Banoo, Sarah Barber, Sameer Barde, Arthur Bird, Carl-Maria Bohny, Kate Bond, James Browder, Regina Brown, Irene Chan, Wen Chang, Philip Chen, Gary Cheng, Jiayi Cheng, Qian Cheng, Nicholas Crisp, Robert Crookes, Sanjay Dave, Raymonde De Vries, Jose Luis Di Fabio, Ke Ding, Jagdish Dore, Albinus D'Sa, Raymond Dugas, Peter Karim Ben Embarek, Ernesto Enriquez, Gao Fang, Gerd Fleischer, Bernadette Franco, Xiao Geng, Débora Germano, Marc Gilkey, Carlos Alberto Goulart, Zhai Peng Gui, Rosane Cuber Guimarães, Qingwu Guo, Margaret Hamburg, Moazzem Hossain, Yinglian Hu, Rong Xiao Hua, Dennis Hudson, Ekopimo Okon Ibia, Anil Jauhri, Ghazala Javed, Arun Jha, Ding Jianhua, Zhang Jinghua, Loveleen Johri, Abhay Kadam, Greg Kalbaugh, Jincheng Kang, Sangeeta Kaul, Bi Kexin, C.B. Kotak, Don Kraemer, Michael Kravchuk, Pramod Kumar, Celestine Kumire, Hector Lazaneo, Li Lei, Sun Lei, David Leishman, Henry Leng, Yu Li, Derick Litthauer, Benny Liu, Patrick Lukulay, Mac Lumpkin, Maeve Magner, Onika Vig Mahajan, Lebo Makgae, Daniel Matlala Malose, R.M. Mandlik, Karen Midthun, Yuan Min, Henri A. Minnaar, Bejon Misra, M. Mitra, Neeraj Mohan, Lauro Moretto, Sana Mostaghim, Guo Nan, Kirti Narsai, Margareth Ndomondo-Sigonda, Skhumbuzo Ngozwana, Thanh Nguyen, Sergio Nishioka, Sarah Olembo, Adriana Valenzuela Palma, Janardan Panday, Ana Marisa Cordero Peña, Michael S. Pepper, Sylvia Pereira, Xu Yan Ping, Teizhinha de Jeusus Andreolli Pinto, Manuel Neto Pinto, Ajay Pitre, Amanda Poldi, Devendra Prasad, Rajeev

Raizada, Raquel Ramilo, Ailton José Rebelo, Mike Robach, Chen Rui, S.K. Saxena, Nirupa Sen, D.G. Shah, Zuo Shuyan, Sarah Simons, G.N. Singh, Jasvir Singh, Ritambhara Singh, Rajinder Sood, Renato Spindel, John T. Sproul, Nick Starke, Gavin Steel, Marco Antonio Stephano, Silvia Storpirtis, Wei Sun, Pramod Swaich, Marta Taniwaki, Asit Tripathy, Pieter Truter, Mary Lou Valdez, Tarun Vij, Amelia Villar, Tanya Vogt, Liz Wagstrom, Sun Wei, Raymond Wigenge, Haiyan Xu, Lily Xu, Guo Xueping, Alice Yang, Steve Yang, Zhang Yi, Ji Yingping, Ma Yong, Worasuda Yoongthong, Li Yu, Penggui Zai, Jainkang (Jack) Zhang, Libin Zhao, Qiang Zheng, and Janette Zhou.

The committee and staff thank U.S. Food and Drug Administration for generously funding this study.

Acronyms and Abbreviations

ADR	adverse drug reaction
AFDO	Association of Food and Drug Officials
AMRH	African Medicines Regulatory Harmonization
Anvisa	National Health Surveillance Agency (Brazil)
AOAC	Association of Official Analytic Communities
APEC	Asia Pacific Economic Cooperation
APEDA	Agricultural and Processed Food Products Export Authority
API	active pharmaceutical ingredient
ASEAN	Association of Southeast Asian Nations
AUIBAR	African Union Interafrican Bureau for Animal Resources
BIO	Biotechnology Industry Organization
CDC	Centers for Disease Control and Prevention
CDSCO	Central Drugs Standard Control Organization (India)
CFSAN	Center for Food Safety and Applied Nutrition
COE	Centers of Excellence
CPSI	Center for Science in the Public Interest
CRADA	Cooperative Development and Research Agreement
DHS	Department of Homeland Security
DNA	deoxyribonucleic acid
DOE	Department of Energy
DOJ	Department of Justice
EDQM	European Directorate for the Quality of Medicines and Healthcare
EFSA	European Food Safety Authority
EIC	Export Inspection Council of India
EMA	European Medicines Agency
EPA	Environmental Protection Agency
EU	European Union
EURASFF	European Union's Rapid Alert Systems for Food and Feed
FAO	Food and Agriculture Organization of the United Nations
FBI	Federal Bureau of Investigation
FDA	Food and Drug Administration
FIAE	Food Industry Association Executives
FICCI	Federation of Indian Chambers of Commerce and Industry
FSMA	FDA Food Safety Modernization Act
FSSAI	Food Safety and Standards Authority of India
G20	The Group of 20
GAO	Government Accountability Office
GAP	Good Agricultural Practices

GHTF	Global Harmonization Task Force
GIZ	Gesellschaft für Internationale Zusammenarbeit (Society for International Cooperation)
GMP	Good Manufacturing Practices
GPhA	Generic Pharmaceutical Association
HACCP	Hazard Analysis and Critical Control Points
HIV	human immunodeficiency virus
HPV	human papillomavirus
HS	Harmonized System Codes
IAEA	International Atomic Energy Agency
IANPHI	International Association of National Public Health Institutes
IBA	International Biopharmaceutical Association
ICDRA	International Conference of Drug Regulatory Authorities
ICH	International Conference on Harmonisation of Technical Requirements for Registration of Pharmaceuticals for Human Use
ICMSF	International Commission on Microbiological Specifications for Food
IICA	Inter-American Institute for Cooperation on Agriculture
IPPC	International Plant Protection Convention
ISO	International Organisation for Standardization
MCC	Medicines Control Council of South Africa
MDMA	Medical Device Manufacturers Association
MRA	Medicines Regulatory Authority
NEPAD	New Partnership for Africa's Development
NMRA	National Medicines Regulatory Authority
OECD	Organization of Economic Co-operation and Development
OIE	World Organization for Animal Health
PAHO	Pan American Health Organization
PhRMA	Pharmaceutical Research and Manufactures of Amrica
PREDICT	Predictive Risk-based Evaluation for Dynamic Import Compliance Targeting
SEAICRN	Southeast Asia Infectious Disease Clinical Research Network
SFDA	State Food and Drug Administration (China)
SIT	sterile insect technique
SPPA	Strategic Partnership Program Agroterrorism
SPS	Sanitary and Phytosanitary Measures
SPS	Strengthening Pharmaceutical Systems
SRA	stringent regulatory authority
TBT	Technical Barriers to Trade
TRIPS	Trade-related aspects of intellectual property rights

UN	United Nations
UNICEF	United Nations Children's Fund
UNIDO	United Nations Industrial Development Organization
USAID	United States Agency for International Development
USDA	United States Department of Agriculture
USFDA	United States Food and Drug Administration
USP	United States Pharmacopeia
USTR	United States Trade Representative
WHO	World Health Organization
WTO	World Trade Organization

Contents

Summary

Food and medical product safety is crucial for public health. The food and medical products regulatory system (hereafter, the regulatory system) is a key piece of the public health system. In the United States, the Food and Drug Administration (FDA) protects consumers from unsafe food and drugs, an ever more complicated task as increasingly food and medical products travel through complex international supply chains. The last 10 years have seen contaminated heparin and pet food reach the American market from foreign factories. Thousands of Americans die every year from food poisoning and, although much of it is home-grown, foodborne epidemics are increasingly international. This is small compared to the product safety calamities in developing countries, where fake drugs and poisoned excipients kill tens of thousands against a constant background of aflatoxin poisoning and foodborne disease.

Product safety in the United States depends on systems in faraway places. The FDA estimates that over 80 percent of active pharmaceutical ingredients and 40 percent of finished drugs come from abroad, as does 85 percent of its seafood. Congress has reacted to these trends by requiring that the FDA inspect more producers. Meeting Congress's new inspection targets will be a great effort for the FDA. More importantly, Congress's most ambitious inspection plan still monitors only a small fraction of foreign manufacturers.

The FDA cannot do its job well without substantive improvements in the capacity of its counterpart agencies in emerging economies. With this in mind, the FDA commissioned this study to identify the core elements of food, drug, medical product, and biologics regulatory systems in developing countries; to identify the main gaps in these systems; and to design a strategy the FDA and other stakeholders can use to strengthen food and medical products regulatory systems abroad.

In preparing this report, the committee heard from stakeholders from many low- and middle-income countries at conferences in Washington, DC, Beijing, São Paulo, Pretoria, and New Delhi. A brief summary of its findings and recommendations follows.

CORE ELEMENTS OF REGULATORY SYSTEMS

The committee identified the main characteristics of successful regulatory systems. First, a robust system is responsive; it can respond quickly in a crisis, and it can respond appropriately to new science and new ideas. Such a system also focuses on the outcomes and does not become overly concerned with prescribing methods that might get in the way of innovation. A robust regulatory system is a predictable system; rules are applied consistently and fairly and are designed to favor neither small nor large companies, neither imports nor domestic products. The system allocates controls proportionate to risk and regulates products with similar risks in similar ways. Finally, a robust regulatory system is independent; it is not unduly influenced by politics or money.

The main duties of a medical products regulatory authority are: product registration; the publication of clear licensure requirements; the provision of unbiased information; market entry notification; safety and effectiveness surveillance; quality control testing; inspection of manufacturers against good manufacturing practices; inspection of distributers against good distribution practices; and the evaluation of medical product performance through trials. In countries that produce vaccines, the regulatory authority is also responsible for the systematic lot release of the vaccine. The main duties of a food regulatory system are providing unbiased education and advice to all stakeholders; inspecting food production sites and processing plants against good agricultural practices and good manufacturing practices; evaluating hazard analysis and critical control points (HACCP) plans; physical, chemical, and microbiological analysis of food; and epidemiological surveillance. These responsibilities make the regulatory system a main piece of the public health system.

Low- and middle-income country regulatory authorities are not able to execute all of these responsibilities. With this in mind, the committee identified minimal elements for a regulatory system. At a minimum, the country must have a rule-making process. This rule-making system should be open enough to allow all stakeholders to comment on new regulations. A minimally functional system also has a protocol for different agencies involved in product regulation to work together. It also has a way to identify when regulatory action is necessary. The minimal elements of a regulatory system emphasize the processes that let the system run well. Product safety is, of course, the goal of any food and medical products regulatory system. However, at a minimum there must be a process in place that allows the system to run. When this administrative framework is in place regulators have a way to execute their product safety responsibilities.

Cooperation with counterpart regulatory agencies is a core element of a modern regulatory system. Coordination among the different regulatory agencies within a country is also necessary for product safety, including coordination at different levels of government. The use of HACCP principles to control the food system and the regulation of active pharmaceutical ingredients are examples of areas where different regulators work together to their mutual benefit.

CRITICAL ISSUES IN DEVELOPING COUNTRY FOOD AND MEDICAL PRODUCT SAFETY SYSTEMS

The committee identified nine common problems that cut across developing country product safety systems. A brief summary of these nine critical issues follows.

1. Adherence to international standards is a clear problem; it requires good infrastructure and expensive equipment. The least developed countries often lack the scientific expertise to send active advocates to international standard setting meetings. Because their representatives do not participate in any meaningful way, the countries become standard-takers, not participants in standard setting.
2. There are many related problems in controlling supply chains. Food spoils quickly without refrigeration or proper storage, and it takes too long to get to market over poor roads. The vaccine supply chain and, to a lesser extent, the medicine supply chain are prey to breaks in the cold chain and to wastage. Inventory planning and demand management are difficult in places that have neither reliable transportation infrastructure nor sufficient managerial expertise in the health workforce.
3. Problems controlling supply chains are difficult to separate from infrastructure deficits. There are serious shortcomings in the market infrastructure in low- and middle-income countries, such as lack of pest control and refrigeration. Quality-control laboratories are woefully few, and the ones that do exist have outdated equipment and often have to depend on an unreliable power supply. Local manufacturing is complicated by more basic sanitation problems. Information technology could improve the jobs of regulators and industry in developing countries, but bandwidth is far too expensive and unreliable.

All elements of the system require trained personnel, which is often scarce in developing countries.

4. A strong legal foundation is a prerequisite for food and medical product regulation. Some of the poorest countries have no laws governing product safety; others have a surfeit of confusing and contradictory ones. Enforcing product safety laws is a monumental task, one that is often neglected or executed unevenly. Product liability laws are often essentially non-existent.

5. Government regulators have too few staff, problems retaining their staff, and problems with morale. Corruption is both a cause and an effect of many of the workforce problems. Some staff are fired for political reasons; others grow frustrated and quit.

6. Regulatory responsibilities in low- and middle-income countries are often scattered among many different agencies. This is true in the United States and in many other developed countries as well, but it becomes a problem in places where the same responsibilities are assigned to different agencies or when there is no way for different agencies to communicate. Sometimes the agencies have limited authority to enforce laws; others have authority, but problems coordinating with other agencies.

7. Poor surveillance systems prevent regulators from evaluating emerging safety signals. They cannot monitor medical product safety, track epidemics, or do risk analysis without reliable surveillance data. Weaknesses in the vaccine safety surveillance system can aggravate vaccine scares. Pharmacovigilance systems are also weak; often doctors and pharmacists are not aware of their responsibilities to report adverse drug events.

8. Strong communication can do much to assuage the problems of fragmentation in a regulatory authority, but there are problems with communication among the different agencies responsible for regulation in developing countries. There are also problems communicating within agencies, especially from subordinate to senior staff. Often there is no appropriate forum for regulators to communicate with industry. Consumer groups, which communicate the public's needs to both government and industry, are often missing.

9. A push for product safety can come from the public, especially in large markets with good communications systems. When governments are accountable to their citizens, public opinion can drive political will. Politicians in emerging economies are often more concerned with economic growth. Some regulators are assigned a job that has both product promotion and regulatory responsibilities; they can do neither fully or well. Product safety is not a high priority in countries with skeletal health systems, poor sanitation, and high mortality. Ironically, the vast increase in foreign aid for health over the last 10 years has had an unintended consequence of decreasing national governments' allocations to health, to the detriment of food and medical product safety.

STRATEGY FOR BRIDGING THESE GAPS

After analyzing the nine main gaps in food and medical product regulatory systems in developing countries, the committee developed a strategy to bridge these gaps. This strategy emphasizes public health, market incentives, risk-based investments, and international coordination.

Unsafe food and medical products are at the root of many public health problems in poor countries. Foodborne disease often causes diarrhea, which in turn aggravates malnutrition. Malnutrition compounds the many infectious diseases common in developing countries, diseases that go untreated because of an unsafe or unreliable drug supply. No one would argue that improving public health is less than essential for international development, and the regulatory system is a key piece of the public health system. Yet, donors are disinclined to invest in regulatory systems, preferring to fund disease-specific programs or improve the primary health system.

There is much room for improvement in the way donor agencies, foundations, non-governmental organizations, and multilateral organizations invest in regulatory systems, not the least of which is an emphasis on risk. It is neither good management nor good sense to divide resources equally among all regulated products. Risk assessment is the foundation of modern regulatory science. An understanding of the same should guide investments in product safety.

The market can also drive improvements to regulatory systems, but not without deliberate incentives. The American food and medical products market is strictly controlled, as are all of the most lucrative markets. In emerging economies, small- and medium-sized businesses dominate much of the pharmaceutical supply chain and vastly more of the food supply chain. Economies of scale make it difficult for these industries to adhere to the standards that would allow them to export to hard currency markets. Proper monetary incentives can help developing country producers stay competitive in the global marketplace. Similarly, stricter product liability laws can work to the advantage of producers who make safety a priority.

Product safety cannot improve without international cooperation. Universities and multilateral organizations are often adept at collaborating across borders. Regional collaboration is an efficient form of collaboration that allows less technologically advanced countries to benefit from the systems in place in neighboring countries.

INTERNATIONAL ACTION

Because of international trade, product safety failures in any one country can have ramifications around the world. The global foodborne disease outbreaks and contaminated drug scares have driven this point home over recent years. International trade is also a vehicle for economic development; jobs in high-value agriculture and manufacturing are ways out of poverty for many. Because everyone has a stake in product safety, everyone needs to take action to build regulatory systems. The committee's proposed international action will: increase investments in regulatory systems; encourage open dialogue among government, industry, and academia in emerging economies; work towards voluntary sharing of inspection results; and support surveillance.

> **Recommendation 5-1: In the next 3 to 5 years, international and intergovernmental organizations should invest more in strengthening the capacity of regulatory systems in developing countries. The United States should work with interested countries to add it to the G20 agenda. Investments in international food and medical product safety should be a significant and explicitly tracked priority at development banks, regional economic communities, and public health institutions. International organizations should provide assistance to achieve meaningful participation of developing country representatives at international harmonization and standardization meetings.**

There is common ground where food and medical product safety, public health, trade, and economic development are mutually reinforcing. The development banks and regional economic communities work in this common ground; they should invest more in building regulatory systems in low- and middle-income countries. In particular, their investments should aim to improve the participation of scientists from these countries in international standard setting. The G20 is an excellent forum for industrialized and emerging economies to work together on development. In 2012, Mexico will host the G20 meeting. An emerging manufacturing nation with a vigorous export economy, Mexico would be an ideal leader for a global initiative on food and medical product safety. The United States and other G20 nations should support Mexico in this effort.

Recommendation 5-2: In emerging economies, national regulatory authorities, regulated industry, and industry associations should engage in open and regular dialogue to exchange expert scientific and technical information before policies are written and after they are implemented. Starting in the next 3 to 5 years, these regulatory authorities should identify third parties, such as science academies, to convene the three pillars of a regulatory system—government, industry, and academia—in ongoing discussion to advance regulatory science, policy, and training.

A robust regulatory system depends on input from industry and academia; government simply cannot shoulder the burden alone. In some counties this will require a cultural shift. Science academies are one neutral venue that can bring stakeholders together for open dialogue; public health institutes, though usually governmental, are another. Regardless of the venue that regulatory authorities use, they need to collaborate with industry and academia when designing their policies and when reviewing them.

Recommendation 5-3: Countries with stringent regulatory agencies[1] should, within the next 18 months, convene a technical working group on sharing inspection reports with the longer-term goal of establishing a system for mutual recognition of inspection reports.

Sharing inspection reports is an important first step in mutual recognition and international regulatory harmonization. In the next 18 months countries with stringent regulatory agencies should share their inspection reports of facilities in developing countries. This is a simple step that could reduce a great deal of waste. There is no need for American and European inspectors to duplicate each other's work, especially when a vast number of facilities go uninspected. Over the next decade, these agencies should participate in a working group on mutual recognition of inspection reports. In time, regulatory authorities in emerging economies would also be able to contribute.

Recommendation 5-4: Industry associations should, over the next 3 years, define an acceptable protocol for sharing of internal inspection results among their members. After agreeing on the methods, they should regularly share their results among their members.

---

[1] Countries with stringent regulatory agencies include the United States, European Union member states, and Japan. For the purposes of this report the committee includes ICH Observers and Associates, Australia, New Zealand, Norway, Iceland, Switzerland, and Canada in the category.

Sharing inspection results is sensitive but crucial to an efficient product safety system. In the next 3 to 5 years, food and medical product industry associations can work with their members to decide what information to share and how to share it. They could also encourage members to make use of modern data management, and to rely less on hand-written inspection reports.

Recommendation 5-5: Starting in the next 5 years, USAID, FDA, CDC, and USDA should provide (both directly and through WHO and FAO) technical support for strengthening surveillance systems in developing countries. This technical support could include development of surveillance tools, protocols for foodborne disease surveillance and post market surveillance of medical products, and training of national regulatory authority staff and national experts.

There is a wealth of surveillance expertise in the United Nations (UN) system; the U.S. government and universities have substantial technical depth in the same. These organizations need to strengthen surveillance systems in low- and middle-income countries. The CDC's PulseNet program, for example, is a surveillance program that has expanded to Latin America, Asia, the Middle East, and Europe. In the next 3 years, USAID, FDA, CDC, and USDA can work with their host country counterparts to develop manageable systems for pharmacovigilance. Within 5 years, an expansion of the CDC PulseNet program could elicit meaningful improvements in the foodborne disease surveillance systems in the poorest countries. Building a cadre of trained epidemiologists will take time, probably 10 years or longer, but is an important step of strengthening surveillance systems.

DOMESTIC ACTION

The Food Safety Modernization Act and the FDA's new *Pathway to Product Safety* make it clear that the agency is prepared to change its operations to keep pace with globalization. The committee recommended specific actions that the FDA and other government agencies should take to improve the capacity of regulatory authorities in low- and middle-income countries. The committee's proposed domestic action will: use risk as a guiding principle; use information technology; bridge training gaps; lead in adaptation of international standards; expand the one-up, one-back track and trace requirements; research inexpensive technology; give market incentives for supply chain management; and increase civil liability.

Recommendation 6-1: The FDA should use enterprise risk management to inform its inspection, training, regulatory cooperation, and surveillance efforts. Enterprise risk management should apply to the Agency's entire operation, and it should incorporate a number of set criteria such as country of manufacture or production, volume and type of product, facility inspection history, and trends or data shared from other regulatory authorities.

A comprehensive use of risk management should guide the FDA, and it should employ risk management for its entire operation, not merely for inspections as is often advised. In the next 3 to 5 years, the FDA should use risk to run its international programs: to choose which offices to scale up, what trainings to run, and where to run them. In the next 10 years, the agency should use risk to determine how it allocates its resources to both domestic and international programs. To this end, it may need to ask Congress to revise the law governing it.

Recommendation 6-2: The FDA should develop an information and informatics strategy that will allow it to do risk-based analysis, monitor performance metrics, and move toward paperless systems. In the next 3 to 5 years, the FDA should propose, in all its international harmonization activities, a standardized vocabulary, a minimum dataset to be collected, and the frequency of data collection.

The use of an enterprise-wide risk management system depends on efficient and reliable data management and on using a data format that lends itself to appropriate international sharing. In the next 3 to 5 years, the FDA can articulate a standard data collection format and vocabulary. The FDA should work at international forums such as the World Wide Web Consortium and the Institute of Electronics and Electrical Engineers to work out a minimum key data set that it and its counterparts can collect and share. These are steps to the goal of having a paperless system in the next decade.

Recommendation 6-3: The FDA should facilitate training for regulators in developing countries. The purpose is workforce training and professional development through an ongoing, standing regulatory science and policy curriculum. In the 3 to 5 years, the FDA should broaden the scope of FDA University to educate FDA staffers on international compliance with its regulations. In the long term, the FDA should consider the options the committee puts forth in Chapter 6.

The FDA should use its diplomatic staff abroad and its gravity at international forums to facilitate the training of foreign regulators, though not necessarily to host it. There should be a predictable, standing regulatory science and policy curriculum that regulators from abroad could work through. Training-of-trainers will also be an invaluable way to educate in all languages and reach students in remote places. Over the next 3 to 5 years, the FDA can work through existing networks, such as the Asia Pacific Economic Cooperation's Partnership Training Institute Network, to train trainers. There is also value in an apprenticeship program akin to the CDC's Field Epidemiology Training Program. The committee understands that training regulators at an international regulatory college and developing an apprenticeship program will take about a decade. In the next 3 to 5 years the FDA can broaden the scope of classes at its staff college to better educate American regulators on the international effects of and international compliance with U.S. regulations.

Recommendation 6-4: U.S. policy makers should integrate food and medical product safety objectives into their international economic development, trade, harmonization, and public health work. To this end, the FDA should lead in the development and adoption of international and harmonized standards for food and medical products.

The FDA is an accepted gold-standard regulatory agency; it should lead by example in the use of international standards. Harmonized standards facilitate trade and simplify compliance with product safety rules. The FDA should also work with other industrialized countries to streamline the criteria they use to evaluate conformance with standards. The FDA can also work with the U.S. Trade Representative to use international forums to promote harmonized standards for foods and medical products. In the next 3 to 5 years, the FDA can begin adopting harmonized international standards, but the full realization of integrating product safety into the larger U.S. international policy agenda will take a decade.

Recommendation 6-5: The FDA, which currently requires one-up, one-back track and trace requirements for food, should, in the next year, hold a multi-sector, international, public workshop on applying it to medicines, biologics, and (when appropriate) to devices.

Laws require food producers to identify the immediate prior and immediate subsequent recipient of all products in their supply chains. This is called one-up, one-back traceability. Expanding one-up, one-back requirements to drugs will be complicated, but all stakeholders need to think seriously about the costs and benefits of doing this. The FDA can demonstrate its commitment to strengthening global supply chains by hosting a public hearing on this topic in the next year.

Recommendation 6-6: Starting in the next 2 years, the FDA and USDA should implement Cooperative Research and Development Agreements and other programs to encourage businesses and academia to research and develop innovations for low-cost, appropriate fraud prevention, intervention, tracking, and verification technologies along the supply chain.

The U.S. government needs to encourage research into frugal technologies that would be useful in poor countries. The USDA and FDA should pursue Cooperative Research and Development Agreements with private companies to work together in research and development; the first of these could be issued in the next two years. They can also collaborate directly with researchers in developing countries. The technologies developed in these collaborations would also benefit small- and medium-sized producers in the United States into the future.

Recommendation 6-7: FDA should ensure an adequate mix of incentives to importers of food and medical products that are confirmed to meet U.S. regulatory standards. One such promising initiative is the 2-year FDA Secure Supply Chain pilot program. The FDA should evaluate this program immediately after its pilot phase (scheduled to end in 2014). The program should be expanded, if successful, to include a greater number of importers and food.

The FDA does not have the authority to regulate all the upstream activities in complex international supply chains of food and medical products. The Secure Supply Chain program rewards firms that trace their products thoroughly from manufacture to entry into the United States. The results from this pilot program should be evaluated when the pilot phase is over in 2014 with the goal of expanding the project to include more importers and more products in the next 3 to 5 years.

Recommendation 6-8: Over the next 10 years, U.S. government agencies should work to strengthen the ability of those harmed by unsafe food and medical products to hold foreign producers and importers liable in civil lawsuits.

Importers carry a great deal of product liability risk when they bring products into the American market. The U.S. government should give clear guidance to producers in low- and middle-income countries on the rights of consumers and the importance of product liability laws to trade and to health. In the next decade, U.S. government agencies including, but not limited to, the U.S. Trade Representative, the Department of Treasury, and the Department of Justice should work to increase liability for unsafe food and medical products.

CONCLUSION

Over the last 30 years, international trade, outsourcing, and improvements in telecommunication have created a more unified world economic system. This system benefits many, but it also presents new challenges. Individual countries can no longer depend on their national regulatory authorities to guarantee product safety in the domestic market. This report identifies the most pressing problems facing food and medical product regulators in developing countries. It outlines a strategy that can guide investments in regulatory capacity. It also recommends 13 specific actions the U.S. government and others could take to improve product safety and public health around the world.

The strategy for building regulatory systems and the 13 specific recommendations put forth in this report could do much to improve food and medical product safety in the United States and abroad. It was clear to the committee that product safety is a dynamic problem; it requires agile systems to respond to changing needs. The system should use enterprise risk management to inform its decisions. It is also clear that the FDA cannot act alone; it must develop ways to make the most of its extensive expertise and limited resources. Pooling data and planning inspections with other stringent regulatory agencies is an important first step. Other international organizations and regional communities are well-positioned to lead in training and education—key pieces of the solution. Finally, it has become clear that the FDA needs to refocus resources and attention on modern threats to the food and medical product supply. This will probably require rebalancing programs to give more attention to foreign producers and suppliers.

1

Introduction

The world has changed rapidly in the last 30 years, and will continue to change for the foreseeable future. Some of these changes are evident to any keen observer. Globalization of infectious agents over recent decades has contributed to the well-publicized spread of HIV, avian influenza, SARS, and multi-drug resistant tuberculosis. The globalization of the world's food and drug supplies is less obvious, perhaps because it has been so rapid and less dramatic to the average consumer.

International commerce is a reality of modern food production and medical product manufacture. The U.S. Food and Drug Administration (FDA) oversees 20 million import lines, including close to seven million import lines for medical devices alone, a three-fold increase in regulated imports from a decade ago (Figure 1-1) (Gill, 2011). Around 85 percent of the seafood, 39 percent of the fruits and nuts, and 18 percent of the vegetables that Americans buy come from abroad, as do 80 percent of active pharmaceutical ingredients and 40 percent of finished drugs (Figure 1-2) (Pew Health Group, 2011; USDA-ERS Alberto Jerardo, 2011).

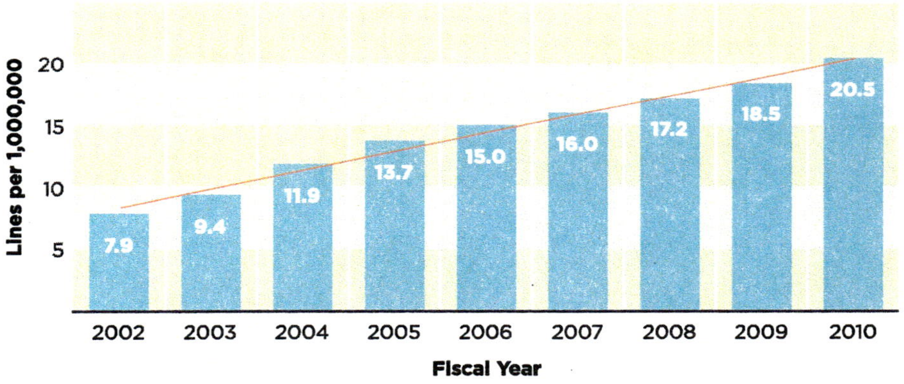

FIGURE 1-1 Imports of regulated products increased nearly threefold between 2002 and 2010.
SOURCE: Gill, 2011.

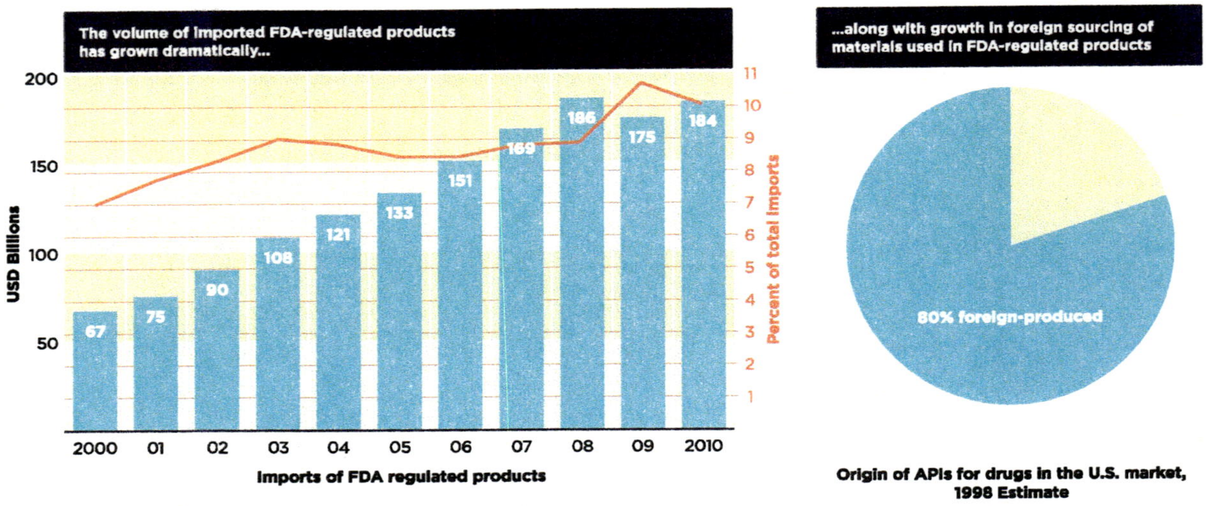

FIGURE 1-2 Increases in global trade are increasing the exposure of U.S. consumers to foreign products and source materials.
SOURCE: FDA, 2011b.

Even to say that American foods and drugs come from abroad is an oversimplification. Prepared foods and fixed dose pharmaceuticals, end products in the market place, are themselves mixtures of dozens of ingredients, often each one from a different country, prepared and repackaged by intermediaries around the world before their final sale. Modern supply chains are complex and reach every corner of the globe. Figure 1-3 shows the path tuna fish may travel to reach an American supermarket and Figure 1-4 describes a modern drug supply chain and the many potential points of vulnerability. As the FDA *Pathway to Global Product Safety* pointed out, the distinction between foreign and domestic producers is no longer clear (FDA, 2011b).

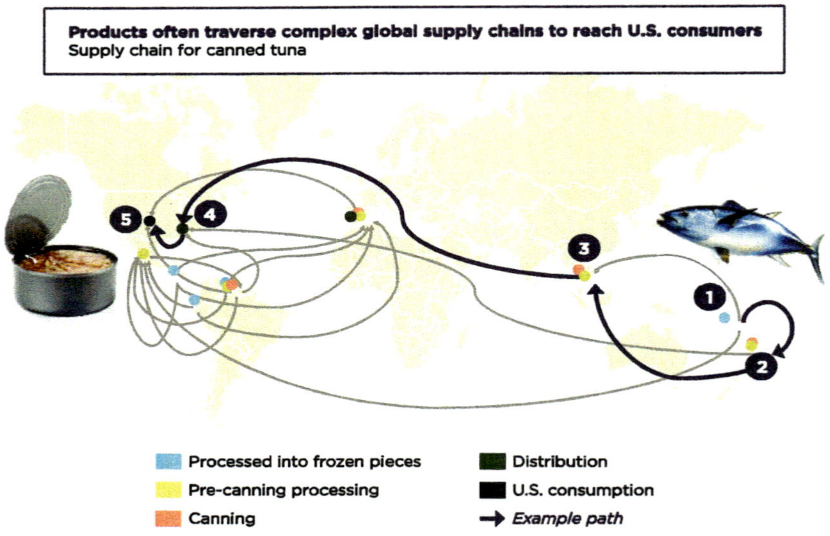

FIGURE 1-3 Canned tuna travels the global supply chain before reaching American tables.
SOURCE: FDA, 2011b.

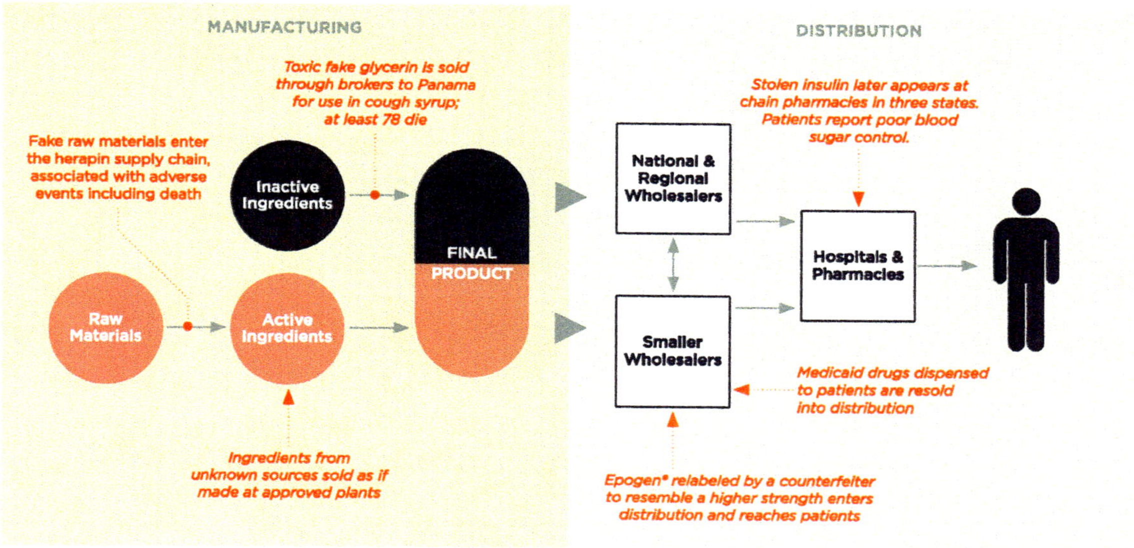

FIGURE 1-4 In complex global drug supply chains, there are many opportunities for unsafe products to be introduced before reaching the consumer. Figure reprinted with permission from the PEW Health Group.
SOURCE: Pew Health Group, 2011.

For the same reasons, through international travel and trade, the health and safety of the American public is now intricately linked to health and safety of people around the world. Recognition of this reality is the cornerstone of the Department of Health and Human Services' (HHS) 2011 *Global Health Strategy*. Secretary of Health Kathleen Sebelius called for the new strategy to guide the Department in realizing its own goals and those of other countries explaining that "only through … multiple and collaborative efforts will [HHS] truly make a mark by improving global health" (HHS, 2011, p. 3). The strategy lays out three interconnected goals for HHS, the parent agency of the FDA. They are protecting and promoting the health of Americans through global health action; providing leadership and technical expertise to improve global health; and advancing U.S. interests through global health action (HHS, 2011). (See Figure 1-5.)

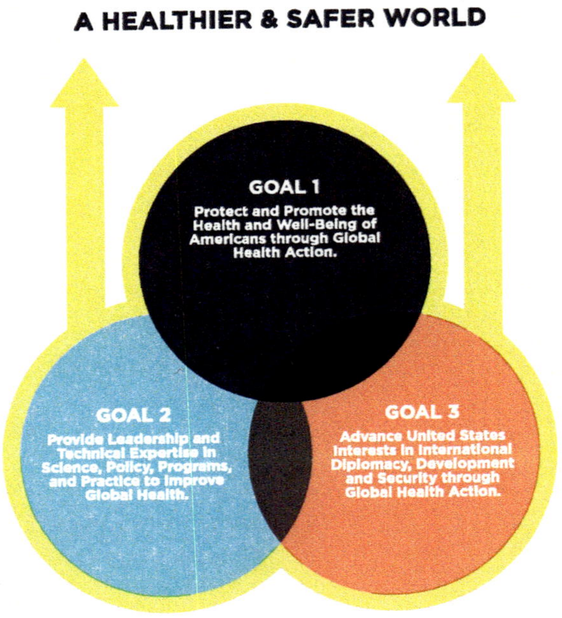

FIGURE 1-5 The HHS's *Global Health Strategy* lays out three interconnected goals.
SOURCE: HHS, 2011.

The *Global Health Strategy* marks a departure from the traditional conception of HHS and its agencies, including the FDA, as purely domestic organizations with an almost exclusive domestic focus. For the FDA in particular, the new HHS strategy aims to "strengthen regulatory capacity on a global basis. Extending … surveillance, regulatory, and program activities beyond the U.S. borders enables more effective protection of Americans' health through improving the health of the world's population" (HHS, 2011, p. 19). This is consistent with the evolving scope of the FDA's work presented in the *Pathway to Global Product Safety and Quality*. This report explains the changes the FDA sees as necessary to "transform itself from a domestic agency operating in a globalized world to a truly global agency fully prepared for a regulatory environment in which product safety and quality know no borders" (FDA, 2011b, p. 3). To this end, the FDA plans to work more with its counterpart agencies to create global coalitions of regulators; to develop international data sharing systems; to expand its intelligence system; and to work with public and private third parties and industry to increase the returns on their mutual efforts (FDA, 2011b).

THE CHANGING FACE OF THE FDA

According to its website, the FDA "is responsible for protecting the public health by assuring the safety, efficacy and security of human and veterinary drugs, biological products, medical devices, our nation's food supply, cosmetics, and products that emit radiation" (FDA, 2010). Because of globalization, its responsibilities now require more international work. The changes put forth in the *Pathway to Global Product Safety and Quality* and the HHS *Global Health Strategy* are the culmination of a gradual shift in the FDA's way of operating, the ramifications of which might not yet be widely recognized, as the American regulatory system moves from mainly reacting to crises to preventing them (Olson, 2011). The 2011 Food Safety Modernization Act improves the FDA's ability to prevent and respond to outbreaks and gives the

FDA the authority to recall foods (Stewart and Gostin, 2011). The act also aims to improve the safety of imported foods by requiring importers to verify that their plants overseas adhere to U.S. safety standards, and by establishing a way for qualified third parties to certify that producers abroad meet quality standards (FDA, 2011b). The act also increases the number of foreign inspections required of the FDA to 600 in 2011, doubling every year for the next five years after that (FDA, 2011b).

The FDA is also under pressure to increase the number of foreign inspections it does of medical product manufacturers. In 2008 the Government Accountability Office (GAO) estimated that at the rate FDA was inspecting drug factories overseas, it would take 13 years to inspect every exporter once (GAO, 2008a). A complementary study reported that high-risk medical device factories were inspected once every 6 years and medium-risk devices about once every 27 years (GAO, 2008b). The FDA responded by creating a group of U.S. staff who exclusively inspect manufacturers overseas and by placing inspectors in FDA's foreign offices (GAO, 2010a). More recent analyses suggest that improvements to the agency's import databases would allow for more efficient management of inspections abroad (GAO, 2010a, 2011). The FDA's current data management system is often criticized; a recent *New York Times* editorial called it "antiquated" and a 2007 FDA Science Board review found it "obsolete" (Dangerous imports, 2011; FDA Subcommittee on Science and Technology, 2007; GAO, 2011).

The FDA's public image is mostly a function of infrequent and controversial debates. The FDA suffers from what former Deputy Commissioner Joshua Scharfstein calls "competing narratives" of its work and mission (Sharfstein, 2011). To some observers, the agency's new emphasis on working across borders and markets to advance the emerging field of regulatory science may be at odds with a conservative understanding of the agency as a domestic enforcer of product safety regulations. The FDA commissioned this report to advance its global mission and promote the necessity of working across borders for product safety.

CHARGE TO THE COMMITTEE

This report, the HHS *Global Health Strategy*, and the FDA's *Pathway to Product Safety and Quality* draw on a common implicit conceptual framework: no country protects its citizens by working alone. In July 2010 the FDA Office of International Programs wrote to the IOM and provided background on the challenges they faced in improving food and drug regulation in developing countries (see Appendix H). This background, which complemented the statement of task, emphasized that the FDA was seeking assistance in developing a broad global health and development vision for the agency. Beyond the traditional statutory food and drug safety mission focused on protecting the U.S. population, the FDA request noted that, "equally important, strengthening regulatory capacity in the developing world will reap tremendous benefits for the health and quality of life of individuals and communities in those countries. Stronger regulatory systems in other countries can help to bolster current U.S. government (USG) investments being made in public health and development, e.g. through the President's Global Health Initiative and USG Agencies, as well as contributions through multilateral organizations, and the broader global health and development community. These efforts increasingly embrace the principles of health systems strengthening, government ownership, and universal coverage." (See Appendix H.)

With this request, the FDA asked the Institute of Medicine (IOM) to convene a committee of international experts to identify the core elements that should be in common among regulatory systems in developing countries, to explain the main gaps in developing country regulatory systems, and to recommend a strategy for the FDA and other stakeholders to work with regulators around the world to improve product safety.

In the course of discussing the initially proposed statement of task with the FDA, there was concern that because the term "developing countries" includes a heterogeneous group of about 150 low- and middle-income countries, the committee's data gathering needed to be focused on a more manageable sample. Thus for the purposes of this study it was agreed that emphasis in formulating cross-cutting insights would be based on looking at commonalities found in a sample of five or six countries that currently are or are expected to soon become major pharmaceutical and agricultural trading partners with the USA (e.g., Mexico, Brazil, South Africa, India, Thailand, and China). Language to that effect was added to the statement of task originally proposed by the FDA. Box 1-1 shows the final statement of task for this study.

BOX 1-1
Statement of Task

The FDA has requested that the Institute of Medicine convene a consensus study to assist FDA in:

(A) Identifying the core elements of needed pharmaceutical, biologics, medical device, and food safety regulatory systems development in developing countries; and in

(B) Prioritizing these needs and recommending a strategic approach to FDA's moving forward to address regulatory capacity needs in the context of globalization.

In addition to identifying and prioritizing the core elements of regulatory systems development, the consensus study would also identify:

(C) Potential areas in which progress could be made in a 3-5 year time frame;

(D) Priorities for FDA engagement;

(E) Areas to which others (bilateral donors, development banks, foundations, academia, industry and non-governmental organizations) are best suited to contribute; and

(F) How FDA might best "partner" with these other institutions to bring to their efforts the expertise that FDA has in an effort to leave a more sustainable "footprint" from both their and our resource commitments.

Specific questions to be explored by the Consensus Study Committee shall at least include:

1. What critical issues do developing country regulatory authorities face and how are they prioritized?
2. In what ways do they participate in standard-setting processes, organizations and harmonization efforts?
3. What issues do they face in utilizing/implementing standards in a sustainable way?
4. What are the core elements of their regulatory systems and are there others that should be considered?
5. What are the major gaps in systems, institutional structures, workforce and competencies?
6. In what ways could those gaps be addressed?
7. In what ways could the U.S. FDA help address those gaps?
8. In what ways could others (as delineated above) help meet those gaps?
9. In what ways could FDA partner with others to help meet those gaps?
10. What recommendations have already been put forward to strengthen regulatory systems?
11. What obstacles exist to implement those recommendations?
12. What steps could be taken to remove those obstacles?
13. What incentives and controls would be needed to support efforts?

Given that "developing countries" include a heterogeneous group of about 150 low- and middle-income countries, for the purposes of this study emphasis will be given to understanding in some depth the issues for a limited number of countries that currently are or are expected to soon become major pharmaceutical and agricultural trading partners with the United States (e.g., Mexico, Brazil, South Africa, India, Thailand, and China).

To address this task the IOM brought together *The Committee on Regulatory Systems Capacity in Developing Countries* with expertise in global public health, pharmaceutical science and practice, agricultural science and practice, food safety, product quality assurance, risk assesment and risk management, supply chain management, globalization and trade, information technology, medical product regulation, food regulation, regulatroy agency leadership, and regulatory or international health law. Box 1-2 describes the committee's process and its domestic and international workshops.

BOX 1-2
The Committee Process

In February 2011, the Institute of Medicine formed a 12-person committee to complete the task given by the FDA. See Appendix F for committee member biographies.

The full committee met in March, July, and October of 2011 to hear from outside speakers and make its recommendations for this report. At the March meeting, the committee heard from eight senior staff at the FDA, including Commissioner Hamburg; it also heard from 11 others, including a representative of the Mexican Ministry of Health. In July the committee heard from an information systems expert and had a public phone call with Anvisa, the Brazilian food and drug regulatory authority. The October meeting was entirely closed to the public. See Appendix E for meeting agendas.

In addition, travel delegations made up of committee members and IOM staff travelled to China, Brazil, South Africa, and India to meet with regulators, representatives of regulated industry, academics, and health and development workers. In China, Brazil, and South Africa the travel delegation had one day in each country of open public workshops and one day of small group meetings or office visits. In India, the travel delegation did not have a large public workshop, but instead had three days of small group meetings and office visits. The India meeting had originally been planned to coincide with the China meeting, but visas for most of the travel delegation were withheld for many weeks. The trip had to be cancelled on short notice and rescheduled.

All the overseas workshops were open to the public. Over the course of 10 days of meetings abroad the travel delegations met with 140 stakeholders, including 21 U.S. government staff posted overseas and 46 regulators from China, India, Bangladesh, Thailand, Brazil, Uruguay, Peru, Chile, Tanzania, South Africa, and the African Union. See Appendix E for travel meeting agendas.

At workshops overseas, committee chair Dr. Jim Riviere's opening remarks noted that the committee was not going to suggest ways to restructure any one country's regulatory system or to describe any country's shortcomings, but to identify common problems and common solutions across a range of low- and middle-income countries.

Public testimonies and information provided to the committee by various stakeholders informed its deliberations, the content of this report, and the committee's recommendations to the FDA and other organizations as to how they can build capacity for food and medical product regulation around the world. After hearing public testimony and identifying the main product safety problems in developing countries the committee and IOM staff examined these problems in the published literature, including scientific studies, commentaries, new articles, and books. This literature review gave depth to the committee's findings and more context to its conclusions.

Both the Food Safety Modernization Act and the FDA *Pathway for Product Safety* emphasize collaboration between the FDA and its counterpart agencies abroad (Tanne, 2011). To work with these agencies, it is important to first understand how regulatory systems work and the challenges regulators face in the world's emerging manufacturing nations. The FDA and other stringent regulatory authorities have a stake in building the regulatory infrastructure and workforce in these countries. It is likely, however, that improving food and medical product regulation overseas will require costly investments that the FDA is neither authorized nor funded to make. Nor should the FDA, or any one agency, shoulder the burden of building capacity in low- and middle-income countries' systems alone. Problems resulting from the globalization of the food and medical products supply require global solutions.

The FDA commissioned this study with the frank admission that its methods of ensuring product safety, inspections at factories and ports of entry, are inadequate when regulated products arrive at 300 different ports of entry from over 300,000 factories in 150 different countries (FDA, 2011b). There are also fundamental flaws with a plan to catch violators by inspecting consignments at random. Ensuring the safety of food and medical products imported from around the world is a difficult task, and one that the FDA has executed fairly successfully so far. There is no reason to believe that its luck will hold over the next 10 years without substantive improvements in the capacity of its counterpart agencies abroad.

The committee's first task was to review the statement of task with the study sponsors from the FDA Office of International Programs. It did this in an open discussion at the first committee meeting. At this meeting, Ms. Mary Lou Valdez, Associate Commissioner for International Programs, explained to the committee that the statement of task is not "suggesting the committee do individual assessments of countries, but to look more widely at the [regulatory] landscape.... What are [the] essential elements of any system? ... What key competencies are essential with any viable regulatory system?" The committee and the sponsors discussed a vision for a report describing the commonalities across low- and middle-income countries, identifying the common problems and a general strategy for solving them. It was clear to all parties that the statement of task does not request analysis of specific regulatory codes in different countries. Instead it requires a high-level analysis across food and medical product lines in a broad cross-section of countries. Ms. Valdez, her colleague Dr. Katherine Bond, and Commissioner Margaret Hamburg explained one of the main goals of this study, from the sponsor's perspective, was to integrate the strengthening of regulatory systems building into the global public health and economic development agenda.

Global public health is a broad field, and there are many organizations working in it. Implicit in the statement of task is the recognition that the FDA budget can barely fund its own activities; it cannot be a donor agency. However, this report aims to help the FDA target its capacity building efforts, and to lay out a strategy that the U.S. government, other governments, universities, development banks, and NGOs can use to ensure safe food and medical products around the world.

This is a complicated problem, but by no means a new one. In its analysis of the core elements of a food and medical products regulatory system, the committee gained perspective by first considering how one gold-standard regulatory agency evolved over the last century. The lessons learned from looking at the history of the FDA give a good foundation for understanding the building of similar agencies in developing countries.

THE BUILDING OF A MODERN REGULATORY AGENCY

For much of the last century, Americans have taken safe food and drugs for granted, but this was not always so. Quality assurance is a relatively modern concept and not one applied to foods or medicines until after the Second World War, when technological improvements spurred the growth of the manufacturing sector (American Society for Quality). But starting in the late nineteenth century, industrialization encouraged migration from rural to urban areas, and country people who had once raised their own food were obliged to buy it. Swindlers flourished in the anonymity of city life. Under the leadership of Harvey Wiley, the Department of Agriculture found and reported on endless cases of food adulteration: bleaches and dyes in molasses, charcoal in ground pepper, and metal salts in canned foods, to name a few (Barkan, 1985; Law and Libecap, 2004). Lead, copper, and mercury salts were used to color candy (Jackson, 2009), and patent medicines, many marketed for children, commonly contained lethal doses of opiates (Finch, 1999). Some eastern states took legal action to prevent fraud, and sparsely populated western ones became a dumping ground for spurious products (Kane, 1964).

The public distrusted manufacturers but was ill-equipped to judge the quality of foods and drugs at purchase (Law and Libecap, 2004). A tangible anxiety resonated on the pages of period journals, and readers responded. A *Ladies Home Journal* letter-writing campaign petitioned President Theodore Roosevelt, his cabinet, and members of Congress for food and drug safety laws (Barkan, 1985). Concerns about product quality also took an economic toll. American exports were less competitive in Europe, where many countries had food and drug regulatory systems in place (Barkan, 1985). Public opinion was shifting in favor of regulation, and Upton Sinclair's 1906 novel *The Jungle,* with its horrific depictions of the Chicago meat packing industry, perhaps did more than anything else to push government to act. Only 4 months after the book's publication, during which time President Roosevelt sent inspectors to verify Sinclair's portrayal of stock yards and slaughterhouses, Congress passed the Pure Food and Drug Act and the Meat Inspection Act, banning food adulteration, deceptive statements on labels, and the interstate sale of adulterated foods (Jackson, 2009).

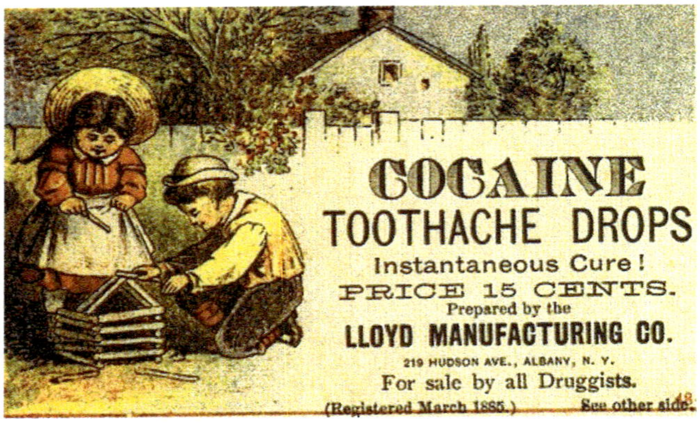

Nineteenth century patent medicines often contained opiates, stimulants, or alcohol.

Around the same time, medicine was also changing. In 1901, a 5-year-old girl died from tetanus in a St. Louis hospital (Junod, 2002). The infection was traced back to a milk wagon horse. Horse blood serum antitoxin was then widely used to treat diphtheria, but there were no controls over its production or requirements for batch testing. When this horse contracted tetanus, its contaminated serum killed 13 children in total (Bren, 2006). As a result, in 1902,

Congress passed the Biologics Control Act, which mandated that producers be licensed for the manufacture and sale of vaccines, serums, and antitoxins (Bren, 2006).

In 1910 the Flexner Report introduced guidelines for medical school accreditation to the United States, requiring doctors to train in anatomy, physiology, and laboratory science and to complete a 2-year hospital internship (Beck, 2004; Flexner, 1910). Standards for accreditation and licensure made the distinctions between medical doctors and quacks clear even to uneducated patients. Over time, the practice of medicine grew more tied to the prescription of controlled drugs. A growing public concern with addiction motivated the Harrison Narcotic Act of 1914, which gave the authority to distribute narcotic drugs and cocaine to licensed physicians only (Spillane and McAllister, 2003).

Legal provisions for food and drug safety still fell short, however. By 1931 the newly formed U.S. Food and Drug Administration (FDA) did not have the authority to inspect farms or factories, and politicians were loath to expand its mandate fearing accusations of socialism (Temin, 1978). The political climate was tense in the early years of the antimicrobial revolution, when the S.E. Massengill Company responded to demand for a liquid sulfa drug preparation with the so-called Elixir Sulfanilamide, a solution of caramel, raspberry extract, water, and the drug sulfanilamide dissolved in diethylene glycol (Ballentine, 1981; Wax, 1995). Over 100 people died from taking it, many of them children who could not swallow the alternative tablet drug (Ballentine, 1981). The Food, Drug, and Cosmetics Act passed in the emotional aftermath of the mass poisoning required drug manufacturers to prove safety before releasing a medicine for sale.

The FDA grew slowly, often in spurts inspired by egregious industry negligence (Figure 1-6). Social changes also drove the need for a government food and drug regulator. Rural to urban migration continued throughout the 20th century and the Great Depression years before the passage of the Food, Drug, and Cosmetics Act saw distinct migration patterns. African Americans left the Jim Crowe South for jobs in northern cities, many in the Chicago meat packing houses; small landholders whose ill-advised farming practices devastated Oklahoma and surrounding states travelled west to California looking for work as day laborers. America changed in the twentieth century: diet and marketing patterns changed, medicine changed, and pharmacology exploded. Designing a regulatory system to adapt to these changes was difficult and expensive, especially during the hard times of the world wars and the Depression.

1862 — The newly formed Department of Agriculture analyzes food and other agricultural products under the Bureau of Chemistry, the early predecessor of today's FDA.

1883 — Harvey Washington Wiley becomes Chief Chemist of the Bureau of Chemistry and expands the Bureau's food adulteration studies. He spends the next two decades as the "Crusading Chemist," reporting on food adulteration while campaigning for a federal law.

1906 — Upton Sinclair publishes *The Jungle* illustrating the horrors of the meat industry.

President Theodore Roosevelt signs the Pure Food and Drugs Act and Meat Inspection Act into law. The laws ban food adulteration, deceptive labels and the interstate sale of illegal food and drugs.

1927 — The Food, Drug and Insecticide Administration is formed from the Bureau of Chemistry to house the food and drug regulatory and enforcement functions.

1931 — The Food, Drug and Insecticide Administration is renamed the Food and Drug Administration.

1937 — Elixir of Sulfanilamide, a solution of the drug sulfanilamide (used to treat streptococcal infections) dissolved in poisonous diethylene glycol and sweetened with raspberry flavor, kills 107 people. There was no law requiring that new drugs be tested for safety.

1938 — In the wake of public outcry around Elixir of Sulfanilamide incident, the Food, Drug and Cosmetic Act becomes law. It requires manufacturers to prove safety before selling new drugs and bring medical devices and cosmetics under federal control.

1958 — The Food Additives Amendment requires manufactures of new food additives to prove safety.

1962 — A sleeping pill that the FDA blocked from entering the United States is identified as the cause of thousands of birth defects in Europe. Public support for tougher drug regulation increases.

1976 — The Medical Device Amendments classify medical devices in three categories based on risk levels and regulate them accordingly. The amendments are passed after thousands of women are injured by the Dalkon Shield intrauterine device.

2011 — The Food Safety Modernization Act expands the FDA's powers with the goal of building a food safety system based on prevention.

FIGURE 1-6 The Evolution of Regulation: History of the U.S. Food and Drug Administration.

Similar Changes and Similar Hurdles in Emerging Economies

Now over 150 other countries are facing the same problems, but globalization has magnified them tenfold. Every week one and a half million people leave the countryside for urban centers (FDA, 2011b), and today's migratory workers are as likely to find work in foreign cities as the provincial capital. Doctors around the world train against similar standards and want to treat their patients with modern medicines. Donor organizations sometimes supply these drugs, but some are sold at market prices. Firms in middle-income countries export medicines cheaply when tariffs allow. Even vaccines, though exceedingly complicated to manufacture, are available around the world, in part because of a combination of technological sophistication and low overhead in India, Indonesia, and Brazil.

The global recession has hit poor counties hard. By World Bank estimates, another 90 million people live on less than $1.25 a day because of the 2008-2009 financial crisis (UN, 2009; World Bank, 2010). The added financial stress came at a bad time for countries transitioning away from a state-controlled economy. Some post-colonial and former communist country governments see a tension between embracing free market capitalism and wanting a government check on industry.

Many of the problems are logistical. Packaged and prepared foods are popular even in traditional societies (Unnevehr, 2007), and these foods are vulnerable to contamination; microbes on only one ingredient can easily contaminate a large amount of food during processing. It is difficult to sanitize equipment without plentiful, clean water (Bester, 2011). It is also hard to enforce sanitary standards when these standards are at odds with prevalent ideas about hygiene.

Fraud is another old problem aggravated by globalization. Fake medicines are a lucrative business worth between $75 and $200 billion a year (Poison pills: Fake drugs, 2010). The trade in them is worst in countries with weak regulatory and law enforcement systems (Siva, 2010). In 2008 *New York Times* reporters Walt Bogdanich and Jake Hooker won the Pulitzer Prize for their investigative series, "A Toxic Pipeline," that tracked adulterated medicine from China to Panama, where over-the-counter cough syrup mixed with diethylene glycol killed hundreds (Bogdanich and Hooker, 2007; The Pulitzer Prizes, 2008). The same network fed solvents to Haiti, India, Nigeria, Argentina, and Bangladesh, killing thousands in countries where the poor die at home, without seeking medical care, outside the reach of surveillance and reporting systems (Bogdanich et al., 2007). Bogdanich and Hooker reported on a crisis similar to the aforementioned Elixir Sulfanilamide tragedy in everything but scale; they found that distance and delay made it almost impossible to trace toxic adulterants through international webs of forged certificates and missing receipts. For criminals dodging accountability, it is easy to hide in the global village.

MODERN FOOD AND DRUG CONTAMINATS TRAVEL FAR AND FAST

In January 2008 the Centers for Disease Control and Prevention (CDC) investigated a spike in reported severe allergic reactions among dialysis patients taking heparin, a blood thinner sold by Baxter International. The CDC and the FDA traced the problem to over sulfated chondroitin sulfate in the heparin active ingredient from China (GAO, 2010b). The adulterated heparin mimicked the properties of the authentic drug in standard screening tests, though it cost roughly 100 times less to manufacture (Pew Health Group, 2011). Neither Baxter nor the FDA was ever able to pinpoint the exact source of the adulteration (GAO, 2010b; Pew Health Group, 2011).

In a report to Congress, the Government Accountability Office (GAO) concluded that the FDA had handled the crisis well, taking speedy and appropriate action to protect the American public from contaminated heparin (GAO, 2010b). The limitations the report identified were in the FDA's ability to inspect and investigate heparin producers in China (GAO, 2010b). While a clear weakness in the FDA's reaction to crisis, the inability to quickly inspect foreign firms is not entirely within its control. The FDA did not have staff permanently stationed in China until November 2008 (FDA, 2011a). Even if it had, and even if the agency's entire inspectorate devoted itself only to inspecting the workshops making heparin in China, it would still have been nearly impossible to identify the source of the problem. Sellers of the contaminated product made between $1 and $3 million by adding over sulfated chondroitin sulfate to the active ingredient (Villax, 2008). The prospect of such payoffs will surely continue to motivate criminal behavior.

The American public became more aware of its vulnerability after the heparin incident, though a Harris poll suggested public confidence in the FDA had been waning much earlier (Harris Interactive, 2008). In March 2007, the FDA recalled 60 million packages of pet food containing Chinese wheat gluten tainted with melamine, a cheap additive that mimics protein in testing (Barboza and Barrionuevo, 2007). In September 2008, the same adulterant was found in the Chinese domestic milk supply. An estimated 300,000 children were sickened from the contaminated milk, many suffering permanent kidney damage (Branigan, 2008). The enormity of the dairy companies' actions drew public attention to weaknesses in the Chinese food industry (Branigan, 2008; Sternberg, 2008). In an interview with *Voice of America*, WHO food safety scientist Peter Ben Embarek attributed much of the problem to a lag between private sector production capability and the public sector's ability to regulate (Schlein, 2008).

REPORT STRUCTURE

This report aims to identify ways to protect the safety of the food and medical product supply around the world. This includes protecting U.S. consumers from nefarious suppliers and poorly controlled imports and building regulatory capacity in low- and middle-income countries. This report will describe ways to work towards standards that will protect both foreign and domestic markets.

There are manifold gaps in the public sector's ability to regulate food and medical products, both in developing and developed countries. This report examines these gaps using examples from specific countries to illustrate common trends. The report presents a strategy for bridging gaps in developing country regulatory systems and ways in which the U.S. government and other stakeholders can work together to bridge these gaps.

This report responds to the statement of task by first describing, in Chapter 2, the core elements of food and medical product regulatory systems as well as the minimal elements of a functional system in a low- or middle-income country. Chapter 2 also describes the common elements in food, drug, and medical device regulatory systems across countries. Chapter 3 summarizes the critical issues regulators in developing countries face. These issues fall into the main categories of adherence to standards, controlling supply chains, problems with infrastructure, legal problems, workforce development, institutional fragmentation, surveillance, communication, and the lack of political will. Chapter 4 lays out the committee's strategic approach to bridging the gaps in developing country regulatory systems. Chapter 5 contains the committee's recommendations to various international organizations and outlines partnerships the FDA could have with these stakeholders. Chapter 6 recommends domestic action that could improve the capacity of food and medical product regulation around the world. Chapter 7 discusses which of the recommendations can be implemented in 3 to 5 years and discusses the report's consistency with the objectives outlined in the *Global Health Strategy*.

REFERENCES

American Society for Quality. *The history of quality: Overview.* http://asq.org/learn-about-quality/history-of-quality/overview/overview.html (accessed April 2, 2012).

Ballentine, C. 1981. Taste of raspberries, taste of death: The 1937 elixir sulfanilamide incident. *FDA Consumer magazine*, http://www.fda.gov/AboutFDA/WhatWeDo/History/ProductRegulation/SulfanilamideDisaster/default.htm (accessed October 25, 2011).

Barboza, D., and A. Barrionuevo. 2007. Filler in animal feed is open secret in China. *The New York Times*, April 30.

Barkan, I. D. 1985. Industry invites regulation: The passage of the pure food and drug act of 1906. *American Journal of Public Health* 75(1):18-26.

Beck, A. H. 2004. The flexner report and the standardization of American medical education. *JAMA: The Journal of the American Medical Association* 291(17):2139-2140.

Bester, A. 2011. The importance of food safety in Africa. http://www.howwemadeitinafrica.com/the-importance-of-food-safety-in-africa/5043/ (accessed June 14).

Bogdanich, W., and J. Hooker. 2007. From China to Panama, a trail of poisoned medicine. *The New York Times*, May 6.

Bogdanich, W., J. Hooker, H. Kumar, A. Giridharadas, and J. Ali Manik. 2007. As FDA tracked poisoned drugs, a winding trail went cold in China. *The New York Times*, June 17.

Branigan, T. 2008. Chinese figures show fivefold rise in babies sick form contaminated milk. *The Guardian*, December 2.

Bren, L. 2006. The road to the biotech revolution: Highlights of 100 years of biologics regulation. *FDA Consumer magazine*, http://www.fda.gov/AboutFDA/WhatWeDo/History/FOrgsHistory/CBER/ucm135758.htm (accessed October 25, 2011).

Dangerous imports. 2011. *The New York Times*, June 25.

FDA. 2010. *About FDA: What we do.* http://www.fda.gov/aboutfda/whatwedo/default.htm (accessed March 1, 2012).

———. 2011a. *FDA's international posts: Improving the safety of imported food and medical products.* http://www.fda.gov/forconsumers/consumerupdates/ucm185769.htm#TheChinaOffice (accessed November 22, 2011).

———. 2011b. *Pathway to global product safety and quality.* Washington, DC: U.S. Food and Drug Administration.

FDA Subcommittee on Science and Technology. 2007. *FDA science and mission at risk: Report of the subcommittee on science and technology.* US Food and Drug Administration.

Finch, L. 1999. Soothing syrups and teething powders: Regulating proprietary drugs in Australia, 1860-1910. *Medical History* 43(1):74-94.

Flexner, A. 1910. *Medical education in the United States and Canada.* NY, New York: The Carnegie Foundation for the Advancement of Teaching.

GAO. 2008a. *Drug safety: Better data management and more inspections are needed to strengthen FDA's foreign drug inspection program* GAO-08-970.

———. 2008b. *Medical devices: Challenges for FDA in conducting manufacturer inspections.* GAO-08-428T.
———. 2010a. *Drug safety: FDA has conducted more foreign inspections and begun to improve its information on foreign establishements but more progress is needed.* GAO-10-961.
———. 2010b. *Food and Drug Administration: Response to heparin contamination helped protect public health; controls that were needed for working with external entities were recently added.* GAO-11-95.
———. 2011. *Drug safety: FDA faces challenges overseeing the foreign drug manufacturing supply chain.* GAO-11-936T.
Gill, L. 2011 March 2. *Addressing the challenges of medical device safety in a global environment.* Paper presented at Strengthening Core Elements of Regulatory Systems in Developing Countries: Meeting One, Washington, D.C. .
Harris Interactive. 2008. *Confidence in FDA hits new low, according to WSJ.com/Harris Interactive study.* http://www.harrisinteractive.com/vault/Harris_Interactive_News_2008_04_22.pdf (accessed November 30, 2011).
HHS. 2011. *The global health strategy of the U.S. Department of Health and Human Services.* Washington, DC.
Jackson, L. S. 2009. Chemical food safety issues in the United States: Past, present, and future. *Journal of Agriculture and Food Chemistry* 57(18):8161-8170.
Junod, S. W. 2002. Biologics centennial: 100 years of biologics regulation. *Update*(November-December), http://www.fda.gov/aboutfda/whatwedo/history/productregulation/selectionsfromfdliupdateseriesonfdahistory/ucm091754.htm (accessed October 25, 2011).
Kane, R. J. 1964. Populism, progressivism, and pure food. *Agricultural History* 38(3):161-166.
Law, M. T., and G. D. Libecap. 2004. *The determinants of Progressive Era reform: The Pure Food and Drugs Act of 1906.* Cambridge, MA: National Bureau of Economic Research.
Olson, E. D. 2011. Protecting food safety: More needs to be done to keep pace with scientific advances and the changing food supply. *Health Affairs* 30(5):915-923.
Pew Health Group. 2011. *After heparin: Protecting consumers from the risks of substandard and counterfeit drugs.* Washington, DC: Pew Health Group.
Poison pills: Fake drugs. 2010. *The Economist*, September 4.
Schlein, L. 2008. China's melamine milk crisis creates crisis of confidence. *Voice of America*, September 26.
Sharfstein, J. M. 2011. The FDA—a misunderstood agency. *JAMA: The Journal of the American Medical Association* 306(11):1250-1251.
Siva, N. 2010. Tackling the booming trade in counterfeit drugs. *The Lancet* 376:1725-1726.
Spillane, J., and W. B. McAllister. 2003. Keeping the lid on: A century of drug regulation and control. *Drug and Alcohol Dependence* 70(3, Supplement 1):S5-S12.
Sternberg, J. 2008. Notes on a milk scandal. *The Wall Street Journal*, October 10.
Stewart, K., and L. Gostin. 2011. Food and Drug Administration regulation of food safety. *Journal of the American Medical Association* 306(1):88-89.
Tanne, J. H. 2011. FDA seeks global partners to improve safety of imported food, medicines, and devices. *BMJ* 342(d4106).
Temin, P. 1978. *Working paper: The origin of compulsory drug prescription.* Cambridge, MA.

The Pulitzer Prizes. 2008. *The 2008 pulitzer prize winners: Investigative reporting.* http://www.pulitzer.org/citation/2008-Investigative-Reporting (accessed December 20, 2011).

UN. 2009. *Rethinking poverty: Report on the world social situation 2010.* New York, NY: United Nations.

Unnevehr, L. J. 2007. Food safety as a global public good. *Agricultural Economics*:149-158.

USDA-ERS Alberto Jerardo. 2011. Summary-import share of U.S. Food consumption. Washington, DC.

Villax, G. 2008 May 29. *Business of counterfeit heparin and its implications*. Paper presented at 3rd EFCG Pharma Business Conference, Lisbon, Portugal

Wax, P. M. 1995. Elixirs, diluents, and the passage of the 1938 Federal Food, Drug and Cosmetic Act. *Annals of Internal Medicine* 122(6):456-461.

World Bank. 2010. *Fact sheet: Impact of the global financial crisis on fragile and conflict-affected countries.*

2

Core Elements of Regulatory Systems

Having safe food and medical products is a cornerstone of public health around the world. The Food and Drug Administration (FDA) protects U.S. consumers from tainted products, and increasingly it works with its counterpart agencies abroad to the same ends. Before identifying the common gaps in developing country food and medical product regulatory systems, and before making a strategy to bridge these gaps, the committee identified the core elements of a functional regulatory system. The committee concluded that the most basic elements of a regulatory system are the same around the world. Therefore, the core elements of regulatory systems are the same in developed and developing countries. This chapter describes these elements as well as the minimal pieces necessary for an effective food and medical product regulatory system.

There is more than one right way to organize a regulatory system. In its analysis, the committee considered a number of different policy and administrative tools governments can use to ensure the safe manufacture, labeling, distribution, and marketing of food and medical products. While the mechanisms employed can vary between countries, effective regulatory programs have a number of common characteristics.

This chapter lays out the characteristic and practical elements of a good regulatory system. It also describes the minimal elements necessary to ensure food and medical product safety. It gives an overview of the organization of food and medical product regulatory systems in developing countries, paying special attention to the importance of harmonized standards in these countries. The importance of international cooperation among regulators is introduced; this will be a theme the committee concentrates on in this report. This chapter ends with a discussion of two important points of international cooperation: the use of risk and hazard analysis in food safety and the regulation of active pharmaceutical ingredients (API).

COMMON ATTRIBUTES OF EFFECTIVE REGULATORY PROGRAMS

The first step in understanding the core elements of food and medical product regulatory systems is identifying the underlying attributes of successful systems. The committee identified five main characteristics of good systems: they should be responsive, outcome-oriented, predictable, risk-proportionate, and independent. These attributes are consistent with those outlined in the World Trade Organization (WTO) Agreement on the Application of Sanitary and Phytosanitary Measures (SPS), especially in their emphasis on the protection of human, plant, and animal health without the application of regulations that would "arbitrarily or unjustifiably discriminate between countries where identical or similar conditions prevail" (WTO, 1998). Similarly, the WTO relies on a scientific evidence base for decision making. Its preference is to use international standards whenever possible; it does allow countries to set their own standards so long as their standards comply with the basic tenets of the WTO rules.

The major attributes the committee identified are common in all highly functioning regulatory systems. These attributes are not the system's main duties, which will be discussed later, but are scientific and philosophical underpinnings of a robust system.

Responsive

The responsiveness of a regulatory system involves two related functions. The first is the ability to respond rapidly to a crisis. The regulatory system should be able to contain and correct any product safety lapse that has occurred, minimizing the health effects. Responsiveness also includes the ability of the system to promptly modify its policies. Responsive regulation keeps pace with the emergence of new hazards, changes in technology, expanding evidence base, and evolving consumer expectations. This attribute also includes the ability of the system to stay up-to-date and knowledgeable about new science. Responsiveness refers to the ability of the regulatory agency to continually expand its knowledge base, to be a learning organization that has internal scientific depth and effective collaboration with academics, and to draw on the technical and business expertise of regulated industry.

Outcome Orientation

A robust regulatory system focuses on product safety outcomes, not on the details of how to arrive at the outcomes. That is not to say that a strong system is not concerned with process. On the contrary, strong regulatory systems often stipulate manufacturing standards and inspection processes. Rather, the outcome-oriented system issues regulations that do not get in the way of innovation. Furthermore, in an outcome-oriented system industry has a clear avenue to petition the regulatory authority to use alternative processes, and this process is not unduly onerous. An outcome-oriented regulatory agency has the scientific expertise to be abreast of changes in food and medical product technology and the modern equipment to analyze it.

Predictable

The regulatory agency has a clear framework guaranteeing that the regulators' decisions are neither arbitrary nor capricious. Predictable regulatory systems make their procedures readily available to the public. The rules are applied consistently, enforced fairly, and are based on the best scientific evidence available at the time of the decision. Predictability assumes a level playing field and describes a function in the regulatory system that is vigilant against bias. A fair and predictable system does not work for or against large industry or small industry; regulations are applied the same way to imported and domestic products.

Proportional

A proportional or risk-based system allocates controls based on threat to public health: product lapses with serious health consequences are monitored stringently, while those with few or insignificant risks receive less attention. Products with similar risks are regulated in similar ways. Proportionality depends first and foremost on the ability of the regulatory agency to assess risk. It also assumes that the agency will consider a cost-to-benefit analysis when measuring the impact of potential risk management options. A proportional regulatory system actively sets priorities ensuring that the agencies' programs give the most attention to the most pressing public health threats.

Independent

Regulatory policies are the combination of scientific decisions and societal expectations. This is especially true of the system's legislative oversight. However, once its legal authority is set, the agency functions best when it is independent of the political process. The predictability of a regulatory system also relies on independence: regulated industry cannot predict how and when regulations will be enforced if the enforcer changes every time the political regime does. Consumer trust depends on independence. The public needs to know that the agency is devoted to its best interests and is not unduly influenced by politics or money.

Approaches to Regulation

Good food and medical product regulation strikes a balance between protecting public health and not unfairly restricting market access. To this end, governments need to ensure that companies comply with regulations, but governments do not function alone. Industry, academia, and consumers give important feedback to the regulatory system, which includes the legal and health systems. The best regulatory model is one that engages all stakeholders. Box 2-1 describes approaches to food and medical product regulation that emphasize the role of consumers and regulated industry.

BOX 2-1
Approaches to Regulation

Informational Approaches

One technique for ensuring strong product safety regulation is education. An informational approach directly educates the consumer on product safety, and it assumes that consumers will use this information to make the best decisions for themselves. This approach assumes that having more information, particularity about the concealed characteristics of products, will cause people to change their behavior and buy safe products (IOM, 2006). Governments, industry, academia, or other organizations can provide this information, although the British government's Department for Business, Innovation and Skills explains that consumer education is best done by non-governmental organizations, leaving the government free to enforce regulations (BIS). Labeling, warnings, and safety rating systems are important tools in informational regulation (BIS; Sunstein, 2011).

Market Approaches

Market approaches to regulation use monetary rewards and punishments to modify behavior. Market regulation gives government control of the final regulatory action while putting industry in charge of the route there. Proponents of the market approach maintain that market controls also empower consumers to make their own cost-benefit estimates and choose products based on these decisions. Taxes on products with negative externalities, such as soft drinks, are a market approach to regulation. Bonded warranties are another market tool sometimes used in food and drug regulation ensure product safety (BIS, 2011; Office of Information and Regulatory Affairs, 2003).

Regulated Standards

Government regulatory authorities choose and enforce product standards based on scientific evidence. They use either performance standards or design standards. Performance standards set the final product requirements, but do not mandate the techniques industry must use to meet these standards. Design standards dictate the means as well as the end product of the product requirements. Proponents of performance standards explain that they encourage innovation, while advocates of design standards emphasize the process as much as the product (IOM, 2006; Office of Information and Regulatory Affairs, 2003).

CORE ELEMENTS OF A STRONG REGULATORY SYSTEM

Responsiveness, outcome orientation, predictably, proportionality, and independence are the underpinnings of strong food and medical product regulatory systems. A regulatory system grounded in these values will be able to execute its core responsibilities. The main duties of a medical products regulatory system are: the registering of medicines; the publishing of clear requirements for licensure; the provision of unbiased information; market entry notification; safety and effectiveness surveillance; quality control testing; the inspecting of manufacturers for compliance with good manufacturing practices; inspection of distributors; and the evaluation of performance through authorized trials (WHO, 1999, 2001, 2003a). In countries that manufacture vaccines, the regulatory authority is also responsible for the systematic lot release of the vaccine (WHO, 1999). The main duties of a food regulatory system are: providing unbiased education and advice to all stakeholders; inspecting food production and processing plants; evaluating hazard analysis and critical control point (HACCP) plans; physical, chemical, and microbiological analysis of food and food additives; and epidemiological surveillance (FAO/WHO, 2003). Essentially, the regulatory system is an important piece of the public health system. By providing manufacturers and producers with unbiased information, guaranteeing the use of best practices, and inspecting producers and manufacturers, the regulatory authority protects the safety of food and medical products.

The committee also identified the core elements of a food and medical products regulatory authority system, as described in Box 2-2. Whether some or all of the core elements noted in Box 2-2 are part of a country's regulatory system depends heavily on wealth and infrastructure. It is difficult for companies to manage their supply chains without reliable transportation systems, for example. Political will to enforce product safety laws can also be variable. A more detailed analysis of the issues developing country regulators face in implementing safety controls follow in Chapter 3.

BOX 2-2
Core Elements of a Food and Medical Product Regulatory System

Government is the foundation for a strong regulatory system. As the national standard-setting body, governments:

- Use science and risk as a basis for developing policy;
- Participate in international cooperation and harmonization of standards;
- Make ethical decisions; and
- Recognize, collect, and transmit evidence when breaches of law occur.

A food and medical product regulatory system integrates:

- Product safety through good manufacturing, clinical, laboratory, and agricultural practices;
- Staff development and training for employees;
- Monitoring and evaluation of product quality using laboratories;
- Inspection and surveillance of products throughout the supply chain;
- Risk assessment, analysis, and management; and
- Emergency response.

Protecting the public's health is crucial in a food and medical product regulatory system. The system needs to quickly communicate information to the public in emergencies to ensure the public's safety.

SOURCES: (Ratanawijitrasin and Wondemagegnehu, 2002; WHO, 2003a; WHO Regional Committee for Africa, 2006)

MINIMAL ELEMENTS OF A REGULATORY SYSTEM

The ideal regulatory system described above depends on funding, infrastructure, workforce, and political commitment. One or more of these is usually missing in low- and middle-income countries (Brown et al., 2006). With this in mind, the committee also identified the minimal elements of a regulatory system that protects public health and ensures product safety. The minimal elements of regulation should be the top priority for developing countries trying to build product safety systems.

A Rule-Making System

The minimal requirements outlined in Box 2-3 focus on the process regulators use to make regulations and on the data they use to enforce them. An open rule-making system ensures that people governed by a new regulation have a chance to publically comment on it (U.S. Department of State). Through an open rule-making process, consumers and industry are informed of proposed food and medical product regulations before they take effect. An open system for rule making involves stakeholders in a regulatory dialogue and lays the ground work for risk communication.

For example, a rule-making process is critical to establishing effective food safety laws. In many developing countries there are food safety rules in place, but there is a lack of processes to ensure their implementation and effectiveness. In Canada, the European Union (EU), and the United States, rule processes have been established to assess risks, to analyze cost-benefit and cost-effectiveness, and to assess the environmental impact of food safety regulations (DOE; European Commission; Health Canada and Canadian Food Inspection Agency, 2007; USDA, 2009). Many developing countries including China, India, the Philippines, Vietnam, and Thailand are in the process of re-organizing their food safety systems (Fairclough, 2009; FAO, 2004; Ramos and Oblepias, 2002; Smart, 2011; WHO, 2009). Box 2-4 discusses the changes India has made to its food safety rules to develop a farm-to-table approach.

BOX 2-3
Minimal Elements of a Regulatory System

At a minimum, a food and medical product regulatory system should include

- An established process for rule making;
- A protocol to coordinate work within and across the agencies responsible for regulation, especially during a crisis;
- A system for stakeholder public comment on regulations and the review process;
- A way to identify when a regulatory action is necessary; and
- A means to enforce their regulations.

To this end, regulators need to have surveillance data and understand their data sources. They also should have a strong enough understanding of their system's weaknesses that they can identify data gaps and know what assumptions to make about unknowable data and when to rely on the private sector for additional information. Crisis early warning systems are invaluable tools to make the most of limited surveillance data.

BOX 2-4
Rule Making in India

In 2006, the Indian government established the Food Safety and Standards Act. The Act "aims to establish a single reference point for all matters relating to food safety and standards" (Palthur et al., 2009). This act formed the Food Safety and Standards Authority of India (FSSAI). FSSAI's mandate is to consolidate previous food laws, make science-based food standards, and regulate and monitor the manufacturing, processing, storage, distribution, sale, and import of foods to ensure safe food for human consumption (FSSAI, 2011; Palthur et al., 2009).

Although India has made strides to improve its food safety rules, implementing the rules is difficult. Small-scale producers, who do not know how to make the changes required by law, cannot comply with the act (Palthur et al., 2009). Some producers are unclear about the terms of the act; others simply cannot implement HACCP and good manufacturing processes. In a 2010 survey of the Indian food processing sector, 28.51percent of respondents identified bottlenecks in the implementation of food safety laws as a concern (FICCI, 2010). Many of the quality control laboratories lack proper equipment and reliable power, complicating the task of surveillance. There are also not nearly enough of them (Palthur et al., 2009).

In January 2011, the FSSAI published a final draft of the Food Safety and Standards rules. In the draft, it specifies how to implement the rules established by the 2006 Food Safety and Standards Act. The new rules replace the country's outdated food adulteration rules from 1955 (Singh, 2011). Other changes include the establishment of state-level licensing authorities, the addition of batch numbers to processed foods for easy product recalls, laboratory expansion, and the requirements for producers to have a surveillance plan (Smart, 2011). India is clearly making progress toward a farm-to-table approach.

Openness in rule making is not part of the political tradition in some countries, particularly one-party governments or countries with an authoritarian history (Dalpino, 2000). This is a challenge to the regulation of food and medical products. By definition food and medical product safety laws govern regulated industry; it is imperative that the regulated understand the rules governing them. Without a public comment period it is doubtful manufacturers are even aware of the regulations affecting them. Regulators are also held back if they cannot have feedback on their practices from a range of stakeholders. In the United States for example, there is an open comment period where all stakeholders can submit comments on proposed rules including those of the FDA (U.S. Government).

Involving All Stakeholders

Part of the problem in developing countries is that the food and, to lesser extent, the medical products industry are made up of many small producers. In China, 80 percent of the food producers have fewer than 10 employees (Roth et al., 2008); India has more than 20,000 drug manufacturers (KPMG International, 2006). Involving so many stakeholders in public forums is challenging, especially when the communication system is not strong and the tradition of two-way comment on law making is not entrenched. Chapter 3 will discuss these gaps in more detail.

Legal Basis to Enforce Regulations

The end goal of an orderly rule making process that involves industry, government, consumers, and academics, is to have a set of enforceable regulations. The committee believes that, at a minimum, the regulatory agency needs to have the legal authority to enforce its rules. To this end, the regulations made need to be enforceable by the national regulatory authority. Box 2-5 describes the goals of food and medical product legislation. As Chapter 3 describes, many developing countries have problems with enforcing or even developing coherent product safety laws.

BOX 2-5
Food and Medical Product Legislation

The World Health Organization (WHO) and the Food and Agriculture Organization of the United Nations (FAO) give good guidance on what a food and medical product legal framework should include. The following summary of the role of food and medical product safety legislation comes from the WHO's *Effective medicines regulation: Ensuring safety, efficacy and quality*, and the FAO and WHO's *Assuring Food Quality and Safety: Guidelines for strengthening national food control systems*.

- State the purpose of regulation;
- Define the categories of products and activities to be regulated;
- Ensure legal provision for the creation of a regulatory authority;
- Coordinate responsibilities when the regulatory authority includes more than one agency;
- Create mechanisms for ensuring transparency and accountability of regulation;
- Define the roles, responsibilities, rights and functions of all parties involved in the manufacture, trade of food and medical products, and also in the use of medicines;
- Set the qualifications and standards required for all those who handle medicines and biologics;
- Define the norms, standards, specifications to be applied in assessing product quality, safety and (in the case of medicines and biologics) efficacy;
- Include clear provisions that the primary responsibility for product safety and quality lies with the producers and processors;
- State the terms and conditions for suspending, revoking or cancelling activity and product licenses;
- Define prohibitions, offenses, penalties and legal sanctions;
- Create mechanisms for government oversight to asses implementation of regulations;
- Recognize the country's international obligations in relation to trade; and
- Include provisions for the rights of consumers to have access to accurate information.

SOURCES: (FAO/WHO, 2003; WHO, 2003b).

FOOD AND MEDICAL PRODUCT REGULATION IN DEVELOPING COUNTRIES

There is a continuum of regulatory capacity in the world. On one end, there are the so-called stringent regulatory agencies of the United States, Canada, Western Europe, Australia, New Zealand, and Japan, agencies with high standards and consistent enforcement. These agencies may struggle to monitor all of their regulated products, especially their imports, but they are nonetheless considered gold standards for product safety. At the other end, there are the regulatory agencies of the least developed countries, many in sub-Saharan Africa and in South and Southeast Asia that may not have a single food control laboratory or a system for medicines registration, one of the most basic functions of a drug regulatory authority. In the middle there are many emerging manufacturing nations including India, China, Brazil, South Africa, Mexico, and Thailand, representatives of which the committee heard from during this study. These countries are leaders in regional harmonization efforts, but they have problems with training and regulatory infrastructure. Across low- and middle-income countries there are some common gaps in the ability to enforce standards, monitor producers for use of best practices, run surveillance systems, issue product recalls, or respond to emergencies. Chapter 3 will describe these gaps.

Medical Products Regulatory Oversight

The Organisation of Economic Cooperation and Development (OECD) Regulatory Policy Committee stressed the importance of regulatory oversight bodies in government to ensure fair and quality regulation (Organisation of Economic Co-Operation and Development, 2009).

Drug and Vaccine Regulation and WHO Prequalification

Oversight bodies are a core element of proper food and medical products regulation, yet according to WHO, less than 20 percent of its 191 member states have well-developed drug regulatory agencies (Ratanawijitrasin and Wondemagegnehu, 2002). In the African region, the WHO found only 10 percent of medicines regulatory authorities have a full system in place (WHO Regional Committee for Africa, 2006). Box 2-6 describes how South Africa restructured its drug regulatory authority.

In some countries, the WHO Prequalification Programme is an important piece of the drug and vaccine regulatory oversight. This program was established in 2001 to ensure that the medicines supplied by the United Nations (UN) agencies were safe and efficacious (WHO, 2010). The prequalification process has five steps. First, the WHO or another UN agency invites drug or vaccine companies to submit a product for prequalification. Products considered are either on the WHO essential medicines list, applied for inclusion on the WHO essential medicines list, or recommended for use in a WHO treatment guideline (WHO, 2010). The manufacturer submits a dossier on the product's safety and efficacy, and a team of experts from regulatory agencies around the world reviews the dossier. Next, inspectors verify that the factory, laboratories, and research mentioned in the dossier all meet international best practices. If the manufacturer passes all inspections, the WHO grants prequalification (WHO, 2010).

BOX 2-6
Restructuring the Drug Regulatory Authority in South Africa

For years, the Medicines Control Council (MCC) of South Africa has worked under cumbersome legislation. Because of a poor legislative framework and complex emerging health products, the council had become inefficient and ineffective, with extensive backlogs delaying regulatory decisions on vital medicines (*Report of the ministerial task team*, 2008). Thus, to significantly improve drug regulation in South Africa, the government is restructuring the council. A rigorous review of other national models and global regulatory trends guided the formation of the South African Health Products Regulatory Authority (*Report of the ministerial task team*, 2008).

The new regulatory authority is different from the MCC in many ways. Consistent with other mature and credible national regulatory authorities, it will regulate medical devices and in vitro diagnostics as well as medicines. The agency will be a national public entity, meaning that it is outside of any specific department but still part of the government. This will help ensure the agency's independence and foster public confidence in its objectivity. Its staff will inspect all plants and enforce regulations on all health products, but will not be involved in pricing, procurement, distribution, wholesaling, or logistics (Crisp).

The restructuring process is ongoing. The parliament passed the Medicines Amendment Act in 2008 and President Motlanthe signed it into law in 2009. However, the implementation team is still working out practical details about the body's management. The transition is expected to begin in late 2011 (Crisp, 2011).

The large-scale restructuring of the medicines regulatory system in South Africa has far-reaching benefits. In addition to the great benefits within South Africa, the development of the new agency is a great opportunity for sharing training, information technologies, inspection, and enforcement within the Southern African region (Crisp). Still, growing pains come with the transition. The new agency now has far too few staff and relies heavily on part-time consultants. It will also take time to get the electronic medicines management system working. Most importantly, the agency's registrar is a subordinate employee in the health ministry and lacks the authority of a chief executive.

Originally WHO prequalification was granted only to HIV, tuberculosis, and malaria drugs (WHO, 2010). Now UN agencies procure over 240 medicines, vaccines, and contraceptives through the prequalification program (WHO, 2010, 2011e). As part of the program, WHO provides training for national regulators and for manufacturers from private companies, and improves quality control laboratories in developing countries (WHO, 2010). In places where the regulatory authority lacks technical depth, this program is a welcome guarantee of medicines quality.

In countries that manufacture vaccines, WHO prequalification depends on the country having a competent national regulatory authority (Brhlikova et al., 2007). The United Nations Children's Fund (UNICEF) procures vaccines for 80-100 countries in the world; 64 of the poorest receive all of their vaccines from UNICEF (Rosnbom, 2010; UNICEF, 2011). The WHO has programs to strengthen oversight from national regulatory authorities, and it gives highest priority to those emerging manufacturing nations that supply vaccines to many other countries; their second priority is building the systems of countries that procure directly from manufacturers without going through UN procurement (WHO, 2011b). Countries that rely fully on UN procurement are lower priority. Though vaccines make up only about 3 percent of the global pharmaceutical market (Wilson, 2010), they require disproportionate regulatory oversight, especially for post-marketing surveillance. Inadequate regulatory oversight of vaccines is a common problem in low- and middle-income countries, and one discussed more in Chapter 3.

The WHO prequalification of vaccine manufacturers in China was not granted easily. In March 2011 WHO recognized China's regulatory system for complying with its vaccine production standards. During an approval period that took 19 months, China's regulators worked to develop a plan that followed WHO's advice on how to strengthen vaccine regulation. A team of experts from various countries assessed China's regulatory system against WHO indicators. Meeting international standards created opportunities for China to apply for WHO prequalification and in the next few years supply vaccines to UN agencies (WHO, 2011d).

Medical Device Regulatory Oversight

The regulation of medical devices is more variable in low- and middle-income countries. The regulation of devices is often in the purview of the drug regulatory authority. In the United States and Europe, the national drug regulatory authorities have monitored device safety since the mid-1970s; Australia, Canada, and Japan followed course in 1989, 1998, and 2002, respectively (Gropp, 2011). Today, 85 countries regulate devices (Gropp, 2011). Figure 2-1 describes the varying levels of comprehensiveness and international consistency or harmonization in different countries device regulation (Gropp, 2011). In many parts of the world, devices are overwhelmingly imported; Latin American countries import more than 80 percent of their medical devices (PAHO, 2010a). Even countries with a strong manufacturing base import most medical devices: India imports about 75 percent of them; Malaysia 90 percent (Chigullapalli and Tandulwadikar). Marketing and post-market oversight of medical devices is important nonetheless, yet often neglected.

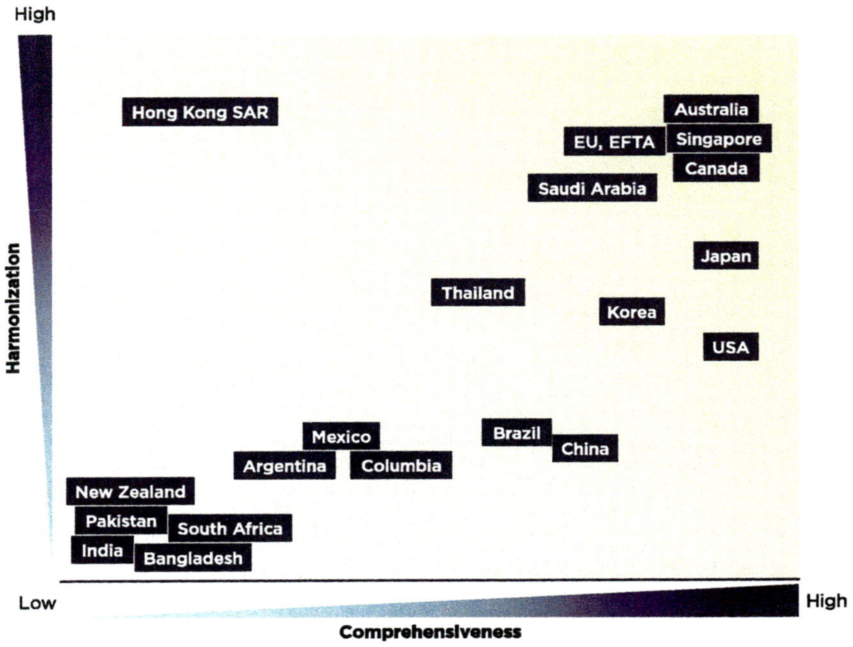

FIGURE 2-1 Conceptual qualitative overview of current national medical device regulatory systems.
SOURCE: Gropp, 2011.

Food Regulatory Oversight

Food safety regulatory oversight is historically more complicated than medical product regulation. In the United States, as in other countries, the government constructed a food safety system in pieces as its understanding of foodborne hazards grew (Dyckman, 1999). Around the world, the food regulatory authority often rests with both the departments of health and agriculture. There is a trend in many parts of the world to combine all aspects of food regulation into the purview of one agency. Canada, Denmark, Ireland, the United Kingdom, Germany, the Netherlands, and New Zealand have all consolidated their regulatory authority in the last decade (GAO, 2005). Nevertheless, regulatory oversight for food is commonly split between health and agriculture sectors.

HARMONIZATION

Harmonization of food and medicines regulations can both increase product safety and promote trade. When countries harmonize their systems, they eliminate the need for redundant testing and reduce registration times, allowing products to enter the market more quickly (Lelieveld and Keener, 2007). Harmonization facilitates fair competition, thereby promoting trade. It can also ensure that imports meet internationally recognized standards for quality and safety (Anand et al., 2010). Because of globalization, international harmonization of product standards is increasingly important (ICDRA, 2010).

Harmonization is of particular value in developing countries where there are infrastructure problems and deficits in regulatory laws. Harmonized and simplified requirements for medicines registration can ensure life-saving medicines are more quickly available in poor countries (Ndomondo-Sigonda and Ambali, 2011). Figure 2-2 describes the value of harmonizing medicines regulations to different stakeholders. Many regional economic communities are active in harmonizing their food and medical product regulations.

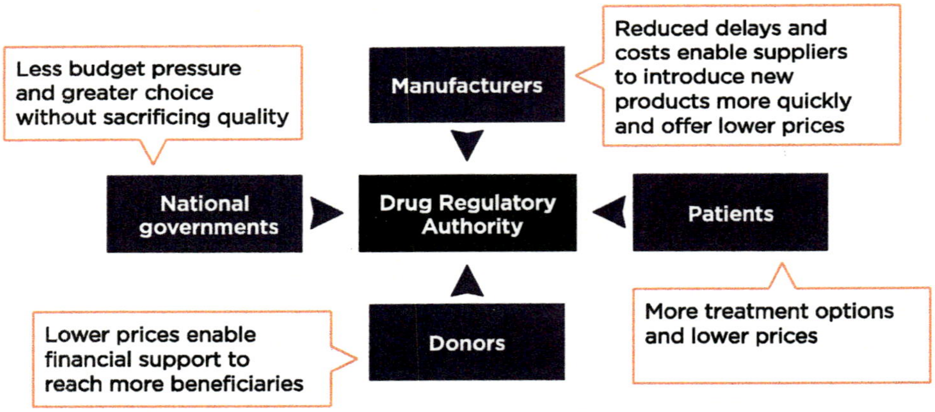

FIGURE 2-2 Benefits of harmonization by stakeholders.
SOURCE: Ndomondo-Sigonda and Ambali, 2011.

Since 1980, the WHO has provided a forum for drug regulatory authorities to come together and discuss strengthening their collaborations (WHO, 2011c). The Pan American Health Organization (PAHO) is also a leader in the Americas in medicines regulatory harmonization. PAHO is conducting technical cooperation projects in conjunction with national regulatory authorities and national control laboratories in the regulation and control of pharmaceutical products, vaccines, and other biologics (PAHO, 2010b).

The Association of Southeast Asian Nations (ASEAN) is active in harmonization in Southeast Asia. In 1992, the ASEAN economic ministers formed the Consultative Committee for Standards and Quality with the goal of harmonizing regulation across multiple sectors, including food and medical products (Ramesh and WG3 Chair). ASEAN's regulatory harmonization focuses on four areas: quality, efficacy, safety, and administration. The committee has established guidelines for many aspects of food and medicines regulation, including labeling, pesticide control, and traditional medicines. It can be difficult to put the guidelines into practice, however. ASEAN member countries range from some of world's least developed (Cambodia and Laos) to some of the most developed (Singapore). ASEAN standards are more stringent than the national standards of some of its member states. However, through collaboration and capacity building, the member states have developed a system of using different timelines for implementing different standards based on national readiness (ASEAN, 2005; Ratanawijitrasin and Wondemagegnehu, 2002).

The African Medicines Regulatory Harmonization Initiative (AMRHI) is an effort to strengthen regulatory capacity in Africa (Ndomondo-Sigonda and Ambali, 2011). Within Africa, there are several ongoing harmonization efforts. The Southern African Development Community, the East African Community, the Economic and Monetary Union of West Africa, the Economic Community of West African States, and the Economic Community of Central African States all work on harmonization. The AMRHI coordinates the process (AMRH, 2010). Regional partners in Africa work around different languages, varying levels of development, and a lack of an information-sharing system. To further complicate the matter, some countries are active in multiple international harmonization efforts. The countries that have made the best progress on harmonization have political will, legal frameworks for cooperation, and common language or currency or both (WHO Regional Office for Africa, 2005).

The International Conference on Harmonization of Technical Requirements for Regulation of Pharmaceuticals for Human Use (ICH) brings together drug regulatory authorities and pharmaceutical trade associations for the harmonization of standards (ICH, 2010). Regulatory authorities that participate in the ICH, either as observers or participants, or regulatory authorities that have legally binding recognition agreements with a conference member are considered stringent regulatory authorities (WHO, 2011a). The United States, Japan, EU member counties, Switzerland, Canada, Australia, Norway, Iceland, and Liechtenstein are all stringent regulatory authorities (Stop TB, 2009). ICH guidelines are widely recognized as high-quality and scientifically sound, though some object to an organization with a relatively narrow membership setting standards used internationally (Abraham, 2002; Molzon et al., 2011). Through its Global Cooperation Group, the ICH involves stakeholders from countries outside of the membership (ICH, 2011).

COOPERATION AMONG REGULATORY AGENCIES

Because of the international trade and multi-country distribution systems described in Chapter 1, the committee concluded that cooperation with other regulators both within county and among neighboring countries is a core element of a modern regulatory system in any country. Cooperation is critical for protecting the health and safety of consumers and for consistent enforcement of national policies (Kraemer et al., 2011).

Cooperation within a Country

The best regulatory systems work at different levels of government (the national, provincial and municipal levels, for example), but this does not happen without cooperation and coordination. When coordination is lacking, multi-level engagement can lead to duplicating work and overlapping responsibilities (Ratanawijitrasin and Wondemagegnehu, 2002). Poor coordination is a common problem in many low- and middle-income countries. For example, in China, food safety regulation falls to multiple agencies including the Ministry of Agriculture; the State Administration for Quality Supervision, Inspection, and Quarantine; the State Administration of Industry and Commerce; the Ministry of Health; and the State Food and Drug Administration. This lack of regulatory coordination for food safety is not unique to China and can be found in developed and developing countries around the world (Otsuki and Wilson, 2001; Stewart and Gostin, 2011). Chapter 3 discusses this problem in more detail.

Regulation of medical products is often simpler, but still requires extensive inter-governmental coordination. For example, many Asian nations have more than one regulatory body overseeing the safety and registration of drugs and other medical products (Pacific Bridge Medical). China is particularly complicated with an overall agency, the State Food and Drug Administration, housing 10 departments responsible for various aspects of medical product regulation and a decentralization of authority that grants relative independence to provincial authorities (SFDA; Tsoi, 2007). A particularly stark example of troubled coordination is Pakistan, which, in June 2011, abolished its national health ministry leaving drug regulatory responsibility to the provinces without any apparent system of coordination (Punjab refuses to accept drug regulatory authority, 2011; Seventeen federal ministries devolved to provinces, 2011).

It is not uncommon to have drug regulatory powers divided between federal and the state levels, as in India. Each Indian state has its own drug control organization that is responsible for the quality of the drug as well as licensing the manufacture, sale and distribution of drugs within that state (CDSCO). Federal agencies are responsible for coordinating states' activities, as in Australia, Malaysia, and Venezuela, for example. Both Australia and Malaysia have a coordination mechanism in place to ensure that federal and state regulatory agencies communicate (Ratanawijitrasin and Wondemagegnehu, 2002). Venezuela has poor coordination between agencies resulting in a fragmented regulatory system (Ratanawijitrasin and Wondemagegnehu, 2002). One way to improve coordination is to bring agencies together. Taiwan recently consolidated its Bureaus of Pharmaceutical Affairs, Food and Drug Analysis, and Controlled Drugs into one agency known as the Taiwan Food and Drug Administration that now regulates drugs, medical devices, and other health products (Pacific Bridge Medical).

The Canadian government is an uncommon example of coordinating multiple agencies in a country efficiently. The Canadian Food Inspection Agency coordinates regulators from the federal, provincial or territorial, and municipal authorities (Health Canada and Canadian Food Inspection Agency, 2007). The federal government agencies (Health Canada and the Canadian Food Inspection Agency) work with the provincial and territorial agencies to facilitate national harmonization, streamline the inspection process, and reduce regulatory pressures on industry (FAO/WHO, 2003).

Evaluating the Regulatory System

The WHO, FAO, and other international organizations have tools that allow regulators to evaluate their agencies' effectiveness and identify weak spots in their systems. For example, the World Organization for Animal Health, known as the OIE,[1] has developed a tool for assessing the veterinary services in a country against international standards (OIE, 2010). The Phytosanitary Capacity Evaluation, an International Plant Protection Convention management tool, aids countries in identifying the strengths and weaknesses in their phytosanitary systems. Table 2-1 lists other capacity evaluation tools; the WTO has complied an extensive list of the same (Standards and Trade Development Facility, 2011).

TABLE 2-1 Overview of Capacity Evaluation Tools

Tool	Developed by	Focus
Strengthening National Food Control Systems: Guidelines to Assess Capacity Building Needs	**FAO**	Food safety
Food Safety Toolkit (IFC, 2011)	**IFC**	Food safety and food hygiene
Performance, Vision and Strategy (PVS) for Food Safety	**IICA**	Food safety
Performance of Veterinary Services (PVS) Pathway	**OIE**	Animal health
Performance, Vision and Strategy (PVS) for National Veterinary Services	**IICA**	Animal health
Phytosanitary Capacity Evaluation (PCE) Tool	**IPPC**	Plant health
Performance, Vision and Strategy (PVS) for National Plant Protection Organizations	**IICA**	Plant health
Guide to Assess Biosecurity Capacity	**FAO**	Biosecurity
Performance, Vision and Strategy Tool for SPS	**IICA**	Food safety and agricultural health
Food safety and agricultural health assessments and action plans	**World Bank**	Food safety and agricultural health
Approach to Evaluate Conformity Assurance Infrastructure	**UNIDO**	Conformity assessment
National capacity self assessment tool for the Convention on Biological Diversity (CBD)	**CBD**	Global environmental commitments
Diagnostic tool for analysis and assessment of trade and health	**WHO**	Trade and health
Data collection tool for the review of drug regulatory systems (WHO, 2007)	**WHO**	Data collection
Computer-Assisted Drug Registration (WHO, 1998)	**WHO**	Drug regulation efficiency
Strengthening National Regulatory Authorities (WHO, 2003)	**WHO**	Capacity building

SOURCE: Adapted from Standards and Trade Development Facility, 2011.

[1] An acronym for its earlier name, Office International des Epizooties.

Cooperation Among Countries

Ensuring safety and quality are the main goals of food and medical product regulation. Globalization and international trade have made the world smaller; countries can no longer expect their national regulatory authority to guarantee product safety. The modern food and medical product supply is shared among many countries, and protecting it requires global action (Guenther and McCormick, 2011). Tables 2-2 and 2-3 give information about international programs building food and medical product safety capacity.

International agreement on minimum product standards is an important piece of international cooperation. International collaboration can lead to more timely detection of problems, promote cross-fertilization of ideas, and eliminate redundant expenses.

A good example of collaboration is the One Health Initiative. This worldwide movement works toward expanding collaboration and communication among specialists in human, animal, and environmental health. This initiative involves individual clinicians and researchers and has the endorsements of the American Medical Association, American Veterinary Medical Association, the American Society of Tropical Medicine and Hygiene, the Centers for Disease Control and Prevention (CDC), the U.S. Department of Agriculture (USDA), and the U.S. National Environmental Health Association (One Health Initiative).

A growing international interest in food defense, the prevention of intentional food supply contamination, has encouraged international cooperation among food regulators (Guenther and McCormick, 2011). The Asia-Pacific Economic Cooperation (APEC) is a forum for that brings together regulators from 21 countries that account for 43.7 percent of the world's trade (Guenther and McCormick, 2011). APEC member countries include representatives of every level of regulatory system capacity, ranging from some of the most developed (the United States, Japan, and Canada) and some of least developed (Papua New Guinea and Indonesia). Technical cooperation is integral to the APEC mission, and APEC symposia are invaluable venues for regulators from across a wide spectrum of nations to meet and exchange knowledge (APEC, 2012).

Much as work against fraud has encouraged international collaboration among food regulators, preventing pharmaceutical fraud demands the cooperation of medicines regulators from around the world. Building "coordinated networks across and between countries" to stop drug counterfeiting was the goal of the WHO's International Medical Products Anti-Counterfeiting Taskforce (WHO, 2012). However, the fight against pharmaceutical fraud has been held back by, among other things, the inability of stakeholder governments to agree on common definitions of substandard, counterfeit, and falsified drugs (Shepherd, 2010). The need for international cooperation is no less pressing among drug regulators than among food regulators, but in this case communication has drawn to a halt.

The committee believes that international cooperation and communication will be an even more important piece of regulatory agencies' responsibilities in the future. Sometimes the venues to bring together regulators can be hard to find. Centers of excellence and national science academies can bring academia, industry, and government together. The Department of Homeland Security Science & Technology Directorate Centers of Excellence (COE) network is a good example of this. The centers of excellence are comprised of 12 centers, each directed or co-directed by a university in collaboration with partners from other agencies, laboratories, or the private sector (Department of Homeland Security, 2011). National academies can convene meetings and bring together differing perspectives. Ultimately, the science academy is a useful neutral forum to come to consensus on controversial problems facing food and medical product regulators.

RISK AND SHARED REGULATORY RESPONSIBILITY

This chapter described some differences in the food and medical product regulatory systems in developed and developing countries. International trade and modern manufacturing bring these systems together, however. Regulators from many different countries debate microbial contamination risks in food and how to best manage the regulation of pharmaceutical ingredients. An overview of these two issues is important to understanding this report.

Risk, Hazard, and Food Regulatory Philosophy

During the past five years there has been increasing discussion about differentiating food safety systems based on whether they are hazard-based or risk-based. Before defining these two systems, it is important to note that there are two primary ways to manage food safety hazards and risks: good hygienic practices and Hazard Analysis Critical Control Point (HACCP) (Juneja and Sofos, 2010). The best systems rely on a combination of both, as it is impossible to implement HACCP without strong underlying good hygienic practices. Box 2-7 describes the basic principles of HACCP.

Good hygienic practices are the methods that ensure hygienic manufacturing in any food manufacturing plant. This includes sanitary practices, facility design, and employee hygiene. HACCP is a supplemental management tool loosely based on systems engineering, failure mode, and effect analysis. HACCP stresses attention to the critical steps in production, processing, distribution, marketing, and preparation that have a reasonable likelihood of failing, as well as the likelihood that the failure causes harm. These points are identified and control measures are put into place to prevent such failures. HACPP programs are divided into two phases: hazard analysis and hazard management. The application of good hygienic practices is a prerequisite to the use of HACCP (NACMCF, 1997).

There are no universally accepted definitions of hazard-based and risk-based safety systems. Though Codex publications such as *Guidelines for the Control of Campylobacter and Salmonella in Chicken Meat* and *Principles and Guidelines for the Conduct of Microbiological Risk Management* offer commentary on these terms, they give no formal definitions (CAC, 2007). In general, hazard-based systems consider the mere presence of a hazard sufficient reason to conclude contamination in the end products. A risk-based system considers the extent of exposure in relation to the likelihood that the exposure causes harm. Some experts go further, suggesting that a hazard-based system is grounded in the application of good hygienic practices or HACCP or both. In their estimation, only food safety programs that have undergone a formal risk assessment should be considered hazard-based. Some food safety experts consider the hazard analysis conducted as the first step in developing a HACCP program distinctly different from a risk assessment (Wallace et al., 2011).

BOX 2-7
HACCP

Hazard Analysis and Critical Control Points (HACCP) is a systematic approach to controlling food safety hazards as food moves through supply chains. Pillsbury developed HACCP in the 1960's while working on the food supply for the space program. There are seven principles in this system, listed below. The goal is to prevent hazards from occurring rather than removing them after the fact.

In 2005, the International Standards Organization developed the ISO 22000 standard for food safety management. ISO 22000 integrates into HACCP auditable requirements. Suppliers identify and assess the hazards as they move along the supply chain. ISO 22000 also requires supply chains have a system management program and interactive communication program to ensure the foods pass through the supply chain with minimal risk. The seven principles of HACCP are:

- Principle 1: Conduct a hazard analysis.
- Principle 2: Identify critical control points.
- Principle 3: Establish critical limits for each critical control point.
- Principle 4: Establish critical control point monitoring requirements.
- Principle 5: Establish corrective actions.
- Principle 6: Establish procedures for ensuring the HACCP system is working as intended.
- Principle 7: Establish record keeping procedures.

SOURCE: (Faergemand, 2008; NACMCF, 1997)

There is wide consensus, however, that HACCP hazard analysis is qualitative or semi-quantitative risk assessment. This idea is further evidenced by the guidance describing HACCP's focus on significant hazards (Hazard analysis and critical control point principles and application guidelines, 1998). Codex gives similar guidance (CAC, 1999). The FDA's National Advisory Committee on Microbiological Criteria for Foods explains, "The HACCP team conducts a hazard analysis and identifies appropriate control measures. The purpose of the hazard analysis is to develop a list of hazards which are *of such significance that they are reasonably likely to cause injury or illness if not effectively controlled....* Hazards that are not reasonably likely to occur would not require further consideration within a HACCP plan" (emphasis added) (NACMCF, 1997).

Clearly, the developers of HACCP plans need to consider risk—the probability and severity—of different threats. Most developed countries have effectively adopted HACCP as the primary risk management system for essentially all foods (Satin, 2005; Unnevehr and Jensen, 1999). The European Union requires food companies to implement HACCP principles. It is a required in the United States, Australia, New Zealand, and Canada. As an outcome of HACCP's adoption in developed countries, some developing countries have also adopted HACCP principles in order to export their products to developed countries (Satin, 2005; Unnevehr and Jensen, 1999).

There are differences in the ways that countries use HACCP and even differences among regulatory agencies within a country. For example, both the United States and the European Union use risk analysis for managing food safety concerns. Both have pre-market and post-market safety protocols. The EU recognizes the precautionary principle (Box 2-8), however. They withhold premarket approval from food additives and novel ingredients when there is not absolute proof of safety, a logical impossibility. In the United States, regulatory agencies build an appropriate caution into their standards based on the degree of uncertainty in the science. When there is evidence that a risk to human health exists but scientific data are insufficient to understand it, the Codex Alimentarius Commission should not proceed to elaborate a standard but should consider elaborating a related text, such as code of practice, provided that such a text is supported by the available scientific evidence (CAC, 2003). However, the difficulty in all these cases is that there is often a lack of agreement on when scientific data are sufficient and complete.

BOX 2-8
The Precautionary Principle

The precautionary principle has roots in a philosophy of risk management that stresses anticipation of, preparedness for, and prevention of harm. Most applicable in the fields of environmental safety and human health, the precautionary principle states that scientific evidence of a threat, rather than indisputable proof, is sufficient grounds for action to prevent harm. The precautionary principle has been invoked to justify the discontinuation of certain pesticides that present a possible health hazard (SEHN, 1998). The general philosophy of the principle is widely accepted among national and international organizations, but its applications and the degree of precaution expected vary greatly. The precautionary principle can take several forms, from a weak, triply negative statement that a lack of proof of danger does not necessitate inaction, to the much stronger version that requires action in the case of suspected hazard. Used wisely, the principle can facilitate rapid and effective response to hazards without the burden of scientific proof (Europa, 2011).

In the European Union, a strict interpretation of the precautionary principle states that it "applies where scientific evidence is insufficient, inconclusive or uncertain and preliminary scientific evaluation indicates that there are reasonable grounds for concern that the potentially dangerous effects on the environment, human, animal or plant health may be inconsistent with the high level of protection chosen by the EU (UNESCO, 2005)." The EU's conservative stance on genetically modified organisms is evidence of this. While the United States relies heavily on genetic modification of food crops, including close to 90 percent of all corn, soybeans, and cotton grown in the country, few genetically modified crops are authorized in the European Union. Several EU countries, including Austria, Greece, Germany, and France, abide by even stricter guidelines that place a complete or near complete ban on GMOs (European Commission; GMO Compass, 2009).

In a speech given in 2003 in New York, Tony Van der Haegan, Minister-Counselor of the Agriculture, Fisheries, Food Safety and Consumer Affairs office of the European Commission Delegation, spoke about the history of the precautionary principle in Europe. He recalled the 1989 U.S. ban on the import of cattle and beef products from the United Kingdom during the Bovine Spongiform Encephalopathy (BSE) crisis as an example of early, effective use of the precautionary principle, and suggested that had the United Kingdom been as proactive in its safety measures, it may have prevented the subsequent spread of BSE throughout Europe (EU, 2003). While proponents of the principle insist that it protects human health and encourages development of new, safer products, critics maintain that it stifles innovation.

The United States and EU also differ on their standards for foodborne pathogenic microorganisms. The EU has moved to define microbiological standards for a number of pathogens, thereby establishing clear, non-zero requirements that recognize the inherent residual risk in all food safety plans (Huss et al., 2004). The equivalent requirements in the United States are established through relatively vague, non-numerical standards. Instead of detailed end-product standards, the U.S. regulators publish official sampling plans and the analytical methods they will use when testing for pathogenic microorganisms (Domesle and O'Keefe, 2011). This allows them to achieve a similar level of control as their European counterparts without having to officially recognize the trace contamination allowed even when the system is operating well.

However, the U.S. food industry generally relies much more on microbiological testing as a food safety verification tool than the European industry does. During the past decade there has been an increased effort to develop measures of microbial food safety to harmonize the companies' different approaches to risk management. The International Commission on Microbiological Specification for Foods gives three metrics[2] as a means to link the stringency of the food safety system to public health outcomes (ICMSF, 2002). This allows more traditional metrics to be set based on the level of public health protection desired and achievable. Conversely, these risk management measures allow for prediction of the likely change in public health protection brought about by the use of different microbiological criteria. The Codex Alimentarius' principles on microbial risk management also give guidance on the use of the metric (CAC, 2007).

Regulation of Active Pharmaceutical Ingredients

Most pharmaceutical products are manufactured in two basic steps. The first step converts chemical intermediates and starting materials into an API using chemical synthesis, fermentation, or other synthesis processes. The second step is final formulation where active ingredients and excipients are mixed to form a drug (pills, tablets, capsules, injectables, etc.). Driven by lower costs and easier environmental compliance standards, over 80 percent of API manufacture is done in India and China, even for formulations that are manufactured in the United States or Europe (FDA, 2011).

The FDA regulates the manufacture of APIs. It requires the manufacturer of the final drug formulation to provide details on which manufacturer they will buy their API from when they file a New Drug Application, Abbreviated New Drug Application, or a change notification. The FDA also requires manufacturers of APIs to submit a drug master file describing the manufacturing facility, processes, and materials used in the production of the active ingredients. Much of the information in the master file is confidential. When a formulator specifies in an application to the FDA that it will be using API from a certain manufacturer, it refers to that manufacturer's master file. The FDA then schedules a site inspection for the API manufacturer. This inspection verifies the information in the master file and ensures compliance with good manufacturing practices. Companies must notify the FDA of any change in their API providers. If the active ingredient manufacturer has not been inspected before, then FDA will start the process again.

In addition to the first time inspection, the FDA also routinely inspects API manufacturing facilities. However, it is not feasible to carry out these routine inspections frequently, especially for manufacturers in India, China, and other foreign countries.

---

[2] Food Safety Objectives, Performance Objectives, and Performance Criteria.

Before the 2008 Olympic Games, the Chinese government temporarily shut down a large number of API factories around Beijing to improve air quality. This caused API shortages and drove up prices on the international market.
SOURCE: PETER PARKS/AFP/Getty Images/Newscom.

Economies of scale drive the manufacture of API. Some companies manufacture both API and final formulations, but no firm can manufacture every active ingredient it could need. Therefore, companies that manufacture both APIs and final formulations buy and sell active ingredients on the merchant market. This creates a complex web of buying and selling that becomes difficult to trace.

Often multiple drug applications reference the same API manufacturer because many different companies use the same source for their API. Other times, a drug application references multiple API manufacturers because one manufacturer gets APIs from several sources. In such cases the FDA's routine inspection covers only the portion of the factory that makes the API in question.

The FDA and other regulatory agencies can regulate API production, but the formulation manufacturers themselves need to audit their API suppliers frequently against international good manufacturing practices. It would also help to coordinate inspections with the EMA or other stringent regulatory authorities. This would allow for more frequent inspections and better inspection coverage all around, as was shown by a pilot collaboration among the FDA, European Medicines Agency (EMA), and Australian medicines regulatory authority (EMA, 2011).

It is also possible to enable existing manufacturers to set up high-quality GMP manufacturing for drugs for serious infectious diseases, such as HIV, tuberculosis, and malaria on the same site where cheaper, less complicated drugs like acetaminophen are manufactured. By using existing facilities, developing country manufacturers can work to WHO prequalification without starting from scratch.

CONCLUSION

As Chapter 1 describes, the United States has built its regulatory system in spurts for over 100 years, largely influenced by product safety disasters. Developing countries are now struggling to design systems that ensure food and medical product safety. This chapter describes the characteristic underpinnings governments should consider in designing food and medical product regulatory systems. A good system should be responsive; it should be able to act in a crisis and able keep pace with changing technology. It should also be focused on outcomes and not hinder innovation. The system must be predictable; that is, regulatory decisions should be fair, not arbitrary or capricious. The amount of regulatory oversight given to a product should be proportional to the product's likelihood of causing harm. Finally, the regulatory system should be independent and not unduly influenced by politics or money.

At its core, an effective food and medical product regulatory system uses science and risk to develop policy. Regulators should participate in international harmonization, and they should value international cooperation. The ethical enforcement of laws is a crucial piece of a regulatory system. A strong regulatory system protects against public health emergencies, yet it can communicate promptly and accurately with the public during an emergency. At the very least, food and medical product regulation depends on a system for rule making. All stakeholders should have a way to communicate with the regulatory authority about the rules governing product safety.

International cooperation is an important part of a modern food and medical product regulatory system. There are many examples of countries working together on harmonization, but there is always room for improvement. Differences in understanding of microbiological hazards in the food chain and inconsistencies in the regulation of APIs can present challenges to international cooperation.

TABLE 2-2 Food Safety Capacity Building Programs

Organization	Project	Objective	Activities	Where
WHO	Global Foodborne Infections Network (GFN)	To promote integrated, laboratory-based surveillance and foster collaboration among human health, veterinary and food-related disciplines, thereby enhancing the capacity of countries to detect, respond and prevent Foodborne and other infection enteric diseases.	• Technical support • Quality control systems for reliable laboratory testing • Training (microbiology, epidemiology, risk assessment)	Worldwide
WHO/FAO	International Food Safety Authorities Network (INFOSAN)	To promote rapid exchange of information during food safety events, share information of global interest, promote partnerships, help countries strengthen their capacity to manage food safety risks, and to respond to requests for assistance during food safety emergencies.	• Improving response capacity of emergency contact points • Training on risk assessment • Guidance and training on developing national food safety emergency response plans • Tools for outbreak investigation	Worldwide
FAO	Food Quality Standards Service (AGNS)	Enhancing food safety and quality along the supply chain at the international, regional and national levels with the aim of protecting consumers and promoting the production and trade of safe quality food.	• Establish and improve national regulatory frameworks • Technical advice on integrated food control systems • Independent scientific advice • Guidelines and tools on food safety risk assessment • Emergency assistance	Worldwide

TABLE 2-2 *Continued*

Organization	Project	Objective	Activities	Where
World Bank	Incorporated into a wide range of regional and country-level programs	Protecting public health and preventing malnutrition; educating the technical staff necessary for a competitive agriculture sector; and improving trade and market access for developing countries.	• Partnerships - Part of the WTO's Standards and Trade Development Facility - Manages the Global Food Safety Fund • Technical advice - Publications such as "Food Safety and Agricultural Health Standards: Challenges and Opportunities for Developing Country Exports - Conducts SPS capacity and needs assessments • Larger scale agricultural and development projects - The World Bank's 2010-2012 *Action Plan* includes helping countries develop infrastructure and institutions for food safety and to better implement SPS; training, knowledge sharing and analytical research on food safety standards; and directing money across the supply chain including logistic and advisory services for food safety standards	Worldwide
United Nations	United Nations Conference on Trade and Development (UNCTAD)	Provides food safety capacity building as part of trade promotion.	• Training good agricultural and manufacturing practices, ISO 9000, ISO 22000, and HACCP standards for farmers in developing countries • Research on SPS standards in least developed countries to assess the barriers to enter markets and strengthen capacity to bridge these gaps	Worldwide
APEC	Food Safety Cooperation Forum	To improve and strengthen information sharing in food safety by enhancing cooperation among member economies; and to identify, prioritize and coordinate capacity building the APEC region, taking other regional activities into account.	• Regulatory frameworks: establish government endorsed food regulatory systems; develop, implement and enforce food safety standards • Food inspection and certification programs: develop legislative frameworks for food management; establish communication systems to support food inspection including education and training • Training in food safety management and risk assessment • Establishing relevant forums, encouraging collaboration and creating surveillance systems for transparent information sharing	Asia Pacific

TABLE 2-2 *Continued*

Organization	Project	Objective	Activities	Where
ASEAN	Cooperation in Food & Agriculture (under the Ministers of Agriculture)	To coordinate and implement food safety measures and to balance the concerns of food security and market access.	• Issues guidelines and standards on food handling, quarantine and testing procedures, GMOs, pesticide residue limits • Formulate common Codex positions • Harmonize ASEAN standards according to Codex • ASEAN Food Safety Network: an integrated platform for sharing food safety information among ASEAN countries, especially related to Codex, OIE and IPPC	Southeast Asia
	Cooperation in Standards & Conformance (under the Ministers of Economics)	To coordinate and implement food safety measures and to balance the concerns of food security and market access.	• Implementation of the ASEAN Framework Agreement on Mutual Recognition Arrangements, moving towards mutually accepted standards and inspections • Harmonize standards • Ensure transparency of standards, technical regulations and conformity assessments	Southeast Asia
	Expert Group on Food Safety	To improve food safety of ASEAN countries, but also to facilitate food trade and formulate a strategic plan to address important food safety issues for mutual benefits.	• Provides assistance to ASEAN governments to develop and strengthen food safety infrastructure and programs • Food Safety Improvement Plan: identifies 10 priority areas for cooperation including a center of excellence for inspection and certification, consumer participation in food safety, education and training, and increased sharing of food safety information.	Southeast Asia
Asian Development Bank	Incorporated into a wide range of regional and country-level programs	Protection of public health through sustainable access to safe foods and promotion of economic development.	• Technical assistance on developing and improving national systems, use of food safety technologies • Research – Publications such as: "Impact of Food Safety Standards on Processed Food Exports from Developing Countries" and "Food Safety and ITC Traceability Systems: Lessons from Japan for Developing Countries" • Promotes regional cooperation in standards	Asia and the Pacific

TABLE 2-2 *Continued*

Organization	Project	Objective	Activities	Where
PAHO	PAHO Regional Program on Food Safety	To build capacity in risk assessment, risk management, risk communication and education and to mobilize and optimize the use of resources.	• Training courses in surveillance, risk assessment, and the application of good manufacturing practices, HACCP, etc. • Updating and harmonizing legislation • Consolidating regional INFOSAN activities • Improving countries' ability to use of systematic risk assessment and develop integrated food safety programs • Supporting active involvement in Codex • Improving national capacity to maintain communication flow between public and private sectors • Improving the technical capability of member states to implement systematic approaches to food safety and to adopt evidence-based decisions • Strengthening farms-to-table links • Associations and partnerships with UN agencies, Organization of American States, etc.	South America
Mercosur	Incorporated into its broader goals of regional integration and increased market access	To create a food safety and hygiene system and phytosanitary area in the Mercosur region and to increase market access for exports, especially with the EU.	• Identifies food safety as a priority for its members and sets regional standards • Cooperative agreement with the EU (up to €15 million) for cooperation and harmonization of veterinary and phytosanitary procedures. Includes: - Strengthening institutions responsible for food safety - Improving food hygiene control systems - Common food hygiene policies for the region	Latin America
African Development Bank	Incorporated into a wide range of regional and country-level programs	To support improved health and nutrition through access to safe foods and to promote economic growth through market access and income generation.	• Training in SPS measures, handling and processing techniques, quality standards • Improving infrastructure such as hygienic meat slaughtering facilities • Improving supply chains with roads and cold chains • Promotes regional standards harmonization	Africa

TABLE 2-2 *Continued*

Organization	Project	Objective	Activities	Where
African Union	Inter-African Bureau for Animal Resources	Building both AU and member country capacity to participate in Codex and other standard setting organizations.	• Participation of African Nations in SPS Standard Setting Organizations (PAN-SPSO) Project • Institutional support • Regional and continental harmonization • Technical capacity building • Information collection and sharing	Africa
	Better Training For Safer Food	African Union and EU collaboration to support food security through the transfer of technical expertise to improve food safety and quality.	• Assess veterinary services and strengthen national capacity to meet international sanitary standards • Improve legal frameworks for animal health and food safety • Strengthen laboratory capacity via twinning • Training of both food safety professionals and regional officials through regional workshops, twinning and visiting experts	Africa
FDA	Office of International Programs, Technical Cooperation and Capacity Building	Defines regulatory capacity, the ability of national regulatory authorities to perform regulatory their core functions to ensure the availability of high quality and safe food and medical products as part of the FDA mission to ensure safe products in the United States.	• Strengthening information and evidence so the FDA can make informed decisions about how to allocate resources • Transferring expertise and identifying training efforts that do not require FDA resources • Encouraging global information networks to strengthen detection, surveillance and assessment systems and strengthen capacity to address food safety problems	Worldwide
USAID	Incorporated into country-level development projects		• Technical assistance to producer groups and exporter associations • Training on good manufacturing and agricultural practices and food safety and laboratory analysis training • Public-private partnership support (gave $1 million as starting money for the Global Food Safety Fund) • Food safety crisis management	Worldwide

TABLE 2-2 *Continued*

Organization	Project	Objective	Activities	Where
USDA	Foreign Agriculture Service	Leads USDA's efforts to help developing countries improve their agricultural systems and trade capacity and develop market-institutions and science based regulatory frame works.	• Trade and scientific exchanges - i.e. Cochran Fellowship Program: provides participants from middle-income countries, emerging markets, and emerging democracies with high quality training to improve local agricultural systems and strengthen and enhance trade links with the United States	Worldwide
UK Department for International Development	Incorporated into country-level development projects and research	Safe food is part of DFID's overall mission to promote health and economic development in low income countries. Access to safe food is critical for health and compliance with safety regulations is necessary to export food to wealthy countries.	• Research: funds a wide range of research of improving food safety systems in developing countries • Country level training and technical assistance - Food control laboratory capacity building - Training African trainers to implement food safety programs based on HACCP	Worldwide
GIZ	Food Quality and Food Safety	To advise public and private actors on the process of setting national and international standards and integrating international standards into their own legislation and quality operations management.	• Advise governments on WTO food standards like SPS • Training for governments to develop food safety systems • Support countries in developing risk assessment and risk management by extending food monitoring programs • Training laboratory personnel	Worldwide

TABLE 2-3 Medical Product Capacity Building Programs

Organization	Project	Objective	Activities	Where
WHO Quality and Safety of Medicines Program	Regulatory Support	To develop internationally recognized norms, standards and guidelines; and to provide guidance, technical assistance and training to support national medical regulatory agencies	• Assessing national medicines regulatory systems • Regulatory information and practical manuals • Training • Model website for regulatory authorities • Model system for computer-assisted medicines registration • Certification scheme on quality of pharmaceutical products • International Conference of Drug Regulatory Authorities	Worldwide
	Safety, Efficacy and Utilization	To develop norms and standards for pharmacovigilance, promote information exchange on medicines safety and provide country support	• WHO Advisory Committee on Safety of Medicinal Products • Monitoring medicines (FP-7): 42 month project launched in 2010 including the WHO, the Uppsala Monitoring Centre and other partners. The Project has four key components: 1. Strengthening consumer reporting. 2. Identification of problems by national pharmacovigilance centers. 3. Better use of existing global data. 4. Developing active and focused systems to address urgent safety questions in priority diseases. Projects to improve pharmacovigilance in drugs for Chagas, TB, HIV and Malaria	Worldwide
	Quality Assurance	To develop norms, standards and guidelines for quality assurance including quality control, production, distribution and inspections	Publications: • WHO good manufacturing principles: main principles for pharmaceutical products (2011) • Good distribution practices for pharmaceutical products (2010) • Quality system requirements for national GMP inspectorates (2003)	Worldwide

TABLE 2-3 *Continued*

Organization	Project	Objective	Activities	Where
WHO Quality and Safety of Medicines Program *(continued)*	The International Pharmacopeia	To provide the source material for reference or adaptation by any member state who wants to establish pharmaceutical requirements	Outlines quality specifications for: • active ingredients and excipients • dosage • general methods of supporting analysis	Worldwide
WHO Department of Immunization, Vaccines and Biologicals	Vaccine Safety	To identify and consolidate consensus opinions on key vaccine regulatory issues; and to communicate the these opinions to national authorities and manufacturers through guidance documents	WHO Technical Report Series (TRS) informs members and manufacturers of up-to-date methods; releases international reference materials for the standardization of assays and testing	Worldwide
	Regulatory Pathway Initiative	To improve developing countries' ability to regulate new vaccines by supporting the development and implementation of regulatory strategies for assessing clinical trial applications and establishing regulatory mechanisms for licensing new vaccines that are not registered in the country of manufactures	• Developing Countries' Vaccine Regulators Network – WHO established the network and plays a secretariat role – Forum for discussion of and exposure to policies and procedures for the evaluation of clinical trial proposals and clinical trial data • Collaboration with the European Medicines Agency, FDA, and other developed regulatory authorities to develop new regulatory strategies for licensing of novel vaccines • Establishment of regional regulatory authority and research center networks to address the short term need for review of clinical protocols, monitoring trials and evaluation of trial data • Training and technical assistance for NRAs which have not developed the expertise to review license applications	Worldwide

TABLE 2-3 *Continued*

Organization	Project	Objective	Activities	Where
WHO Department of Essential Health Technologies	Global initiative on health technologies	To establish a framework for the development of national health technology programs; and to support World Health Assembly resolution 60.29 which urges member states to have guidelines for good manufacturing and regulatory practices, to establish surveillance systems and to participate in international harmonization [other major objectives not related to safety or regulatory capacity buidling]	• Establish guidelines for national health technology programs • Develop methodologies to help member states conduct assessments • Identify national, international and global standards for countries to identify their gaps and future needs Worldwide • Create tools to implement gaps in policies • WHO publications on designing and implementing effective medical device regulatory systems	Worldwide
World Bank	Incorporated into a wide range of projects, primarily in its Health, Nutrition and Population sector (HNP)	To assist countries in improving the health, nutrition, population outcomes of poor people via strengthening the health care systems and securing sustainable health financing. To protect the most vulnerable from the impoverishing effects of illness, malnutrition, and high fertility by developing health policies that enhance the knowledge, skills, and values leading to equitable economic and human development.	• Partnerships - Partner in the African Medicines Regulatory Harmonization initiative • Research • Overall HNP strategy includes improving health governance, health systems strengthening, supply chain management, access to medicines • Country-level investment	Worldwide

TABLE 2-3 *Continued*

Organization	Project	Objective	Activities	Where
PAHO	Pan American Network for Drug Regulatory harmonization	To maintain a constructive dialogue among drug regulatory authorities and other stakeholders, adopt guidelines on specific aspects of regulation, and to promote technical cooperation among countries	Harmonization and capacity building efforts in: • Bioequivalence • Biotechnological products • Counterfeit medicines • Good clinical, laboratory and manufacturing practices • Medicine manufacturing plants • Medicines classification and registration • Pharmacopeia • Pharmacovigilance • Vaccines	The Americas
APEC	APEC Harmonization Center	Increase regulatory harmonization among member states with the goals of supporting access to best practices, information exchange, clinical trials that meet international standards and to improve the quality, safety and efficacy of medical products to enhance health outcomes and facilitate international trade	• Research on harmonization policies and best practices • Education and training, including fellowship programs • Establish strong information exchange networks • Maintain online publications • Develop and disseminate harmonization models • Support international cooperation	Asia Pacific
ASEAN	ACCSQ Pharmaceutical Product Working Group	The harmonization of pharmaceutical regulations to facilitate the goals of the ASEAN Free Trade Area, particularly eliminating technical barriers to trade, without compromising the quality or safety of medicines	• GMP training • Implementation of common technical requirements • Mutual recognition agreements for GMP inspections • Shared post-market surveillance information • Vaccine regulation capacity building	Southeast Asia

TABLE 2-3 *Continued*

Organization	Project	Objective	Activities	Where
NEPAD, WHO, World Bank, Gates Foundation, DFID, Clinton Health Access Initiative	African Medicines Regulatory Harmonization Initiative	To improve health by increasing access to safe and effective medicines of good quality through strengthening the technical and administrative capacity of national medicines regulatory authorities	• Create a collaborative network of regional regulatory authorities • Harmonize technical requirements of medical products and build confidence so that standards are respected by participating authorities • Establish a framework for joint evaluations of applications and inspections of manufacturing sites • Strengthen the capacity for regulatory oversight • Develop information management systems and promote the exchange of regulatory information	Sub-Saharan Africa
South African Development Community (with support from the African Development Bank)	SADC Pharmaceutical Programme	To strengthen the capacity of member states and to mitigate the threat of diseases that are major public health concerns by increasing access to quality medicines	• Harmonizing regional regulations • Strengthening regulations and enforcement infrastructure • Education and retaining competent pharmaceutical staff; strengthen regional training centers • Promoting joint procurement of quality essential medicines • Maximizing research and production capacity of quality, generic essential medicines • Gap assessments of national regulatory authorities and laboratories	Southern Africa
FDA	Office of International Programs, Technical Cooperating and Capacity building	Defines regulatory capacity, the ability of national regulatory authorities to perform regularly their core functions, to ensure the availability of high quality and safe food and medical products, as part of the FDA mission to ensure safe products in the United States	• Strengthening information and evidence so the FDA can make informed decisions about how to use its resources • Transferring its expertise and identifying training efforts globally that do not require the use of FDA resources • Encouraging global information networks to strengthen detection, surveillance and assessment systems • Support surveillance and tracking efforts for global supply chains • Support pharmacovigilance capacity	Worldwide

TABLE 2-3 *Continued*

Organization	Project	Objective	Activities	Where
USAID and Management Sciences for Health	Strengthening Pharmaceutical Systems	To build capacity within poor countries to effectively manage pharmaceutical systems, successfully implement USAID priority services and protect public health by improving access to and use of quality assured medicines	• Improving governance in the pharmaceutical sector • Strengthening pharmaceutical and laboratory management systems • Containing the mergence and spread of antimicrobial resistance • Expanding access to medicines	Worldwide
USP	Promoting Quality of Medicines	A five year, USAID funded project to address poor quality medicines in developing countries and to assure the quality, safety and efficacy of medicines for USAID priority diseases	• Strengthen national quality control programs: – Build the capacity of national quality control laboratories – Support medicines registration, inspections, laboratory testing and post-market surveillance • Increase supply of quality assured medicines by offering technical assistance to manufactures on WHO prequalification • Combat substandard and counterfeit medicines by developing testing mechanisms, conducting quality research on essential medicines and providing technical assistance on detecting and monitoring substandard medicines • Provide technical leadership and global advocacy on the dangers of substandard medicines	Worldwide
Brighton Collaboration		A non-profit, scientifically independent partnership with the goal of conducing and promoting high quality vaccine safety research.	• Set vaccine safety research standards and provide common terminology • Build research capacity • Joined with the WHO and Gates Foundation to build vaccine safety monitoring • Developed network of local vaccine experts to serve as a global vaccine safety resource • Developed pilot infrastructure (with the European Center for Disease Prevention control) to link electronic records and an online classification tool • Established a virtual online research institute to facilitate communication • Plans to develop a vaccine training program	Worldwide

REFERENCES

Abraham, J. 2002. The pharmaceutical industry as a political player. *The Lancet* 360(9344):1498-1502.

AMRH. 2010. *African medicines registration harmonisation newsletter: Issue 3.* NEPAD and WHO.

Anand, K., K. Saini, S. Binod, and Y. Chopra. 2010. To recognize the use of international standards for making harmonized regulation of medical devices in Asia-Pacific. *Journal of Young Pharmacists* 2(3):321-325.

APEC. 2012. *Agricultural technical cooperation.* http://www.apec.org/Home/Groups/SOM-Steering-Committee-on-Economic-and-Technical-Cooperation/Working-Groups/Agricultural-Technical-Cooperation.aspx (accessed February 1, 2012).

ASEAN. 2005. *ASEAN policy guideline on standards and conformance.* Manila, Philippines.

BIS. *Choose the alternative.* http://www.bis.gov.uk/policies/bre/better-regulation-framework/alternatives-to-regulation/choose-the-alternative (accessed October 5, 2011).

———. 2011. *Market / economic instruments.* http://www.bis.gov.uk/policies/bre/better-regulation-framework/alternatives-to-regulation/choose-the-alternative/market-economic-instruments (accessed 2011, Decemeber 7).

Brhlikova, P., I. Harper, and A. Pollock. 2007 July 2-3. *Good manufacturing practice in the pharmaceutical industry.* Paper presented at Working paper 3, prepared for Workshop on 'Tracing Pharmaceuticals in South Asia', University of Edinburgh.

Brown, A. C., J. Stern, B. Tenenbaum, and D. Gencer. 2006. *Handbook for evaluating infrastructure regulatory systems.* Washington, DC: The International Bank for Reconstruction and Development/The World Bank.

CAC. 1999. *Codex alimentarius food hygiene basic texts- second edition.* Rome: World Health Organization and the Food and Agriculture Organization of the United Nations.

———. 2003. *Principles for the risk analysis of foods derived from modern biotechnology.*

———. 2007. *Principles and guidelines for the conduct of microbiological risk management (MRM).* Rome: World Health Organization and the Food and Agriculture Organization of the United Nations.

———. 2011. *Guidelines for the control of campylobacter and salmonella in chicken meat.*

CDSCO. *List of state drugs controllers.* http://cdsco.nic.in/html/state%20drugs1.htm (accessed November 11, 2011).

Chigullapalli, R., and A. Tandulwadikar. Asian medical device markets - emerging regulations *Asian Hospital and Healthcare Management,* http://www.asianhhm.com/Knowledge_bank/articles/asian-medical-device-markets.htm (accessed November 11, 2011).

Crisp, N. *Changes to South African medicines regulation body.*

———. 2011 May 31. *SAHPRA: Progress regarding establishing the entity and impact/relevance for medical device industry.* Paper presented at 2nd Annual South African Medical Devices Industry Association (SAMED) Conference, Midrand, South Africa.

Dalpino, C. E. 2000. *Deferring democracy: Promoting openness in authoritarian regimes.* Washington, DC: The Brookings Institution.

Department of Homeland Security. 2011. *Homeland security centers of excellence.* http://www.dhs.gov/files/programs/editorial_0498.shtm (accessed November 9, 2011).

DOE. The national environmental policy act of 1969. In *Title I*, edited by Department of Energy. Washington, DC.

Domesle, A., and M. O'Keefe. 2011. *United States national residue program: 2011 scheduled sampling plans.* Washington, DC: USDA/FSIS/OPHS.

Dyckman, L. J. 1999. *U.S. Needs a single agency to administer a unified, risk-based inpsection system: Statement of Lawrence J. Dyckman.* Government Accountability Office.

EMA. 2011. *Final report on the international API inspection pilot programme.* London: European Medicines Agency, Australian Government, and the Food and Drug Administration.

EU. 2003. *EU view of precautionary principle in food safety.* http://www.eurunion.org/news/speeches/2003/031023tvdh.htm (accessed February 14, 2012).

Europa. 2011. *Summaries of EU legislation: The precautionary principle.* http://europa.eu/legislation_summaries/consumers/consumer_safety/l32042_en.htm (accessed February 14, 2012).

European Commission. *General food law - principles.* http://ec.europa.eu/food/food/foodlaw/principles/index_en.htm (accessed November 21, 2011).

———. *Rules on GMOs in the EU - ban on GMOs cultivation.* http://ec.europa.eu/food/food/biotechnology/gmo_ban_cultivation_en.htm (accessed February 14, 2012).

Executive summary: Report of the ministerial task team on the restructuring of the Medicines Regulatory Affairs and Medicines Control Council and recommendations for the new regulatory authority for health products of South Africa. 2008. Ministry of Health of South Africa.

Faergemand, J. 2008. *The ISO 22000 series: Global standards for safe food supply chains.* International Organization for Standardization.

Fairclough, G. 2009. *Beijing tightens food-safety laws: New measures call for tougher penalties and more oversight.* http://online.wsj.com/article/SB123591044294303161.html (accessed November 21, 2011).

FAO. 2004. *Foodborne diseases: Situation of diarrheal diseases in Thailand.* ftp://ftp.fao.org/docrep/fao/meeting/006/ad703e/ad703e00.pdf (accessed November 18, 2011).

FAO/WHO. 2003. *Assuring food safety and quality: Guidelines for strengthening national food control systems.*

FDA. 2011. *Pathway to global product safety and quality.* Washington, DC: U.S. Food and Drug Administration.

FICCI. 2010. *Bottlenecks in Indian food processing industry.* New Delhi, India: Federation of Indian Chambers of Commerce and Industry.

FSSAI. 2011. *About FSSAI.* http://www.fssai.gov.in/AboutFSSAI/introduction.aspx (accessed November 17, 2011).

GAO. 2005. *Food safety: Experiences of seven countries in consolidating their food safety systems.* Washington, DC: Government Accountability Office.

GMO Compass. 2009. *USA: Cultivation of gm plants.* http://www.gmo-compass.org/eng/agri_biotechnology/gmo_planting/506.usa_cultivation_gm_plants_2009.html (accessed February 14, 2012).

Gropp, M. 2011 March 2-3. *Core elements of medical device regulatory systems in developing countries*. Paper presented at Strengthening Core Elements of Regulatory Stystems in Developing Countries: Meeting One, Washington, DC.

Guenther, J. C., and K. J. McCormick. 2011. U.S. Government efforts to build global food defense capacity. Paper read at Strategies for Achieving Food Security in Central Asia, Bishkek, Kyrgyzstan.

Hazard analysis and critical control point principles and application guidelines. 1998. *Journal of Food Protection* 61(6):762-775.

Health Canada and Canadian Food Inspection Agency. 2007. *The food regulatory system in Canada.*

Huss, H. H., L. Ababouch, and L. Gram. 2004. *Assessment of seafood safety and quality.* Rome, Italy: FAO.

ICDRA. 2010 Novemer 30-December 3. *14 ICDRA recommendations*. Paper presented at the Fourteenth International Conference of Drug Regulatory Authorities, Singapore.

ICH. 2010. *The value and benefits of ICH to drug regulatory authorities: Advancing harmonization for better health.* Geneva, Switzerland.

———. 2011. *ICH harmonisation for better health: Official website*. http://www.ich.org/ (accessed October 4, 2011).

ICMSF. 2002. *Microorganisms in foods 7: Microbiological testing in food safety management*. New York: Kluwer Academic/Plenum Publishers.

IOM. 2006. *Valuing health for regulatory cost-effective analysis*. Edited by W. Miller, L. A. Robinson and R. S. Lawrence. Washington, DC: The National Academies Press.

Juneja, V. K., and J. N. Sofos. 2010. *Pathogens and toxins in foods: Challenges and interventions*. Washington, DC: American Society for Microbiology Press

KPMG International. 2006. *The Indian pharmaceutical industry: Collaboration for growth.* The Netherlands: KPMG International.

Kraemer, D. W., Deputy Director for Operations, Center for Food Safety and Applied Nutrition, and Food and Drug Administration. 2011. *Challenges faced by food safety regulatory systems in developing countries*. Paper presented at Strengthening Core Elements of Regulatory Systems in Developing Countries: Meeting One, Washington, DC.

Lelieveld, H., and L. Keener. 2007. Global harmonization of food regulations and legislation--the Global Harmonization Initiative. *Trends in Food Science & Technology* 18:S15-S19.

Molzon, J. A., A. Giaquinto, L. Lindstrom, T. Tominaga, M. Ward, P. Doerr, L. Hunt, and L. Rago. 2011. The value and benefits of the international conference on harmonisation to drug regulatory authorities: Advancing harmonization for better public health. *Clinical Pharmacology and Therapeutics* 89(4):503-512.

NACMCF. 1997. *Hazard analysis and critical control point principles and application guidelines.* http://www.fda.gov/food/foodsafety/HazardAnalysisCriticalControlPointsHACCP/ucm114868.htm (accessed December 13, 2011).

Ndomondo-Sigonda, M., and A. Ambali. 2011. The African medicines regulatory harmonization initiative: Rationale and benefits. *Clinical Pharmacology and Therapeutics* 89(2):176-178.

Office of Information and Regulatory Affairs. 2003. *Regulatory impact analysis: A primer.*

OIE. 2010. *The new tool for the evaluation of performance of veterinary services (pvs tool) using OIE international standards of quality and evaluation*

http://web.oie.int/eng/OIE/organisation/en_vet_eval_tool.htm (accessed October 5, 2011).
One Health Initiative. *One Health Initiative will unite human and veterinary medicine.* http://www.onehealthinitiative.com/index.php (accessed November 9, 2011).
Organisation of Economic Co-Operation and Development. 2009. *Indicators of regulatory management systems: 2009 report* OECD.
Otsuki, T., and J. S. Wilson. 2001. *Global trade and food safety: Winners and losers in a fragmented system.* Washington, DC.
Pacific Bridge Medical. *Asian medical regulatory agencies.* http://www.pacificbridgemedical.com/asian-medical-regulatory-agencies.php (accessed November 9, 2011).
PAHO. 2010a. *Medical devices regulation.* http://new.paho.org/hq/index.php?option=com_content&task=view&id=3418&Itemid=1272 (accessed November 11, 2011).
———. 2010b. *Quality and regulation.* http://new.paho.org/hq/index.php?option=com_content&task=view&id=2384&Itemid=1179 (accessed October 5, 2011).
Palthur, M. P., S. S. Sajala, and S. K. Chitta. 2009. The Food Safety and Standards Act, 2006 : A paradigm shift in Indian regulatory scenario. *Pharmainfo* 7(5).
Punjab refuses to accept drug regulatory authority. 2011. *The Peninsula*, October 9.
Ramesh, S. V., and WG3 Chair. *Accsq working group on standards and technical regulations (WG3) – standards harmonization and technical regulations.* http://www.asean.org/14889.htm (accessed November 21, 2011).
Ramos, A. C., and C. A. Oblepias. 2002. *Country report proposed by the philippines.* Marrakech, Morroco: FAO-WHO.
Ratanawijitrasin, S., and E. Wondemagegnehu. 2002. *Effective drug regulation: A multicountry study.* The World Health Organization.
Rosnbom, K. A. 2010 February 3. *Developments in UNICEF vaccine procurement.* Paper presented at Global Immunization Meeting.
Roth, A. V., A. A. Tsay, M. E. Pullman, and J. V. Gray. 2008. Unraveling the food supply chain: Strategic insights from China and the 2007 recalls. *Journal of Supply Chain Management* 44(1):22-39.
Satin, M. 2005. *Quality enhancement in food processing through haccp* Tokyo, Japan: Asian Productivity Organization.
SEHN. 1998. *Wingspread conference on the precautionary principle.* http://www.sehn.org/wing.html (accessed February 14, 2012).
Seventeen federal ministries devolved to provinces. 2011. *Pakistan Today*, July 1.
SFDA. *Internal structure* http://eng.sfda.gov.cn/WS03/CL0764/ (accessed November 15, 2011).
Shepherd, M. 2010. Beef up international cooperation on counterfeits. *Nature Medicine* 16(4):366-366.
Singh, R. 2011. *FSSAI publishes food safety and standards rules 2011.* New Delhi, India: USDA Foreign Agricultural Service- Global Agricultural Information Network.
Smart, P. 2011. *Features of new rules set by food safety and standards authority.* http://www.dnaindia.com/mumbai/report_features-of-new-rules-set-by-food-safety-and-standards-authority_1595836 (accessed November 16, 2011).

Standards and Trade Development Facility. 2011. *SPS-related capacity evaluation tools: An overview of tools developed by international organizations.* Geneva, Switzerland: World Trade Organization.

Stewart, K., and L. Gostin. 2011. Food and Drug Administration regulation of food safety. *Journal of the American Medical Association* 306(1):88-89.

Stop TB. 2009. *List of countries considered as stringent regulatory authorities.* http://www.stoptb.org/assets/documents/gdf/drugsupply/List_of_Countries_SRA.pdf (accessed December 12, 2011).

Sunstein, C. R. 2011. *Memorandum for the heads of independent regulatory agencies: Executive order 13579, "regulation and independent regulatory agencies".* Washington, DC: Office of Informationa and Regulatory Affairs.

Tsoi, A. 2007. *Pharmaceutical policies and regulations in China.* http://www.deacons.com.hk/eng/knowledge/knowledge_290.htm (accessed November 14, 2011).

U.S. Department of State. *Rulemaking: What is the rulemaking process?* http://www.state.gov/m/a/dir/rulemaking/c42660.htm (accessed October 4, 2011).

U.S. Government. *Home: Let your voice be heard.* http://www.regulations.gov/#!home (accessed January 20, 2012).

UNESCO. 2005. *World Commission on the Ethics of Scientific Knowledge and Technology (COMEST): The precautionary principle.* http://unesdoc.unesco.org/images/0013/001395/139578e.pdf (accessed 2012, February 14).

UNICEF. 2011. *Supplies and logistics: GAVI.* http://www.unicef.org/supply/index_gavi.html (accessed November 11, 2011).

Unnevehr, L. J., and H. H. Jensen. 1999. The economic implications of using haccp as a food safety regulatory standard. *Food Policy* 24(6):625-635.

USDA. 2009. Federal crop insurance reform and department of agriculture reorganization act of 1994. In *Section 304*, edited by United States Department of Agriculture. Washington, DC.

Wallace, C. A., W. H. Sperber, and S. E. Mortimore. 2011. *Food safety for the 21st century: Managing haccp and food safety throughout the global supply chain.* Oxford, United Kingdom: Whiley-Blackwell.

WHO. 1999. *Regulation of vaccines: Building on existing drug regulatory authorities.* Geneva, Switzerland: WHO Department of Vaccines and Other Biologics.

———. 2001. *The impact of implementation of ICH guidelines in non-ICH countries: Report of a WHO meeting.* Geneva: WHO.

———. 2003a. *Aide-memoire: Strengthening national regulatory authorities.* Geneva.

———. 2003b. Effective medicines regulation: Ensuring safety, efficacy and quality. *WHO Policy Perspectives on Medicines* 007:1-6.

———. 2009. *Food safety background.* http://www.wpro.who.int/vietnam/sites/dhp/food_safety/ (accessed November 16, 2011).

———. 2010. *Prequalification of medicines by WHO.* http://www.who.int/mediacentre/factsheets/fs278/en/index.html (accessed November 14, 2011).

———. 2011a. *Guideline on submission of documentation for prequalification of multisource (generic) finished pharmaceutical products (FPPs) approved by stringent regulatory authorities (SRAs).* WHO.

———. 2011b. *Immunization standards: Strengthening national regulatory authorities.* http://www.who.int/immunization_standards/national_regulatory_authorities%20/strengthening/en/index.html/ (accessed November 11, 2011).

———. 2011c. *International conference of drug regulatory authorities.* http://www.who.int/medicines/areas/quality_safety/regulation_legislation/icdra/en/index.html (accessed October 5, 2011).

———. 2011d. *National regulatory authority of China meets international standards for a vaccine regulation.* http://www.who.int/immunization_standards/vaccine_regulation/nra_china_functional/en/index.html (accessed February 2, 2012).

———. 2011e. *WHO list of prequalified medicinal products.*

———. 2012. *Impact: Frequently asked questions.* http://www.who.int/impact/impact_q-a/en/index.html (accessed February 1, 2012).

WHO Regional Committee for Africa. 2006. *Medicines regulatory authorities: Current status and the way forward- report of the regional director.*

WHO Regional Office for Africa. 2005. First African medicines regulatory authorties conference: Final report. Paper read at Conference of African Medicine Regulators, October 31– November 3, 2005, Addis Ababa, Ethiopia.

Wilson, P. 2010. *Giving developing countries the best shot: An overview of vaccine access and R&D.* Geneva, Switzerland: Oxfam.

WTO. 1998. *Understanding the WTO agreement on sanitary and phytosanitary measures.* http://www.wto.org/english/tratop_e/sps_e/spsund_e.htm (accessed November 9, 2011).

3

Critical Issues

From March to September 2011, the committee heard from various stakeholders in the United States and abroad. In the foreign workshops the travel delegations met government regulators from a dozen different low- and middle-income countries (see Appendix E). It also met with representatives of multinational and national food and medical companies, NGOs, regional economic organizations, donor organizations, and universities (see Appendix E). In its deliberations the committee synthesized what it learned in these workshops, identifying nine common problems that cut across countries and industries. These are the nine main problems that the committee focused its discussions on. This input and background research informed its analysis of the main issues developing country regulators face.

The committee found that regulators abroad face problems with: adhering to international standards, controlling supply chains, infrastructure, their laws, their workforce, institutional fragmentation, surveillance, communication, and political will. A detailed analysis of each of these gaps follows.

ADHERENCE TO INTERNATIONAL STANDARDS

One of the main responsibilities of a regulator is to ensure the food and medical product supply meets agreed upon standards for safety and quality. National regulatory authorities are entitled to set their own standards, but established international norms are expedient to use; they also facilitate trade. Some standards are set into a country's legal code, others are set by private organizations or corporations (Giovannucci and Purcell, 2008). Standard setting is one of the regulatory authority's main responsibilities, separate from their responsibilities to enforce standards. For the purposes of this section, standards means "established norms or codified requirements for a product, such as material specifications or technical standards for performance. Standards may be developed by regulatory agencies, public organizations, or industry associations" (Marucheck et al., 2011, 714). Tables 3-1 and 3-2 list some important organizations and describe their work in standard setting.

Proponents of standards maintain that their use helps traceability through the supply chain, eliminates redundant audits, and when, harmonized across markets, decreases bureaucracy. Others see standards as little more than fines on poor countries because of the high costs of compliance (Marucheck et al., 2011). A debate on this topic is outside the scope of this report. Regardless of the reasons these standards exist, quality assurance and adherence to international norms are essential as developing countries introduce regulated goods into the global marketplace.

TABLE 3-1
International Standard Setting Organization for Food

Organization	Year Established	What they do	What they set standards in
United States Pharmacopeial Convention (USP)	1820	"USP establishes documentary and reference standards to ensure the quality and consistency of medicines, dietary supplements, and food ingredients" (USP, 2008).	• Purity and identity of food ingredients (USP, 2011a)
AOAC International	1884	AOAC International provides science-based expertise to develop voluntary consensus standards or technical standards through stakeholder consensus and working groups (AOAC).	• Single laboratory validation for botanicals • Study validation • Food microbiology • Characterization of antibodies used in immunochemical methods of analysis for mycotoxins and phycotoxins (AOAC, 2009)
International Organization for Standardization (ISO)	1947	A network of national standards institutes from 162 countries (ISO, 2011a), that sets trade standards and fosters standardization activities (Giovannucci and Purcell, 2008b).	• Food Products • Good Management Practices • Management systems for food safety
International Plant Protection Convention (IPPC)	1952	"The IPPC provides an international framework for plant protection that includes developing international standards for phytosanitary measures for safeguarding plant resources" (IPPC, 2011).	• Procedures and references • Pest surveillance, survey and monitoring • Import regulations and pest risk analysis • Compliance procedures and phytosanitary inspection methodologies • Pest management • Post entry quarantine • Exotic pest emergency response, control and eradication • Export certification (IPPC, 2011)
International Commission on Microbiological Specifications for Food (ICMSF)	1962	ICMSF provides science-based guidance to both government and industry on evaluating and controlling the microbiological safety of foods (ICMSF). *ICMF is not a standard setting organization. They are included here because of their valuable advisory role.*	• Microbiological limits and criteria in food (ICMSF)

TABLE 3-1 *Continued*

Organization	Year Established	What they do	What they set standards in
Codex Alimentarius Commission	1963	Codex is responsible for developing "food standards, guidelines and related texts such as codes of practice under the Joint FAO/WHO Food Standards Program" (CAC, 2011). "The purpose of the program is to protect the health of consumers, ensure fair trade practices in food trade, and promote the coordination of all food standards work undertaken by international governmental and non-governmental organizations" (CAC, 2011).	• Food quality and safety • Codes of hygienic or technological practice • Pesticide and food additive evaluation • Limits for pesticide residue • Guidelines for contaminants (Henson and Humphrey, 2009)

TABLE 3-2 International Standard Setting Organizations for Medical Products

Organization	Year Established	What they do	What they set standards in
United States Pharmacopeial Convention (USP)	1820	"USP establishes documentary and reference standards to ensure the quality and consistency of medicines, dietary supplements, and food ingredients" (USP, 2008).	• Identification testing • Limit testing for impurities or related compounds • Assays for drug substances and formulations • System suitability testing (USP, 2011c) • Product quality verification services for drug substances and excipients used to make over-the-counter and prescription pharmaceuticals (USP, 2011d)
International Organization for Standardization (ISO)	1947	A network of national standards institutes from 162 countries (ISO, 2011a), that sets trade standards and fosters standardization activities (Giovannucci and Purcell, 2008b).	• Requirements and testing methods for medical devices (ISO, 2011b)
International Conference on Harmonization (ICH)	1990	The ICH "makes recommendations toward achieving greater harmonization in the interpretation and application of technical guidelines and requirements for pharmaceutical product registration" (ICH, 2011).	• Good Clinical Practices • Good Manufacturing Practices of medicines, biologics, and vaccines • Standards for the transfer of regulatory information
The Global Harmonization Task Force (GHTF)	1992	The GHTF encourages the harmonization of regulatory practices related to ensuring the safety, effectiveness, performance and quality of medical devices, promoting advancements in technology and assisting international trade. This is accomplished through the publication and dissemination of harmonized guidance documents on basic regulatory practices (GHTF, 2007).	• Medical device safety, effectiveness, performance, and quality (GHTF, 2007)
European Directorate for the Quality of Medicines and Healthcare (EDQM)	1996	The EDQM "protects public health by enabling the development, supporting the implementation, and monitoring the application of quality standards for safe medicines and their safe use (EDQM)."	• Quality and safety of medical products (EDQM)

Adherence to Food Standards

Adherence to international standards is a problem in the agri-food industry in many low- and middle-income countries. In these countries there is a large domestic market for products that stringent regulatory authorities would reject. People in developing countries often do not demand, for example, process certification or assurance of minimal pesticide residues. This may be because they are often not aware of the public health risks international standards aim to protect against. They may also assume, sometimes incorrectly, that it is possible to assess the producer's quality practices at point of purchase when the market has few middle men. More importantly, these countries still struggle to feed their citizens; concerns about trace pesticide residues seem frivolous in comparison to hunger. The threat of death from starvation in the next month will dwarf theoretical cancer risks in fifty years.

In China, for example, food safety has only been an official priority for the last 12 years (Gale and Buzby, 2009). It is especially difficult in such a large country to keep their estimated 200 million farmers working plots of 2 acres or less abreast of good agricultural practices (Gale and Buzby, 2009). China's roughly 400,000 cottage industry food processers face similar challenges (Gale and Buzby, 2009).

The involvement of the least developed countries and their institutions in international standard-setting organizations such as Codex is often nominal. The Codex Trust Fund aims to correct this by supporting scientists from the least developed countries and small island nations to participate better at Codex (WHO, 2011a). Still, the poorest countries do not have representatives with sufficient expertise to participate meaningfully in standard setting meetings (The African Union Interafrican Bureau for Animal Resources). Sometimes logistical constraints complicate participation in these meetings. International travel is too expensive for regulatory agencies to fund (World Bank, 2008).

There is also evidence that, especially in Sub-Saharan Africa, the food producers have no way to give input into standard development (World Bank, 2003). This means that small- and medium-size enterprises, and even some larger firms, rely on their importing agents or their national regulatory authority to make information available. There are also too few scientists qualified to analyze the standards. Without advocates these countries become "standard takers" rather than active participants in the dialogue (World Bank, 2003).

It is expensive to adhere to international standards. At the very least it requires a supplier to be able to trace products through the supply chain, and show proof of adherence to best practices at all stages of production. This proof usually takes the form of a certificate of inspection, audit, or accreditation. Producers pay for inspections and certification, and for small producers these costs are prohibitively high (Giovannucci and Purcell, 2008). Some agri-food standards, those on pesticide residues for example, rely on technical skills and laboratory equipment that are essentially missing in many developing countries (Jaffee and Henson, 2004; World Bank, 2003). For all these reasons, the World Trade Organization (WTO) called for donor aid to improve developing countries adherence to standards in their Sanitary and Phytosanitary (SPS) agreement. Bilateral and multilateral agencies spent between $65-$75 million a year in the years after the agreement on building capacity for agri-food health management (Jaffee and Henson, 2004). The full benefit of these investments is yet hard to measure. There is a learning curve when new technology is introduced to a sector, as well as a time lag when new staff need to be trained to use it (World Bank, 2003).

In the meantime, the inability to adhere to standards deepens inequalities in market access between counties (Belton et al., 2010). Only eight countries, most of them in Latin American, account for two-thirds of all fruit and vegetable exports from emerging economies (Stcichele et al., 2006). Even these Latin American countries, with relatively advanced systems for maintaining standards, can be subject to border rejections, and rejections cost middle-income countries about $1.8 billion in 2001 (Jaffee and Henson, 2004). Border rejections are only a fraction of the income lost. Econometric analysis indicates that China alone lost an estimated $8 billion in lost export income in 2002 because of failure to meet standards (Lu, 2005). The individual financial losses are also heavy. Vietnamese farmers who can comply with supermarket standards earn about 400 percent higher profits than those who cannot (M4P, 2006).

Access to export markets could improve the economies in some of the least developed countries, and the health and social benefits of adhering to standards cannot be understated. Aflatoxin, a food contaminant, accounts for an estimated 25,200-155,000 cases of liver cancer a year, overwhelmingly in countries without strict food standards (Liu and Wu, 2010). Even in the United States roughly 3,000 people die every year from foodborne illness (CDC, 2011). The CDC estimates that food imported to the United States caused 2,348 illnesses between 2005 and 2010 (CDC, 2012). Half of these outbreaks happened in 2009 or 2010, and about 45 percent of them have a probable source in Asia (CDC, 2012).

Globally, there are an estimated 155,000 deaths from foodborne *Salmonella* infections alone (Majowicz et al., 2010). Adherence to manufacturing and agriculture standards would improve working conditions and protect the environment in many countries. Farming in accordance with good agricultural practices, for example, improves soil quality and prevents erosion (Poisot et al., 2004).

Adherence to Medical Product Standards

In many ways, problems in adhering to international standards in the medical products industry are similar to those in agriculture and food. Regulators in low- and middle-income countries depend on standards developed abroad; they often have minimal input into the standard setting process. Even more so than with agri-food standards, adhering to drug, biologics, and device standards demands sophisticated testing laboratories, and control of complicated supply chains.

The International Conference on Harmonization of Technical Requirements for Registration of Pharmaceuticals for Human Use (ICH) is a standard setting organization for drugs; it has membership from European, Japanese, and U.S. pharmaceutical industry associations, and the drug regulatory agencies of 17 countries (Abraham, 2002; ICH, 2011a). ICH activities generally focus on their member countries, but they are increasingly working to improve good manufacturing practices around the world. It held a training on the same for southern African regulators in Tanzania in June of 2011, for example (ICH, 2011b).

As in the agri-food sector, developing countries are standard-takers rather than standard makers. This can cause problems. Until recently the ICH guidelines on medicine shelf life, for example, failed to account for stability in hot, humid climates (Kopp, 2006). A working group of Southeast Asian nations remedied this and brought attention to the problems of accepting ICH guidelines outside of ICH regions (Kopp, 2006). In other cases, the solutions for the standard takers are not as clear. Far more rich countries than poor ones regulate diagnostics; of those that do only 68 percent require regulatory review of clinical trial data, and trial data with as few as 15 subjects are often acceptable (Peeling et al., 2010). When clinicians in developing countries use diagnostics developed abroad they base their understanding of the tests' predictive value on product inserts, values that are not accurate if the disease prevalence in the trial population is different from that in the population tested.

Even when international standards are available to regulators and are appropriate, there are problems in adhering to quality standards if the medical regulatory authority has insufficient funding or trained staff or both. For example, one essential function of drug and biologic standards is to answer the questions, "Is this drug what is says it is, in the stated strength, and is it free of contaminants?" (Kenyon et al., 1994, p. 615). Quality control laboratories answer these questions, but many countries cannot afford to set up and staff these laboratories (Leng and Matsoso, 2008). Outsourcing quality control is one way around this; private companies can do quality control for a national drug supply, as is the case in the United Kingdom. Leng and colleagues recounted hesitation to use private laboratories in both South Africa and Algeria though because of concerns about conflicts of interests given that the quality control laboratories in question worked for both government and industry (Leng and Matsoso, 2008).

Developing countries also face challenges in implementing good manufacturing practices; the standards that ensure all manufacturing steps can be reproduced and result in the desired products. These are of critical importance in the production of vaccines and other biological products, given the inherent variability in testing a biologically active product (Milstien et al., 2009). The World Health Organization (WHO) Prequalification of Medicines and Vaccines Program facilitates access to quality medicines and vaccines for treating priority diseases. As Chapter 2 describes, this program evaluates product safety, quality, and efficacy, and serves as the grounds for donor procurement. The vaccine and medicine companies that pass the evaluation must meet good manufacturing practices and be overseen by a competent national regulatory authority; it is the government regulator's responsibility to enforce manufacturing standards (Brhlikova et al., 2007). In 2009 the WHO announced that it would withhold new prequalification evaluations from Indian companies barring improvements to their national regulatory authority (Milstien et al., 2009).

In the same way, some consumers see WHO prequalification as an international vote of confidence in the national regulatory authority. On March 1, 2011, the WHO recognized the Chinese State Food and Drug Administration as compliant with international regulatory standards, a decision that will allow for the eventual introduction of Chinese vaccines into international use (Jia and Carey, 2011). This may help restore public confidence in Chinese vaccine companies after a year of scandals: substandard rabies and hepatitis B vaccines were rumored to have killed about 100 babies in Shanxi province in 2010; shortly afterwards a company in Jiangsu province also produced substandard rabies vaccine (Jia and Carey, 2011).

WHO prequalification drives compliance with international good manufacturing practices and gives incentive to improve government regulation. Economies of scale keep small countries out of the vaccine prequalification system. Similarly, WHO drug prequalification encourages adherence to international standards, at least in emerging economies large enough to support a manufacturing sector. Smaller countries depend on prequalification in their drug procurement.

Pharmaceutical manufacture in most emerging economies was designed for generics, and their drug innovation system suffers. Some developing countries do not regulate human subjects' protection in trials or require peer review of human subjects protocols by institutional review boards, perhaps because governments see trials as a way for some of their citizens to get medical care (Kelleher, 2004). Still, the richest countries are home to 15 percent of the world's population and 75 percent of drug trial participants (Herring, 2011). Consistent adherence to international research standards could change this, and would give depth to the results of drug trials, increase understanding of drug development, benefit patients in the developing world, and improve the economies of least developed countries (Herring, 2011).

CONTROLLING SUPPLY CHAINS

Food and medical product supply chains are complex and far-reaching. In the United States, the 2002 Bioterrorism Act requires all parties in the food supply chain to identify the immediate previous source of their products and the immediate recipient; known as one-up, one-back traceability (Gessner et al., 2007). When every actor is responsible for one-up, one-back reporting, it is possible to re-create the entire supply chain, even if no one party has a complete picture of it. Traceability requirements are less clear in medical products supply chains. During the 2008 heparin crisis neither the Food and Drug Administration (FDA) nor Baxter was able re-create the heparin supply chain quickly; it took weeks to even get close to the source. The exact identification of the responsible actors was never possible (Pew Health Group, 2011). Multinational companies are exploring radio frequency identification tags and two dimensional bar codes to trace products through their supply chains (McMeekin et al., 2006). In developing countries, controlling supply chains is even more of a problem.

The Food Supply Chain

Large multinational corporations such as Wal-Mart, Archer Daniels Midland, ConAgra, Nestle, Cargill, and Unilever control a great deal of the international food market. These companies have close relationships with their suppliers; they can trace their supply chains in developing countries, a considerable accomplishment considering that a granola bar contains ingredients from half a dozen different countries (Figure 3-1) (Carey, 2007). These companies monitor their supply chains using the principles of Hazard Analysis and Critical Control Points (HACCP), described in Chapter 2. There are five main links in the food supply chain: the farm, the packing house, the transportation, the market, and the consumer (UC Davis Department of Plant Sciences, 2011).

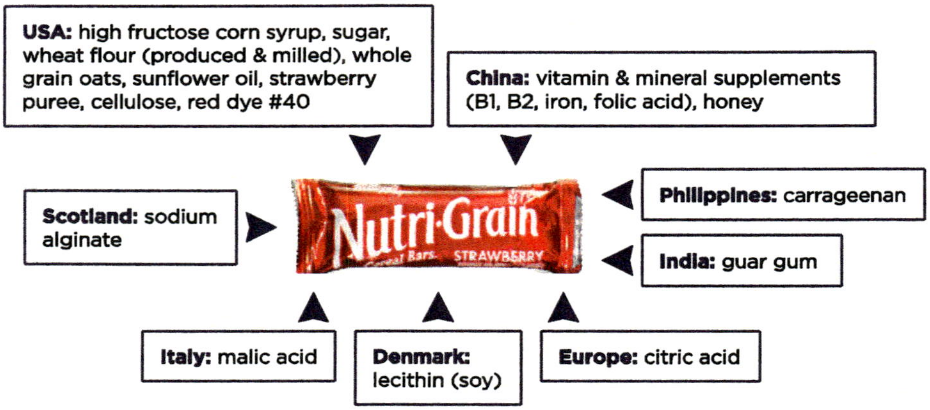

FIGURE 3-1 Global sourcing of food ingredients.
SOURCE: Roth et al., 2008.

Over the last decade there has been a rapid growth in production of high value agriculture, premium products such as vegetables, fruits, and animal products. Much of Africa's high-value exports are grown in countries with high altitudes and year-round growing seasons, and exported to Europe (Okello et al., 2007). There are usually separate supply chains feeding the export and domestic markets, with relatively little crossover. High value agricultural products are highly perishable; logistics, in particular the availability of airfreight space, play a significant role in their trade (Okello et al., 2007). Orders from retailers come in late at night once the European markets are closed, but the crops are picked earlier in the day. When the export order does not match what the supplier packed, the order may end up in the local market, though usually the exporters cannot get the same price that they would have had in the European market (Henson and Humphrey, 2009).

With the notable exception of one participant from Uruguay, the guests at the various site visits for this study explained that there are two supply chains in their countries: one for export and one for local consumption. Standards are generally lower for the domestic market (Broughton and Walker, 2010; Llana, 2010). At the New Delhi meetings for this report, Indian participants mentioned that having two food safety standards does not trouble them; some stressed that Indians take care to avoid food spoilage at home by marketing daily and boiling their milk every hour. Others believe Indians have higher innate immunity to foodborne disease than Westerners. Similar misconceptions are common in China (Roth et al., 2008).

Workers in Honduras wash thousands of bananas a day, preparing them for evaluation. Bananas that are exactly the right weight, length, and color are packaged and shipped to the United States; those that are not acceptable are sold in Honduras.
SOURCE: © 2007 Sarah Axelson, Courtesy of Photoshare.

Spoilage is one of the main problems in the domestic supply chain of developing countries. Often it takes too long for products to get to market over poor roads and without refrigeration. There are, for example, 280,000 refrigerated trucks transporting food in the United States, while China, with its vastly larger population, has only 30,000 (Barboza, 2007). As much as 35 to 40 percent of fresh produce in India spoils because of lack of refrigeration in the wholesale or retail markets (Godfray et al., 2010; Kader, 2010). Some experts predict that this will change. The Indian grape business has had recent success by bringing small grape farmers together in Mahagrape, an association of grape growing collectives (Roy and Thorat, 2008). These for-profit collectives give farmers access to cooling and storage infrastructure. The Indian agricultural cold chain business has an estimated net value of $2.6 billion, expected to more than quadruple by 2015 (Narula, 2011).

High-value agricultural products, such as tomatoes and green beans, need to be kept at chill temperatures; they can spoil quickly in heat or cold. Grains have a longer shelf life, but rats will eat them if they are not stored in silos or grain safes; one third of the grain stores in Southeast Asia are lost to pests (Godfray et al., 2010). According to an expert at the International Fund for Agriculture and Development, these losses could be reduced by half with proper refrigeration and post-harvest storage (Waste not, want not, 2011). Figure 3-2 shows the relative food lost between the farm and fork in different regions of the world. Notably, household waste is a small fraction of the food lost in most regions (Figure 3-2). Reductions in post-harvest losses would be of tremendous value to the poor in developing countries. Less than 5 percent of agricultural research funding goes to post-harvest losses (Kitinoja et al., 2011).

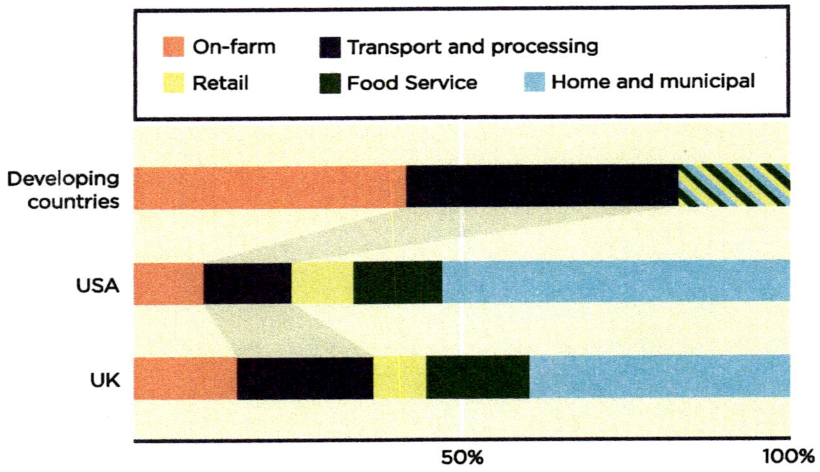

FIGURE 3-2 Makeup of total food waste in developed and developing countries. Retail, food service, and home and municipal categories are lumped together for developing countries.
SOURCE: Godfrey et al., 2010.

Protecting the transportation and storage steps of the supply chain becomes increasingly important as the population in developing countries becomes more urban. Supermarkets, which generally have high quality standards and interest in their branding, are increasingly the food markets of choice in middle-income countries, such as Vietnam, and middle-class shoppers in low-income countries, such as India (M4P, 2006). Small farmers struggle to meet supermarket standards; supermarkets will reject produce only for cosmetic reasons that have nothing to do with safety or nutritional value (Gustavasson et al., 2011). Cities in the least developed countries have fewer supermarkets and more wholesale and street markets that "are often small, overcrowded, unsanitary, and lacking in cooling equipment" (Gustavasson et al., 2011, p. 13). Food spoils quickly in these markets, but poor shoppers have little choice but to buy it anyway. This is offset, in part, by daily marketing, a common practice in developing countries.

Disorganized retail supply chains hurt farmers as well. Desperation often drives poor farmers to sell under-ripe crops during the pre-harvest hungry season, sabotaging their income and the nutritional value of the food (Gustavasson et al., 2011). In Rajasthan, a large onion-growing state in west India, farmers routinely dump part of their crop along the highway, as their revenues do not even cover the costs to bring the crop to market (Maheshwar and Chanakwa, 2006). The use of relatively simple technologies could increase small farmer's incomes and reduce waste in developing countries. Drying and juice making near the farm could preserve expensive fruits and vegetables, for example, provided there is equipment to pasteurize and package the food.

The Medical Products Supply Chain

A typical pharmaceutical supply chain consists of: the primary manufacture of chemicals from their raw state; several steps of secondary manufacture from processed products; market warehouses and distribution centers; wholesalers; retailers; hospitals, clinics or pharmacies; and, finally, patients (Yu et al., 2010). Drug regulatory authorities in developing countries often lack the ability to monitor the steps on this supply chain. These drug regulatory authorities are often supported partly from the government and the rest from user fees (Yadav, 2009). They are focused on the most pressing tasks: licensing and registering products and giving marketing approvals (Yadav, 2009). There is little attention to factory inspections; quality control tests at retail or wholesale points are almost unknown. As mentioned in the section on standards, there is little post-marketing surveillance. It is also difficult to control imports, especially in parts of the world where there are many small, neighboring, landlocked countries. These factors make for a porous pharmaceutical supply chain. Fake drugs are a common problem.

A full analysis of the problem of counterfeit, falsified, and sub-standard drugs is outside the scope of this report, but medicines regulators in the countries visited for this study repeatedly raised it as a concern (Box 3-1). In September 2011 the FDA commissioned the IOM to convene a consensus study entitled *Understanding the Global Public Health Implications of Substandard, Counterfeit, and Falsified Drugs*. This report, which will be released in 2013, will aim to clarify the terms used to discuss pharmaceutical fraud, describe the scope of the problem, and recommend action to reduce the public health consequences of fake drugs in developing countries.

By WHO estimates, between 20 and 90 percent of antimalarials in Sub-Saharan Africa and 38-53 percent of the same drugs in Southeast Asia fail quality testing (Newton et al., 2010; WHO, 2005). Fraud also affects medical devices and in vitro diagnostics, a topic reported on in the Asian press (Mori et al., 2011). Tampering with expiry dates on in vitro diagnostics in Vietnam was the subject of *Lancet* correspondence (Day et al., 2004; Watt, 2004). There are a variety of sophisticated techniques that can prevent this fraud, but many are expensive and impractical in developing countries (Newton et al., 2010). Organizations such as Sproxil have made some progress recently with using mobile phones and paper watermarking to authenticate bar codes (Sharma et al., 2008; Sproxil, 2011). There is a need for more inexpensive ways to secure medical products supply chains in developing countries, however.

BOX 3-1
Counterfeit, Falsified, and Substandard Drugs

There are no universally accepted definitions for counterfeit, falsified and substandard drugs (Clift, 2010a, 2010b). A single product can be simultaneously counterfeit, falsified and substandard, or some combination of the three (Oxfam, 2011).

The World Health Organization defines counterfeit drugs as "deliberately and fraudulently mislabeled with respect to identity or source" (WHO, 2011b). Counterfeit applies to "both branded and generic products [and] may include products with the correct ingredients or with the wrong ingredients, without active ingredients, with insufficient active ingredients or with fake packaging" (WHO, 2011b). This definition has been a source of ongoing controversy. It conflates the definition of counterfeit, which has a specific legal meaning in the context of intellectual property, with the drug quality and safety (Clift, 2010a). According to the WHO, however, whether "a good is considered counterfeit from a public health perspective is independent of whether the product infringes on intellectual property rights" (WHO, 2010b, p. 3). A counterfeit medicine, following the WHO definition, may or may not violate intellectual property rights.

The term falsified evolved, primarily in Europe and Latin America, as a way of distinguishing between intellectual property or trademark violations and fake drugs (Clift, 2010a). It refers to drugs "falsified in relation to their identity, history or source. Those products usually contain sub-standard or falsified ingredients, or no ingredients or ingredients in the wrong dosage, including active ingredients, thus posing an important threat to public health" (EU, 2011).

The definition of substandard is generally agreed upon as drugs that fail to meet quality specifications established by WHO standards (Clift, 2010a; Oxfam, 2011). What is not agreed upon, however, is whether or not the category of substandard drugs includes counterfeit and falsified medicines. In 2003, the WHO stated that substandard medical products may be a "result of negligence, human error, insufficient human and financial resources, or counterfeiting. Counterfeit medicines are part of the broader phenomenon of substandard pharmaceuticals. The difference is that they are deliberately and fraudulently mislabeled with respect to identity or source" (WHO, 2003b). In 2009, however, it revised this definition to specifically exclude counterfeiting (Clift, 2010a). The revised definition defines substandard drugs that do not meet quality specifications produced by manufacturers authorized by a given national medical regulatory authority.

As in the food supply chain, some of the problems with medical products supply chains are related to infrastructure. There is a lack of hard data on where in the pharmaceutical supply chain bottlenecks exist (Oluka et al., 2010). In an assessment of the pharmaceutical sector in East Timor, Norris and colleagues described small warehouses and medicines being kept in tropical heat and humidity at every point between entering the country and the patients' hands (Norris et al., 2007). In 2008, the Global Fund identified similar problems with medicine storage and inventory control in an audit of its Indian grant programs (The Global Fund, 2008).

Vaccines are particularly vulnerable to spoilage in developing countries. An incomplete cold chain was the probable cause of a polio outbreak in South Africa in the mid-1990s (Schoub and Cameron, 1996; Setia et al., 2002). The problems are not confined to tropical climates: Lugosi and colleagues found that cold weather damaged 38 percent of vaccines sampled in Hungary (Lugosi and Battersby, 1990). By 2019 another dozen vaccines may be introduced in developing countries, but without fast-moving, temperature controlled supply chains, these vaccines will not be effective (Kauffmann et al., 2011). By some estimates, the demands on the vaccine cold chain will increase 20-fold during this time (see Figure 3-3) (Sabot et al., 2011). Box 3-2 describes the vaccine supply chain in developing countries.

Even considering only routine immunization using the currently available vaccines, the vaccine cold chain capacity is insufficient, outdated, and broken—a serious bottleneck in increasing immunization rates. The poor cold chain compromises vaccine efficacy and, in some cases, vaccine safety as well. The projected expansion of the immunization program will surely aggravate this problem (Sabot et al., 2011). In 2007 PATH and the WHO launched the Optimize Project, with funding from the Bill and Melinda Gates Foundation (PATH, 2012a). Optimize aims to identify sustainable solutions for building cold chain capacity for future vaccines (PATH, 2012b).

There are also promising improvements in the heat stability of vaccines. A high throughput screening process for identifying thermostable formulations promises to improve the stability of a number of new and existing vaccines, while developments in controlled-temperature vaccines can mitigate the problems of cold chain breaks (Chen and Kristensen, 2009; Schlehuber et al., 2011). Other simple technologies have the potential to improve the strength of the vaccine cold chain. Temperature-sensitive labels, for example, that change color to indicate when a vaccine has been exposed to damaging temperatures are currently being procured by the United Nations Children's Fund (UNICEF) (PATH, 2012c). New investments in cold chain capacity coupled with new technological advances such as thermostable vaccines, will be invaluable tools to meet increased demands on the vaccine cold chain over the next decade (Chen and Kristensen, 2009; Sabot et al., 2011). Developing country regulatory authorities need to be kept informed of these developments.

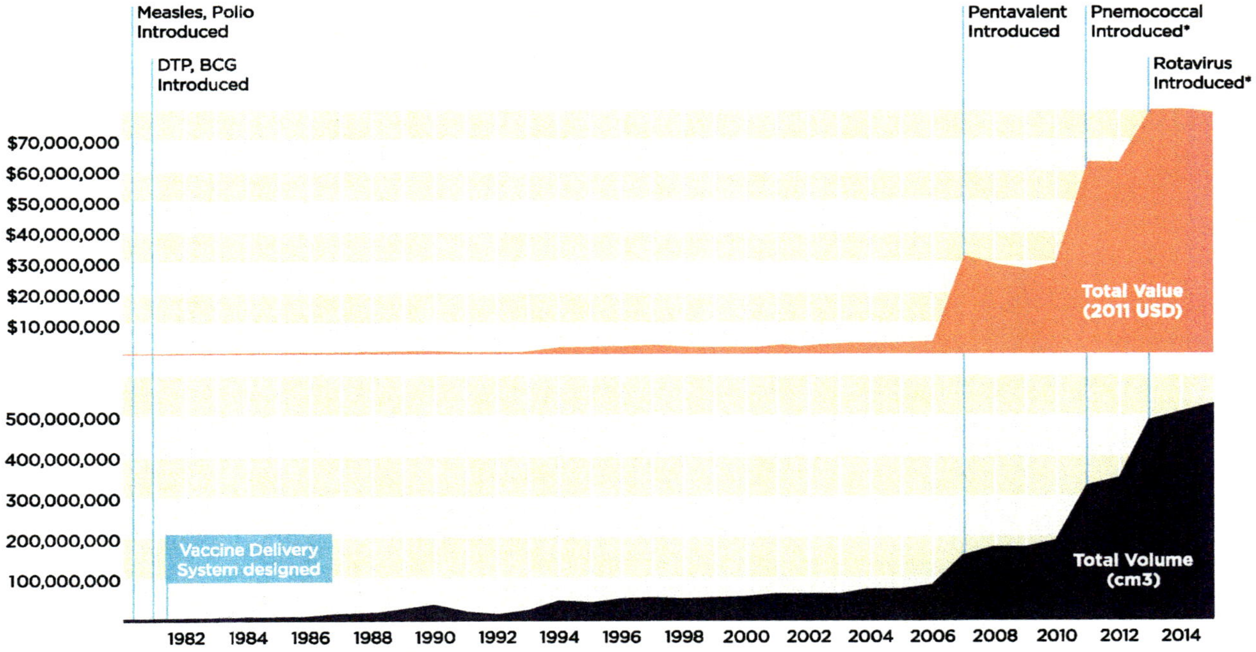

FIGURE 3-3 Demands on vaccine delivery systems are rising dramatically
Cumulative value and volume of vaccines used in routine childhood immunization: Ethiopia.
SOURCE: Sabot et al., 2011.
*Planned introduction date

BOX 3-2
Vaccine Supply Chains in Low- and Middle-Income Countries

Vaccines usually need to be stored between 2° and 8°C (Chen and Kristensen, 2009). Some are heat-sensitive, rendered inactive at high temperatures; others are cold sensitive, rendered inactive by freezing. Maintaining temperature control in places without electricity is challenging and gets more complicated when health workers carry the vaccine for miles to give immunizations in remote villages. Vaccines also have a short shelf life that leaves little room for forecasting errors, inefficient management, or slow distribution. Many countries waste as much vaccine as they use. This will have to change over the next decade when more and costlier vaccines come into use. Trained logisticians and supply chain managers will be invaluable to this effort, but they are hard to find in the places that need them most.

There are two vaccine supply chains in developing countries: one that carries the vaccines from the factory to the developing country port of entry and one that carries the vaccines from the port of entry to the patient. The supply chain that carries the product from the supplier to the port of entry is generally strong, thanks to UNICEF and the shipping companies they contract with. Within the recipient country, immunization program managers decide how and where to store the shipments and when to release them to regional or provincial storehouses.

In their analysis of vaccine supply chains Kauffman and colleagues stress the importance of moving vaccines to patients, and discourage the common practice of holding large inventories in case of emergency. To this end, they suggested removing unnecessary storage levels. Warehouse management is complicated and introduces opportunities for the supply chain to breakdown. The Thai government reorganized its vaccine supply chain in 2009, removing three levels of store housing, and began shipping directly from the central warehouse to health centers.

Donors could also help by not insisting on separate shipments, storage, and handling for donated vaccines. Kauffmann and colleagues describe a Kenyan health center that takes shipment from five warehouses, 13 procurement agencies, and 18 donor organizations. Such redundancy hinders the development of integrated, efficient supply chains.

SOURCE: (Kauffmann et al., 2011)

A nurse vaccinates a 4-month-old baby outside her home in Nueva Segovia, Nicaragua.
SOURCE: © 2008 Adrian Brooks, Courtesy of Photoshare

There are also problems with the points on the medicine supply chain closest to the patient. In 2002 the consulting firm A.T. Kearney estimated that half of the medicine shortages in Mexico were because of poor inventory management and demand planning (Box 3-3) (A.T. Kearney, 2004a; Sarley et al., 2006). Hospital administrators or pharmacists can estimate their demand for medicines either by modifying previous years' records or by calculating the number of patients presenting with a given condition from national morbidity data (A.T. Kearney, 2004b). Either way, supply chain planning requires reliable surveillance and some managerial proficiency in the health care workforce, common shortcomings that will be discussed later in this chapter.

Once the hospital or pharmacy has an estimated medicines projection, they need to communicate their need to the warehouse, distribution center, or whole seller. Sometimes the ordering system slows down this process. In both Tanzania and South Africa, for example, the Ministry of Health requires health workers to report detailed patient summaries to a central pharmacy when ordering the essential medicine acyclovir (Corbell et al., 2010). This extra step slowed procurement and led to frequent stock-outs (Corbell et al., 2010). Communication with central distribution is a common bottleneck, one that modern information technology and supply chain management could do much to unblock (Oluka et al., 2010). Figure 3-4 highlights other supply chain gaps.

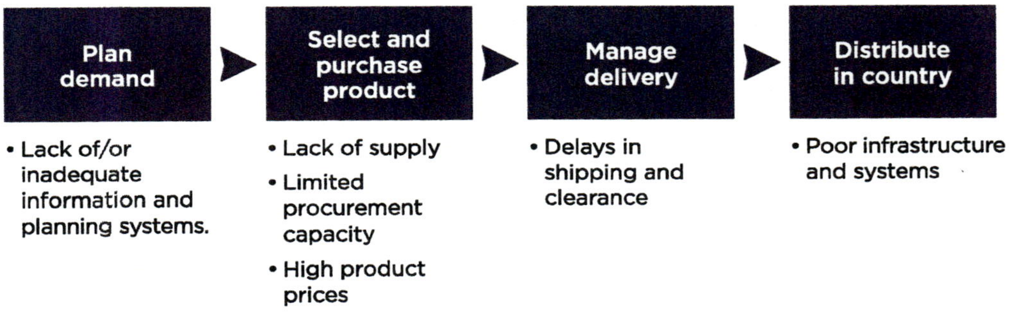
Plan demand
Select and purchase product
Manage delivery
Distribute in country
• Lack of/or inadequate information and planning systems.
• Lack of supply
• Limited procurement capacity
• High product prices
• Delays in shipping and clearance
• Poor infrastructure and systems

FIGURE 3-4 Challenges and bottlenecks in a drug supply chain.
SOURCE: Oluka et al., 2010.

BOX 3-3
Supply Chain Management in Mexico

Frequent stock-outs were a problem at Mexican pharmacies and health centers in 2002 when President Vincente Fox enlisted the help of the management consulting firm A.T. Kearney to improve the Mexican pharmaceutical supply chain (A.T. Kearney, 2004a). Working with the Mexican government, A.T. Kearney developed solutions that relieved the pressure of health care budgets, reduced the cost of medicine and improved the efficiency of the drug supply chain (A.T. Kearney, 2004b). This included adopting a consistent demand-planning methodology, streamlining the drug procurement process, and improving inventory management (A.T. Kearney, 2004a).

The consultants found that more than half of the medicine shortage in Mexico was because of poor inventory management. They recommended calculating drug demand using morbidity data (A.T. Kearney, 2004a). That is, health center staff estimated the number of patients they would treat for a given disease and combined the estimated number of patients with the approximate amount of medicine required to treat them. The forecasts were adjustable, to account for local differences in morbidity and local treatment preferences. The adoption of this method resulted in an 80 percent accuracy rate in Mexico's drug forecasting (A.T. Kearney, 2004a).

Long delays in drug procurement were still a problem, however. The procurement process took four months, causing a drug shortage in the first quarter of every year (A.T. Kearney, 2004a). Poor communication among many small hospitals and clinics prevented them from pooling their drug orders. Working together and using a standardized, public bidding process these institutions switched to a system of large drug orders placed less frequently (A.T. Kearney, 2004a). They also switched to a pull system* where hospitals and health centers could order their own medicines. By adopting this system, health officials were able to improve the management of their drug inventory and reduce costs (A.T. Kearney, 2004a).

In 2002, much of the Mexican drug legislation was out-dated and poorly understood, even by health professionals (A.T. Kearney, 2004a). This led to confusion and an overall frustration with the system as a whole. A.T. Kearney worked with officials to eliminate unnecessary rules that hampered the purchasing of drugs from suppliers.

Within two years of making these simple changes and restructuring the value chain, the percentage of Mexicans receiving full prescriptions rose from 70 percent to more than 90 percent, with no added costs to the consumer or manufacturer (A.T. Kearney, 2004a).

*In a pull system, each level of the supply chain determines its drug needs using a formula that takes costs, demand, distribution, and the level of inventory into consideration. Orders of medicines are based on real consumption data.

There is also often an erratic lead-time between placing the order and having it delivered (Jahre et al., 2010). When dispensary managers cannot predict how long it will take to refill their drug supply, they stockpile drugs. Stockpiling in turn encourages other supply chain problems, such as using drugs past their expiry date. Stockpiling in one dispensary often causes shortages in another (Corbell et al., 2010).

The expanded use of anti-retroviral drugs in Sub-Saharan Africa has brought attention to the problems of supply chain management. The National University of Rwanda's pharmacy department includes pharmaceutical management in its pre-service curriculum. Makerere University in Uganda and Muhimbili University of Health and Allied Sciences in Tanzania both have plans to develop master's programs in pharmaceutical supply chain management (Matowe et al., 2008). The United States Agency for International Development's (USAID's) Supply

Chain Management program is also working in PEPFAR countries to build the existing drug supply chain to better handle the increase brought on by anti-retroviral drugs (USAID, 2011).

INFRASTRUCTURE

It is difficult to separate problems controlling supply chains from problems with infrastructure. Inadequate storage for foods, medicines, and vaccines are infrastructure deficits. The vaccine supply chain described in Box 3-2, for example, aims to move vaccines swiftly from the airport to the patient; it depends on reliable electricity for temperature control, strong telecommunications systems to facilitate timely orders, and decent roads, all common infrastructure gaps in poor countries. A strong food and medical products regulatory system is itself a key piece of the public health infrastructure. Similarly, a surveillance system is part of the regulatory infrastructure. Without surveillance and staff trained in management and causal inferences, countries are vulnerable to vaccine safety scares, for example (Black et al., 2010). But for the purposes of organizing this report, the infrastructure gaps the committee identified in developing countries fall into the categories of laboratory, manufacturing, and market infrastructure, and information and communication infrastructure.

Laboratory, Manufacturing, and Market Infrastructure

Food and medical product regulators in poor countries do not have the quality control and reference laboratories that their counterparts in rich countries take for granted. In India, for example, the site visitors heard repeatedly that Indian food production was totally compliant with the International Standards Organization, but there was little evidence of a sufficient testing infrastructure to confirm this. A World Bank analysis confirmed that India's four national and 79 state food safety laboratories had neither the equipment nor the personnel to properly collect and analyze food samples (World Bank, 2009). The same assessment found that of the 19 drug testing laboratories in India, only seven had the ability to run a full range of assays (World Bank, 2009). Some countries work around their infrastructure shortages. In South Africa, the drug regulatory authority contracts universities to do quality control testing for biologics and drugs (Essack et al., 2011). But in some of the poorest countries there are no accredited safety testing laboratories (Abegaz, 2006). Some countries, such as Pakistan, need to rely on regional analytic labs, and sending samples regularly to distant labs is time consuming, expensive, and slow (Hao, 2012). There are only five WHO-prequalified medicine quality control laboratories in Sub-Saharan Africa, two in India, two in Singapore, and one in Vietnam (WHO, 2011h). Building laboratory capacity is a priority for the Asia Pacific Economic Cooperation's Food Safety program (APEC, 2008). Box 3-4 describes recent success in laboratory capacity building in Southeast Asia.

BOX 3-4
Strengthening Laboratory Capacity in Southeast Asia

A solid laboratory system is essential for medicines regulation, but is missing even in many middle-income manufacturing counties. U.S. Pharmacopeia, USAID, and Asian universities are all working to improve regulatory and laboratory capacity. Their efforts are improving reference laboratories and supporting pharmacists in good clinical practice and good pharmacy practice.

The Southeast Asia Infectious Disease Clinical Research Network (SEAICRN) is increasing laboratory capacity through collaborative partnership. The network brings together hospitals, universities, and other research organizations from Thailand, Vietnam, Indonesia, and Singapore to improve laboratories, equip them well, train scientists, and ensure quality laboratory management. Through the integrated, collaborative model, countries in the network are responding more rapidly to emerging disease issues, such as the assessment of oseltamivir resistance in A/H1N1 in 2008 (Wertheim et al., 2010).

U.S. Pharmacopeia and USAID's Promoting the Quality of Medicines program is also active in laboratory capacity building. Promoting the Quality of Medicines works to improve post-market surveillance for product quality and safety (Lukulay, 2011). Southeast Asian police have drawn on the program's data and closed more than 100 illicit drug vendors in the region (USP, 2011). The map below shows sentinel surveillance sites in the Mekong Delta region as of 2008 that are staffed by two scientist each and use portable mini-laboratories to test medicine quality (Global Pharma Health Fund; Lukulay, 2011). Some sites also monitor the efficacy of malaria treatments.

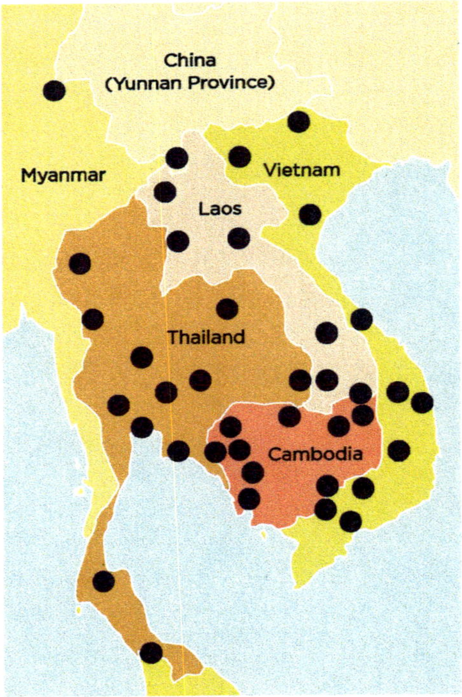

SOURCE: Promoting the Quality of Medicines (USAID and USP Cooperative Agreement).

In his March presentation to the committee Paul Young, Director of Chemical Analysis Operations at Waters Corporation, described visiting food safety laboratories in a number of developing countries while working as a food regulator in Europe and finding donated equipment stored under plastic sheets, because no one had been trained in its use, the people trained to use it no longer worked at the lab, or because basic infrastructure to run the equipment was inadequate. Tropical climates and power surges are hard on sensitive electronics. In many ways the challenge of supporting laboratory infrastructure is complicated by the more basic deficits of sanitation and a stable power supply.

Shortages of laboratory infrastructure in turn encourage other gaps in regulatory systems. At the Pretoria visit for this study, the Tanzanian Food and Drug Authority's Raymond Wigenge explained that Sub-Saharan African countries' limitations in laboratory science cause their poor participation in Codex and other standard setting meetings. He explained that if African scientists were better able to do exposure assessments they would bring to Codex data on the accurate maximum exposure for mycotoxins and contribute to setting the Codex mycotoxin standard.

There are clear ties between problems with water sanitation infrastructure and ensuring safety in food production. Good agricultural practices require deep pit latrines and the separation of defecation and farming fields (Agribusiness and Allied Kenya Ltd et al., 2006). Grains and spices need to be properly dried to reduce risk of mycotoxin contamination. As mentioned in the discussion of supply chain problems, rural roads are poor and transportation is expensive (Hazell and Wood, 2008). Farmers and distributors have higher vehicle operating costs from damages caused by unpaved roads (Donnges et al., 2007). A distribution system that moves foods more quickly from the farm to the market could do much to promote food safety (Kader, 2010).

Market infrastructure is also lacking in the growing cities of Africa and Asia. Only 20 percent of markets in the Indian state of Maharashtra have cold storage, compared to 5 percent in Tamil Nadu, and none in Orissa or Uttar Pradesh (Umali-Deininger and Sur, 2007). The majority of the same markets surveyed have no system for pest control (Umali-Deininger and Sur, 2007). Pest infestation in markets is a clear disease risk and can introduce other contaminants, such as heavy metals, to food (Sharma et al., 2009).

A woman and child prepare a vegetable harvest for transport in western China.
SOURCE: © 2008 Xiaobo Zhang, Courtesy of Photoshare.

Local manufacture and sale of processed foods is part of life around the world, but the manufacture of medical products is more controversial. In 2005 some experts discouraged local medicines production in the poorest countries, believing the energy and raw materials costs of domestic manufacture to be prohibitively high for them (Attridge and Preker, 2005). Local manufacture is sometimes thought to put economic and industrial development before public health in the name of self-sufficiency (Anderson, 2010). Others maintain that as long as one third of the world, mostly in Africa and Asia, does not have access to essential medicines, local drug manufacture can build crucial industrial infrastructure, and that the least developed countries have a brief window to do so before the TRIPS agreement binds them to observe pharmaceutical patents (Anderson, 2010; Chaudhuri et al., 2010; Losse et al., 2007). Local manufacture of essential medicines could also guarantee a more reliable local medicine source in countries otherwise dependent on trade or foreign aid. A full analysis of this dynamic controversy is outside the scope of this report. But recently the WHO prequalified artemisinin combination therapy manufacturers in Uganda and a Kenyan antiretroviral manufacturer (Manson, 2011; WHO, 2011g). Nevertheless, local production of medical products depends on having decent industrial infrastructure and factories that are designed to facilitate meeting international manufacturing standards (Milstien et al., 2009). When the manufacturing infrastructure lags behind, regulators in the developing countries face a harder job in enforcing safety controls.

Information and Communication Technology

Low- and middle-income countries do not have the technology necessary to track and trace products through their supply chains. This is not surprising, as traceability in the food and pharmaceutical industries is difficult even for immensely profitable multinational conglomerates with a stake in protecting their brand names. Food and medicines are made from ingredients that are processed and aggregated at different steps in manufacture, often in different countries (Roth et al., 2008). Guy Blissett, the head of consumer products at the IBM Institute for Business Value, has described traceability as "a global information management problem" (Roth et al., 2008, p. 32).

In India, the Agricultural and Processed Food Export Development Authority has invested in traceability systems when there is a clear commercial benefit to doing so, such as tracing grapes for the European market. The pressure to trace foods through the domestic market is not strong, however. Some speculate that nothing will change until domestic consumers show interest and willingness to pay for traceability (Roth et al., 2008; Umali-Deininger and Sur, 2007). Even if emerging economies had traceability systems in place, they do not have the ability to issue rapid recalls. Recalls depend as much on transportation and communication infrastructure as they do on product tracing.

Farmers in poor countries are usually obliged to sell their crops at harvest, when the market is glutted and prices are lowest, because the spoilage process starts quickly, as mentioned above in the discussion of supply chains. Investments in silos and temperature controlled storage are one way around this, as is preserving the perishable foods. Information technology can also help farmers manage their inventory. For example, the Indian agricultural commodities firm ITC Ltd. trained soybean farmers to use the internet to monitor the weather forecast, to learn about best agricultural practices, and to track soy prices and the Chicago Board of Trade ten-day global market outlook. Armed with better information, farmers could schedule their marketing to coincide with periods of demand (Upton and Fuller, 2004). There are transferable lessons in ITC's experience for food regulators interested in monitoring the food supply from farm to table.

Most Indian farmers still rely on their own or their friends' observations for their information about crop prices (Umali-Deininger and Sur, 2007). Using simple information technology to monitor commodity prices is a way to involve farmers in the agricultural extension system. The ITC trainers found that by making information technology available they built trust with the soybean farmers and had a strong foundation on which to build future collaborations (Upton and Fuller, 2004). The use of information technology is a simple way to build trust with rural suppliers and encourage ownership in food safety technology.

In the ITC model, farmers connected to the internet though landlines or very small aperture terminals (Upton and Fuller, 2004). The bandwidth available was not high, but was sufficient for the project. Poor bandwidth limits more ambitious use of information technology in developing countries. Food and drug safety information is available online, but still not accessible to developing country regulators. Even universities, whose informatics infrastructure is often better than the government's, are "digitally isolated from the rest of the world. [Their internet capacity is] equivalent to 30,000 people trying to use a single connection. Bandwidth can be exorbitantly expensive, and services are often unreliable. The result is that faculty and students rarely have access to the latest knowledge, and universities cannot form effective partnerships with academics and institutions in other countries. High-speed access to the Internet—at a minimum of 1 gigabyte per second—would serve as a lifeline for universities and help to drive a country's economic renewal" (Juma, 2008, p. 17). Without internet access the WHO's vast and useful library of handbooks for regulators are beyond the reach of regulators in the poorest countries, the people who need them most.

LAWS

Relevant and enforceable laws are the foundation of food and medical production regulation (FAO/WHO; WHO, 2007). Governments pass food and medical product laws to protect public health, prevent fraud, and promote fair trade (WHO, 2003a). The laws governing food and medical products invariably reflect a country's political, economic and cultural history. Muslim countries may include halal criteria in their national food law, for example. Box 3-5 describes the political and historical influences on Indian intellectual property and drug legislation.

Some developing countries have no laws governing food or drug safety; others have a surfeit of confusing and contradictory ones (Vapnek and Spreij, 2005; WHO, 2005). Participants at the São Paulo and Pretoria meetings for this study explained that in many of their countries the regulatory legislation dates from the turn of the last century and is not suitable for the modern world. Governments should periodically revisit their laws governing product safety to ensure they are up-to-date and cogent (WHO, 2003a). Poorly coordinated legislation can also create fragmentation by assigning the same responsibilities to several agencies. The subsequent section on fragmentation discusses this problem in more detail.

BOX 3-5
Historical and Political Influences on Indian Drug Legislation

At the time of Indian independence, Western multinational corporations controlled 80-90 percent of the Indian pharmaceutical market (Greene, 2007). In an effort to foster self-sufficiency and create an independent supply of pharmaceutical products, the Indian government enacted high tariffs and import restrictions to encourage domestic production. As part of this program, the 1970 Patent Act ended Indian recognition of product patent protection. The Patent Act allowed Indian drug companies to reverse engineer expensive, patented drugs without paying licensing fees. In the absence of legal patent protection, most foreign manufacturers left India. As of 2005, foreign companies held less than 20 percent of the Indian drug market (Greene, 2007).

Indian government policy long encouraged small- and medium-sized drug companies to enter the market. Consequently, today's market in India is fragmented and competitive—there are more than 20,000 drug manufacturers (KPMG International, 2006). Roughly 300 of these account for 70 percent of the market; the top 10 firms account for 30 percent (KPMG International, 2006).

The industry changed in 2005 when the Indian government amended the Patents Act to comply with the TRIPS Agreement and Indian pharmaceutical companies could no longer reverse engineer patented drugs. Indian firms sought to replace lost revenues in several ways. First, they increased generic exports. As of 2007, generics accounted for 60-100 percent of sales in India's top ten firms (Greene, 2007). In addition, most have entered into contract research and manufacturing agreements with foreign drug companies. Indian companies have costs far below those of Western ones—one-eighth for research and development and one-fifth for manufacturing (Nauriyal, 2006). Low costs, both in labor and capital, coupled with India's recognition of foreign patent laws, have made India an attractive destination for clinical trials and drug discovery and research. Indian companies are now building more and better factories and working to comply with international manufacturing standards in an effort to secure manufacturing contacts from multinational pharmaceutical corporations (Nauriyal, 2006).

Enforcement of Existing Regulations

One of the main problems developing country regulators have with their laws is with implementing punitive measure for violators. Participants at the São Paulo, Delhi, and Beijing workshops all noted that small producers can easily close their operations and re-open under a different name to avoid penalty. A 2010 Government Accountability Office (GAO) report described the FDA's helplessness to the same problem (GAO, 2010). An FDA effort to verify foreign producers in 2010 found that of 43 drug manufacturers visited, 7 did not exist at the address in FDA's data base (GAO, 2010).

There was consensus in the Delhi and Beijing workshops that both India and China have a thorough legal regulatory framework in place. In these countries, as in many other emerging economies, regulatory authorities face more problems enforcing their laws than creating them. It is difficult to strengthen law enforcement in the face of poor staffing, inadequate infrastructure, and lack of political will (Bollyky, 2009). A World Bank appraisal of food and drug regulatory oversight identified weak enforcement of existing regulations as one of India's four main problems in both food and drug safety (World Bank, 2009). They found the food system had "traditionally … depended on spot checks of manufacturing conditions and random sampling of final products. Even this system was not evenly enforced "(World Bank, 2009, p. 1). Of the drug system, they concluded, "enforcement of good manufacturing practice was highly variable. The quality of training for drug inspectors was uneven ... [and there was] anecdotal evidence of lack of transparency in granting licenses"(World Bank, 2009, p. 2).

In an analysis of food safety law enforcement in China, Ni and Zeng compared China's food safety laws to its environmental laws. The laws increase in number as the environment degrades and the government focuses on punishing offenders (Ni and Zeng, 2009). This is consistent with the committee's observation that the Chinese government prefers to enforce its laws by punishing offenders and is less interested in rewarding compliance. This tactic is itself a limiting factor in a country as large as China with so few inspectors (see section on Workforce). Competing societal forces will also undermine the government's best efforts at punishment. Global business is increasingly the purview of large corporations operating on narrow profit margins, especially in the food sector (Garrett and Huang, 2011). Their suppliers are under pressure to cut costs; too often they do so by using unsafe ingredients and cutting corners on good practices (Garrett and Huang, 2011). Sometimes industry's interest in protecting their brand and a fear of liability laws are enough to prevent fraud and adulteration, but in many low- and middle-income countries it is not so.

Civil Liability

Appendix B, "A Review of Tort Liability's Role in Food and Medical Product Regulation," describes the role of product liability in regulatory systems and an overview of the different systems in place in South Africa, Brazil, China, and India.

WORKFORCE

During the public meetings for this study the committee repeatedly heard that regulatory authorities in developing countries have too few staff, insufficient technical training for staff, and an inability to retain staff. They cannot offer private sector salaries, and, perhaps more importantly, there is little *espirit de corps* among regulators. Some are sacked for political reasons; others grow frustrated and quit. While they are serious concerns for government regulators, these workforce problems reverberate in the public sector.

Too Few Staff in the Regulatory Authority

In an interview for this study, FDA China staff explained that at first glance China has an army of food and drug inspectors, 400,000 by some estimates (Becker, 2008), but that most of them work part time and many perform an average of one inspection a year. Chinese Minister of Health Chen Zhu gives a much lower estimate of the number of food safety inspectors in China: approximately 133,000, or fewer than 1 for every 10,000 people (LaFraniere, 2011). In a 2010 assessment of medicines regulatory authorities in Sub-Saharan Africa, the WHO found that all 26 of the countries evaluated reported a shortage of qualified inspectors (WHO, 2010a). Indian drug regulatory authorities, especially at the state level responsible for most inspections, have far too few staff to enforce their laws (Langer, 2008).

The inspectorate is only one arm of the workforce in a regulatory authority. Regulatory science and its constituent fields are new areas of study in most of the world. Ahuja and Sharma summed up the problem in India with one example, "the supply-demand situation for skilled manpower is highly skewed in favor of the demand, as this field [e.g., pharmacovigilance] is new in India and elsewhere" (Sharma and Ahuja, 2010, p. 1). Despite having over half a million physicians, India has less than 200 investigators trained in good clinical practices (Prakash, 2009).

If China and India, with their massive populations, cannot staff a regulatory authority, the problem is even more serious in smaller countries. In many low- and middle-income countries environmental health inspectors often do the job of food safety inspectors, and analytical positions in both food and medical product quality control laboratories often go unfilled (FAO/WHO, 2003; WHO, 2010a). A 2002 comparative analysis of 10 different drug regulatory authorities found the shortage of qualified staff to be the main problem facing medicines regulatory authorities around the world (Ratanawijitrasin and Wondemagegnehu, 2002).

Insufficient Technical Training for Staff

The problem of too few staff at regulatory agencies is closely related to the problem of staff competency. In China, for example, many of the inspectors have only a middle-school education; they lack the scientific background to do more than a superficial inspection, a problem more pronounced in the central and western part of the country (UN, 2008). The technical proficiency of the Chinese inspectorate is concern enough that both the FDA and GIZ, the German government's aid agency, train inspectors or train trainers. The WHO has also encouraged the Chinese government to develop a central training institute for food safety, but the government has balked at this suggestion because of difficulties in implementing such a large project.

These problems are by no means unique to China. A study of food inspectors in Andhra Pradesh, India found limited knowledge of food microbiology in the inspectorate, a weakness attributed to lack of in-service training (Sudershan et al., 2008). A joint Food and Agriculture Organization of the United Nations (FAO) and WHO report recommended offering in-service training for regulatory staff as a way to strengthen food safety systems (FAO/WHO, 2003). The FAO has also recommended a central food safety training center for South America, and participants at the IOM meeting in São Paulo were eager to see such a center open because it would enrich training for people from small countries. Such institutions would be most useful if their curricula were designed specifically for the school's region. In a systematic review of problems facing the pharmacy workforce, Hawthorne and Anderson reported that curricula developed in North America or Europe are used in developing countries with the best intentions, but this practice contributes to job dissatisfaction as pharmacists trained on a foreign curriculum are not prepared for the reality of work in developing countries (Hawthorne and Anderson, 2009).

The need for a properly trained regulatory staff will increase in the next decade. In the past, the review process for new chemical entities took place most in industrialized countries; low- and middle-income countries only had to register or give market approval to a drug tested abroad (Moran et al., 2011). Now there is more interest in developing treatments for neglected diseases; in 2007 over $2.5 billion was invested globally in research on neglected tropical disease (Moran et al., 2009). These products are now coming up for regulatory review in Asia, Sub-Saharan Africa, and parts of Latin America, and it is imperative that the regulatory work force has the depth to register and review these new products.

Therefore, education in regulatory science is a particular need. Regulatory science is a relatively new field that includes training in basic sciences that relate to the regulatory system; the development and validation of regulatory tests; screening and compliance testing; investigation of test results; and submission of dossiers for government or in-house review (Irwin et al., 1997). Increasingly, any food production house or medical manufacturer needs to have a regulatory affairs specialist on staff. Until recently, developed countries generally relied on on-the-job training for regulatory affairs personnel, but this created important blind spots, such as poor understanding of how international organizations work to harmonize standards (Gundersen, 2001). There are now a few, but only a few, universities that train in regulatory science, some of which also offer distance-education classes (Gundersen, 2001). Improved education in regulatory science is a need around the world, and there is increasing attention to its international importance (Hamburg, 2011).

The problem of inadequate training extends to the workforce as a whole, not just government regulators. In 2011 an African business newsletter reported that staff at African food companies often fail to follow proper food safety protocols because they have never been trained in them (Bester, 2011). Similarly, the non-profit organization Engineering and World Health identified lack of trained staff as a serious barrier to the use of high-tech medical devices in the poorest countries, explaining, "In countries where the literacy rate can be 50 percent, eligible workers can be difficult to find" (Malkin, 2007, p. 579). Chinese participants at the public meeting for this report agreed that while much adulteration in China is frank criminal behavior, some is attributable only to worker ignorance, which can have disastrous consequences. In 2011 Chinese farmers used the chemical forcholfenuron to speed the growth of melons and caused the entire crop to explode in the fields (Watts, 2011).

Donor organizations can fill training gaps, but donor training is sporadic and short-term. A World Bank analysis of capacity for food safety in Zambia, found that beyond a few workshops for street vendors, donors were not interested in food safety in Zambia (Abegaz, 2006). In larger countries, and in countries that export foods, there is much more donor involvement. Last year in China, for example, the World Bank committed $100 million to increasing and improving safety in a single Chinese province. The $100 million was accompanied by matching grants for producers to set up 200-300 training sites for good agricultural practices (World Bank, 2010). Additionally, the WHO has a permanent food safety presence in China. With funding from the Asian Development Bank, it advises the State Food and Drug Administration on food safety management, policies and international standards (WHO, 2008b).

At the Pretoria workshop for this study, the participants agreed that donor trainings, no matter how technically rigorous, are not helpful unless donors coordinate their plans with the appropriate central government agencies. There have also been calls for donors to coordinate at the international level. The lack of a clear international consensus on how to best support the poorest countries holds back biotechnology development, and the same can be said of general regulatory systems development (Byerlee and Fischer, 2002).

Donor trainings are also vulnerable to problems in recruiting the proper audience. Opportunities to travel and collect per diem, i.e. donor trainings, are too often a reward to senior staff for their years of service. More junior implementing staff are harder to reach. Reaching and training the proper staff for a variety of jobs in the food and drug regulatory authority are of special concern to this report. At all the international workshops for this study, participants mentioned a need for training, specifically, training in risk analysis to inform their regulatory work. The importance of more rigorous training for regulatory staff cannot be understated. If regulators had similarly rigorous training they would develop comparable systems. Ongoing professional development is itself an incentive that could be used to keep technical expertise in government service. This is one reason American government and universities are able to keep their staff despite the higher salaries offered in industry.

A more sustainable solution to the training problem in developing countries depends on academia (Lupien, 2007). At their workshops abroad, the site visitors heard many times that academia does not contribute to food or medical product safety: they neither research public health problems nor do they emphasize real world experience in their teaching. Part of this convention may come from the way people think about education, especially in Asia. In China, for example, anything seen to distract students from their studies is frowned upon (A tale of two expats: Business in China and the west, 2011); this extends even to professional internships. Technical internships are lacking in India as well; an Asian Development Bank publication reported that only a quarter of Indian engineering graduates had the skills they needed to find work without further training (Xiaoguang and Fengqiao, 2010). Professors can hardly be expected to train students for careers they have had no exposure to themselves. Except for the elite Indian Institutes of Technology, Indian universities do little research and development work (World Bank, 2007). Some of the problem may stem from a "passive national learning system" in post-colonial countries, where policy has encouraged copying technology developed abroad and failed to foster home-grown innovation (Morel et al., 2007, p. 180; Viotti, 2002).

The links between industry, government, and academia appear to be stronger in Latin America (Juma, 2008; Sutz, 2000). At the São Paulo workshop for this study, Rosane Cuber Guimarães, Good Practices Manager at Biomanguinhos, the technical and scientific unit of vaccine production at Fiocruz, Brazil's national public health institute, discussed her institute's training program. She explained that they have a rigorous training program and enrolled about 30 masters and 2 doctoral students in 2011. The problem at Biomanguinhos, and at many public institutions, is retaining their graduates in public service.

Problems Retaining Staff

Government jobs in food and medical product regulation do not pay as well as positions of comparable seniority and scientific expertise in the private sector. This is true in rich countries as well, although in 2007 Congress authorized incentive pay for government scientists in an effort to close this pay gap (Bridges, 2007). The WHO assessment of medicines regulation in Sub-Saharan Africa found a universal lack of sustainable funding for staff salaries; only 8 percent had a staff development plan (WHO, 2010a). Almost without exception the government regulators who took part in workshops for this study mentioned an internal brain drain, where talented staff leave government service. In countries with a robust private sector, such as China, India, and Brazil they commonly leave for positions in industry, while in the least developed countries they are more likely to find work on donor projects or with NGOs.

At the São Paulo workshop for this study, participants raised the concern that government regulators can lose their jobs for political reasons, when a newly elected politician wants to slim down the government payroll, for example. Valuable training is wasted when scientific staff are dismissed arbitrarily. It also impairs institutional memory when entire cohorts of senior staff leave an organization in unison. Anvisa, the Brazilian equivalent of FDA, has put systems into place that insulate their staff from political patronage (Box 3-6) (Prado, 2006). Government agencies in the countries visited for this study were slow to adopt modern management principles or implement succession plans, however.

BOX 3-6
Brazilian Regulatory Restructuring

Independent regulatory agencies are a relatively new phenomenon in Latin America. In a regulatory authority, independence means that there are systems in place to protect scientific decision making from political actors (Prado, 2008). This includes having certain safeguards in place. The president of the country should not be able to remove the agencies' leaders and the senate should approve the commissioner. Decisions should be made by a board, agency commissioners should have pre-defined terms of office and these terms should be staggered, so that all leadership does not retire at the same time. Finally, independent agencies should have independent funding (Prado, 2008).

In the 1990s, Brazil established nine independent regulatory agencies adopting many institutional formulas from the United States (Prado, 2008). At the time, Brazil was in a process of privatizing state-owned companies and changing regulatory oversight, in part to be more attractive to investors. The government understood that a stable, independent regulatory authority was important to economic development: investors are reluctant to fund industry if the regulations governing it change with every election.

The National Health Surveillance Agency (Anvisa) was created in 1999 as part of Brazil's regulatory restructuring; its bylaws were approved in 2000. Anvisa's mission is to protect the health of the Brazilian people by exercising sanitary control over production and marketing of products and services subject to sanitary surveillance (Anvisa, 2003; Aragão, 2010). Structured within the Brazilian federal public administration and linked to the Ministry of Health, the agency is managed by a collegiate board of directors, comprised of five members with staggered three year terms (Anvisa, 2003). It is an independent, financially autonomous regulatory agency (Anvisa, 2003; Aragão, 2010).

At the public workshops in India and South Africa, participants hinted at concerns with corruption, a reality of work in many countries that can push professionals to look for other jobs. In China, a senior Ministry of Health official, spoke with great candor about a desire to develop the professional ethic in both the inspectorate and in industry. In India, the 2003 Mashekellar report on spurious drugs cited government corruption as a factor encouraging the trade in fake drugs (Government of India, 2003). Corruption is a sensitive topic, one that industry, government employees, and academics are all understandably hesitant to discuss. Corruption is hard to measure, but is prevalent in places "without robust institutional checks, [where] government regulators can make discretionary decisions rather than decisions based on uniform criteria" (Cohen, 2005, p. 78). A culture of accepting bribes does not encourage trust in government or respect of civil servants; staff who are not respected or have no pride in their agency have little reason to refuse bribes. Working in a vicious cycle, corruption is both a cause and an effect of the staff retention problems at many regulatory agencies.

FRAGMENTATION

Regulatory systems in both developed and developing countries often suffer from fragmentation, "the assign[ing] of different responsibilities to different regulatory bodies"

(Ratanawijitrasin and Wondemagegnehu, 2002, p. 2). There is also sometimes a similar problem of assigning the same responsibilities to different regulatory bodies. Even in the United States, there are a dozen different federal agencies enforcing 35 different food safety laws (Martin, 2007). This is a commonly cited complaint about the U.S. food safety and, to a lesser extent, drug safety systems (CSPI, 2007; The Genetics and Public Policy Center, 2010). Fragmentation is often a consequence of historical compromises. This kind of fragmentation is common in developed and developing countries alike. The FDA, for example, began as an office within U.S. Department of Agriculture (USDA), the differentiation of their responsibilities continues to evolve today. The strongest regulatory systems can evolve to match changing production practices. For example, in 2011 Commissioner Hamburg reorganized the FDA's reporting chain and added an Office of Operations and a Deputy Commissioner for Global Regulatory Operations and Policy, in order to help the agency respond to the challenges of globalization (May, 2011).

In its overseas workshops, however, the committee identified a different fragmentation in the regulatory systems of emerging economies, a fragmentation without a clear assignment of responsibilities, an established protocol for enforcement, or an articulated chain of command. This confuses already complicated systems. Appendix C shows the sprawling organization of food and drug safety systems in South Africa, Brazil, India, and China.

Fragmentation is even more serious a problem in the poorest countries. In its analysis of medicines regulatory authorities in Sub-Saharan Africa, the WHO found that an organizational chart was missing in four countries; nine had unclear or missing job descriptions for key positions (WHO, 2010a). Though, as the figures in Appendix C show, drug safety laws are scattered among fewer agencies than food safety laws are.[1] In many of the countries visited, the lack of established communication channels between and within agencies confounds the fragmentation problem. This is discussed in more detail below.

Many countries, the United States included, have recently attempted to unify their food or medical product safety regulation. The Brazilian government's work on Anvisa is an example of one such successful project (Box 3-6). Ambitious legal restructuring of food and drugs regulation is not usually an option, however. When the Brazilian government created Anvisa it was part of a larger restructuring and privatization movement happening across Latin America (Prado, 2008). Rarely do governments have the money or the political capital to support such a large effort. In the United States, for example, the division of responsibility between the USDA and the FDA is a patchwork of historical compromises. The system works, however, because the delegation of responsibility between the agencies is clear and because they work together and with their counterparts in other government agencies. Both agencies also have clearly articulated chains of command; they coordinate their efforts to avoid duplicating each other's work.

In their analysis of drug regulatory systems in ten different countries, Ratanawijitrasin and Wondemagegnehu concluded that fragmentation is either a problem of delegation with no authority to enforce the laws or delegation with full authority but no coordination with other regulatory agencies (2002). Large countries tend to face the former problem: their provincial and local governments staff local regulatory authorities with limited authority to enforce federal regulations.

In both China and India, every regulatory authority has offices at multiple levels of government. That is, the national drug regulatory authority has provincial and municipal levels as well. There are different regulations at the federal, provincial, and municipal levels;

[1] See Appendix D for more detailed notes on the Chinese food safety system.

sometimes these regulations overlap, other times they conflict. For example the Drugs Controller General of India, a federal office, approves all drugs sold in the country, but state authorities, whose standards vary widely, issue manufacturing licenses (Jeffery and Santhosh M.R., 2009). Once a drug is licensed in one state, it is automatically approved for sale throughout the country. There are over 70,000 drugs for sale on the Indian market, many of them sold in irrational fixed-dose combinations, stressing the already bursting quality control laboratories (Jeffery and Santhosh M.R., 2009). If every agency had a clearer delineation of its responsibilities, then there would be more efficient use of the government's limited staff (Lu and Kjeldsen-Kragh, 2008).

Routine reporting from local to provincial and state governments is of the utmost importance in larger countries. In Malaysia, for example, the Deputy Director of Health in each state reports directly to the Pharmaceutical Services within the National Pharmaceutical Control Bureau. This ensures communication between the state and federal level within the government hierarchy (Ratanawijitrasin and Wondemagegnehu, 2002).

In the public workshops for this report, the committee learned that different agencies often repeat each other's testing. In South Africa, for example, the Departments of Health and Agriculture are both required to test unprocessed foods, though both agencies have insufficient laboratory capacity to do so (Chanda et al., 2010). Different agencies regulating food and medical products frequently lack an established protocol to share data. This makes surveillance as much a political task as a scientific one.

Small countries more commonly face the problem of delegation of responsibilities with full authority, but poor coordination. At the São Paulo meeting for this report, Claudio Poblete, a consultant retired from the Chilean agricultural service, explained that he had seen some uncoordinated delegation in the Chilean food safety systems, particularly in that the ministries of health and agriculture are meant to enforce food safety laws codified in the Animal Health and Protection Code, a decree released by the Ministry of Finance in 1963 as part of land reform.

Pakistan is another country where uncoordinated delegation is a problem. In January 2012 over 100 heart patients died from adulterated medicine at the Punjab Institute of Cardiology in Lahore (Guerin, 2012). There is a greater risk for such disasters since July 2011, when the government devolved the country's drug regulations to the provinces (The Daily Times, 2012). With no central drug regulatory agency, there is no way to coordinate provincial regulatory work (Abudhoo, 2012; The Daily Times, 2012).

SURVEILLANCE

Surveillance is one of the essential functions of the regulatory and public health systems. The WHO's International Health Regulations-2005 define surveillance as, "systematic ongoing collection, collation and analysis of public health information…assessment and public health response as necessary" (WHO, 2008a, p. 10). Surveillance depends on a strong health infrastructure, established methods for data collection, and epidemiologists and statisticians to analyze and interpret data and disseminate their findings. If data quality is not good, then the analysis and interpretation are doomed, but rigorous data collection is difficult in low- and middle-income countries, especially in remote places. Regulators in developing countries struggle to maintain affordable surveillance systems that produce reliable data. Too often data collection is difficult and data quality uneven, calling into question the returns on the investments developing countries make in surveillance systems (Frerichs, 1991). In the era of global supply chains, anti-microbial resistance, and international epidemics, "all countries … have a stake in the success or failure of surveillance and response capacity development in any one country" (Kimball et al., 2008, p. 1464). This realization has driven growth in global and regional surveillance networks over the last 10 years (Castillo-Salgado, 2010). At every overseas workshops for this study, the participants told the committee that their regulatory authorities have problems conducting risk assessment. Risk assessment identifies hazards and their sources, the characteristics of theses hazards and their health risks, and projects the impacts of different ways to control hazard (Todd and Narrod, 2006; WHO, 2012). Some of the problems regulators face in conducting risk analysis stem from insufficient training for their staff, a gap discussed earlier in this chapter. Poor surveillance also limits risk assessment. While training regulators abroad in risk assessment is an excellent goal, this training should accompany improvements to national food and medical product surveillance systems.

Food Safety Surveillance

Food safety surveillance depends on the reporting of cases of foodborne disease to a central data repository; the epidemiological investigation of foodborne disease; laboratory identification of the pathogen that differentiates it from similar agents; trace-back capability to the source of the contamination; and the recall of contaminated products from the market when necessary. While the health surveillance system is seldom part of the regulatory agency (the CDC is a separate agency from USDA's Food Safety Inspection Service, for example) surveillance is still part of the regulatory system.

It is difficult to trace back through a supply chain that includes many anonymous transactions (Todd and Narrod, 2006). In its outline for the food safety system for India, the International Life Sciences Institute emphasized that monitoring contaminants in food and water is a prerequisite for monitoring disease in the population (International Life Sciences Institute-India, 2007).

Foodborne disease is extremely common in developing countries. By WHO estimates, 2.2 million people, more than half of them children, die from diarrheal disease every year, most of it caused by contaminated food and water (UNICEF; UNICEF and WHO, 2009). Disease surveillance is poor in most countries, especially for mundane diseases like diarrhea, so these estimates are almost certainly too low (Todd and Narrod, 2006).

In passive surveillance systems, health workers or patients identify what they suspect to be an adverse event due to a drug and then report it to the regulatory authority. Passive disease surveillance cannot effectively detect foodborne outbreaks: diarrhea is not often treated in clinics, biospecimens are collected for microbiological analysis, and health workers do not report serious cases or deaths into a central repository (Zaidi et al., 2008). It is difficult to identify clusters of similar cases in an area over a short time when many cases are out of reach of the health system. It is also difficult to report a spike in illness without first knowing the baseline disease prevalence. Foodborne listeriosis, for example, is closely monitored in the United States, but its prevalence is unknown in developing countries, even in the Middle East where experts assume it to be a public health problem given the popularity of cold, cooked meats and soft cheeses (Todd and Notermans, 2011).

Twenty years ago, foodborne outbreaks often came from improper food handling in the kitchen (Swaminathan et al., 2001). An outbreak at a restaurant or party was easy to identify. Nowadays, when food is contaminated at or near the farm or in processing, the global food supply chain can quickly spread the pathogen. Modern outbreaks can be far removed from their triggers in time and place. From May to July 2011, an epidemic of bloody diarrhea and hemolytic-uremic syndrome sickened over 4,000 people and killed 50, mostly in Germany, but also in Sweden and other parts of Europe (Blaser, 2011; Reuters, 2010). Epidemiologists eventually traced the epidemic to Egyptian fenugreek seed contaminated by human or animal feces either in storage or transport, possibly as early as 2009 (Blaser, 2011). Because contaminated food can look, taste, and smell normal, identifying contaminants requires sophisticated microbiological assays. DNA fingerprinting and molecular subtyping are part of the modern epidemiologic investigation of a foodborne outbreak (Swaminathan et al., 2001). The CDC's gold-standard technique, pulsed field gel electrophoresis, depends on laboratory infrastructure that is often missing in developing countries. The WHO's Global Foodborne Infections Network is working to improve laboratory serotyping of enteric pathogens in its member countries (WHO, 2011e). Continued extension of PulseNet, the CDC's molecular subtyping network, would do much to advance the science of molecular epidemiology in developing countries and could improve the speedy investigation of outbreaks around the world (Swaminathan et al., 2006).

In countries that have the capacity to do molecular epidemiological investigation of outbreaks, the information gained from them is invaluable. Serotyping and pulsed field gel electrophoresis of *Salmonella* in Thailand identified a geographically disparate cluster of the same pathogen in Thailand and the United States (Pornruangwong et al., 2011). Mexico also has an integrated food chain surveillance system; it has identified *Salmonella* clusters and their animal reservoirs, the baseline *Salmonella* contamination in retail meats, and the prevalence of asymptomatic *Salmonella* infection in different parts of the country (Zaidi et al., 2008).

There are also surveillance techniques that do not depend on the laboratory. The emerging field of public health informatics analyzes search patterns on the Internet to give early warning of outbreaks (Castillo-Salgado, 2010). Private companies such as Voxiva use mobile phones for electronic surveillance in remote places (Castillo-Salgado, 2010; Voxiva, 2011). These novel surveillance methods can be especially useful in low- and middle-income countries.

Improvements to food safety surveillance systems within developing countries can be motivated by the demands of foreign importers or by the rising expectations of local consumers. In recent years, increasing concern with bioterrorism and imported zoonotic diseases is an example of how the concerns of rich countries may, as a consequence, drive improvements that also benefit poor ones. Some of these improvements, like food chain security and information sharing, can also lead to mutually beneficial effects on intentional and accidental food contamination (Alpas and Smith, 2011). Related improvements in global disease monitoring can also assist with the control of antimicrobial resistance.

Drug and Device Surveillance

Medical products go through safety and efficacy evaluations before they come to market. Even large-scale trials, however, cannot identify rare or latent problems with the product, nor do trials have the power to assess product safety in small sub-populations. Through post-market surveillance, regulators monitor for known side-effects and detect and investigate new signals. The science of detecting, assessing and preventing adverse of effects of medicines, and by extension, all medical products, is called pharmacovigilance (WHO, 2011f). Ensuring the safety of all drugs sold in a country is the responsibility of the drug regulatory authority. The regulatory authority should cooperate with health workers to monitor for drug safety signals. After identifying a possible signal, the regulatory authority should be able to evaluate the relationship between the drug and the adverse event. Finally, it should be able to take action if it verifies a problem. That action might be changing the drug label, issuing warnings, or, in rare cases, withdrawing it from the market (Bandekar et al., 2010; Kshirsagar et al., 2010). Pharmacovigilance is a common problem in poor and middle-income countries (Bakare et al., 2011; Olsson et al., 2010; Pirmohamed et al., 2007).

The Uppsala Monitoring Center is the WHO's international pharmacovigilance center (UMC). As of the summer of 2011, 106 countries had joined the WHO drug monitoring program, 34 other countries are waiting to for full membership (UMC, 2011). Drug regulators from participating countries report possible adverse drug reactions to Uppsala, where the information is pooled and analyzed (Bandekar et al., 2010; Kshirsagar et al., 2010). To ensure that all the data can be pooled and analyzed, drug regulators need to collect and transmit data in a standard way. Bandekar and colleagues identified serious inconsistencies in the adverse event reporting forms used in 10 different countries, finding for example, that many forms failed to account for the patient's pregnancy status or known allergies (Bandekar et al., 2010). This problem is not limited to developing countries, however. By their scoring, Malaysia had the most thorough spontaneous reporting form reviewed, exceeding that of the United States or Britain (Bandekar et al., 2010).

Less than 27 percent of lower-middle income and low income countries have pharmacovigilance systems in place, compared to 96 percent of the wealthier countries in the Organization for Economic Cooperation and Development (Pirmohamed et al., 2007). The poorest countries generally do not have drug regulatory authorities with a sufficient pharmacovigilance system to become full members of Uppsala. Table 3-3 describes drug safety surveillance systems in different low- and middle-income countries.

The most frequent approach to surveillance for adverse effects to medicines in developing countries is passive or spontaneous adverse event reporting. Passive reporting systems rely on patients or health workers to report adverse events. Spontaneous reporting systems have important limitations. Most obviously, they cannot capture events that happen outside of the formal healthcare system, or even events within the system if the health workers do not report them (UNAIDS and WHO, 2011). It is also impossible to calculate the rates of the event without knowing the number of people in the same population using the drug without problems, i.e. the denominator. Spontaneous reporting is time consuming and adds to the workload of already overburdened health professionals (Bakare et al., 2011).

Active surveillance can add depth to the background passive surveillance systems. Cohort event monitoring is a useful surveillance technique in developing countries. This type of surveillance enrolls a group of people taking a medication in a prospective cohort study and systematically records data on all adverse events that happen to the patients in the cohort (UNAIDS and WHO, 2011). While this is often impractical for large-scale surveillance, active surveillance can let regulators detect signals early and keep missing data and reporting bias to a minimum (Bakare et al., 2011).

Because they monitor a complete sample, active surveillance methods allow for the calculation of true event rates. Active surveillance also allows for risk factor analysis and generally a fuller picture of the drug effects. Sentinel surveillance programs, i.e. surveillance by a few select sites, usually hospitals or universities, can also provide a depth of data from a small population and has the added benefit of logistical ease (SPS, 2010b). Sentinel surveillance can use active or passive surveillance methods.

TABLE 3-3 Comparison of postmarketing drug safety surveillance or pharmacovigilance status among selected countries

Countries	Regulatory Agency	Pharmacovigilance Center/ADR Reporting Center	Number of ADR Reports Received	Regulatory Guidelines	Electronic ADRs reporting possible?	ADR Reports by Market Authorization Holders	Dedicated Safety Staff present?	Risk Management Strategies	Communication to the public by bulletins, drug alerts
Low-income countries									
Tanzania	Tanzania Food and Drugs Authority	National ADR Monitoring Center	From 117 (in 2002) to 79 (in 2004–2005)	Yes	Yes	No reports	No	None	Information not available
Zambia	Pharmaceutical Regulatory Authority	Plan to set up Zambia pharmcacovigilance Center	N/A	No	No	Not yet done	N/A	None	N/A
India	Central Drugs Standard Control Organization	National Pharmacovigilance center	9,964 (in 2005–2006)	Yes	Yes	Mandatory	No	None	Yes
Lower-middle-income countries									
Cuba	Health Ministry	National Coordinating Unit of Pharmacovigilance	From 16,500 (in 2001) to 7,100 (in 2005)	No	Yes	Voluntary	No	None	N/A
Ukraine	Ministry of Health	Ukrainian Pharmacovigilance Center	From 122 (in 1996) to 667 (in 2002)	No	N/A	N/A	N/A	None	N/A
China	State Food and Drug Administration	National Center for Adverse drug Reaction monitoring	From 4,700 (in 1988–1999) and 173,000 (2005)	Yes	Yes	Mandatory	No	None	Yes

TABLE 3-3 *Continued*

Countries	Regulatory Agency	Pharmaco-vigilance Center/ADR Reporting Center	Number of ADR Reports Received	Regulatory Guidelines	Electronic ADRs reporting possible?	ADR Reports by Market Authorization Holders	Dedicated Safety Staff present?	Risk Management Strategies	Communica-tion to the public by bulletins, drug alerts
Upper-middle-income Countries									
South Africa	Ministry of Health	National Adverse Drug Event Monitoring Center	Approx. 200 (in 1997) to over 500 (1999)	Yes	Yes	Voluntary	No	None	Yes
Malaysia	Drug Control Authority	Malaysian Adverse Drug Reaction Advisory Committee	From 787 (2001) to 2,363 (in 2005)	Yes	Yes	N/A	Yes	None	Yes
Chile	Health Authority	National Drug Information and Pharma-covigilance Center	424 (200) to 771 (2002)	No	N/A	N/A	N/A	None	N/A

SOURCE: Vaidya et al., 2010.

Ideally, active surveillance following drug or device safety lapses or the introduction of a new product would complement the background passive surveillance system. However, at the USAID conference on national pharmacovigilance systems in Nairobi in 2010, participants agreed that establishing a minimal functional pharmacovigilance system is a good goal for most countries, and that active surveillance may be beyond the minimum requirements (SPS, 2010a). A study in South Africa found that most health professionals, including pharmacists, do not understand what to report as an adverse event (Suleman, 2010). Less than half of the 88 national pharmacovigilance centers surveyed by Uppsala require health workers to report adverse events (Benabdallah et al., 2011).

Less than half of the 55 low- and middle-income countries responding to a 2008 survey had budget support for pharmacovigilance; 13 percent[2] had no pharmacovigilance system at all (Olsson et al., 2010). Of the countries that did have a pharmacovigilance center, 69 percent were a part of the drug regulatory authority, 20 percent were part of the Ministry of Health, and 9 percent were part of a university or scientific center (Olsson et al., 2010). It is not surprising that the poorest countries have weak pharmacovigilance systems, but it is a more striking regulatory gap in emerging manufacturing powers. Both the Indian and Chinese drug industries were developed for production of generic drugs. Since generic drug companies do not run clinical trials or develop drugs, they tend to have weaker overall systems for safety surveillance. Since 2005 the World Bank has sponsored a national pharmacovigilance program in India with more than 26 peripheral reporting centers around the country (Kumar, 2011). This program has fostered a reporting culture among Indian health workers and built up the woefully small cadre of pharmaco-epidemiologists who can advise the drug regulatory authority in the future (Kumar, 2011). This will become a more important need as India becomes more active as a larger clinical research hub for neglected tropical diseases.

The WHO and the Global Fund describe the minimum requirements for a national pharmacovigilance system and lay out clear steps regulators can take to ensure medicines safety (WHO and Global Fund, 2010). These are: having a national pharmacovigilance center, a spontaneous reporting systems, a central database, an pharmacovigilance advisory committee, and a strategy to communicate with the public (WHO and Global Fund, 2010).

The post-market surveillance for medical products is complicated, and it is a wide gap in developing countries. Medical device surveillance is not optimal even in the United States (Rumsfeld and Peterson, 2010). While the FDA keeps records of device failures, they do not have adequate data on total device usage that would allow them to calculate a failure rate (Rumsfeld and Peterson, 2010). Many developing country regulatory authorities will authorize use of a device if it is registered for use by a stringent regulatory authority. Device surveillance is not a priority and device recalls depend entirely on the manufacturer. When 21 Croatian kidney patients died immediately after dialysis in 2001, the Ministry of Health suspected a problem, but the faulty blood filters that caused the deaths were not removed from the market until Baxter International recalled them several months later (Reuters, 2001). Venezuela, Uruguay, and Costa Rica also have problems with medical device surveillance, and none has the legal ability to recall a device (Morroney et al., 2010).

[2] Bangladesh, Ecuador, Liberia, Malawi, Mauritius, East Timor, and United Arab Emirates.

Vaccine Surveillance and Public Trust

Post-marketing surveillance of vaccines is important because vaccines are biologically active. They are given to large numbers of healthy people, often children. There is a likelihood of a reaction at the injection site. Live attenuated vaccines may elicit a mild form of the disease, or, in rare instances, a full-blown case (GACVS and WHO Secretariat, 2009). More commonly, vaccines are the target of emotional scare campaigns. In places where childhood diseases are well-controlled, rumors fly that immunization causes autism (Cheng, 2010; Freed et al., 2010). In India, Nicaragua, the Philippines, and Nigeria, conspiracy theorists have speculated that vaccines are part of government plot to sterilize children or spread HIV (Larson et al., 2011). Regulators need to respond to these rumors quickly and with accurate information, or they risk losing the public's trust and jeopardizing immunization programs. They cannot respond without data collected from safety surveillance.

The WHO's Developing Country Vaccine Regulator's Network is a useful forum for representatives of drug regulatory agencies of Brazil, China, Cuba, South Korea, India, Indonesia, South Africa and Thailand to come together to share their knowledge and experience (Chocarro et al., 2011). The WHO also runs the Global Advisory Committee on Vaccine Safety to advise them on vaccine safety, analyze, and interpret vaccine surveillance data. The committee also advises the WHO on how to strengthen vaccine monitoring in developing countries (GACVS and WHO Secretariat, 2009; WHO, 2011c). The advisory committee's analysis of vaccine safety can be limited by the quality of the data collected in the poorest countries, few of which have proper vaccine safety monitoring systems (Brighton Collaboration, 2010). Furthermore, detecting rare events after immunization also requires sample sizes in excess of 100 million, pooled from comparable sources from different countries. The Global Vaccine Safety Blueprint Project, funded by the Bill and Melinda Gates Foundation, aims to improve vaccine surveillance in low- and middle-income countries and to support international information exchange (WHO, 2011d). The Brighton Collaboration, a global research network on vaccine safety, together with WHO and the Bill and Melinda Gates Foundation, works to improve the ability to collect safety data in the poorest countries. They also promote electronic data sharing, and the linking of exposure and event data (Brighton Collaboration, 2010).

Brazil has a strong system for reporting adverse events after immunization (Martins et al., 2010). Brazil also develops vaccines for tropical diseases at Bio-Manguinhos Fiocruz, the national institute for vaccine production and development, and is active in regional vaccine surveillance as part of SANEVA (Box 3-7). Other emerging economies are not as strong in vaccine safety surveillance. An anonymous executive at one of China's largest vaccine companies told *Nature Biotechnology* that Chinese vaccine companies fear reporting side effects, and they do not collect or report data on adverse events (Jia and Carey, 2011). The Indian government also has problems responding to distrust of vaccine trials. In 2010 the Ministry of Health and Family Welfare suspended a demonstration project, a kind of bridging trial required to introduce a vaccine tested abroad into a different country, of human papillomavirus (HPV) vaccine in response to claims that the vaccine had killed four girls (Larson et al., 2010). Later investigations revealed that the deaths were unrelated to the trial (Larson et al., 2010). An open discussion of the surveillance data and investigation into the deaths might have assuaged public fears and hastened the use of a lifesaving vaccine in India. The Indian HPV scandal is a reminder that even if developing country regulators improve their capacity for pharmacovigilance, it will be of little value without complimentary improvements in communication.

BOX 3-7
SANEVA: A Model of International Collaboration for Vaccine Safety Monitoring

In 2006, with the goal of improving vaccine safety, Argentina, Brazil, Mexico, Panama, and Venezuela formed SANEVA, a collaborative pharmacovigilance program. SANEVA is working both to strengthen existing passive surveillance systems and to develop a regional active surveillance system (GACVS and WHO Secretariat, 2009). To meet its objectives, the network is tasked with:

- Monitoring adverse events attributed to the introduction of rotavirus vaccines;
- Maintaining a system capable of both early identification of potential risks and efficient information sharing;
- Developing a rapid alert system for reporting severe and unanticipated adverse events;
- Recommending corrections;
- Supporting other countries that introduce vaccines that SANEVA is monitoring; and
- Boosting national, regional, and global surveillance capacities (PAHO, 2011).

Because of SANEVA's efforts, better data on adverse events after vaccination are now available, allowing Latin American scientists to distinguish more accurately between real reactions to vaccines and problems that coincidentally followed vaccination. An example of this improvement is the monitoring of the RotaShield vaccine in Mexico and Brazil. In 1999, RotaShield was withdrawn from U.S. markets because of associations with intussusception. Mexican and Brazilian regulators were therefore cautious when introducing the vaccine into their countries in 2006 and 2007. Through improved surveillance capabilities, reliable data were collected rapidly and across a broad base following the vaccine's introduction. The data showed that the number of deaths and hospitalizations averted because of the vaccine far exceeded the number of intussusception cases potentially associated with the vaccination (Patel et al., 2011).

As exemplified by the surveillance of RotaShield, SANEVA's approach is improving vaccine safety monitoring in Latin America. To further increase the effectiveness of this program, SANEVA plans to expand beyond its original five members to include more Latin American countries (GACVS and WHO Secretariat, 2009).

COMMUNICATION

For food and medical product regulators, who are privy to trade secrets and confidential information on product development, trial results, and inspections, the balance between sharing information and building trust in confidentiality can be hard to strike. Even the FDA, widely considered a gold-standard regulatory agency, has been criticized for lack of openness (Hampton, 2011) and, "an internal culture that stifles dissent" (Okie, 2010, p. 1493).

Communication is a broad term. In this report it refers to the need to share information, the strategy to do so appropriately, and the culture that supports open dialogue. Unlike many other components of a regulatory system, communication is less linked to international standards and more linked to local customs and policy. In liberal democracies governments report to their citizens; they have established protocols for communicating with the public and for making government business public. This tradition is less entrenched in some post-colonial (even those that are liberal democracies, such as South African and India) and former communist countries, leading to a communication gap.

The communication problems developing country regulators face fall into four broad categories: communication within a regulatory authority and across government agencies that share regulatory responsibility; communication between regulatory authorities and those they regulate; communication to the public; and communication with counterpart regulatory agencies abroad.

Communication Within a Regulatory Authority and Across Government Agencies That Share Regulatory Responsibility

When multiple agencies within a country share oversight and responsibility for regulation, the need for communication among all the agencies is paramount. The foreign regulators who met with the committee for this study were often unaware of the need for information sharing between government agencies. For others, the political environment of their agency is not one that fosters dialogue. Even if staff may realize the need for communication across sectors, changing communication patterns can only happen from the top. This influences the ability of a government to address major safety problems; it also inhibits the prospective development of risk mitigation plans. Especially in China, the cultural imperative to be indirect is at odds with modern management principles that stress the need to acknowledge problems and respond to them promptly (Roth et al., 2008).

Communication Between Regulatory Authorities Regulated Industry

At the overseas workshops for this report, representatives from regulated industry raised concerns that there are few, if any, forums for regulators and industry to share information on general product policy and the development of regulations. At an Asian Productivity Organization conference on reducing post-harvest waste, Iranian participants saw the lack of two-way communication between the government and other stakeholders as the main problem in their horticulture supply chain (Asian Productivity Organization, 2006). In most cases, there is not a good venue for dialogue between industry and regulators. Regulation is more effective when industry has a voice in the development of the regulations. For example FDA and PhRMA, the Pharmaceutical Research and Manufacturers of America, have regular conferences on drug development policy. Recently, their conference dealt expressly with improving communication between sponsors during drug development (FDA, 2011).

The communication gap that exists in poor countries between industry and regulators can be blamed to some extent on weak or non-existent industry associations in developing countries. Industry associations allow companies to collaborate on meeting regulations that affect them all. They also allow regulators to hear input from the people who implement their regulations. Industry associations also have a useful, if unintended, effect of encouraging adherence to standards through subtle peer pressure. Strong industry associations can support regulators. In places were these groups are discouraged, and in the least developed countries where there is little industry, the lack of robust associations hinders communication.

Communication Between the Regulatory Authority and the Public

The regulatory authority has a duty to communicate promptly and clearly with the public during an emergency. This is a difficult task, even in developed countries with a tradition of openness. In developing countries, it is more complicated. Sometimes a culture of saving face prevents admission of problems; other times the regulatory authority may question the utility of taking public action, such as issuing a recall, if they lack the muscle to implement it. Most commonly, the regulatory agencies simply do not have accurate data to know when a crisis is brewing. A culture of keeping safety threats quiet is a clear failure of communication between regulators and the public. In 2010 the agriculture bureau of Hubei province in south China destroyed 3.5 tons of black-eyed peas found contaminated with a toxic pesticide and issued a national warning about the same (Wong, 2010). Contaminated peas were eventually discovered in three other Chinese provinces, but the provincial regulators were not rewarded for whistle blowing. On the contrary, they were criticized for, "breaking the 'unspoken rule' that officials in different cities and provinces report problems to another rather than telling the public" (Wong, 2010).

In China, the political structure discourages any but the most senior government officials from communicating with the public. A change in organizational thinking might be needed so that admission of safety problems would be seen as accountability rather than humiliation. Government regulators might also be understandably reluctant to admit safety lapses to a public that does not have sufficient understanding of food and drug safety to process the information. The World Bank's 2003-2009 food and drug capacity building project in India cited lack of public awareness as a major safety barrier (World Bank, 2009).

The public also needs to have a system to communicate with government regulators. There is a lack of active consumer organizations in the countries the committee visited for this report. In general, Sub-Saharan African countries, "do not have culture of consumer complaints" (Bester, 2011). This is true in all the least developed countries as poor education is one of the main barriers to consumer communication with government (Affin, 1993). Consumers in middle-income countries may be more vocal, but grassroots consumer advocacy is still in its early stages. At the Delhi meetings for this report, Bejon Misra, founder of Partnership for Safe Medicines, India, estimated that of the roughly 2,500 consumer groups in India, only about four have the staff and management structure to effectively advocate for public safety. Regulators in developing countries often do not see consumer participation as a priority; consumer education is a sliver of the food safety budget in Asia and Pacific countries (Affin, 1993).

Communication with Counterpart Regulatory Agencies Abroad

Regulators need to be able to share information with their counterparts abroad, especially during international emergencies. International communication is especially difficult; it depends on trust and willingness to share such information and on geopolitical factors beyond the regulatory authority's control. Governments may fear "expos[ing] their data to interpretations other than those published by their official statisticians" (Pisani and AbouZahr, 2010, p. 463). In post-colonial countries, there is a suspicion that pharmaceutical companies could exploit health surveillance data to their profit (Pisani and AbouZahr, 2010).

At this study's international workshops in São Paulo and Pretoria participants repeatedly mentioned that the Institute of Medicine meeting brought them together with people whom they had never met, despite working in the same field in neighboring countries. There are international forums that bring regulators together, however. The WHO's International Food Safety Authorities Network and its International Conference of Drug Regulatory Authorities both bring together regulators to strengthen international collaboration. Some changes in the education of the workforce would help stress that communication is key part of modern regulatory system.

One factor that will continue to hold back international communication is the need for trust and confidentiality. In 2011 the FDA and the European Medicines Agency (EMA) completed a pilot study of sharing inspections for good clinical practices inside the European Union. Both agencies found this collaboration useful allowing them to, "identify the gaps in each agency's inspection processes and to fill in those gaps" (EMA and FDA, 2011, p. 17). The agencies' future plan includes expanding the program to sites outside of the United States and Europe (EMA and FDA, 2011). The FDA, EMA, and Australia's Therapeutic Goods Commission are also in the early stages of collaboration on inspecting factories producing active pharmaceutical ingredients (EMA, 2011). Such exemplary communication between regulatory authorities is the result of confidentiality agreements and trust. This can be difficult to cultivate, even among developed countries with established historical alliances and comparable regulatory standards.

POLITICAL WILL

Compared to most emerging economies, the United States has roughly a 100 year head start on enforcing food and medical product safety laws and a large, educated, vocal middle class to demand as much. Even so, American support for government regulation has waned since the 2008-2009 economic crisis (Newport, 2010). During a recession public opinion tends towards encouraging business and reducing unemployment, not asking industry to spend money complying with regulations. A 2010 Gallup poll found that 57 percent of Americans fear too much government regulation; only 37 percent fear too little (Newport, 2010). Public opinion will change promptly during a crisis, however. Even during the recession, public outcry over *Salmonella*-contaminated peanut butter and eggs contributed to Congress passing the Food Safety Modernization Act (Harris and Neuman, 2010).

Public opinion can drive political will, especially in a democracy. This is why a press that is free to publish investigative journalism is an important part of the political process. Independent consumer groups serve a similar purpose. Both are essential for an accountable product safety system. In its deliberations, the committee identified problems with political will, acknowledging that sometimes this is difficult to separate from the public opinion that drives political will.

Competing Priorities, Limited Budgets

In developing countries, even more than in the United States, food and medical product safety often takes a backseat to economic development. In China, for example, 70 percent of local government officials' annual review comes from the GDP growth in their districts (Roth et al., 2008). Enforcing product safety regulations would shut down many companies and hurt local politicians (Box 3-8). Furthermore, in some developing countries, the regulatory authorities have non-regulatory responsibilities (WHO, 2007). In Cuba, the drug regulatory authority is also in charge of manufacturing drugs; in India the drug regulatory authority runs the Pharmacopeia Commission. In some emerging economies there is reluctance to enforcing product safety regulations that might stifle the economic growth (Bamberger and Guzman, 2008).

BOX 3-8
Enforcing Drug Regulation in China

State control of the pharmaceutical industry has receded in China since the 1980s. At the same time, decentralization has encouraged local governments to develop their own economies. The 1984 China Pharmaceutical Administration Law gave drug approval and production licensing power to local governments (Liu, 2010). During the same time, government funding to hospitals decreased, and drug sales were a way for clinics to cover costs. To survive clinics needed to minimize cost and maximize profit. Selling many inexpensive drugs was a way to do that (Liu, 2010). The Chinese government is trying to change this, but hospitals still get 25-60 percent of their revenue from drug sales (U.S. Commercial Service, 2002).

In 1998, the State Drug Administration, later reorganized into the State Food and Drug Administration (SFDA), was created as an independent medicines regulator (Zhen, 2004). The SFDA is in charge of "the administrative and technical supervision of the research, production, distribution, and utilization of drugs, bulk chemicals, medical devices, medical dressings, and pharmaceutical packaging materials" (Zhen, 2004, p. 347).

In recent years, the Chinese government has launched a series of crackdowns on shoddy drug regulation. Its 2007 anti-counterfeiting campaign shutdown 300 hundred drug and medical device manufacturers and rescinded 150 certificates of good manufacturing practices (Bate and Porter, 2009). Shortly thereafter, Zheng Xiaoyu, former head of the SFDA, was executed for accepting bribes from drug and medical equipment companies (Bate and Porter, 2009). After Xiaoyu's sentence, the Ministry of Health took over the SFDA, and SFDA employees were required to divest of pharmaceutical stock (Liu, 2010).

Despite publicized campaigns, SFDA has a pervasive problem enforcing regulations. To begin with, the counterfeit drug business employs 3 to 5 million people and brings in an estimated $40-80 billion annually (Clark, 2003). In some estimations "counterfeiting is now so huge [that] radical action would crash the economy overnight and even destabilize a government where counterfeit factories and warehouses are often owned by local military and political grandees" (Bate and Porter, 2009, p. 3). The low penalties for counterfeiting, a fine of about $15-580, suggest that SFDA penalties do not reflect the magnitude of public outrage over the crime (Bate and Porter, 2009).

In some large developing countries food and medical product safety programs are the purview of the same agencies responsible for either promoting commerce or assuring drug availability through price controls. For example, the Ministry of Commerce, whose principal goal is to increase exports, is responsible for food safety in India. In China, final responsibility for product safety resides with the local Communist party, whose primary goal is economic development. Both India and Brazil maintain price control agencies with the laudable goals of assuring drug availability throughout society. In India these agencies also assure the productivity of small drug firms. These well-intentioned systems may put economic growth at odds with medical product and food safety actions. This is especially true at municipal government levels, where the very existence of the food safety system depends on funding that comes from commerce. Similarly, in the attempt to assure drug availability for the poorest, governments can cut prices to point cutting quality out of the system. Both of these scenarios also encourage bypassing proper distribution channels, inadvertently promoting substandard products.

The conflict of interest in promoting exports and regulating export safety may trouble India and China's trading partners. Their own citizens have different concerns. In most countries, the Ministry of Health has a great deal of medical product regulatory responsibility; they often have food regulatory responsibility as well. Ministers of Health in these countries have many problems: malnutrition, child mortality, infectious disease, water shortages, health financing, and poor sanitation to name a few. With so many demands on their attention, they do not always see food and medical product safety as a high priority. Even when they do, the heads of government may be more concerned with agriculture, labor, or commerce.

Donors, on the other hand, are enthusiastic funders of the health sector; health aid is an important piece of many countries' foreign policy. Development aid for health grew over $16 billion between 1990 and 2007 (The Lancet, 2009). In the same time, government spending on health dropped from 24.3 to 20.9 percent in low-income countries, and from 52.2 to 48.6 percent in middle-income countries (Farag et al., 2009). By some analyses, every dollar donor's spend on health accompanies a $0.46 decrease in government health spending (Lu et al., 2010). The substitution of donor aid for government spending is also common in agriculture, although less so in infrastructure building and education (Farag et al., 2009).

Reallocating money from health and agriculture to other sectors is an understandable choice for low- and middle-income countries facing a rare windfall of donor generosity. Heads of government can justify their budgets, explaining that national projects on HIV, malaria, and tuberculosis are still better off than they would have been on public money. Health and medical product regulatory systems are a clear loser in this equation, however. With notable exceptions such as USAID's Strengthening Pharmaceutical Systems Program, the African Medicines Regulatory Harmonization Initiative (a joint effort including the WHO, World Bank, NEPAD, the Clinton Health Access Initiative and the Gates Foundation), and the FAO's Food Quality and Standards Service, donors are not interested in building regulatory systems. Smaller budgets for health and agriculture mean less support for food and medical product safety.

The United States government has recognized a need to shift from health aid for specific diseases, also called vertical programs, to broader-based health systems aid, or horizontal programs. The 2008 *Global Health Initiative Strategy Document* describes Obama administration's commitment to strengthening health systems, in particular the goal of "improved research and regulatory capacity to support clinical trials, bring new, high-quality innovations to partner country markets; and monitor the quality, safety, and efficacy of the supply chain" (GHI, p. 21).

Corruption and Accountability

The previous section on gaps in the regulatory workforce describes the ways in which corruption contributes to staff retention problems in the government. Similarly, corruption saps political will to enforce regulations. Mexico, China, and Thailand are the second, third, and fourth largest food suppliers to the United States (Muchmore, 2010). Transparency International rates all three as having serious corruption problems (Muchmore, 2010). It is difficult for a regulatory authority to prevent its inspectors from taking bribes in these countries, especially when the bribe is accompanied with a threat (Muchmore, 2010, p. 403).

There are reasons for optimism, however. The middle class is growing in India, China, Mexico, Brazil, South Africa, Thailand, Indonesia, and many other countries. According to the Asian and African Development Banks the middle class now accounts for roughly one-third of the population of Africa, a quarter of India, three-quarters of Latin America, and 90 percent of China[3] (Politics in emerging markets: The new middle classes rise up, 2011; Chun, 2010).

[3] The development banks define the middle class as those earning between $2-20 a day, a definition that includes people only barely out of poverty. It is a particularly rough measure in China, where the value of the currency is set

Middle class voters tend to be disproportionately urban; they are concerned with health care and generally distanced from farming (ADB, 2010). They buy medicines in pharmacies or dispensaries and buy food in markets. Public health and product safety are more important to the middle class than to the poor. In August 2011, China saw its largest popular uprising since Tiananmen Square over a toxic chemical plant in the wealthy city of Dalian (Politics in emerging markets: The new middle classes rise up, 2011).

Indian customers at a Big Apple convenience store in New Delhi.
SOURCE: AFP/Getty Images.

Eliminating corruption is also important to middle class voters. In 2011 Brazilian president Dilma Rousseff sacked numerous corrupt officials, including the second in command at the Ministry of Agriculture, in a house cleaning *The Economist* attributes in part to her country's changing demographics and priorities (Dilma tries to drain the swamp, 2011; Politics in emerging markets: The new middle classes rise up, 2011). In August 2011, Indian activist Anna Hazare's four-day hunger strike protested government corruption with support from the middle class (Denyer and Lakshmi, 2011).

The momentum against corruption and in support of food and medical product safety is likely to grow as communication gets easier. In China, blogging services such as Sino Weibo have 140 million users; China has half a billion cell phone users (Politics in emerging markets: The new middle classes rise up, 2011; Freeman, 2009). The priorities of a growing and technologically active middle class are driving change.

CONCLUSION

In its deliberations the committee identified nine main critical issues facing developing country regulators. Problems adhering to international standards endanger product safety in low- and middle-income countries. It also hedges them out of lucrative export markets. International

---

at 7 Yuan to 1 dollar. By more modest estimates, there are only 80 million middle class consumers in China (Hodgson, 2007).

standards assume control of supply chains. In places where there are many, sometimes anonymous, transactions that occur over long supply chains this is particularly difficult. Poor roads, unreliable power, water shortages, poor sanitation, and other infrastructure problems make supply chain management difficult. Companies in low- and middle-income countries cannot track and trace their products without improvements in information technology infrastructure.

Laws are at the foundation of food and medical product regulation, and many countries lack the ability to enforce their product safety laws. Law enforcement might be easier if regulatory authorities had more and better trained staff. It is hard to keep trained scientists in government service in low- and middle-income countries. Better salaries on projects and in industry draw many away. Others grow frustrated and quit.

The job of a government regulator in a developing country is often frustrating, in part because regulatory responsibilities are usually scattered among many different government agencies. And, while this is often true in rich countries as well, fragmented responsibilities can cripple an agency without strong communication systems. Communication with the public and with regulated industry is also common weakness in low- and middle-income countries. During emergencies prompt and accurate communication is essential. The regulatory authority needs to draw on accurate data to inform their message. Poor surveillance systems prevent them from forming clear and accurate messages to share with the public. Poor surveillance also impedes an important part of the regulator's job. Modern regulatory systems use risk assessment to inform their decisions, and regulators in emerging economies have neither the reliable data to inform risk analysis or personnel with the mathematics and epidemiology training to do it.

In some cases, the very structure of the regulatory system encourages these problems. Regulatory systems in emerging economies assign to their staff conflicting responsibilities; a regulator given both product safety and commerce promotion jobs can do neither job well. More commonly, food and medical product safety slip through the many cracks in nascent health systems. Ironically, the last decade of donor support for health programming has encouraged governments to spend their money in other sectors. Food and medical product regulation have suffered because of this. There is reason to believe that this will change in the future, as the middle class continues to grow in the world's emerging manufacturing nations.

There are many root causes of the nine main gaps discussed in this chapter. Poverty and a lack of a strong government infrastructure are two of the main ones. The regulatory systems in Latin America, for example, benefit from greater wealth and good school system. These are advantages that cannot be immediately replicated in South Asia or Sub-Saharan Africa. The committee's recommendations are for improvements that could elicit a meaningful change across a wide range of countries at different levels of development.

REFERENCES

A.T. Kearney. 2004a. *Healing Mexico's health-care system.* Chicago, Illinois.

———. 2004b. *An imperative for public health care: Improving the medicine supply chain.* Chicago, Illinois.

Abegaz, M. 2006. *Working paper on: Assessment of the capacity of food safety and quality in Zambia.* The World Bank.

Abraham, J. 2002. The pharmaceutical industry as a political player. *The Lancet* 360(9344):1498-1502.

Abudhoo, S. 2012. Devolution of drug regulations to raise manufacturing cost. *The Nation.*

ADB. 2010. *The rise of Asia's middle class.* Mandaluyong City, Philippines: The Asian Development Bank.

Affin, A. b. 1993. Food control and consumer affairs in developing countries. *Food, Nutrition and Agriculture* 8/9.

Agribusiness and Allied Kenya Ltd, Standards and Solutions Consulting Ltd, and The International Centre of Insect Physiology. 2006. *Generic manual on quality management system for smallholder horticultural farmer groups in Kenya for certification to EUREPGAP option 2.* GlobalG.A.P.

Anderson, T. 2010. Tide turns for drug manufacturing in Africa. *The Lancet* 375(9726):1597-1598.

Anvisa. 2003. *Overview.* http://www.anvisa.gov.br/eng/institution/introduction.htm (accessed October 21, 2011).

APEC. 2008 February 25-26. *Draft implementation plan for strengthening food safety standards practices in APEC economies for 2008-2011 (agenda item 4(5)).* Paper presented at First Sub-Committee on Standards and Conformance Meeting, Lima, Peru.

Aragão, A. 2010. As agências reguladoras independentes brasileiras: O caso da agência nacional de vigilância sanitária. *Revista de Direito Sanitário* 10(3):77-89.

Asian Productivity Organization. 2006. *Postharvest management of fruit and vegetables in the Asia-Pacific region.* Tokyo Japan.

Attridge, C. J., and A. S. Preker. 2005. *Improving access to medicines in developing countries: Applicaiton of new institutional economics to the analysis of manufacturing and distribution issues.* Washington, DC: The World Bank's Human Development Network.

Bakare, N., I. R. Edwards, A. Stergachis, S. Pal, C. B. Holmes, M. Lindquist, C. Duncombe, A. Dodoo, J. Novendstern, J. Nwokike, R. Kuchenbecker, J. A. Aberg, V. Miller, and J. Strobos. 2011. Global pharmacovigilance for antiretroviral drugs: Overcoming contrasting priorities. *PLoS Med* 8(7):e1001054.

Bamberger, K. A., and A. T. Guzman. 2008. Keeping imports safe: A proposal for discriminatory regulation of international trade. *California Law Review* 96(6):1405-1447.

Bandekar, M. S., S. R. Anwikar, and N. A. Kshirsagar. 2010. Quality check of spontaneous adverse drug reaction reporting forms of different countries. *Pharmacoepidemiology and Drug Safety* 19(11):1181-1185.

Barboza, D. 2007. Food-safety crackdown in China. *The New York Times*, June 28.

Bate, R., and K. Porter. 2009. The problems and potential of China's pharmaceutical industry. *American Enterprise Institute for Policy Research*(3):1-10.

Becker, G. S. 2008. *Food and agricultural imports from China.* Congressional Research Service.

Belton, B., M. M. Haque, D. C. Little, and L. X. Sinh. 2010. Certifying catfish in Vietnam and Bangladesh: Who will make the grade and will it matter? *Food Policy* 36(2):289-299.

Benabdallah, G., R. Benkirane, A. Khattabi, I. R. Edwards, and R. S. Bencheikh. 2011. The involvement of pharmacovigilance centres in medication errors detection: A questionnaire-based analysis. *The International Journal of Risk and Safety in Medicine* 23(1):17-29.

Bester, A. 2011. The importance of food safety in Africa. http://www.howwemadeitinafrica.com/the-importance-of-food-safety-in-africa/5043/ (accessed June 14).

Black, S., K. Mulholland, and N. A. Halsey. 2010. Developing sustainable funding for vaccine safety infrastructure. *Vaccine* 28(5):1133-1134.

Blaser, M. J. 2011. Deconstructing a lethal foodborne epidemic. *New England Journal of Medicine* 365(19):1835-1836.

Bollyky, T. J. 2009. Global health interventions for U.S. Food and drug safety: CSIS Global Health Policy Center.

Brhlikova, P., I. Harper, and A. Pollock. 2007 July 2-3. *Good manufacturing practice in the pharmaceutical industry*. Paper presented at Working paper 3, prepared for Workshop on 'Tracing Pharmaceuticals in South Asia', University of Edinburgh.

Bridges, A. 2007. FDA bonuses spending to draw scrutiny. *USA Today*, July 17.

Brighton Collaboration. 2010. *What we do: Capacity building*. https://brightoncollaboration.org/public/what-we-do/capacity.html (accessed November 3, 2011).

Broughton, E. I., and D. G. Walker. 2010. Policies and practices for aquaculture food safety in China. *Food Policy* 35(5):471-478.

Byerlee, D., and K. Fischer. 2002. Accessing modern science: Policy and institutional options for agricultural biotechnology in developing countries. *World Development* 30(6):931-948.

Carey, J. 2007. Not made in China. *Business Week*, July 30, 41-43.

Castillo-Salgado, C. 2010. Trends and directions of global public health surveillance. *Epidemiologic Reviews* 32(1):93-109.

CDC. 2011. *CDC estimates of foodborne illness in the United States.* National Center for Emerging & Zoonotic Infectious Diseases; Division of Foodborne, Waterborne, and Environmental Diseases.

———. 2012. *CDC research shows outbreaks linked to imported foods increasing.* http://www.cdc.gov/media/releases/2012/p0314_foodborne.html (accessed March 16, 2012).

Chanda, R. R., R. J. Finchman, and P. Venter. 2010. A review of the South African food control system: Challenges of fragmentation. *Food Control* 21(6):816-824.

Chaudhuri, S., M. Mackintosh, and P. G. M. Mujinja. 2010. Indian generics producers, access to essential medicines and local production in Africa: An argument with reference to Tanzania. *European Journal of Development Research* 22(4):451-468.

Chen, D., and D. Kristensen. 2009. Opportunities and challenges of developing thermostable vaccines. *Expert Review of Vaccines* 8(5):547-557.

Cheng, M. 2010. Britain bans doctor who linked autism to vaccine. *Associated Press*, May 25.

Chocarro, L., P. Duclos, K. Senouci, and J. Southern. 2011. Consultation on interactions between national regulatory authorities and national immunization technical advisory groups. *Expert Review of Vaccines* 10(9):1265-1270.

Chun, N. 2010. *Middle class size in the past, present, and future: A description of trends in Asia.* Mandaluyong City, Philippines: The Asian Development Bank.
Clark, D. J. 2003. Product counterfeiting in China and one American company's response, National Defense University.
Clift, C. 2010a. *Combating counterfeit, falsified, and substandard medicines: Defining the way forward?* London, UK: Chatham House.
———. 2010b. *Meeting summary: Combating counterfeit, falsified, and substandard medicines.* London, UK: Chatham House.
Cohen, J. C. 2005. Corruption in the pharmaceutical sector. In *Corruption in health.* Boston: Boston University. Pp. 76-102.
Corbell, C., A. Stergachis, F. Ndowa, P. Ndase, L. Barnes, and C. Celum. 2010. Genital ulcer disease treatment policies and access to acylovir in eight Sub-Saharan African countries. *Sexually Transmitted Diseases* 37(8):1-6.
CSPI. 2007. *Combine all U.S. Food safety functions into a single agency, the food safety administration: Support s. 654, h.R. 1148 -- the safe food act.* Washington, DC: Center for Science in the Public Interest.
Day, J. N., T. T. Hien, and J. Farrar. 2004. Expiry-date tampering. *The Lancet* 363(9403):172.
Denyer, S., and R. Lakshmi. 2011. Anna Hazare inspires young, middle-class awakening in India. *The Washington Post*, August 19.
Dilma tries to drain the swamp. 2011. *The Economist*, August 20.
Donnges, C., G. Edmonds, and B. Johannessen. 2007. *Rural road maintenance: Sustaining the benefits of improved access.* Geneva: International Labour Organization.
EMA. 2011. *Final report on the international API inspection pilot programme.* London: European Medicines Agency, Australian Government, and the Food and Drug Administration.
EMA, and FDA. 2011. *Report on the pilot EMA-FDA GCP initiative: September 2009-March 2011.* London.
Essack, S. Y., N. Shchellack, T. Pople, L. v. d. Merwe, F. Suleman, J. C. Meyer, A. G. S. Gous, and D. Benjamin. 2011. Antibiotic supply chain and management in human health. *South African Medical Journal* 101(8).
EU. 2011. *Directive 2011/83/EC of the European Parliament and of the council of 8 June 2011 amending Directive 2001/83/EC on the Community code relating to medicinal products for human use, as regards to the prevention of the entry into the legal supply chain of falsified medicinal products.*
FAO/WHO. 2003. *Assuring food safety and quality: Guidelines for strengthening national food control systems.*
Farag, M., A. K. Nandakumar, S. S. Wallack, G. Gaumer, and D. Hodgkin. 2009. Does funding from donors displace government spending for health in developing countries? *Health Affairs* 28(4):1045-1055.
FDA. 2011. FDA-industry PDUFA V reauthorization meeting, Teleconference.
Freed, G. L., S. J. Clark, A. T. Butchart, D. C. Singer, and M. M. Davis. 2010. Parental vaccine safety concerns in 2009. *Pediatrics* 125(4):654-659.
Freeman, C. W. 2009. *China's capacity to manage infectious diseases: Global implications.* Washington, DC: Center for Strategic and International Studies.
Frerichs, R. R. 1991. Epidemiologic surveillance in developing countries. *Annual Review of Public Health* 12(1):257-280.

GACVS, and WHO Secretariat. 2009. Global safety of vaccines: Strengthening systems for monitoring, management and the role of GACVS. *Expert Reviews Vaccines* 8(6):705-716.

Gale, F., and C. J. Buzby. 2009. Imports from China and food safety issues. 52(Journal, Electronic):January 14, 2011, http://www.ers.usda.gov/publications/eib52/ (accessed.

GAO. 2010. *Drug safety: FDA has conducted more foreign inspections and began to improve its information on foreign establishments but more progess is needed.* GAO-10-961.

Garrett, L., and Y. Huang. 2011. *Food and drugs: Can safety be ensured in a time of increased globalization?* Council on Foreign Relations.

Gessner, G. H., L. Volonino, and L. A. Fish. 2007. One-up, one-back ERM in the food supply chain. *Information Systems Management* 24(3):213-222.

GHI. *The United States government global health initiative: Strategy document.*

Giovannucci, D., and T. Purcell. 2008. *Standards and agricultural trade in Asia.* Tokyo: Asian Development Bank Institute.

Global Pharma Health Fund. *The GPHF-Minilab® - protection against counterfeit medicines.* http://www.gphf.org/web/en/minilab (accessed November 9, 2011).

Godfray, H. C. J., J. R. Beddington, I. R. Crute, L. Haddad, D. Lawrence, J. F. Muir, J. Pretty, S. Robinson, S. M. Thomas, and C. Toulmin. 2010. Food security: The challenge of feeding 9 billion people. *Science* 327(5967):812-818.

Government of India. 2003. *Report of the expert committee on a comprehensive examination of drug regulatory issues, including the problem of spurious drugs.*

Greene, W. 2007. *The emergence of India's pharmaceutical industry and implications for the U.S. Generic drug market.* Washington, DC: Office of Economics, U.S. International Trade Comission.

Guerin, O. 2012. Lahore grieves over heart pill deaths. *BBC News*, January 29.

Gundersen, L. E. 2001. Training needs in regulatory science for the biopharmaceutical industry. *Nature Biotechnology* 19(12):1187-1188.

Gustavasson, J., C. Cederberg, U. Sonesson, R. v. Otterdijk, and A. Meybeck. 2011. *Global food losses and food waste: Extent, causes, and prevention.* Dusseldorf, Germany: Food and Agriculture Organization.

Hamburg, M. A. 2011. Advancing regulatory science. *Science* 331(6020):987-987.

Hampton, T. 2011. European drug agency under fire: Critics charge that trial data are too inaccessible. *JAMA - Journal of the American Medical Association* 306(6):593-595.

Hao, Z. 2012. *Substandard cardiac drugs claim over 100 lives in pakistan* http://english.cntv.cn/20120206/113321.shtml (accessed Febuary 12, 2012).

Harris, G., and W. Neuman. 2010. Senate passes sweeping law on food safety. *The New York Times*, November 30.

Hawthorne, N., and C. Anderson. 2009. The global pharmacy workforce: A systematic review of the literature. *Human Resources for Health* 7.

Hazell, P., and S. Wood. 2008. Drivers of change in global agriculture. *Philosophical Transactions of the Royal Society B: Biological Sciences* 363(1491):495-515.

Henson, S., and J. Humphrey. 2009. *The impacts of private food safety standards of the food chain and on public standard-setting processes: Paper prepared for FAO/WHO.* FAO/WHO

Herring, J. 2011. Consistent clinical research standards benefit patients around the world. *Nat Med* 17(9):1036-1036.

Hodgson, A. 2007. *China's middle class reaches 80 million.* Euromonitor International.

ICH. 2011a. *ICH harmonisation for better health: Official website.* http://www.ich.org/ (accessed October 4, 2011).

———. 2011b. *SADC workshop, 27-30 june 2011, Arusha, Tanzania.* http://www.ich.org/trainings/ich-trainings/good-manufacturing-practices.html (accessed September 30, 2011).

International Life Sciences Institute-India. 2007. *A surveillance and monitoring system for food safety in inida (under food safety and standards act- 2005).* International Life Sciences Institute.

Irwin, A., H. Rothstein, S. Yearley, and E. McCarthy. 1997. Regulatory science - towards a sociological framework. *Futures* 29(1):17-31.

Jaffee, S., and S. Henson. 2004. Standards and agro-food exports from developing countries: Rebalancing the debate. *World Bank Policy Research Working Paper No. 3348.*

Jahre, M., L. Dumoulin, L. B. Greenhalgh, C. Hudspeth, P. Limlim, and A. Spindler. 2010 September 30-October 1. *Improving health systems in developing countries by reducing the complexity of drug supply chains.* Paper presented at The 8th International Conference on Logistics and SCM Research, Bordeaux, France.

Jeffery, R., and Santhosh M.R. 2009. Architecture of drug regulation in India: What are the barriers to regulatory reform? *Journal of Health Studies* II:13-32.

Jia, H., and K. Carey. 2011. Chinese vaccine developers gain WHO imprimatur. *Nature Biotechnology* 29(6):471-472.

Juma, C. 2008. Learn to earn. *Nature* 456(n1s):15-17.

Kader, A. A. 2010. Handling of horticultural perishables in developing vs. Developed countries.

Kauffmann, J. R., R. Miller, and J. Cheyne. 2011. Vaccine supply chains need to be better funded and strengthened, or lives will be at risk. *Health Affairs* 30(6):1113-1121.

Kelleher, F. 2004. The pharmaceutical industry's responsibility for protecting human subjects of clinical trials in developing nations. *Columbia Journal of Law and Social Problems* 38(1):67-106.

Kenyon, T. A., A. S. Kenyon, and T. Sibiya. 1994. Drug quality screening in developing countries: Establishment of an appropriate laboratory in Swaziland. *Bulletin of the World Health Organization* 72(4):615.

Kimball, A. M., M. Moore, H. M. French, Y. Arima, K. Ungchusak, S. Wibulpolprasert, T. Taylor, S. Touch, and A. Leventhal. 2008. Regional infectious disease surveillance networks and their potential to facilitate the implementation of the International Health Regulations. *Medical Clinics of North America* 92(6):1459-1471.

Kitinoja, L., S. Saran, S. K. Roy, and A. A. Kader. 2011. Postharvest technology for developing countries: Challenges and opportunities in research, outreach and advocacy. *Journal of the Science of Food and Agriculture* 91(4):597-603.

Kopp, S. 2006. Stability testing of pharmaceutical products in a global environment. *The Regulatory Affairs Journal*:4.

KPMG International. 2006. *The Indian pharmaceutical industry: Collaboration for growth.* The Netherlands: KPMG International.

Kshirsagar, N. A., S. Olsson, and R. E. Ferner. 2010. Consideration of the desirable features and possible forms of practical indicators of the performance of pharmacovigilance centres. *The International Journal of Risk and Safety in Medicine* 22(2):59-66.

Kumar, A. 2011. Past, present and future of pharmacovigilance in India. *Systematic Reviews in Pharmacy* 2(1):55-58.
LaFraniere, S. 2011. In China, fear of fake eggs and 'recycled' buns. *The New York Times*, May 7.
Langer, E. S. 2008. Biologics regulation in India. *BioPharm International* 21(3).
Larson, H. J., P. Brocard, and G. Garnett. 2010. The India HPV-vaccine suspension. *The Lancet* 376(9741):572-573.
Larson, H. J., L. Z. Cooper, J. Eskola, S. L. Katz, and S. Ratzan. 2011. Addressing the vaccine confidence gap. *The Lancet* 378(9790):526-535.
Leng, H. M. J., and M. P. Matsoso. 2008. Pharmaceutical and analytical quality control services: Ownership or outsourcing - a South African case study. *Drug Information Journal* 42(2):161-173.
Liu, P. 2010. From decentralised developmental state towards authoritarian regulatory state: A case study on drug safety regulation in China. *China: An International Journal* 8(1):110-137.
Liu, Y., and F. Wu. 2010. Global burden of aflatoxin-induced hepatocellular carcinoma: A risk assessment. *Environmental Health Perspectives* 118(6).
Llana, S. M. 2010. Food safety: From Mexican farm, to Costco, to your plate. *The Christian Science Monitor*, October 23.
Losse, K., E. Schneider, and C. Spennemann. 2007. *The viability of local pharmaceutical production in Tanzania.* Deutsche Gesellschaft für Technische Zusammenarbeit.
Lu, C., M. T. Schneider, P. Gubbins, K. Leach-Kemon, D. Jamison, and C. J. L. Murray. 2010. Public financing of health in developing countries: A cross-national systematic analysis. *The Lancet* 375(9723):1375-1387.
Lu, W. 2005. *Trade and environment dimensions in the food and food processing industries in Asia and the Pacific: A country case study of China.* Hangzhou, China: Department of Agricultural Economics, Zhejiang University.
Lu, W., and S. Kjeldsen-Kragh. 2008. International food safety standards: Catalysts for increased Chinese food quality? *The Copenhagen Journal of Asian Studies* 26(1):70-90.
Lugosi, L., and Battersby. 1990. Transport and storage of vaccines in hungary: The first cold chain monitor study in europe. *Bulletin of the World Health Organization* 68(4):431-439.
Lukulay, P. 2011 March 3. *Promoting the quality of medicines (PQM) program.* Paper presented at Strengthening Core Elements of Regulatory Systems in Developing Countries: Meeting One, Washington, D.C.
Lupien, J. R. 2007. Prevention and control of food safety risks: The role of governments, food producers, marketers, and academia. *Asia Pacific Journal of Clinical Nutrition* 16(Supplement 1):74-79.
M4P. 2006. *The participation of the poor in supermarkets and other distribution value chains.* Hanoi: The Asian Development Bank.
Maheshwar, C., and T. S. Chanakwa. 2006. Post harvest losses due to gaps in cold chain in India. *IHS Acta Horticulturae* 712:777-784.
Majowicz, S. E., J. Musto, E. Scallan, F. J. Angulo, M. Kirk, S. J. O'Brien, T. F. Jones, A. Fazil, R. M. Hoekstra, and for the International Collaboration on Enteric Disease "Burden of Illness" Studies. 2010. The global burden of Nontyphoidal Salmonella Gastroenteritis. *Clinical Infectious Diseases* 50(6):882-889.
Malkin, R. A. 2007. Design of health care technologies for the developing world.

Manson, K. 2011. Act production: 'The biggest challenge is access to the market'. *The Financial Times*, April 21.

Martin, D. S. 2007. Lawmakers push for change in food safety oversight. *CNN*, May 17.

Martins, R. d. M., M. d. L. d. S. Maia, E. M. d. Santos, R. L. d. S. Cruz, P. R. G. dos Santos, S. M. D. Carvalho, H. K. Sato, M. T. Schermann, R. Mohrdieck, M. d. L. F. Leal, and A. Homma. 2010. Yellow fever vaccine post-marketing surveillance in Brazil. *Procedia in Vaccinology* 2(2):178-183.

Marucheck, A., N. Greis, C. Mena, and L. Cai. 2011. Product safety and security in the global supply chain: Issues, challenges and research opportunities. *Journal of Operations Management* 29(7-8):707-720.

Matowe, L., P. Waako, R. Adome, I. Kibwage, O. Minzi, and E. Bienvenu. 2008. A strategy to improve skills in pharmaceutical supply management in East Africa: The regional technical resource collaboration for pharmaceutical management. *Human Resources for Health* 6(1):30.

May, M. 2011. FDA reorganization inspires hope for better coordination. *Nature Medicine* 17(9):1024-1024.

McMeekin, T. A., J. Baranyi, J. Bowman, P. Dalgaard, M. Kirk, T. Ross, S. Schmid, and M. H. Zwietering. 2006. Information systems in food safety management. *International Journal of Food Microbiology* 112(3):181-194.

Milstien, J., A. Costa, S. Jadhav, and R. Dhere. 2009. Reaching international GMP standards for vaccine production: Challenges for developing countries. *Expert Review of Vaccines* 8(5):559-566.

Moran, M., J. Guzman, A.-L. Ropars, A. McDonald, N. Jameson, B. Omune, S. Ryan, and L. Wu. 2009. Neglected disease research and development: How much are we really spending? *PLoS Med* 6(2):e1000030.

Moran, M., N. Strub-Wourgaft, J. Guzman, P. Boulet, L. Wu, and B. Pecoul. 2011. Registering new drugs for low-income countries: The African challenge. *PLoS Medicine* 8(2):e1000411.

Morel, C. M., J. R. Carvalheiro, C. N. P. Romero, E. A. Costa, and P. M. Buss. 2007. The road to recovery. *Nature* 449(7159):180-182.

Mori, M., R. Ravinetto, and J. Jacobs. 2011. Quality of medical devices and in vitro diagnostics in resource-limited settings. *Tropical Medicine and International Health* 16(11):1439-1449.

Morroney, R., J. Arrieta, A. Belza, M. Biere, G. Castaneda, L. Funari, S. Gilbert, B. Marinaro, and Y. Obando. 2010. *Medical device regulation in Latin America.* Rockville, MD: Regulatory Affairs Professional Society.

Muchmore, A. I. 2010. Private regulation and foreign conduct. *San Diego Law Review, Vol. 47, No. 2, 2010.*

Narula, S. A. 2011. Reinventing cold chain industry in India: Need of the hour. Interview with Mr. Sanjay Aggarway. *Journal of Agribusiness in Developing and Emerging Economies* 1(2).

Nauriyal, D. K. 2006. TRIPS-compliant new patents act and Indian pharmaceutical sector: Directions and strategy in R&D. *Indian Journal of Economics and Business, Special Issue China & India* 1:2-20.

Newport, F. 2010. *Americans leery of too much gov't regulation of business.* Princeton, NJ: Gallup.

Newton, P. N., M. D. Green, and F. M. Fernández. 2010. Impact of poor-quality medicines in the 'developing' world. *Trends in Pharmacological Sciences* 31(3):99-101.

Ni, H.-G., and H. Zeng. 2009. Law enforcement is key to China's food safety. *Environmental Pollution* 157(7):1990-1992.

Norris, P., R. B. Dos Santos, D. Woods, and W. Tobata. 2007. Delivering medicines in a challenging environment: The pharmaceutical sector in east timor (a descriptive study). *Pharmacy Practice* 5(4):145-150.

Okello, J. J., C. Narrod, and D. Roy. 2007. *Food safety requirements in African green bean exports and their impact on small farmers.* Washington, DC: International Food Policy and Research Institute.

Okie, S. 2010. Reviving the FDA. *New England Journal of Medicine* 363(16):1492-1494.

Olsson, S., S. N. Pal, A. Stergachis, and M. Couper. 2010. Pharmacovigilance activities in 55 low-and middle-income countries: A questionnaire-based analysis. *Drug Safety* 33(8):689-703.

Oluka, N., F. Ssennoga, and S. Kambaza. 2010 August 26-28. *Tackling supply chain bottlenecks of essential drugs: A case of Uganda local government health units.* Paper presented at 4th International Procurement Conference, Seoul, South Korea.

Oxfam. 2011. *Eye on the ball: Medicine regulation- not IP enforcement- can best deliver quality medicines.*

PAHO. 2011. *SANEVA - adverse event sentinel surveillance network for new vaccines.* http://66.101.212.220/hq/index.php?option=com_content&task=view&id=1033&Itemid=243 (accessed November 8, 2011).

Patel, M. M., V. R. López-Collada, M. M. Bulhões, L. H. De Oliveira, A. B. Márquez, B. Flannery, M. Esparza-Aguilar, E. I. Montenegro Renoiner, M. E. Luna-Cruz, H. K. Sato, L. d. C. Hernández-Hernández, G. Toledo-Cortina, M. Cerón-Rodríguez, N. Osnaya-Romero, M. Martínez-Alcazar, R. G. Aguinaga-Villasenor, A. Plascencia-Hernández, F. Fojaco-González, G. Hernández-Peredo Rezk, S. F. Gutierrez-Ramírez, R. Dorame-Castillo, R. Tinajero-Pizano, B. Mercado-Villegas, M. R. Barbosa, E. M. C. Maluf, L. B. Ferreira, F. M. de Carvalho, A. R. dos Santos, E. D. Cesar, M. E. P. de Oliveira, C. L. Osterno Silva, M. de los Angeles Cortes, C. Ruiz Matus, J. Tate, P. Gargiullo, and U. D. Parashar. 2011. Intussusception risk and health benefits of rotavirus vaccination in Mexico and Brazil. *New England Journal of Medicine* 364(24):2283-2292.

PATH. 2012a. *Project optimize: At a glance* (accessed January 31, 2012).

———. 2012b. *Rethinking the vaccine supply chain.* http://www.path.org/projects/project-optimize.php (accessed January 31, 2012).

———. 2012c. *World's smartest sticker.* http://www.path.org/projects/vaccine_vial_monitor.php (accessed January 31, 2012).

Peeling, R. W., P. G. Smith, and P. M. M. Bossuyt. 2010. A guide for diagnostic evaluations. *Nature Reviews Microbiology*:S2-S6.

Pew Health Group. 2011. *After heparin: Protecting consumers from the risks of substandard and counterfeit drugs.* Washington, DC: Pew Health Group.

Pirmohamed, M., K. N. Atuah, A. N. O. Dodoo, and P. Winstanley. 2007. Pharmacovigilance in developing countries. *BMJ* 335.

Pisani, E., and C. AbouZahr. 2010. Sharing health data: Good intentions are not enough. *Bulletin of the World Health Organization* 88(6):462-466.

Poisot, A.-S., A. Speedy, and E. Kueneman. 2004. *Good agricultural practices –a working concept: Background paper for the FAO internal workshop on good agricultural practices.* Rome: FAO.
Politics in emerging markets: The new middle classes rise up. 2011. *The Economist*, September 3.
Pornruangwong, S., R. S. Hendriksen, C. Pulrikarn, A. Bangstrakulnonth, M. Mikoleit, R. H. Davies, F. M. Aarestrup, and L. Garcia-Migura. 2011. Epidemiological investigation of *Salmonella enterica* serovar Kedougou in Thailand. *Foodborne Pathogens and Disease* 8(2):203-211.
Prado, M. M. 2006 March 23-25. *Independent regulatory agencies, patronage and clientelism lessons from Brazil.* Paper presented at Primera conferencia internacional sobre corrupcion y transpacencia: debatiendo las fronteras entre estado, mercado y sociedad, Mexico City.
———. 2008. The challenges and risks of creating independent regulatory agencies: A cautionary tale from Brazil. *Vanderbilt Journal of Transnational Law* 41(2):435-503.
Prakash, S. 2009. Evolution of regulatory system in India. *India Journal of Pharmacology* 41(5):207.
Ratanawijitrasin, S., and E. Wondemagegnehu. 2002. *Effective drug regulation: A multicountry study.* The World Health Organization.
Reuters. 2001. Baxter recalls kidney filters after deaths. *USA Today*, October 18.
———. 2010. E coli outbreak blamed on egyptian fenugreek seeds. *The Guardian*, July 5.
Roth, A. V., A. A. Tsay, M. E. Pullman, and J. V. Gray. 2008. Unraveling the food supply chain: Strategic insights from China and the 2007 recalls. *Journal of Supply Chain Management* 44(1):22-39.
Roy, D., and A. Thorat. 2008. Success in high value horticultural export markets for the small farmers: The case of mahagrapes in India. *World Development* 36(10):1874-1890.
Rumsfeld, J. S., and E. D. Peterson. 2010. Achieving meaningful device surveillance. *The Journal of the American Medical Association* 304(18):2065-2066.
Sabot, O., P. Yadav, and M. Zaffran. 2011. *Maximizing every dose and dollar: The imperative of efficiency in vaccine delivery.* Seattle, WA: The National Bureau of Asian Research.
Sarley, D., V. Dayaratna, W. Abramson, J. Gribble, N. Quesada, N. Olson, and V. S. Betancourt. 2006. *Options for contraceptive procurement: Lessons learned from Latin America and the Caribbean.* Arlington, VA and Washington, DC: DELIVER, USAID -Health Policy Initiative for the U.S. Agency for International Development.
Schlehuber, L. D., I. J. McFadyen, Y. Shu, J. Carignan, W. P. Duprex, W. R. Forsyth, J. H. Ho, C. M. Kitsos, G. Y. Lee, D. A. Levinson, S. C. Lucier, C. B. Moore, N. T. Nguyen, J. Ramos, B. A. Weinstock, J. Zhang, J. A. Monagle, C. R. Gardner, and J. C. Alvarez. 2011. Towards ambient temperature-stable vaccines: The identification of thermally stabilizing liquid formulations for measles virus using an innovative high-throughput infectivity assay. *Vaccine* 29(31):5031-5039.
Schoub, B. D., and N. A. Cameron. 1996. Problems encountered in the delivery and storage of OPV in an African country. *Developments in biological standardization* 87:27-32.
Setia, S., H. Mainzer, M. L. Washington, G. Coil, R. Snyder, and B. G. Weniger. 2002. Frequency and causes of vaccine wastage. *Vaccine* 20(7-8):1148-1156.
Sharma, A., L. Subramanian, and E. A. Brewer. 2008. Secure rural supply chain management using low cost paper watermarking, Seattle, WA.

Sharma, R. K., M. Agrawal, and F. M. Marshall. 2009. Heavy metals in vegetables collected from production and market sites of a tropical urban area of India. *Food and Chemical Toxicology* 47(3):583-591.
Sharma, V., and V. Ahuja. 2010. Training in post-authorization pharmacovigilance. *Perspectives in Clinical Research* 1(2):70-75.
Sproxil. 2011. *Sproxil- world-class brand protection for emerging markets.* http://sproxil.com/ (accessed October 19, 2011).
SPS. 2010a. *National pharmacovigilance systems: Ensuring the safe use of medicines august 16-18, 2010 Nairobi, Kenya.*
———. 2010b. *Sentinel site-based pilot active surveillance pharmacovigilance in the Vietnam ART program.* Arlington, VA: USAID.
Stcichele, M. V., S. v. d. Wal, and J. Oldenziel. 2006. *Who reaps the fruit? Critical issues in the fresh fruit and vegetable supply chain (update).* Amsterdam: Centre for Research on Multinational Corporations.
Sudershan, R. V., P. Rao, K. Polasa, G. M. Subba Rao, and M. Vishnu Vardhana Rao. 2008. Knowledge and practices of food safety regulators in southern India. *Nutrition and Food Science* 38(2):110-120.
Suleman, F. 2010. Pharmacovigilance: Who is responsible and why should we care? *South African Pharmaceutical Journal* 77(9).
Sutz, J. 2000. The university–industry–government relations in Latin America. *Research Policy* 29(2):279-290.
Swaminathan, B., T. J. Barrett, S. B. Hunter, R. V. Tauxe, and CDC Pulsenet Taskforce. 2001. Puslenet: The molecular subtyping network for foodborne bacterial disease surveillance, United States. *Emerging Infectious Diseases* 7(3):382-389.
Swaminathan, B., P. Gerner-Smidt, L.-K. NG, S. Lukinmaa, K.-M. Kam, S. Rolando, E. P. Gutierrez, and N. Binsztein. 2006. Building PulseNet international: An interconnected system of laboratory networks to faciliatate timely public health recognition and response to foodborne disesase outbreaks and emerging foodborne diseases. *Foodborne Pathogens and Disease* 3(1):36-50.
A tale of two expats: Business in China and the west. 2011. *The Economist*, January 1.
The African Union Interafrican Bureau for Animal Resources. *Participation of African nations in sanitary and phytosanitary standard-setting organisations* http://www.au-ibar.org/index.php?option=com_flexicontent&view=items&cid=67:projects&id=83:pan-spso&Itemid=39 (accessed October 4, 2011).
The Daily Times. 2012. DRA establishment at federal level demanded. January 27.
The Genetics and Public Policy Center. 2010. *Reproductive genetic testing: A regulatory patchwork.* http://www.dnapolicy.org/policy.international.php?action=detail&laws_id=63 (accessed October 25, 2010).
The Global Fund. 2008. *Procurement, supply chain management and service deliver of the global fund's grants to the government of India.*
The Lancet. 2009. Who runs global health? *The Lancet* 373(9681):2083.
Todd, E. C. D., and C. Narrod. 2006. *Agriculture, food safety and foodborne disease.* International Food Policy Research Institute.
Todd, E. C. D., and S. Notermans. 2011. Surveillance of listeriosis and its causative pathogen, listeria monocytogenes. *Food Control* 22(9):1484-1490.

U.S. Commercial Service. 2002. *Contact China: A resource guide for doing business in the People's Republic of China.* Beijing, China.
UC Davis Department of Plant Sciences. 2011. *Postharvest technology* http://www.plantsciences.ucdavis.edu/plantsciences/outreach/postharvest_tech.htm (accessed January 12, 2011).
Umali-Deininger, D., and M. Sur. 2007. Food safety in a globalizing world: Opportunities and challenges for India. *Agricultural Economics* 37:135-147.
UMC. *The WHO programme.* http://www.who-umc.org/DynPage.aspx?id=98078&mn1=7347&mn2=7252&mn3=7322 (accessed November 4, 2011).
———. 2011. *WHO programme members.* http://www.who-umc.org/DynPage.aspx?id=100653&mn1=7347&mn2=7252&mn3=7322&mn4=7442 (accessed November 28, 2011).
UN. 2008. *Advancing food safety in China.* Office of the United Nations Resident Coordinator in China.
UNAIDS, and WHO. 2011. *Pharmacovigilance for antiretroviral drugs: Rationale for including pharmacovigilance in the proposal.*
UNICEF. *Child survival fact sheet: Water and sanitation.* http://www.unicef.org/media/media_21423.html (accessed November 4, 2011).
UNICEF, and WHO. 2009. *Diarrhoea: Why children are still dying and what can be done.* Geneva.
Upton, D. M., and V. A. Fuller. 2004. The ITC eChoupal initiative. *Havard Business Review* 604(016):20.
USAID. 2011. *Supply chain management: Providing quality medicines for people living with and affected by HIV/AIDS.* http://www.usaid.gov/our_work/global_health/aids/TechAreas/treatment/scms.html (accessed November 29, 2011).
USP. 2011. *PQM in Asia.* http://www.usp.org/worldwide/dqi/regions/asia.html (accessed November 9, 2011).
Vapnek, J., and M. Spreij. 2005. *Perspectives and guidelines on food legislation, with a new model food law.* Rome: Food and Agriculture Organization of the United Nations.
Viotti, E. B. 2002. National learning systems: A new approach to technological change in late industrializing economies and evidences from the cases of Brazil and South Korea. *Technological Forecasing and Social Change* 69:653-680.
Voxiva. 2011. *Voxiva: About.* http://voxiva.com/company/about.html (accessed November 4, 2011).
Waste not, want not. 2011. *The Economist*, February 26.
Watt, G. 2004. Expiry-date tampering. *The Lancet* 363(9403):172.
Watts, J. 2011. Exploding watermelons put spotlight on Chinese farming practices. *The Guardian*, May 17.
Wertheim, H. F. L., P. Puthavathana, N. Ngoc My, H. R. van Doorn, N. Trung Vu, P. Hung Viet, D. Subekti, S. Harun, S. Malik, J. Robinson, M. Rahman, W. Taylor, N. Lindegardh, S. Wignall, J. J. Farrar, and M. D. de Jong. 2010. Laboratory capacity building in Asia for infectious disease research: Experiences from the South East Asia Infectious Disease Clinical Research Network (SEAICRN). *PLoS Medicine* 7(4):1-5.

WHO. 2003a. Effective medicines regulation: Ensuring safety, efficacy and quality. *WHO Policy Perspectives on Medicines* 007:1-6.
———. 2003b. *Substandard and counterfeit medicines.* http://www.who.int/mediacentre/factsheets/2003/fs275/en/ (accessed November 9, 2011).
———. 2005. *African medicines regulatory harmonization initiative (AMRHI): A WHO initiative.*
———. 2007. *Practical guidance for conducting a review.* Geneva.
———. 2008a. *International health regulations (2005).* Geneva: The World Health Organization.
———. 2008b. *What has been achieved so far.* http://www.wpro.who.int/china/sites/fos/achievements.htm (accessed October 4, 2011).
———. 2010a. *Assessment of medicines regulatory systems in sub-saharan African countries.* Geneva.
———. 2010b. *Counterfeit medical prodcuts: International medical products anti-counterfeiting task force: Report by the secretariat.*
———. 2011a. *Codex trust fund: News.* http://www.who.int/foodsafety/codex/trustfund/en/ (accessed November 21, 2011).
———. 2011b. *General information on counterfeit medicines.* http://www.who.int/medicines/services/counterfeit/overview/en/ (accessed November 9, 2011).
———. 2011c. *Global advisory committee on vaccine safety: About us.* http://www.who.int/vaccine_safety/about/indepth/en/index.html (accessed November 3, 2011).
———. 2011d. *Global vaccine safety blueprint: Draft for discussion.*
———. 2011e. *An integrated approach to food safety and zoonoses: Building capacity to detect, control and prevent foodborne infections.* Geneva: The World Health Organization.
———. 2011f. *Pharmacovigilance.* http://www.who.int/medicines/areas/quality_safety/safety_efficacy/pharmvigi/en/index.html (accessed November 28, 2011).
———. 2011g. *WHO list of prequalified medicinal products.*
———. 2011h. *WHO list of prequalified quality control laboratories.* Geneva: WHO.
———. 2012. *Risk assessment.* http://www.who.int/foodsafety/micro/riskassessment/en/index.html (accessed January 18, 2012).
WHO, and Global Fund. 2010. *Minimum requirements for a functional pharmacovigilance system.* Geneva, Switzerland.
Wong, E. 2010. Officials in China at odds over food scandal. *The New York Times*, March 2.
World Bank. 2003. *Standards and global trade: A voice for Africa.* Washington, DC.
———. 2007. *Unleashing India's innovation.* Washington, DC: The World Bank.
———. 2008. *Training regulators in Africa.* Washington, DC: The World Bank.
———. 2009. *Implementation, completion and results report on a credit in the amount of SDR 39.7 million (US$54 million equivalent) to India for food and drugs cpacity building project.*
———. 2010. *World Bank to help improve food safety in China.* http://www.worldbank.org/en/news/2010/05/13/world-bank-help-improve-food-safety-china (accessed November 21, 2011).

Xiaoguang, S., and Y. Fengqiao. 2010. *Higher and professional education in India.* Manila, Philippines: The Asian Development Bank.

Yadav, P. 2009. *Counterfeit drug resistance in the developing world: An assessment of incentives across the value chain and recommendations of policy interventions.* Washington, D.C.: Center for Global Development.

Yu, X., C. Li, Y. Shi, and M. Yu. 2010. Pharmaceutical supply chain in China: Current issues and implications for health system reform. *Health Policy* 97(1):8-15.

Zaidi, M. B., J. J. Calva, M. T. Estrada-Garcia, V. Leon, G. Vazquez, G. Figueroa, E. Lopez, J. Contreras, J. Abbott, S. Zhao, P. McDermott, and L. Tollefson. 2008. Integrated food chain surveillance system for *salmoella* spp. In Mexico. *Emerging Infectious Diseases* 14(3):429-435.

Zhen, L. H. 2004. Drug control authorities in China. *The Annals of Pharmacotherapy* 38(2):346-350.

4

A Strategy to Building Food and Medical Product Regulatory Systems

As Chapter 1 explains, this report is the product of the Food and Drug Administration's (FDA), and the entire Department of Health and Human Services' (HHS'), expanding interest in health beyond U.S. borders. In keeping with its task to speak to the common elements of food and medical products regulation, the common problems across low- and middle-income countries, and the common recommendations that could improve food and medical product safety for a range of stakeholders. After identifying the common gaps in food and medical product regulatory systems in emerging economies, the committee developed a strategic plan for how the FDA and other stakeholders could best work to bridge these gaps. The committee's strategy builds on the nexus of global health, trade, and development. In making its recommendations the committee kept in mind that international trade and modern supply chains mean that every country has a stake in the safety standards of its least developed trading partner.

The committee's strategy also emphasizes that food and medical products regulatory systems are an essential piece of the health system in any country. The deficits in the systems of the poorest countries are, because of global trade, vulnerabilities in the richest. HHS Secretary Kathleen Sebelius commented on this vulnerability when introducing the HHS *Global Health Strategy* on January 5, 2012, explaining, "we can no longer separate global health from America's health" (Sebelius, 2012), mentioning in particular the globalization of the food and medical product supply. The department's new health strategy emphasizes the importance of improving global disease surveillance, increasing the integrity of the food and medical product supply chain, implementing scientifically rigorous international health and safety standards, and advancing health diplomacy (HHS, 2011). The committee recognizes that there are times when the goals of commerce and health will conflict. Some of the gaps Chapter 3 describes, especially the deficits in communication and political will, are a function of this tension. Nevertheless, it would be a mistake to ignore the broad common ground where nations can work together on health programs, development, and trade. The committee believes that food and medical product safety are in this common ground. Investments in food and drug regulation are to the mutual benefit of the investor and the recipient.

GLOBAL HEALTH, TRADE, AND DEVELOPMENT

Adequate regulation aims to assure food and drug safety. Regulatory authorities have a first responsibility to look after the health of their own countries' citizens. But in a larger sense, food and medical product safety is a cornerstone for global health, trade, and economic development (Bollyky, 2009; Fidler, 2001; Unnevehr, 2007).

Food and Medical Product Safety and Global Health

Rich and poor countries alike feel the costs of unsafe food and medical products. Foodborne disease outbreaks have occurred on every continent over the last decade (WHO, 2002). The Centers for Disease Control and Prevention (CDC) estimates that, in the United

States alone, every year roughly 1 out of 6 (48 million people) are sickened, 128,000 are hospitalized, and 3,000 die from foodborne diseases (CDC, 2011). In developing countries, the burden is even greater. More than two million people die each year from diarrhea, much of which is caused by foodborne contaminants (WHO, 2012). At worst, toxically adulterated drugs kill patients; at best they hold back recovery, confuse clinicians, and impede disease control. Though precise estimate are hard to come by, millions of counterfeit prescriptions are probably filled every year in the United States alone (Pew Health Group, 2011). The incidence of counterfeiting is when regulatory and enforcement systems are weak: in Africa, parts of Asia and Latin America, and the former Soviet Union (WHO, 2009).

No national regulatory authority, including the FDA, can totally ensure the safety of food and medical products in its markets. Unsafe foods and drugs cross national boundaries with trade and travel; technology makes international commerce easier. The volume of the global trade in food and drugs and complexity of its supply chains overwhelm border control and inspection efforts. There are legal and practical limits on the ability of an importing country's regulatory authority to inspect foreign food and medical product producers and suppliers (Bollyky, 2009). As a result, the adequacy of the food and drug safety in any one country is dependent on the adequacy of regulation in others.

Food and Medical Product Safety and Trade

Over the last 50 years, barriers to international trade have declined substantially with lower tariffs, reduced quotas, and preferential trade agreements (Bhagwati, 2002). International manufacturing and modern distribution systems have made food and medical products truly global industries. Increased competition, thinning profit margins, and a relentless drive for productivity have pushed multinational food and drug companies to source their production in low- and middle-income countries and through complex, fragmented supply chains (FDA, 2011).

The resulting growth in international food and drug trade volume has been spectacular. Agricultural exports from developing countries nearly doubled between 1990 and 2000 and continue to increase rapidly (Aksoy and Ng, 2010). In the United States alone, imports of FDA-regulated food and drug products have increased by more than 13 percent annually since 2002, with imports from Mexico, India, China, and Thailand increasing the fastest (FDA, 2011). U.S. imports of medical devices quadrupled over the last ten years (FDA, 2011). The international food and drug trade is not unilateral. American companies, for example, sell an increasing amount of drugs and medical devices in low- and middle-income countries (Johnson, 2009). Bilateral food and drug trade between developing countries has likewise expanded (Miller, 2009).

The last decade has seen many food and drug safety crises, some because of contamination in developing countries. As supply chains have grown more complex and food is no longer produced solely in any one country, regulators find their laws, written decades ago, insufficient to protect the modern supply chain. The private sector responded initially by implementing private standards such as Global-gap, Hazard Analysis and Critical Control Points, good manufacturing practices, etc. to ensure product safety, and many of the private standards were stricter than the public standards (Willems et al., 2005). Subsequently many countries such as the United States, European Union (EU) members, Canada, and Japan have found it necessary to modernize their product safety requirements. Suppliers to these countries, and to companies that sell in these countries, need to ensure they are meeting the changing monitoring and traceability requirements. If they do not, they will lose a lucrative market.

Food and Medical Product Safety and International Development

The global food and drug trade has been an engine of international economic development. Many people in low- and middle-income countries earn their livings in farming and manufacturing. Drug manufacturing is an important growth sector in developing countries like India and China (FDA, 2011). Continued trade and investment in the food and drug sector will depend on local governments and producers ensuring that the safety and quality requirements of importing governments and corporations are met.

Unsafe food and drugs hold back economic development in many ways. Foodborne illnesses caused $35 billion in medical costs and lost productivity in the United States in 1997, likely much more today (WHO, 2007). International efforts to improve nutrition in low- and middle-income countries depend on safe, nutritious food and a plentiful, clean water supply (Lupien, 2008). Foodborne illnesses and substandard drugs are most harmful to the most vulnerable: children, pregnant women, the sick, and the elderly. Deliberately and fraudulently misidentified shipments and products undermine the customs, regulations, and rule of law in low- and middle-income countries (Bollyky, 2009).

A functioning regulatory system is a key piece of the public health system and one that is missing in many countries. International development organizations have the funding, staffing, and institutional strength to improve functioning of regulatory systems, but to do this they need technical input from expert regulators. Regulators would benefit from working though the established development networks that aid organizations have implemented. Unfortunately, the two groups often work in relative isolation from each other.

STRATEGY FOR BRIDGING THE GAPS IN FOOD AND MEDICAL PRODUCT REGULATION

A four-part strategy that includes an emphasis on public health, risk-based investments, suitable incentives, and international coordination could help bridge the gaps in food and medical product safety regulation around the world. An explanation of the four pieces of this strategy follows.

Emphasis on Global Public Health

The cornerstone of this strategy is its recognition that adequate regulation of food and medical products is essential for public health, improved well-being, and long lifespan. Public health is itself a predictor of economic development; healthy, strong people can work better and earn more (Strauss and Thomas, 1998). Growth during early childhood predicts adult health and cognitive ability (Case and Paxson, 2008; Richards et al., 2002). Malnutrition and disease rob poor countries of the intellectual capital that could fuel their growth.

Unsafe food and water cause the problem; unreliable and poor quality drug supplies compound it. Childhood disease causes malabsorption of nutrients and poor growth; malnutrition, in turn, aggravates infections (Guerrant et al., 2008). There is an emerging body of evidence that chronic early exposure to aflatoxin, a dangerous mycotoxin produced from fungus that infects grain, also causes childhood stunting (Gong et al., 2002; Wild, 2007). Malaria, bacterial infections, parasites, and vaccine-preventable diseases are all commonplace in developing countries. Their prevention and treatment depends on national regulatory authorities as much as it depends on the primary health care system, but donor investments in health favor disease-specific programming and improving primary health care to the exclusion of developing the food and medical products regulatory system. This is ultimately a short-sighted donor strategy. This report maintains that regulatory systems are an important piece of the public health system, a position taken by the FDA in its *Pathway to Global Product Safety and Quality*.

Risk-based Investments

The committee recognizes that it is neither practical nor sensible for any stakeholder to divide limited resources equally among all regulated products. Modern regulatory science demands an understanding of risk, "the probability of an adverse event ... caused under specified circumstances by exposure to an agent" (IPCS, 2004, p. 13). In 2010 the Institute of Medicine's (IOM's) report *Enhancing Food Safety* expanded on this concept, describing a risk-based system as one that "facilitates decision making to reduce public health risk in light of limited resources and additional factors" (IOM, 2010, p. 79). Data drives a risk-based system; only through surveillance and epidemiological analysis can the risks of a food or medical product lapse be understood. Risk analysis sets out rules that allow for comparison of seemingly disparate problems. The risks with the greatest threat to public health are ranked highest and those with little risk to public health are ranked lower (IOM, 2010). The best risk-based systems involve all the stakeholders in their process and encourage open dialogue (IOM, 2010). A system properly grounded in risk analysis has the ability to respond to a product safety emergency in a way that will not disrupt the background functioning of the system (IOM, 2010).

To this end, the committee's strategy emphasizes risk. National regulatory authorities should give the most attention to the highest risk products. Risk can guide the investments international organizations make in products, industries, countries, and regions. Stringent regulatory authorities have surveillance data that others can share to inform their understanding of risk. Over time, as surveillance systems and risk analysis capacity improves in emerging economies, a wider scope of data will be available and a better understanding of risk in different parts of the world will emerge.

Suitable Market Incentives

The committee's strategy includes building incentives that encourage strong national regulatory authorities and higher compliance with international standards. The United States and EU are examples of markets with much stricter controls than in low- and middle-income countries (Euro Consultants, 2010). Access to lucrative, highly regulated export markets are a powerful incentive for emerging economies to raise their own food and drug standards (Maertens and Swinnen, 2009; Vogel, 1997). Once a producer meets the safety standards required by the export market, spillover effects may occur to local production (Unnevehr et al., 2003; Vogel and Kagan, 2002).

The committee's emphasis on incentives aims to make international standards more attractive for exporters in developing countries. If large, stringently regulated economies, such as the United States, ensure an adequate mix of incentives that offer competitive advantage in their markets, this would benefit trading partners confirmed to meet their higher regulatory standards (Bollyky, 2009). In accordance with World Trade Organization (WTO) law, such incentives should be not favor the applicants of one country over another. Some of the committee's recommendations will address policymakers in importing economies. The committee considered consistent use of international standards as an important guiding principle in its recommendations.

Retailers and manufacturers need to better control their supply chains, and that includes the supply chains of all their suppliers. Retailers and manufacturers are also the ones in the best position to do this in the short term. Already, supermarkets enforce standards and regulate their supply chains; multinational pharmaceutical companies do the same (Havinga, 2006; O'Marah, 2007). To manage its supply chains, industry needs to consider which suppliers are most credible and which ones are compliant with regular inspections. Manufacturers and retailers also have a wealth of expertise that they can share with their suppliers on how to run production efficiently, keep waste low, and other safe ways to maximize profits.

U.S. retailers and manufacturers are in the best position to ensure the safety of their products. They can do this by adopting stronger prevention measures and control of their supply chains. There are already good incentives for U.S. companies to control their suppliers. It is relatively simple and inexpensive to bring a lawsuit to court in the United States and there are no disincentives to sue, encouraging a litigious culture. For the defendant companies, litigation is expensive, and even if the plaintiff settles, a lawsuit can damage the firm's reputation. There are legal and practical limits to the ability of U.S. consumers to hold foreign producers responsible for the harm their products cause in the United States, however. In some cases, U.S. firms can avoid product liability when there is no evidence that they knew or should have known about vulnerabilities in their suppliers' products (Bamberger and Guzman, 2008).

The committee sees value in encouraging retailers and manufacturers to improve oversight of their suppliers by increasing liability for the importation of unsafe food and medical products. In its strategy the committee recognizes that there are different ways to enforce product liability, discussed further in Chapter 6.

Some agricultural economists fear that smallholders will not be able to access high-value agricultural markets given the strict standards (Graffham and MacGregor, 2009; Okello et al., 2011). New economic incentives could help small producers stay competitive in the global marketplace. Narrod et al. (2009) describe how public–private partnerships can encourage farm-to-table connections that can meet demands for food safety, and still retain smallholders in the supply chain. Unfortunately such market incentives often do not exist in many developing countries where there is limited quality testing in the marketplace. In the agri-food sector in particular, much of the food produced by smallholders in poor countries is consumed locally.

Successful multinational corporations understand how to use market incentives with their suppliers. But there are still many retailers and manufacturers that need to better control their supply chains, and that includes the supply chains of all their partners.

International Coordination

Product safety crises know no national borders. The last decade of product safety scares has driven this point home. The committee sees international cooperation as a foundation for effective product safety regulation. The committee also values international collaboration in the capacity building programs that it recommends. Cooperation among all nations and international organizations is one of the main principals the committee considered when making its recommendations. While food and medical product regulation is a national and even local process, but success requires international coordination.

The committee believes that international cooperation will support the building of a cadre of regulators in developing countries. Critics of an international approach might maintain that the national regulatory authority of each nation is solely responsible for its country's product safety. This was true 20 years ago, but this report explains why the rapid increase in global trade has created a worldwide interdependence of regulators. Much as the World Health Organization (WHO) is the backbone of the public health system in developing countries, international product safety cooperation should be the backbone of regulatory systems.

Cooperation among nations does not mean that each country has to do things the same way. What one country considers an emergency may be a routine incident in another (WHO and FAO). However, international cooperation becomes more important during a serious product safety lapse. During the heparin incident of 2008, for example, U.S. and Chinese regulators and industry representatives had to work together to identify the contaminated drug and its source. A stronger framework for international collaboration might have improved this process. Figure 4-1 shows conceptually how more serious events require higher level of international coordination.

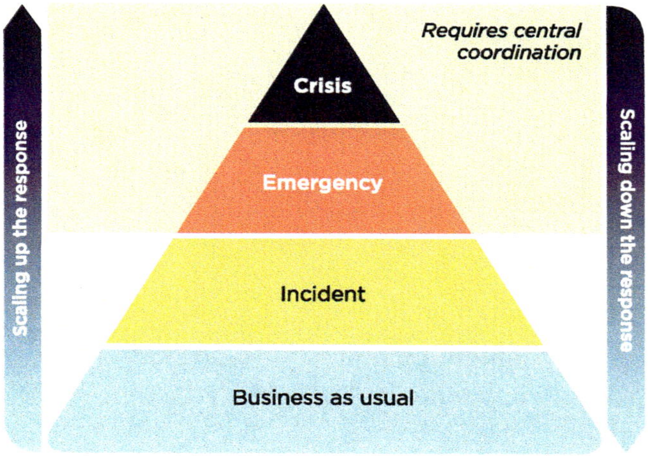

FIGURE 4-1 Product Safety Events.
SOURCE: Adapted from WHO and FAO, 2010. Reprinted with permission from the Food and Agricultural Organization of the United Nations.

Intergovernmental institutions are the experts in the sensitive area of international coordination. The WTO is the leader on coordinating international trade; the WHO has a similar voice in international health. Universities often have collaborative research centers in other countries. International NGOs have expertise in coordinating operations on the same project in different countries. The development banks have long worked on projects at the intersection of health and economic development. The World Bank funded a project on building capacity for food and drug safety in India that contributed to the development of the 2006 Indian Integrated Food Law (World Bank, 2009). The same project also built 13 new food safety labs and 6 new drug testing labs in India and renovated dozens more (World Bank, 2009). Rational pharmaceutical use and medicines registration have long been one of the Inter-American Development Bank's main program areas (Guiffrida, 2001); the bank has implemented a drug inventory and distribution plan in Nicaraguan hospitals (IADB, 2006). The Asian Development Bank is working to build the drug regulatory authority in Mongolia (ADB, 2010). This program established a drug regulatory authority in Mongolia, upgraded the Mongolian drug control laboratories, modernized its laboratory accreditation process, and strengthened post-marketing surveillance (ADB, 2008). The African Development Bank funded a successful project to improve sanitary and phytosanitary (SPS) measures, improve food safety standards, and strengthen SPS institutions (Magalhães, 2010).

In making its recommendations, the committee encourages cooperation among regulatory authorities from industrial and emerging economies. The Group of Twenty (G20) international forum is a venue that brings leaders of these countries together to advance an agenda of a strong, sustainable, and balanced global economy; it would be a useful venue to elevate the priority of food and medical product safety for global health, development, and trade. International and intergovernmental institutions such as the WHO, the Food and Agriculture Organization of the United Nations (FAO), development banks, and other UN organizations, many of which are already promoting good regulatory practices, can be international leaders in facilitating and supporting regulatory cooperation and strengthening. National and local governments, industry, and consumers are also all stakeholders that the committee considers central to its strategy. Its recommendations will have a global focus, in an effort to reduce accusations of double standards for imported and domestic products. This strategy sees the key overlaps among public health, economic development, and trade, and it values the safety of all foods and medical products produced around the world.

The committee also sees regional collaborations, both regional economic partnerships and regional public health networks, as important to international coordination. In its *Resource Guide on Drug Regulation in Developing Countries*, the British government's aid agency observed that "regional cooperation may allow scarce expertise to be more efficiently applied" (Gray, 2004, p. 3). The committee agrees with this sentiment. All countries should work towards a long-term goal of having a reliable health system, and this includes a system for food and medical product safety. But in the short term, regional collaboration will allow smaller and less technologically advanced countries benefit from their neighbors' systems. Box 4-1 describes a successful international collaboration in South America; the South American countries that worked together on medfly eradication were able to improve their agricultural exports and their food security.

BOX 4-1
Mediterranean Fruit Fly Eradication in Chile

The Mediterranean fruit fly, also known as medfly, is a destructive fruit pest that destroys crops when it deposits its eggs on host fruits and vegetables. The larvae damage the fruit as they feed on the pulp and tunnel through it, which encourages the entrance of secondary pathogens (Bergsten et al., 1999).

Although the medfly originated in Africa, it arrived in Latin America in 1901 and rapidly spread throughout the continent. The medfly's destruction of fruit and vegetable crops posed a threat to the region's export industry because it not only lowered the market value of the crop, but it also rendered many crops unfit for human consumption (Vail et al.). The need to minimize economic losses and ensure consumer safety encouraged the development of eradication programs such as Chile's Agriculture and Livestock Service's "Fruit Flies in Chile" project (Labos and Machuca, 1998).

Suppression programs such this one called for collaboration among surrounding countries and international organizations. One exemplary partnership was between Chile and the International Atomic Energy Agency (IAEA). It began in 1987 during the first phase of the usage of the sterile insect technique (SIT) to repress medfly (Labos and Machuca, 1998). Field research demonstrated that bringing sterile males into Chile from Guatemala, Hawaii, and Mexico had been highly effective so the IAEA assisted Chile in building a factory to produce sterile medflies and provided the necessary technical support (IAEA and UNDP, 1998).

Another successful negotiation was the bi-national agreement between Chile and Peru. The Chilean province of Arica borders Peru and had the highest risk of infestation because medflies could enter northern Chile through the southern Peruvian border. It was imperative that Chile and Peru cooperate to eliminate the pest. With Chile's guidance, the Peruvian government effectively introduced sterile males to these regions. This resulted in a dramatic reduction in medfly population densities and reduced the invasion pressure into Chile (Gonzalez and Troncoso, 2005).

Chile finally achieved a medfly free status in November 1995. This allowed it to expand its exports to markets where it had previously been banned such as China and Japan. In 1996, Chile's total agriculture exports were worth $1 billion (Sims, 1996). By 2011, agriculture exports had increased nearly sevenfold (This is Chile, 2011). Chile's medfly-free status allowed it to become the largest fruit exporter in South America (IAEA, 2007).

Chile's success led it to help neighboring countries in eradicate the medfly. The SIT program has been applied in other Latin American countries such as Argentina, Bolivia, Colombia, Uruguay and Ecuador. The goal of these methods is to ensure the complete eradication the medfly pest from the major fruit growing regions of Latin America (IAEA and UNDP, 1998).

THE ORGANIZATION OF THE COMMITTEE'S RECOMMENDATIONS

After identifying the nine main problems in developing country product safety systems and agreeing on a common strategy to solve these problems, the committee formed 13 recommendations. These recommendations suggest actions for the FDA, international organizations, the G20, developing country regulatory authorities, developed country regulatory authorities, industry associations, and other branches of the U.S. government including USAID, the CDC, and USDA. Meaningful change in product safety systems will take time, and success will be measured in increments. With this in mind, the committee suggested actions for the short and long term. See Table 4-1.

TABLE 4-1 Recommended Actions to Address the Nine Main Problems in Developing Country Product Safety Systems

Critical Issue	Recommendations	Timeframe	Action
Adherence to international standards	5-1: Increasing international investments	1 year	Bring regulatory capacity building to the 2012 G20 meeting agenda
		3-5 years	Track investments in regulatory systems and training
	5-3: Working towards shared inspections	18 months	Share inspection reports among stringent regulatory agencies
		~10 years	Establish a system for mutual recognition of inspection reports
	5-4: Sharing inspection results voluntarily	3 years	Share industry inspection results among members
	6-5: Expanding one-up, one-back track and trace	1 year	Convene a public workshop on expanding one up, one back
	6-7: Giving market incentives for supply chain management	2 years	Evaluate the Secure Supply Chain program in 2014
		3-5 years	Scale up the Secure Supply Chain program based on evaluation
Controlling supply chains	5-4: Sharing inspection results voluntarily	3 years	Share industry inspection results among members
	6-2: Using information technology	3-5 years	Articulate a standard data format and vocabulary
		~10 years	Develop an informatics strategy that moves to paperless systems
	6-5: Expanding one-up, one-back track and trace	1 year	Convene a public workshop on expanding one up, one back
	6-6: Researching inexpensive technology	2 years	Issue CRADAs that benefit producers and regulators abroad
		3-5 years	Stimulate industry and academic research on behalf of small producers
	6-7: Giving market incentives for supply chain management	2 years	Evaluate the Secure Supply Chain program in 2014
		3-5 years	Scale up the Secure Supply Chain program based on evaluation

TABLE 4-1 *Continued*

Critical Issue	Recommendations	Timeframe	Action
Infrastructure deficits	5-2: Encouraging open dialogue among government, industry and academia in emerging economies	3-5 years	Identify neutral venues to bring together government, industry, and academia
		Ongoing	Regular, open dialogue on regulatory science and policy
	6-2: Using information technology	3-5 years	Articulate a standard data format and vocabulary
		~10 years	Develop an informatics strategy that moves to paperless systems
	6-4: Leadership in adopting standards	3-5 years	Adopt international standards in the U.S.
		~10 years	Fully integrate product safety into U.S. foreign policy
Strong legal foundation	6-4: Leadership in adopting standards	3-5 years	Adopt international standards in the U.S.
		~10 years	Fully integrate product safety into U.S. foreign policy
	6-8: Increasing civil liability	~10 years	Hold producers and importers liable for unsafe products
Workforce	5-2: Encouraging open dialogue among government, industry and academia in emerging economies	3-5 years	Identify neutral venues to bring together government, industry, and academia
		Ongoing	Regular, open dialogue on regulatory science and policy
	5-3: Working towards shared inspections	18 months	Share inspection reports among stringent regulatory agencies
		~10 years	Establish a system for mutual recognition of inspection reports
	5-5: Strengthening surveillance systems	3 years	Develop pharmacovigilance plans
		5 years	Improve the foodborne disease surveillance systems
		~10 years	Build a cadre of trained epidemiologists

TABLE 4-1 *Continued*

Critical Issue	Recommendations	Timeframe	Action
Workforce, *continued*	6-3: Bridging training gaps at home and abroad	3-5 years	Revise the curriculum at the FDA staff college
			Work through existing networks to train trainers abroad
			Support academic exchanges
		~10 years	Facilitate the development of a standing regulatory science college
			Implement an apprenticeship program like the FETP
	6-4: Leadership in adopting standards	3-5 years	Adopt international standards in the U.S.
		~10 years	Fully integrate product safety into U.S. foreign policy
Fragmentation	5-2: Encouraging open dialogue among government, industry and academia in emerging economies	3-5 years	Identify neutral venues to bring together government, industry, and academia
		Ongoing	Regular, open dialogue on regulatory science and policy
Surveillance	5-5: Strengthening surveillance systems	3 years	Develop pharmacovigilance plans
		5 years	Improve the foodborne disease surveillance systems
		~10 years	Build a cadre of trained epidemiologists
	6-2: Using information technology	3-5 years	Articulate a standard data format and vocabulary
		~10 years	Develop an informatics strategy that moves to paperless systems
	6-4: Leadership in adopting standards	3-5 years	Adopt international standards in the U.S.
		~10 years	Fully integrate product safety into U.S. foreign policy
	6-6: Researching inexpensive technology	2 years	Issue CRADAs that benefit producers and regulators abroad
		3-5 years	Stimulate industry and academic research on behalf of small producers

TABLE 4-1 *Continued*

Critical Issue	Recommendations	Timeframe	Action
Communication	5-2: Encouraging open dialogue among government, industry and academia in emerging economies	3-5 years	Identify neutral venues to bring together government, industry, and academia
		Ongoing	Regular, open dialogue on regulatory science and policy
	5-3: Working towards shared inspections	18 months	Share inspection reports among stringent regulatory agencies
		~10 years	Establish a system for mutual recognition of inspection reports
	5-4: Sharing inspection results voluntarily	3 years	Establish a protocol for sharing anonymous internal inspection results
		Ongoing	Publish these results in association newsletters and other publications
	6-2: Using information technology	3-5 years	Articulate a standard data format and vocabulary
		~10 years	Develop an informatics strategy that moves to paperless systems
	6-6: Researching inexpensive technology	2 years	Issue CRADAs that benefit producers and regulators abroad
		3-5 years	Stimulate industry and academic research on behalf of small producers
Political will	5-1: Increasing international investments	1 year	Bring regulatory capacity building to the 2012 G20 meeting agenda
		3-5 years	Track investments in regulatory systems and training
	5-2: Encouraging open dialogue among government, industry and academia in emerging economies	3-5 years	Identify neutral venues to bring together government, industry, and academia
		Ongoing	Regular, open dialogue on regulatory science and policy
	6-4: Leadership in adopting standards	3-5 years	Adopt international standards in the U.S.
		~10 years	Fully integrate product safety into U.S. foreign policy
	6-7: Market incentives for supply chain management	2 years	Evaluate the Secure Supply Chain program in 2014
		3-5 years	Scale up the Secure Supply Chain program based on evaluation
6-1: Using enterprise risk management to rank priorities		3-5 years	Choose priorities for FDA foreign operations
		~10 years	Lobby Congress to reorganize FDA operations based on risk

REFERENCES

ADB. 2008. *Fourth health sector development project: Improving sector governance: Mongolia* http://pid.adb.org/pid/LoanView.htm?projNo=41243&seqNo=01&typeCd=2&projType=GRNT (accessed January 20, 2012).

———. 2010. *ADB, Mongolia target hospital, drug safety improvements.* http://beta.adb.org/news/adb-mongolia-target-hospital-drug-safety-improvements (accessed November 10, 2011).

Aksoy, M. A., and F. Ng. 2010. *The evolution of agricultural trade flows.* The World Bank.

Bamberger, K. A., and A. T. Guzman. 2008. Keeping imports safe: A proposal for discriminatory regulation of international trade. *California Law Review* 96(6):1405-1447.

Bergsten, D., D. Lance, and M. Stefan. 1999. Mediterranean fruit flies and their management in the USA. *Pesticide Outlook*:207-212.

Bhagwati, J. 2002. *In defense of globalization.* New York: A Council on Foreign Relations book, Oxford University Press.

Bollyky, T. J. 2009. Global health interventions for U.S. Food and drug safety: CSIS Global Health Policy Center.

Case, A., and C. Paxson. 2008. Height, health, and cognitive function at older ages. *American Economic Review* 98(2):463-467.

CDC. 2011. *CDC estimates of foodborne illness in the United States.* National Center for Emerging & Zoonotic Infectious Diseases; Division of Foodborne, Waterborne, and Environmental Diseases.

Euro Consultants. 2010. *Kazakhstan health technology transfer and institutional reform report: Consulting services for food safety and WTO accession in Kazakhstan.*

FDA. 2011. *Pathway to global product safety and quality.* Washington, DC: U.S. Food and Drug Administration.

Fidler, D. 2001. The globalization of public health: The first 100 years of international health diplomacy. *Bulletin of the World Health Organization* 79(9):842-849.

Gong, Y. Y., K. Cardwell, A. Hounsa, S. Egal, P. C. Turner, A. J. Hall, and C. P. Wild. 2002. Dietary aflatoxin exposure and impaired growth in young children from Benin and Togo: Cross sectional study. *British Medicine Journal* 325(7354):20-21.

Gonzalez, J., and P. Troncoso. 2005 May 9-13. *The fruit fly programme in Chile* Paper presented at FAO/IAEA International Conference on Area-Wide Control of Insect Pests: Integrating Sterile Insect and Related and Other Techniques, Vienna, Austria.

Graffham, A., and J. MacGregor. 2009. Impact of GlobalGAP on smallscale vegetable growers in Kenya. In *Standard bearers: Horticultural exports and private standards in Africa*, edited by A. B. d. Battisti, J. MacGregor and A. Graffham. London, UK: International Institute for Environment and Development.

Gray, A. 2004. *Access to medicines and drug regulation in developing countries: A resource guide for DFID.* London, United Kingdom: DFID Health Systems Resource Center.

Guerrant, R. L., R. B. Oriá, S. R. Moore, M. O. B. Oriá, and A. A. M. Lima. 2008. Malnutrition as an enteric infectious disease with long-term effects on child development. *Nutrition Reviews* 66(9):487-505.

Guiffrida, A. 2001. *Learning from the experience: The Inter-American Development Bank and pharmaceuticals.* Washington, DC: Inter-American Development Bank.

Havinga, T. 2006. Private regulation of food safety by supermarkets. *Law & Policy* 28(4):515-533.

HHS. 2011. *The global health strategy of the U.S. Department of Health and Human Services.* Washington, DC.

IADB. 2006. *Project completion report-pcr* Inter-American Development Bank.

IAEA. 2007. *Chile's leading edge.* http://www.iaea.org/newscenter/features/2007/medfly/medflychile.html (accessed October 6, 2011).

IAEA, and UNDP. 1998. IAEA technical co-operation, building development partnerships: Defeating the medfly.

IOM. 2010. *Enhancing food safety: The role of the Food and Drug Administration.* Washington, DC: The National Academies Press.

IPCS. 2004. *IPCS risk assessment terminology.* Geneva, Switzerland: World Health Organization.

Johnson, A. 2009. Drug firms see poorer nations as sales cure. *The Wallstreet Journal*, July 9.

Labos, C., and J. Machuca. 1998. *Eradication of medfly from Chile and joint programme in southern Peru* Paper presented at FAO/IAEA International Conference on Area-Wide Control of Instect Pests: Integrating the Sterile Inscet and Related Nuclear and Other Techniques, Penang, Malaysia.

Lupien, J. R. 2008. *Food and hunger perspectives beyond 2010.* http://www.worldfoodscience.org/cms/?pid=1004531 (accessed November 10, 2011).

Maertens, M., and J. Swinnen. 2009. Food standards, trade and development. *Review of Business and Economics* LIV(3):313-326.

Magalhães, J. 2010. *Regional sanitary and phytosanitary frameworks and strategies: Report for the standards and trade development facility.* Food and Agriculture Organization of the United Nations, the World Organisation for Animal Health, the World Bank, the World Health Organization and the World Trade Organization.

Miller, J. W. 2009. India prepares EU trade complaint. *The Wall Street Journal*, August 6.

Narrod, C., D. Roy, J. Okello, B. Avendaño, K. Rich, and A. Thorat. 2009. Public-private partnerships and collective action in high value fruit and vegetable supply chains. *Food Policy* 34(1):8-15.

O'Marah, K. 2007. *Supply chain leaders.* http://www.forbes.com/2007/01/29/amr-supply-chain-leaders-biz-logistics-cx_kom_0129amr.html (accessed November 11, 2011).

Okello, J. J., C. Narrod, and D. Roy. 2011. Export standards, market institutions and smallholder farmer exclusion from fresh export vegetable high value chains: Experiences from Ethiopia, Kenya and Zambia. *Journal of Agricultural Sciences* 3(4).

Pew Health Group. 2011. *After heparin: Protecting consumers from the risks of substandard and counterfeit drugs.* Washington, DC: Pew Health Group.

Richards, M., R. Hardy, D. Kuh, and M. E. J. Wadsworth. 2002. Birthweight, postnatal growth and cognitive function in a national uk birth cohort. *International Journal of Epidemiology* 31(2):342-348.

Sebelius, K. 2012. *Speech: HHS global health strategy.* http://www.hhs.gov/secretary/about/speeches/sp20120105.html (accessed February 9, 2012).

Sims, C. 1996. Chile says its spraying has suppressed medfly. *The New York Times*, March 26.

Strauss, J., and D. Thomas. 1998. Health, nutrition, and economic development. *Journal of Economic Literature* 36(2):766-817.

This is Chile. 2011. *Chilean fruit exports to increase 7.4 percent in 2011.* http://www.thisischile.cl/7095/2/419/chilean-fruit-exports-to-increase-74-percent-in-2011/Article.aspx (accessed October 6, 2011).

Unnevehr, L., L. Haddad, and C. Delgado. 2003. *Food safety policy issues for developing countries.* Washington, DC: International Food Policy Research Institute.

Unnevehr, L. J. 2007. Food safety as a global public good. *Agricultural Economics*:149-158.

Vail, P. V., I. Moore, and D. Nadel. The Mediterranean fruit fly in Central America. *IAEA Bulletin* 18(3/4):42-46.

Vogel, D. 1997. *Trading up: Consumer and environmental regulation in a global economy.* Cambridge, MA: First Harvard University Press.

Vogel, D., and R. A. Kagan. 2002. National regulations in a global economy. In *Dynamics of regulatory change: How globalization affects national regulatory policies* edited by D. Vogel and R. A. Kagan. Berkley and Los Angelos, CA: University of California Press. Pp. 1-41.

WHO. 2002. *WHO global strategy for food safety: Safer food for better health.* Geneva: WHO Food Safety Programme.

———. 2007. *Food safety and foodborne illness fact sheet.* http://www.who.int/mediacentre/factsheets/fs237/en/ (accessed November 10, 2011).

———. 2009. *Key facts.* http://www.who.int/medicines/services/counterfeit/CfeitsFactSheetJuly09.pdf (accessed November 22, 2011).

———. 2012. *Water-related diseases.* http://www.who.int/water_sanitation_health/diseases/diarrhoea/en/ (accessed January 12, 2012).

WHO and FAO. 2010. *FAO/WHO framework for developing national food safety emergency response plans.* Rome.

Wild, C. P. 2007. Aflatoxin exposure in developing countries: The critical interface of agriculture and health. *Food and Nutrition Bulletin* 28(Supplement 2):372S-380S.

Willems, S., E. Roth, and J. v. Roekel. 2005. *Changing European public and private food safety and quality requirements: Challenges for developing country fresh produce and fish exporters.* Washington, DC: World Bank Agriculture and Rural Development.

World Bank. 2009. *Implementation, completion and results report on a credit in the amount of SDR 39.7 million (US$54 million equivalent) to India for food and drugs cpacity building project.*

5

International Action

Over the last 30 years, international trade, outsourcing, and improvements in telecommunication have created a more unified world economic system. This system presents new challenges. No country can rely solely on its own national regulatory authority to ensure food and medical product safety. Regulators today depend on their counterparts abroad in ways that no one could have foreseen in the 19th and early 20th centuries when many food and medical product regulatory systems were designed.

Changes in trade and manufacturing patterns call for changes in the ways countries work together for safety. The committee recommends that governments, industries, and academics work more consciously across borders to their mutual benefit. This chapter recommends specific areas for international cooperation, namely: increasing international investments in regulatory systems; encouraging open dialogue among government, industry, and academia; working towards voluntary sharing of inspection reports; and supporting surveillance.

INCREASING INTERNATIONAL INVESTMENTS

There is a common ground where food and medical product safety, global health, international trade, and development are mutually reinforcing (Henson and Jaffee, 2008; Horton and Wright, 2008; Maertens and Swinnen, 2009). Chapter 4 describes the nexus of these topics, and this report suggests action that will advance their common goals. Both the health and the economy in developing countries would benefit from investments in their regulatory systems; these investments are also tools for international trade. Intergovernmental institutions and international donor agencies have not yet recognized this or, if they have, their investments do not reflect it.

Recommendation 5-1: In the next 3 to 5 years, international and intergovernmental organizations should invest more in strengthening the capacity of regulatory systems in developing countries. The United States should work with interested countries to add it to the G20 agenda. Investments in international food and medical product safety should be a significant and explicitly tracked priority at development banks, regional economic communities, and public health institutions. International organizations should provide assistance to achieve meaningful participation of developing country representatives at international harmonization and standardization meetings.

One measure of this recommendation will be the extent to which the 2012 G20 meeting in Mexico includes food and medical product safety on its agenda. The amount of discussion at the Mexico meeting and at subsequent Group of Twenty (G20) meetings will be a further measure. Actions from the G20 meeting and increased allocations to regulatory systems can also measure this recommendation. An increased attendance of scientists from developing countries at standard setting meetings and the development of programs that improve their participation would be measures.

Putting this topic on the agenda at the 2012 G20 meeting can be accomplished in the next year. Increasing investments in building regulatory systems and tracking these investments could take longer; this should begin in the next three to five years and continue.

Advancing Safety Standards Through Trade

Safety standards serve many purposes. They protect health by reducing the likelihood of harmful products circulating in the market. They also facilitate trade: countries with disparate product safety regulations use common standards in the international market (Maertens and Swinnen, 2009). International or harmonized standards and certification regimes are useful to both exporters and importers. They lend predictability to regulatory decisions and protect against accusations of arbitrary barriers to trade. International standards also simplify the requirements for export to multiple markets. The committee commends the Global Food Safety Fund, supported by Waters Corporation, Mars Inc., and the United States Agency for International Development (USAID), for their pilot training program in the Asia Pacific Economic Cooperation (APEC) countries. This program draws on funding and expertise from government and the private sector to establish training programs and improve testing in developing countries (Goetz, 2011).

Complying with international safety standards can be expensive, especially when starting from scratch. However, once a producer has invested in meeting standards for one market, his or her marginal compliance costs decrease as the size of the market increases. These economies of scale could drive better safety standards in emerging economies (Henson and Jaffee, 2008; Horton and Wright, 2008). International trade negotiations and agreements such as the World Trade Organization (WTO) Agreements on Application of Sanitary and Phytosanitary Measures (SPS) and the Technical Barriers to Trade (TBT) promote harmonization and encourage the use of international, science-based food and drug standards.[1] [2] Developing countries can obtain guidance on compliance from Codex, the World Organization for Animal Health, the World Health Organization (WHO), and other international organizations.

Ideally, low- and middle-income countries would use international standards in their own regulatory systems. This would protect health in places where foodborne disease and substandard drugs kill many. It would also promote the competitiveness of exports from low- and middle-income countries in hard-currency markets (Henson, 2003; Maertens and Swinnen, 2009; World Bank, 2005). Failure to comply with food and drug safety standards can lead to product border detentions, import bans, and contractual penalties. The costs of failing to meet standards are substantial, especially for producers in low-and middle-income countries (Henson, 2003). Therefore, even developing countries with little public health infrastructure have reason to invest in oversight of food and drug exports.

The prospect of increased trade can motivate developing countries to invest in safety standards and regulatory oversight. Demonstrated ability to adhere to standards can improve their ability to export to tightly-regulated markets (Maertens and Swinnen, 2009). These improvements in turn encourage foreign direct investment in local food and drug processing,

---

[1] Agreement on the Application of Sanitary and Phytosanitary Measures, Apr. 15, 1994, Marrakesh Agreement Establishing the World Trade Organization, Annex 1B, THE LEGAL TEXTS: THE RESULTS OF THE URUGUAY ROUND OF MULTILATERAL TRADE NEGOTIATIONS 121 (1999), 1867 U.N.T.S. 493 (1994), art. 2, 4

[2] Agreement on Technical Barriers to Trade, Apr. 15, 1994, Marrakesh Agreement Establishing the World Trade Organization, Annex 1B, THE LEGAL TEXTS: THE RESULTS OF THE URUGUAY ROUND OF MULTILATERAL TRADE NEGOTIATIONS 59 (1999), 1868 U.N.T.S. 120 (1994), art. 2.4.

exporting, and retailing (Henson and Jaffee, 2008). This arrangement can have spillover benefits for local populations: they can count on safe food and medicine, and their economies thrive (Unnevehr et al., 2003). Investors and multinational companies spread the use of high standards in developing countries to reduce transaction costs in regional distribution and supply chains, and to harmonize production and processing standards across subsidiaries (Henson and Jaffee, 2008; Maertens and Swinnen, 2009).

The mechanism of this spillover benefit is complicated. The committee recognizes that many countries do support higher safety controls on exports products and neglect to implement best practices for their domestic markets. There is reason this could change, and the committee believes the changes will be more quickly realized in the medical products industry than in the food industry. Medical products are complicated to manufacture; cottage industry production of drug ingredients, while not unheard of, is rare.

The spillover benefits of better product standards will take time, probably at least 10 years, and will happen at the company and industry levels and at the level of the regulatory system. First of all, at the company level, there are common manufacturing processes for both the export and domestic markets. The process a company goes through to meet international standards creates greater knowledge, awareness, and experience with the standards throughout the company and industry. Staff who train against international best practices also bring their skills to other firms as they progress in their careers. There is room for cross-fertilization of ideas within companies and, because of job turnover, within industries.

The committee also sees room for spillover at the national level. As regulators inspect companies against domestic standards, they will be exposed to records, book-keeping, and audit reports reflecting international standards. Regulators will become better acquainted with international standards. Furthermore, regulators in low- and middle-income countries are already keen to enforce international standards; the international meetings for this study convinced the committee of this. However, lobbying forces in the domestic industry work to prevent this. The committee believes that pressure at the ministry levels of government could override the lobbying from industry and create momentum for higher domestic standards.

Much of this depends on the demands people in developing countries put on their governments. Chapter 3 explains how increased prosperity in parts of Asia, Africa, and Latin America drives increased attention to food and drug safety. Middle-class consumers will pay more for safer food (Morehouse and Moriarty, 2007). Studies in the United States and Europe indicate that consumers will pay more for higher quality food (Enneking, 2004; Lusk et al., 2003). Improving the ability of producers in low- and middle-income countries to adhere to international standards is to the shared advantage of consumers around the world. As demand for animal-source foods increases and access to medicines improves in low- and middle-income countries, the interests of consumers in developed and developing countries will overlap more (Unnevehr et al., 2003).

Many low- and middle-income countries have a two-tier regulatory model in which products for export are fairly well regulated, but those for domestic consumption are not (World Bank, 2006). Consumers in these countries could come to resent being subjected to lower standards. There is also invariably intermixing of domestic and export product lines. This undermines developed country regulators' confidence in the products they import.

International food and drug safety standards promote trade and global health, but the proliferation of overlapping, often inconsistent national and private standards do not. Adoption of international food standards has been slow and, in high-income countries such as the United

States, poor (Roberts and Josling, 2011). The United States puts great effort into ensuring its standards are close to the Codex ones, but, because of an apparent disconnect between international and domestic priorities, these standards are often not adopted. When large, hard-currency economies disagree on standards, they undermine the efforts to enforce them in low- and middle-income countries (Horton and Wright, 2008). Inconsistent national standards impede market access and breed trade disputes, which in turn undermine developing country support for future multilateral trade agreements (Henson and Jaffee, 2008). The committee advocates for greater consistency in the use of standards on the part of the developed countries. While the SPS Agreement allows signatories to adopt more stringent standards than Codex calls for if they have scientific reason, the committee sees this practice as unnecessarily harmful to emerging economies.

For example, high-value agricultural products are a promising business for farmers in the Horn of Africa. In order to sell on the European market these farmers need to meet requirements for pesticide residues, field and pack house operations, and traceability (Okello et al., 2007). Businesses increasingly rely on private organization standards, voluntary third-party certifications, and their own safety and quality management systems to regulate their suppliers.

This is not an efficient system. It increases the cost of compliance for producers and can lock small- and medium-sized holders out of the market (Maskus et al., 2005). This is a particular problem in low- and middle-income countries, where small- and medium-sized businesses dominate much of the pharmaceutical (and vastly more of the food) supply chain. Public-private partnerships can play a key role in satisfying market demands for food safety while retaining smallholders in the supply chain (Narrod et al., 2009).

Priorities for Future Multilateral and International Engagement

The United States should work with like-minded governments to pursue food and drug safety at intergovernmental trade, development, and global health forums. A global approach to food and drug safety would lessen claims of double standards and reflect the shared interests of developed and developing countries. Intergovernmental venues are important because food and drug regulation in one state is increasingly dependent on the adequacy of that regulation in other states. Linking global health, trade, and economic development objectives can help engage a wide variety of stakeholders. The committee recognizes that many international organizations work to build food and medical product regulatory capacity around the world. Tables 2-2 and 2-3 give examples of some prominent capacity building projects in food and drug safety.

Action for the Group of Twenty (G20)

The G20 brings together leaders from industrialized and emerging economies to work together for global economic stability and development. The support of the G20 would do much to advance the international food and drug safety agenda. As a leaders' summit of the largest economies in the world, the G20 has the political and economic influence to advance food and medical product safety internationally (Kharas, 2011). The G20 membership includes many important stakeholders—representatives of emerging manufacturing economies including India, China, South Africa, Mexico, Thailand, and Brazil, as well as the developed countries in a position to offer technical assistance like the United States and members of the European Union (G20, 2011). The G20 countries need to commit to improving regulatory systems; without their support, change is unlikely (Drezner, 2007). If food and medical product regulatory systems received prominent attention at a G20 meeting it could spur investment from other donors, intergovernmental institutions, and national governments.

Global food and drug safety is well-suited for the G20 agenda. The G20 development priorities include international trade, food security, investment, and job creation in low- and middle-income countries (G20, 2010). The multi-year G20 development agenda already includes many programs that promote food and medical product safety: identifying practical ways to support trade integration; harnessing agriculture to reduce poverty; increasing private sector participation in development; and promoting small business' access to international markets (G20, 2010). The G20 has recognized international development as integral to its "mandate of global economic cooperation" and a critical component of the G20's goal is "strengthening the relationships among high, middle, and low-income countries" (G20, 2010, p. 1). The G20 development priorities include matters dependent on improved food and drug safety: international trade, food security, and investment and job creation in low- and middle-income countries (G20, 2010).

The G20 should take food and drug safety seriously because it has significant implications for public health, trade, and economic development in G20 countries. The means to address this issue—improved regulatory cooperation, information sharing, and adoption of international standards—are also all areas in which consensus among G20 countries is possible despite the diversity of their economies. This should make it easier for G20 members to act (Kharas, 2011).

Mexico will host the 2012 G20 meeting. As a middle-income country with a vigorous export economy, Mexico would be an ideal country to lead an initiative on global food and drug safety. This initiative might include increasing information sharing among stringent regulatory authorities to reduce redundant audits. Another valuable action would be enhancing the meaningful participation of developing country scientists in international standard setting. They might also emphasize supporting small- and medium-sized developing country producers in complying with international standards. The United States, working with other G20 member states, should encourage and support Mexico before, during, and after the 2012 G20 meeting.

Actions for the WTO, Development Banks, and Regional Economic Institutions

The development banks, regional economic communities, and public health institutions need to invest more in food and medical product safety; this includes investments in the systems and processes that ensure product safety. A 2005 World Bank report stressed that capacity building, especially as it relates to product safety standards, should avoid isolated interventions and work to increase broader market competitiveness (World Bank, 2005). The World Bank is gradually increasing such loans. In 2005 it lent Colombia $30 million to improve the competitiveness of its meat and milk exports (Nuthall, 2005), and a 2010 program invested $100 million in China's adherence to good agricultural practices (World Bank, 2010). Some of the regional banks are working on the same issues. A 2009 $95 million Asian Development Bank loan to Vietnam aims to improve the quality of commercial agriculture (ADB, 2009). These loans are a step in the right direction, but they need to reach more countries.

Standard Setting

As Chapter 3 discusses, scientists from developing countries are often not prepared to make meaningful contributions at international standard setting meetings. Their countries clearly suffer as a result, becoming standard-takers, not equal standard-setters. Their silence also undermines the legitimacy of the standard setting process. And, in the end, they are unable to comply with the standards produced (Horton and Wright, 2008).

The committee recognized that the three international food standard-setting organizations recognized by the WTO—Codex Alimentarius, the International Plant Protection Convention (IPPC), and the World Organization for Animal Health (OIE)—are valuable sources of information and training for regulators in developing countries. Nevertheless, more must be done to mobilize resources and provide technical support that can encourage the participation of developing countries. The International Conference on Harmonisation of Technical Requirements for Registration of Pharmaceuticals for Human Use (ICH) should likewise do more to encourage meaningful engagement by low- and middle-income countries, consistent with trends in the global production and consumption of medicines. These organizations should work closely with regional economic and public health institutions such as APEC, the Pan American Health Organization, the Association of Southeast Asian Nations, the American Institute for Cooperation on Agriculture, and the African Union Interafrican Bureau for Animal Resources to engage low- and middle-income countries.

ENCOURAGING OPEN DIALOGUE AMONG GOVERNMENT, INDUSTRY, AND ACADEMIA IN EMERGING ECONOMIES

A robust regulatory system depends on input from industry and academia; government simply cannot shoulder the burden alone. Most developed country regulators describe their system as a stool supported by three legs: industry, government, and academia. The shared responsibility makes for a stronger system with much wider ownership. In low- and middle-income countries, especially in Asia and Africa, it is not so.

It is important for consumer groups and industry to have a chance to comment on regulations before they are made. It is also important that all parties should be able to modify laws if they have scientific evidence to support a change.

Recommendation 5-2: In emerging economies, national regulatory authorities, regulated industry, and industry associations should engage in open and regular dialogue to exchange scientific and technical information before policies are written and after they are implemented. Starting in the next 3 to 5 years, these regulatory authorities should identify third parties, such as science academies, to convene the three pillars of a regulatory system—government, industry, and academia—in ongoing discussion to advance regulatory science, policy, and training.

The number of meetings among industry, academia, and government regulators in low- and middle-income countries will be one measure of this recommendation. Another important measure will be the policy outcomes of the meetings. However, in measuring the impact of open dialogue the process is as important, if not more important, than the outcome. Openness in involving all stakeholders and actively seeking neutral forums for discourse are the most important outcomes of this recommendation.

Communication and Transparency

Lack of communication and transparency are major gaps found within and between regulatory systems around the world (IOM, 2009; IUF, 2009). A lack of openness aggravates the problems, as does poor communication between industry and consumer groups. It is therefore not surprising that there are problems with both transparency and communication across borders. Regulatory systems in low- and middle-income countries have this problem, and similar communication gaps exist in the United States. However, the United States has public reporting requirements, external advisory boards, independent national association meetings, and study panels, such as those convened by the Institute of Medicine, that provide avenues for communication. This kind of open dialogue is essential for progress. These opportunities for open dialogue are often lacking in developing countries.

In low- and middle-income countries, the line between scientific and policy decisions is often blurred. Both often require political clearance at the highest government levels. This hampers efforts to promptly transmit the technical data crucial for assuring product safety. In some countries, so-called independent organizations act as go-betweens for government and industry, but in reality their independence is nominal. In other cases, the lack of suitable venues or personnel to transmit technical data, such as the testing requirements for a new regulation, holds back communication. This gap is especially evident as one goes from national to state and provincial authorities. This problem is complicated by the dearth of scientific staff at the more local levels. Similarly, the regulated industry has little ability to provide input into new regulations or get technical guidance on compliance. Academia can help bridge regulatory agencies and industry, but its involvement is generally minimal.

Avenues to More Effective Dialogue

There are examples in North America, Europe, and Australia where the three independent pillars of well functioning stringent regulatory systems (government, industry, and academia) are brought together to discuss issues of mutual concern (Australian Government, 2011; Global Harmonization Initiative, 2011; Health Canada, 2009; IOM, 2011). For example, the U.S. Department of Agriculture (USDA) and the United States Food and Drug Administration (FDA) worked with the Department of Homeland Security and the Federal Bureau of Investigation to jointly engage states and private industry in food defense (USDA, 2005). These partnerships lead to better protection of the food supply from farm to table.

These partnerships present a number of opportunities. First, stakeholders can discuss technical issues related to standard setting, testing, and approaches to implementation. Second, they provide a mechanism for information dissemination especially on adopting new regulations. Third, international experts could teach satellite courses to educate provincial or municipal staff on implementing regulations from the national regulatory authority. These recommendations are generally concerned with opportunities for training and training trainers, and training sessions are an excellent venue for open dialogue.

In emerging economies, existing regional bodies will be an important venue for communication among neighboring countries facing similar problems. The FDA could help facilitate such meetings by sending its overseas staff when appropriate opportunities arise.

Convening Three Pillars of a Regulatory System

Professional associations and academic institutions are often good places to bring together stakeholders for balanced and open dialogue on regulatory policy (ASM, 2011; IFT, 2011). Although such venues cannot and should not assume decision-making functions of government agencies, they do open lines of communication among regulators, sister agencies, academic experts, and multiple levels of regulated industry.

There are notable glimmers of improving communication in some places. In November 2011, the Indian food regulatory authority took public input from food industry associations in designing its product recall plan (FSSAI, 2011). Even in this case however, academia was notably uninvolved. This is a problem as gaps in basic and regulatory sciences prevent a regulatory authority from doing its job (Mattes et al., 2010).

Regulatory science is a new field (Gundersen, 2001). It is multi-disciplinary and includes elements of basic science, epidemiology, statistics, social science, business management, public policy, and communication. A field of such breadth needs instructors with practical experience. The emergence of such cross-cutting disciplines requires collaboration between universities, industry, and government. The first step to advance regulatory science in emerging economies is to bring these stakeholders together.

National Science Academies

As noted previously, a number of organizations have at various times convened government, industry, and academia on product safety. Science academies are uniquely positioned to serve in this area. Science academies have expertise to draw from among their members, who are elected by their peers. Election to a national academy is an honor. It is also a chance for elite scientists to serve their country, and it gives countries a trusted and independent advisory body. Science academies are, in many countries, a neutral space that can bring together stakeholders from various disciplines. Their focus on evidence-based decision making provides the neutral setting needed to bring together academia, government, and industry.

Public Health Forums

According to the Institute of Medicine's report on the *Future of Public Health*, "[p]ublic health is what we, as a society, do collectively to assure the conditions for people to be healthy" (IOM, 1988, p. 20). Public health agencies work at the intersection of science, government, business, and civil society. They oversee the implementation of health policies and regulations. However, state health agencies in many developing countries lack the infrastructure to carry out standard public health functions such as surveillance (Mok et al., 2010). The Bill and Melinda Gates Foundation funded the International Association of National Public Health Institutes in 2006 to build public health institutes in less developed countries (IANPHI, 2011b). A particular focus of its work has been on improving public health functions like disease surveillance, outbreak investigation and response, and operations research (IANPHI, 2011a).

The Association of Food and Drug Officials (AFDO), established in 1896, works toward public health safety and consumer protection in regulatory areas concerned with food, drugs, devices, cosmetics, and consumer products (AFDO, 2010). Along with promoting education and dialogue among government, industry, and consumers, AFDO also provides "guidance and training programs for regulatory officials and the regulated industry, to promote nationally and internationally uniform inspections, analyses, interpretations and investigations" (AFDO, 2010). Other international organizations such as the WHO, the Food and Agriculture Organization of the United Nations (FAO), and the World Trade Organization (WTO) have provided similar forums and support for discussions on food and medical product regulation (FAO/WHO, 2005; GIFSL, 2010; WHO, 2011; WTO, 2011). In addition, the International Biopharmaceutical Association brings together biopharmaceutical and clinical research institutions and organizations from different countries. All of these organizations could convene and educate students, possibly through their online discussion groups.

WORKING TOWARD SHARED INSPECTIONS

Sharing inspection reports is a first step to international regulatory harmonization. It is also a simple change that could reduce a great deal of waste; there is no need for American and European inspectors to duplicate each other's work, especially when a vast number of facilities go uninspected. Eventually, regulatory authorities in emerging economies would also be able to share inspections.

Recommendation 5-3: Countries with stringent regulatory agencies[3] should, within the next 18 months, convene a technical working group on sharing inspection reports with the longer-term goal of establishing a system for mutual recognition of inspection reports.

This recommendation can be measured by looking at the number of inspections the United States, Canada, Australia, New Zealand, Japan, and European Union countries share and the steps they take towards mutual recognition of inspections. The objectives of these working groups will depend on the relationship between the regulatory authorities and the baseline similarity of their systems.

In the longer term, that is, over the next decade, this recommendation will measured by monitoring the same involvement from emerging economies.

Collaboration Among National Regulatory Authorities

The FDA and other stringent regulatory authorities need to respond to globalization by formally recognizing their dependence on each other. No single regulatory agency can conduct the bulk of the world's food and drug facility inspections. The most technologically advanced regulatory agencies could coordinate on planning inspections and share the results of inspections (GAO, 2010). It is extremely complicated for the FDA to inspect the vast number of food producers and medical product manufacturers outside the United States. Among other things, the FDA's records on foreign manufacturers are often incomplete and inaccurate (GAO, 2008, 2011). All parties could vastly increase the accuracy and breadth of their information with relatively simple collaborations. In the longer term, including developing country regulatory authorities in these collaborations would be a valuable opportunity for sharing knowledge.

The International API Inspection Pilot Programme is an exceptionally promising collaboration among medicines regulatory authorities of the EU countries most active in active pharmaceutical ingredient (API) inspections (France, Germany, Ireland, Italy, and the United Kingdom), the Australian Therapeutic Goods Administration, and the FDA (EMA, 2011). Starting in 2008, all participating regulatory authorities shared their inspection plans using a common template (EMA, 2011). They also shared their retrospective data from 2005, identifying 85 duplicate inspections in three years (EMA, 2011). During the study, participating agencies developed an API facility master list that all agencies would use to plan future inspections and to share the results of each (EMA, 2011). They conducted nine joint inspections and have made a plan to coordinate and share their inspections in the future (EMA, 2011). This is an exemplary step towards efficient international cooperation.

The FDA and European Medicines Agency (EMA) have also worked together on sharing inspections for compliance with good clinical practice. The report on this pilot program

[3] By the ICH definition countries with stringent regulatory agencies include the United States, European Union member states, and Japan. For the purposes of their recommendations the committee includes ICH Observers and Associates: Australia, New Zealand, Norway, Iceland, Switzerland, and Canada, in this group.

concluded that sharing inspections is less time-consuming and more efficient than conducting separate inspections (EMA and FDA, 2011). It also stressed an unforeseen benefit of the pilot program: it allowed regulators to identify gaps in their inspection processes and fill them in (EMA and FDA, 2011). In joint reports, the FDA and EMA praised the pilot programs as efficient and valuable collaborations that have great promise for better future operations (EMA, 2011; EMA and FDA, 2011).

The FDA has confidentiality agreements with Health Canada, the Swiss Medic, Anvisa, and many other regulatory agencies abroad (FDA, 1973, 2003, 2010). A confidentiality agreement is the legal first step in sharing sensitive data, such as inspection reports.

The committee recommends that FDA, USDA, EMA, and other technologically advanced regulatory authorities do a similar pilot study on sharing inspections of farms and food producers. The Food Safety Modernization Act increased the number of overseas inspections required of the FDA to 600 in 2011, doubling every year after that until 2016 (FDA, 2011). Under such high demands, the agency and its counterpart agencies in developed countries need to share inspections. In a joint report, the PEW Health Group and the Center for Science in the Public Interest encouraged the FDA to accept inspection reports from trusted foreign governments with similar regulatory rigor (CSPI, 2011). Sharing inspection reports and conducting joint inspections increases efficiency and helps all parties see ways to improve their systems (NRC, 2011).

The continuation of the International API Inspection program is an invaluable step in the right direction towards better information sharing among regulatory agencies. The committee feels that the larger goals of the program could be well served by forming a standing technical working group on mutual recognition. In the next decade this working group could expand, assuming all confidentially agreements were met, to include low- and middle-income countries. The gradual inclusion of low- and middle-income countries in the working group would be an opportunity for regulators from these countries to learn more about international inspections and best practices. It would also allow them to see close-up how technically advanced regulatory agencies operate. This working group would likely have the unplanned secondary benefit of encouraging cross-fertilization of ideas. The WHO emphasizes a similar idea in the WHO Prequalification Program's guidelines on collaborative inspections. Participating in the WHO Prequalification Inspections is a learning experience for the inspectors nominated by their national regulatory authorities. It also eases the inspection burden on the national regulatory authority (WHO, 2010).

Information Sharing Challenges and Incentives

In order for regulatory agencies to share inspections and work towards mutual recognition, they need to first set up systems for collecting the same data. The API Inspection pilot gave great attention to the design of a common data collection template (EMA, 2011). In the early stages of their work, the regulatory agencies can streamline their data collection tools. The use of handheld computers could make the inspectors' job simpler and protect the reports from careless mistakes. Paper and pencil data collection systems are still shockingly common, however. The 2002 Bioterrorism Act has forced the American food industry and government agencies to use electronic data systems, but this is not so in other parts of the world, even in developed countries (Rosenberg, 2006). At the 2010 International Conference of Drug Regulatory Authorities, drug regulators' stressed their need for a protected electronic system that would allow them to safely share confidential information (ICDRA, 2010).

The committee realizes that one of the first main steps to sharing inspections is negotiating a system by which countries can share confidential information. While the different regulatory laws that govern the stringent regulatory authorities will make this challenging, it is possible to agree to a set of harmonized rules for making information confidential.

The committee also recognizes that, in the long run, in order to share inspection duties with other advanced regulatory authorities, the FDA will need to ask Congress to revise the terms of the inspections it mandates. Currently, FDA is legally obligated to inspect a certain number of foreign producers, but it would be more efficient for Congress to encourage inspection sharing with trusted nations. Other advanced regulatory authorities might have similar legal mandates. In the short term, all parties can increase their efficiency by planning inspections together so as to avoid duplicating work. Furthermore, the committee sees no legal barriers to joint inspections, which are useful for all parties and pave the way for future mutual recognition.

SHARING INSPECTION RESULTS VOLUNTARILY

As recommendation 5-3 describes, regulatory authorities should cooperate better in inspections and work towards mutual recognition. Government collaborations can only advance product safety so far, however. Manufacturers and producers have the most thorough knowledge of their supply chains; they need to share information as well.

Regulated industry has a wealth of information in its internal inspection reports. Once a manufacturer has identified a risk in its system, this knowledge could be made available to others in the industry as a way to avoid repeating the same problem. Industry associations such as the Pharmaceutical Research and Manufacturers Association, the Biotechnology Industry Organization, the Generic Pharmaceutical Association, the Medical Device Manufacturers Association, Food Industry Association Executives, the Grocery Manufacturers Association, and others could work towards making inspection and audit reports available to other association members.

Recommendation 5-4: Industry associations should, over the next 3 years, define an acceptable protocol for sharing of internal inspection results among their members. After agreeing on the methods, they should regularly share their results among their members.

The number of inspection results shared and number of associations working on voluntary sharing programs will be the best measures of this recommendation.

The committee recognizes that it will take food and medical product industry associations 3 years to define a trusted, nonthreatening way for their members to share internal inspection results. Once there is a system in place, the analysis of anonymous reports should be shared in newsletters on an ongoing basis.

Reluctance to Sharing Information

Industry is often reluctant to share its internal data and inspection reports with anyone. This reticence is appropriate: industries have a responsibility to their shareholders to protect proprietary information and avoid harming the brand with rumors. Furthermore, some internal audit reports identify problems, and if it became apparent that an executive had ignored warnings and released a product anyway, the company could face monumental negligence litigation. Economic incentives and limiting liability may encourage greater information sharing, though much depends upon the data that industry is asked to share.

Industry associations are well-positioned to work towards voluntary information sharing among their members. Associations have established relationships with their members, and member dues support their operations. They are also responsible for initiating collaborations between companies that advance their mutual goals. When sharing inspection reports, trust in confidentiality will be critical. This is why industry associations are the ideal leaders: they have established good relationships with their member companies and have an interest in protecting the industry from damaging rumors. A trusted industry association could serve as an information clearinghouse. Association staff could analyze blinded, de-identified data from across the supply chain and disseminate their results at meetings and in association newsletters.

The committee realizes that this raw data will not be accessible to the FDA or any regulatory agency, but it believes in the value of regulated industry sharing information and learning from formal analysis of a wide cross-section of data. Private sector supply chains, especially in the branded food industry, are often excellent. There is a need to draw on industry's knowledge of supply chain management. The conclusions that industry draws from analysis of de-identified inspection reports would be invaluable to government and academic stakeholders, as well as the industry and the suppliers.

It will not be possible to improve product safety without taking advantage of industry's expertise. As Chapter 3 explains, there is no tradition of collaboration between regulatory authorities, industry, and academia in most developing countries. The committee also sees much room for improvement in developed countries when it comes to sharing information and learning from the depth of experience in industry. Industry associations around the world can help fill this gap by sharing the lessons learned from aggregate inspection reports.

Examples of Collaboration

Although voluntary sharing of inspection results within industry is not common, there is precedents for such collaboration in both the food and pharmaceutical industries. The non-profit organization Rx-360 is an industry consortium that brings together regulators and pharmaceutical and supplier executives to improve security in the drug supply chain (Rx-360, 2009). Martin Van Trieste, the former president of Rx-360, described the collaborative's joint audit program in his 2011 Senate testimony (VanTrieste, 2011). This program grew out of a response to the 2008 heparin crisis and allows participating companies to share redacted audit reports via a common database (VanTrieste, 2011). In his testimony, Van Trieste also recommended that excipient and API brokers disclose to manufacturers the exact origin of all their products, something not currently required (VanTrieste, 2011).

Much as the Rx-360 consortium grew out of a response to the heparin crisis, the beef industry has responded to the virulent *E.coli* O157:H7 outbreaks with regular summits that include cattlemen, butchers, retailers, government, and academics (Cattlemen's Beef Board and National Cattlemen's Beef Association, 2003, 2009, 2010, 2011). In January 2003, summit participants developed a plan to control *E. coli* O157:H7 throughout the supply chain, emphasizing the need for "industry to maintain open communication and to share data regarding pre-harvest interventions and good management practices" (Cattlemen's Beef Board and National Cattlemen's Beef Association, 2003).

Clearly, industry stakeholders have an interest in sharing their best practices. Product recalls are costly and logistically complicated. Companies need to protect their brands. Sharing information across the supply chain can help them avoid product safety lapses and thereby strengthen their brands.

STRENGTHENING SURVEILLANCE SYSTEMS

Surveillance is one of the main responsibilities of food and medical products regulatory authorities, and, as Chapter 3 describes, it is a major gap in regulatory systems in emerging economies. Trade and international travel make this a problem for people all over the world. Foodborne pathogens can spread quickly through the supply chain. Similarly, drug adverse events, often a signal of an adulteration, threaten disparate populations.

USAID, FDA, CDC, EMA, and the WHO Prequalification Programme all have technical depth and training capabilities in surveillance. The committee aims to mobilize their expertise to support surveillance systems in low- and middle-income countries. The committee recognizes that regulatory agencies do not generally have the budget or mandate to support intensive capacity building projects. Therefore other agencies and other organizations will need to support surveillance as well.

Recommendation 5-5: Starting in the next 5 years USAID, FDA, CDC, and USDA should provide (both directly and through WHO and FAO) technical support for strengthening surveillance systems in developing countries. This technical support could include development and sharing of surveillance tools, protocols for foodborne disease surveillance and post market surveillance of medical products, and training of national regulatory authority staff and national experts.

The most direct measure of this recommendation will be the number of programs these agencies initiate to improve foodborne disease and post-market surveillance systems in developing countries. Over time, a change in the number of surveillance staff at regulatory agencies in low- and middle-income countries will be another measure of this recommendation.

In addition to measuring these process indicators, the functioning of the surveillance tools developed will all be measured using sensitivity and specificity criteria specific to the tool. The scientists developing these tools will need to articulate the minimum threshold at which the tool is functioning properly.

Building a cadre of trained epidemiologists will take time. This important step of strengthening surveillance systems may take 10 years or longer to develop. In the next 3 years, USAID, FDA, CDC, and USDA can work with their host country counterparts to develop and strengthen manageable systems for post-market surveillance of medical products. Developing a foodborne disease surveillance system will require improvements in laboratory infrastructure and will therefore take longer, but the committee believes meaningful improvements, such as the expansion of the CDC PulseNet program, can begin in the next 5 years.

Surveillance Tools

The most frequent approach to post-market surveillance of medical products in developing countries is spontaneous or passive reporting by health workers. Spontaneous reporting systems have important limitations. Because they rely on overworked doctors and nurses or, even worse, on patient initiative, spontaneous reporting is synonymous with underreporting. Spontaneous reporting systems can generate useful data and give early signals of medical product safety problems, but in the poorest countries even passive reporting systems are not functional (Kuemmerle et al., 2011).

Active surveillance complements spontaneous reporting systems. Active surveillance involves methodically searching for exposures of interest or adverse events at sentinel surveillance sites. These sites, sometimes hospitals or clinics, collect enough data to allow analysts to calculate event rates with an accurate denominator. Sentinel surveillance sites at hospitals and health centers in developing countries need to be improved. These improvements should accompany the development of active surveillance when necessary. For example, drug regulators can engage active surveillance systems after passive event reporting or sentinel sites identify a signal. The WHO and Global Fund have proposed the essential elements of a national pharmacovigilance system (Xueref, 2010). Trainers should work to align their technical support to these systems.

The CDC's Global Disease Detection network builds capacity for active surveillance in developing countries. This researcher in Kibera, Kenya uses a handheld computer to track disease symptoms.
© 2008 Dana Pitts, Courtesy of Photoshare.

Independent laboratories are also essential for functional surveillance systems. Food safety surveillance in particular depends on laboratories for molecular subtyping of pathogens. This is challenging in developing countries, and the committee sees expanding laboratory capacity as a key piece of the technical support U.S. and international organizations should give. The CDC's PulseNet program has given valuable technical support in developing clinical, reference, and food safety laboratories in Asia and Latin America (Swaminathan et al., 2006). The committee encourages this expansion of PulseNet over the next five years and believes every part of the world could benefit from the PulseNet system.

Fortunately, information technology has created a wealth of surveillance tools more easily adapted to middle-income countries. These methods are often described as event-based. That is, they rely on patterns of events: Google searches on symptom clusters, news reports, and discussion threads on blogs and in internet chat rooms. Figure 5-1 describes how these events can be alerts of an epidemic that is still in the early stages. Twitter and other internet-based surveillance tools have been useful in tracking the incidence of dengue fever in Brazil (Gomide et al., 2011). In the poorest countries, the lack of internet access will prevent the reliable use of internet-based surveillance, but the conceptually similar mobile phone surveillance shows promise (Breiman et al., 2008). The CDC's BioSense system is an example of a surveillance tool that uses internet technology to create an online surveillance community (Box 5-1).

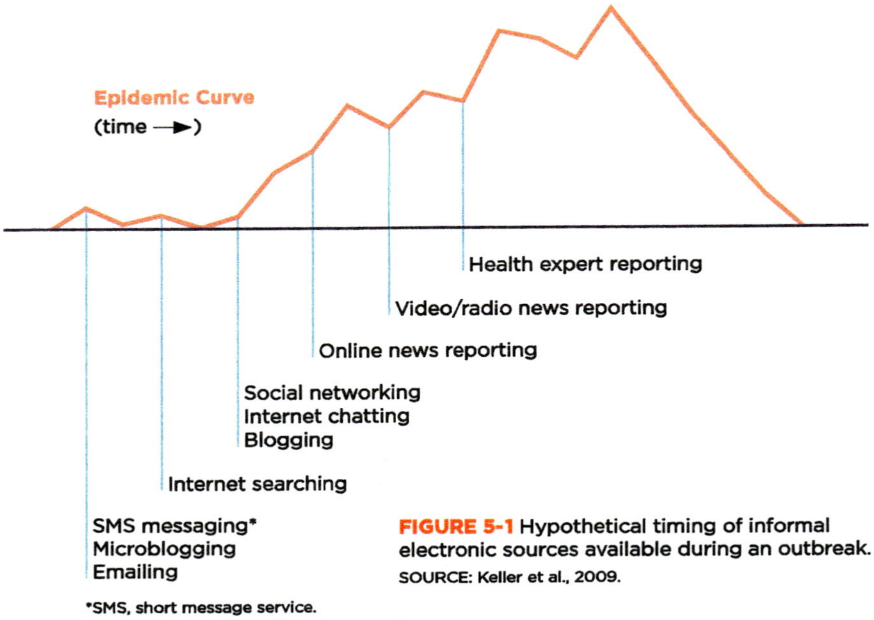

FIGURE 5-1 Hypothetical timing of informal electronic sources available during an outbreak.
SOURCE: Keller et al., 2009.

BOX 5-1
The BioSense Redesign

Following the anthrax attacks of 2001, the U.S. government recognized the need for a more informed and better equipped public health sector to deal with potential and actual bioterrorism threats (SEMP, 2008). In 2002, Congress passed the Public Health Security and Bioterrorism Preparedness and Response Act (FDA, 2002). This act mandated the formation of BioSense, a program housed in the CDC. BioSense is a data collection and analysis program that helps public health officials throughout the U.S. plan for, detect, and respond to disease outbreaks that may be related to bioterrorism. BioSense is used for both prevention and response, making it a multi-faceted tool for the preservation and advancement of national health (CDC, 2012).

After operating for several years as a program focused primarily on bioterror threat detection, in 2010 the CDC began redesigning BioSense to better meet the needs of the public health sector (CDC, 2012). Some users objected to BioSense's narrow focus and insufficient integration with other, similar programs already in use (RTI International, 2011). Guided by the suggestions of public health officials at municipal, state, and national levels, the CDC restructured BioSense to respond to a wider range of health threats. This revamped program, BioSense 2.0, facilitates collaboration within and between the levels of the public health infrastructure, and provides users with the information, analysis, and tools they need to best respond to health threats (BioSense Redesign, 2011; CDC, 2012). In essence, BioSense 2.0 creates a "public health surveillance community" comprised of public health professionals across disciplines, borders, and organizations (BioSense Redesign, 2011). The redesign project will conclude in June 2013 (RTI International, 2011).

The CDC solicited input from a range of stakeholders during the BioSense redesign. A key element of this mission was the BioSense Redesign Collaboration Site, a website that solicited suggestions and asked for feedback on the project's process (CDC, 2012). Through the website, all stakeholders were involved in the work, and their needs were incorporated into the BioSense revisions (RTI International, 2011).

Foodborne disease lends itself to event-based surveillance. The Global Public Health Information Network relies on information from all pertinent news streams. This web-mining surveillance system was instrumental in containing SARS (Brownstein et al., 2009; Keller et al., 2009). Box 5-2 describes how the state of North Carolina uses an early warning system that integrates many types of signals for better food safety. The committee sees web-mining and event-based surveillance as potentially valuable tools for developing country regulators and believes all technical support should draw on this valuable new technology.

The committee believes that Internet-based surveillance tools might be useful in emerging economies with reasonably sophisticated technology infrastructures, such as China, India, Brazil, South Africa, Mexico, and Thailand. In less developed countries, mobile phone technology might be used to the same end: building a novel foodborne disease and drug post-market surveillance system.

BOX 5-2
North Carolina Foodborne Events Data Integration and Analysis Tool

Researchers from the University of North Carolina's Center for Logistics and Digital Strategy at the Kenan-Flagler Business School and the North Carolina Center for Public Health Preparedness in the Gillings School of Global Public Health have developed the *North Carolina Foodborne Events Data Integration and Analysis* (NCFEDA) tool to bridge gaps North Carolina's food safety system (Greis et al., 2011).

The public and private sectors and consumers must all work together for food safety. There are information delays in a standard food surveillance system that can allow months to pass between the time of suspected contamination and the removal of affected products from grocery shelves. New, more timely, and more informative data sources can reduce the latent time between contamination and removal. NCFEDA reduces these latencies by making real-time information available to public health officials—from consumer complaints and emergency hospital rooms visits to social media and FDA recall information—as well as private sector data (Greis et al., 2011).

Public health officials in North Carolina collaborated with Kenan-Flager School faculty in designing the NCFEDA tool. The tool integrates four essential capabilities that contribute to improved situational awareness. First, it integrates data from many different types of signals, such as consumer complaints and emergency room visits. It also relies on analytical tools that help make connections across these signals to better recognize disease or contamination patterns. The tool includes a visualization piece that allows mapping and other graphic data display. Finally, the tool works in real-time; all stakeholders work together on a coordinated response (Greis et al., 2011).

New information systems like NCFEDA can help assure better food safety and minimize the impact of food contamination events—especially for products that originate abroad. NCFEDA is a first step toward integrating a diverse set of stakeholder across North Carolina food safety systems. NCFEDA aligns with current national strategic plans for food safety, such as those outlined in the Food Safety Modernization Act. Other states and countries can use this system as a model.

Surveillance Experts

Web-mining is a promising piece of surveillance development in low- and middle-income countries, but it is not the only remedy the committee suggests. In an interview with *Nature*, the head of animal health at the French food safety agency cautioned against seeing internet-based surveillance systems as an alternative to building a cadre of local epidemiologists (Butler, 2006). In the same article, Peter Roeder, a consultant with the FAO, explained, "No amount of setting international guidelines and publishing global action plans is going to help when you have an organization within the country that doesn't know what to do" (Butler, 2006, p. 6). The committee agrees that training in-country staff in epidemiology and modern surveillance methods should be central to any and all surveillance programs. Similarly, building modern surveillance systems will include building a culture of reporting adverse effects among health workers and advertising the proper pathways for reporting.

CONCLUSIONS

The committee's strategy for building regulatory systems in developing countries emphasizes international cooperation. The unified world market has united countries in many positive ways, but has also introduced new liabilities. No country's regulatory authority can vouch for the safety of all foods and medical products in its market. The committee identified five areas where stakeholders around the world could act to improve food and medical product safety.

First, the development banks, regional economic communities, and public health institutes should ensure that scientists from the least developed countries are better prepared to participate in international standard setting. The G20 is also an excellent forum to discuss how to increase investments in regulatory systems. The United States and other G20 members should support Mexico, the 2012 G20 host, in sponsoring a global initiative on building food and medical product regulatory systems. In the next three to five years, increased investment in strengthening regulatory systems capacity should be explicitly tracked at international organizations.

The committee was struck by the isolation that many developing country regulators work in. They lack the involved support of industry and academia. National regulatory authorities in emerging economies should work to change this in the next 3 to 5 years and foster an open discussion on science and policy with all stakeholders. To this end, they may need to ask their national science academies to convene a stakeholder meeting.

More open communication about policy will benefit all parties, but the changes should not stop there. Stringent regulatory authorities should immediately work toward sharing inspection reports; they should also coordinate their inspections in emerging economies and conduct joint inspections when possible. This collaboration will encourage cross-fertilization of ideas and, more importantly, will prevent duplicating inspections, something nobody can afford. In the next decade, they could work towards a system of mutual recognition of inspection reports, a system developing countries might also join. Industry also has a wealth of information in its internal inspection reports. In the next 3 years, industry associations should develop ways to share this information that are acceptable to their members.

Finally, U.S. agencies and multilaterals with appropriate expertise should support surveillance systems in developing countries. Without reliable data on post-market surveillance of medical products and foodborne disease, risk assessment is meaningless, and risk assessment is the cornerstone of any modern regulatory agency. In the next 3 years, it will be possible to develop a system for the post-market surveillance of medical products, and the expansion of CDC's PulseNet program to more developing countries can start in 5 years. Over the next decade, the training of a cadre of developing-country epidemiologists can complement this surveillance development.

REFERENCES

ADB. 2009. *Viet Nam's drive to improve food safety receives $95M boost from ADB.* http://beta.adb.org/news/viet-nams-drive-improve-food-safety-receives-95m-boost-adb (accessed November 20, 2011).

AFDO. 2010. *The AFDO mission.* http://www.afdo.org/afdo/MissionStatement.cfm (accessed November 22, 2011).

ASM. 2011. ICAAC final program. *51st Interscience Conference on Antimicrobial Agents and Chemotherapy.*

Australian Government. 2011. *International Medical Device Regulators' Forum (IMDRF).* http://www.tga.gov.au/about/international-imdrf-111105.htm (accessed November 22, 2011).

BioSense Redesign. 2011. *BioSense redesign fact sheet.* https://sites.google.com/site/biosenseredesign/file-cabinet (accessed February 9, 2012).

Breiman, R. F., M. K. Njenga, S. Cleaveland, S. Sharif, M. Mbabu, and L. King. 2008. Lessons from the 2006-2007 Rift Valley fever outbreak in East Africa: Implications for prevention of emerging infectious diseases. *Future Virology* 3(5):411-417.

Brownstein, J. S., C. C. Freifeld, and L. C. Madoff. 2009. Digital disease detection — harnessing the web for public health surveillance. *New England Journal of Medicine* 360(21):2153-2157.

Butler, D. 2006. Disease surveillance needs a revolution. *Nature* 440(7080):6-7.

Cattlemen's Beef Board and National Cattlemen's Beef Association. 2003. *E.Coli O157:H7 solutions: The farm to table continuum (executive summary).* San Antonio, TX: Beef Industry E.coli Summit Meeting.

———. 2009. Beef industry safety summit: Executive summary. Paper read at Beef Industry Safety Summit, March 4-6, San Diego, California.

———. 2010. 2010 beef industry safety summit: Executive summary. Paper read at 2010 Beef Industry Safety Summit, March 3-5, Dallas, TX.

———. 2011. 2011 beef safety summit executive summary. Paper read at Beef Safety Summit, March 2-4, Dallas, TX.

CDC. 2012. *BioSense.* http://www.cdc.gov/biosense/ (accessed February 9, 2012).

CSPI, P. a. 2011. *Focus on: Food import safety.* Pew Health Group and the Center for Science in the Public Interest.

Drezner, D. W. 2007. *All politics is global: Explaining international regulatory regimes.* Princeton, NJ: Princeton University Press.

EMA. 2011. *Final report on the international API inspection pilot programme.* London: European Medicines Agency, Australian Government, and the Food and Drug Administration.

EMA, and FDA. 2011. *Report on the pilot EMA-FDA GCP initiative: September 2009-March 2011.* London.

Enneking, U. 2004. Willingness-to-pay for safety improvements in the German meat sector: The case of the Q&S label. *European Review of Agricultural Economics* 31(2):205-223.

FAO/WHO. 2005 December 6-9. *Importance of stakeholder collaboration in Canada's food safety system.* Paper presented at FAO/WHO Regional Conference on Food Safety for the Americas and the Caribbean, San Jose, Costa Rica.

FDA. 1973. *FDA - Canadian Department of National Health and Welfare agreement of cooperation between the Canadian Department of National Health and Welfare and the Food and Drug Administration.*

———. 2002. *Regulatory information: Bioterrorism Act of 2002.* http://www.fda.gov/regulatoryinformation/legislation/ucm148797.htm (accessed February 16, 2012).

———. 2003. *Confidentiality commitment statement of legal authortity and commitment from Swissmedic not to publicly disclose non-public information shared by the United States Food and Drug Administration.*

———. 2010. *Statement of authority and confidentiality commitment from the United States Food and Drug Administration not to publicly disclose non-public information shared by the Agência Nacional de Vigilância Sanitária of Brazil.*

———. 2011. *Pathway to global product safety and quality.* Washington, DC: U.S. Food and Drug Administration.

FSSAI. 2011. *Product recall pilot by FSSAI.* http://www.fssai.gov.in/Product_Recall.aspx (accessed December 15, 2011).

G20. 2010 November 11-12. *G20 Seoul development consensus for shared growth (annex 1).* Paper presented at The G20 Seoul Summit, Seoul, Korea.

———. 2011. *Members.* http://www.g20.org/en/g20/members (accessed February 8, 2012).

GAO. 2008. *Drug safety: Preliminary findings suggest recent FDA initiatives have potential, but do not fully address weaknesses in its foreign drug inspection program.* GAO-08-701T.

———. 2010. *Drug safety: FDA has conducted more foreign inspections and begun to improve its information on foreign establishements but more progress is needed.* GAO-10-961.

———. 2011. *Drug safety: FDA faces challenges overseeing the foreign drug manufacturing supply chain.* GAO-11-936T.

GIFSL. 2010. *International food safety administration programme for senior officials (IFSA).* http://foodsystemsleadership.org/Programs/program.aspx?proID=2 (accessed November 22, 2011).

Global Harmonization Initiative. 2011. *About GHI.* http://www.globalharmonization.net/background (accessed November 22, 2011).

Goetz, G. 2011. *World food safety fund launched at APEC.* http://www.foodsafetynews.com/2011/11/world-food-safety-fund-launched/ (accessed November 15, 2011).

Gomide, J., A. Veloso, W. Meira, F. Benuvenuto, V. Almeida, F. Ferraz, and M. Teixeira. 2011. Dengue surveillance based on a computational model of spatio-temporal locality of Twitter. *Proceedings of the ACM WebSci'11*:1-8.

Greis, N. P., M. Nogueira, P. MacDonald, and R. Wilfert. 2011. *NCFEDA north carolina foodborne events data integration and analysis tool: A new informatics tool for food safety in north carolina.* Research Triangle Park, North Carolina: Prepared by RTI International–Institute for Homeland Security Solutions under contract HSHQDC-08-C-00100.

Gundersen, L. E. 2001. Training needs in regulatory science for the biopharmaceutical industry. *Nature Biotechnology* 19(12):1187-1188.

Health Canada. 2009. *Report on the Health Canada/US-FDA and industry BPA value chain meeting.* http://www.hc-sc.gc.ca/fn-an/securit/packag-emball/bpa/bpa_meet-reunion_20090130-eng.php (accessed November 22, 2011).

Henson, S. 2003. *Food safety issues in international trade.* Washington, DC: International Food Policy Research.

Henson, S., and S. Jaffee. 2008. Understanding developing country strategic responses to the enhancement of food safety standards. *World Economy* 31(4):548-568.

Horton, L. R., and E. Wright. 2008. *Reconciling food safety with import faciliation objectives: Helping developing country producers meet U.S. And EU food requirements through transatlantic cooperation.* Washington, D.C.: International Food and Agricultural Trade Policy Council.

IANPHI. 2011a. *Long-term development projects: Saving lives through NPHIs.*

———. 2011b. *Who we are.* http://www.ianphi.org/who-we-are/ (accessed December 14, 2011).

ICDRA. 2010 Novemer 30-December 3. *14 ICDRA recommendations.* Paper presented at the Fourteenth International Conference of Drug Regulatory Authorities, Singapore.

IFT. 2011. *IFT 12: Annual meeting and food expo.* http://www.am-fe.ift.org/cms/ (accessed November 21, 2011).

IOM. 1988. *The future of public health.* Washington, DC: National Academy Press.

———. 2011. *Food forum.* http://www.iom.edu/Activities/Nutrition/FoodForum.aspx (accessed November 22, 2011).

———. 2009. *Managing food safety practices from farm to table: Workshop summary.* Washington, DC: The National Academies Press.

IUF. 2009. *Melamine poisoning and the death penalty in China: Scapegoats punished to avoid the real scandal* http://asianfoodworker.net/?p=409 (accessed November 22, 2011).

Keller, M., M. Blench, H. Tolentino, C. C. Freifeld, K. D. Mandl, A. Mawudeku, G. Eysenbach, and J. S. Brownstein. 2009. Use of unstructured event-based reports for global infectious disease surveillance. *Emerging Infectious Diseases* 15(5):689-695.

Kharas, H. 2011. *The g-20's development agenda.* Washington, DC: The Brookings Institute.

Kuemmerle, A., A. Dodoo, S. Olsson, J. Van Erps, C. Burri, and P. Lalvani. 2011. Assessment of global reporting of adverse drug reactions for anti-malarials, including artemisinin-based combination therapy, to the WHO programme for international drug monitoring. *Malaria Journal* 10(1):57.

Lusk, J. L., J. Roosen, and J. A. Fox. 2003. Demand for beef from cattle administered growth hormones or fed genetically modified corn: A comparison of consumers in France, Germany, the United Kingdom, and the United States. *American Journal of Agricultural Economics* 85(1):16-29.

Maertens, M., and J. Swinnen. 2009. Food standards, trade and development. *Review of Business and Economics* LIV(3):313-326.

Maskus, K. E., T. Otsuki, and J. S. Wilson. 2005. *The cost of compliance with product standards for firms in developing countries: An econometric study.* Washington, DC: World Bank.

Mattes, W. B., E. G. Walker, E. Abadie, F. D. Sistare, J. Vonderscher, J. Woodcock, and R. L. Woosley. 2010. Research at the interface of industry, academia and regulatory science. *Nature Biotechnology* 28(5):432-433.

Mok, E. A., L. O. Gostin, M. D. Gupta, and M. Levin. 2010. Implementing public health regulations in developing countries: Lessons from the OECD countries. *Journal of Law, Medicine and Ethics* 38(3):508-519.

Morehouse, J., and M. Moriarty. 2007. *Food safety in China: What it means for global companies.* A.T. Kearney.

Narrod, C., D. Roy, J. Okello, B. Avendaño, K. Rich, and A. Thorat. 2009. Public-private partnerships and collective action in high value fruit and vegetable supply chains. *Food Policy* 34(1):8-15.

NRC. 2011. *The potential consequences of public release of food safety and inspection service establishment-specific data* Washington, DC: The National Academy Press.

Nuthall, K. 2005. Columbia: World Bank to make food production more competitive. *Just Food*, July 11.

Okello, J. J., C. Narrod, and D. Roy. 2007. *Food safety requirements in African green bean exports and their impact on small farmers.* Washington, DC: International Food Policy and Research Institute.

Roberts, D., and T. Josling. 2011. *Tracking the implementation of internationally agreed standards in food and agricultural production.* International Food and Agricultural Trade Policy Council.

Rosenberg, S. 2006. *Meeting the 2005 requirements for the Bioterrorism Act.* Voluntary Interindustry Commerce Solutions.

RTI International. 2011. *BioSense strategic plan.* https://sites.google.com/site/biosenseredesign/file-cabinet (accessed February 9, 2012).

Rx-360. 2009. *About Rx-360.* http://www.rx-360.org/AboutRx360/tabid/55/Default.aspx (accessed November 22, 2011).

SEMP. 2008. *CDC's BioSense biosurveillance program: Performance update.* http://www.semp.us/publications/biot_reader.php?BiotID=570 (accessed February 9, 2012).

Swaminathan, B., P. Gerner-Smidt, L.-K. NG, S. Lukinmaa, K.-M. Kam, S. Rolando, E. P. Gutierrez, and N. Binsztein. 2006. Building PulseNet international: An interconnected system of laboratory networks to faciliatate timely public health recognition and response to foodborne disesase outbreaks and emerging foodborne diseases. *Foodborne Pathogens and Disease* 3(1):36-50.

Unnevehr, L., L. Haddad, and C. Delgado. 2003. *Food safety policy issues for developing countries.* Washington, DC: International Food Policy Research Institute.

USDA. 2005. *USDA, FDA, DHS and FBI join states and private inudstry to protect nation's food and agriculture supply from agroterrorism.* http://www.usda.gov/wps/portal/usda/usdahome?contentidonly=true&contentid=2005/07/0279.xml (accessed November 22, 2011).

VanTrieste, M. 2011. *Testimony before the Senate Health, Education, Labor, and Pensions Committee: Securing the pharmaceutical supply chain.* Washington, DC.

WHO. 2010. *Guidance: Collaborative procedure between World Health Organization Prequalification of Medicines Programme (WHO-PQ) and selected National Medicines Regulatory Authorities (NMRAs) in inspection activities.* Geneva, Switzerland.

———. 2011. *International conference of drug regulatory authorities.* http://www.who.int/medicines/areas/quality_safety/regulation_legislation/icdra/en/index.html (accessed October 5, 2011).

World Bank. 2005. *Food safety and agricultural health standards: Challenges and opportunities for developing country exports.* Washington, DC: The World Bank.

———. 2006. *China's compliance with food safety requirements for fruits and vegetables: Promoting food safety, competitiveness, and poverty reduction.* Washington, DC.

———. 2010. *World Bank to help improve food safety in China.* http://www.worldbank.org/en/news/2010/05/13/world-bank-help-improve-food-safety-china (accessed November 21, 2011).

WTO. 2011. *WTO public forum 2011: Topics for discussion.* Geneva, Switzerland.

Xueref, S. 2010 June 11. *Towards a global strategy on pharmacovigilance*. Paper presented at Global Surveillance of Anitretroviral Drug Safety meeting, Washington, DC.

6

Domestic Action

In its *Pathway to Product Safety* the U.S. Food and Drug Administration (FDA) emphasizes the importance of operating as a "truly global agency fully prepared for a regulatory environment in which product safety and quality know no borders" (FDA, 2011b, p.3). To this end, the agency must bridge the many gaps within regulatory systems abroad. In this chapter, the committee recommends actions the FDA and other U.S. government agencies can take to increase the efficiency of their own operations while improving the systems of their counterpart agencies abroad.

USING RISK AS A GUIDING PRINCIPLE

Chapter 4 describes the committee's strategy in forming its recommendations, and emphasizes that the FDA should let risk guide its efforts to build food and medical product regulatory systems abroad. In keeping with its focus on risk, the committee recommends that the FDA divide its limited resources according to risk. An understanding of risk will allow FDA to choose what problems are their highest priorities.

There are tradeoffs implicit in all decision making. Especially in capacity building, managers need to choose between different risks effecting different populations. When working across many countries, choosing to work with one population means less attention for others. Through the use of an enterprise risk management framework, the FDA can determine which risks are the most serious and have an objective way to rank its priorities.

Recommendation 6-1: FDA should use enterprise risk management[1] to inform their inspection, training, regulatory cooperation, and surveillance efforts. Enterprise risk management should apply to the agency's entire operation, and it should incorporate a number of set criteria such as country of manufacture or production, volume and type of product, facility inspection history, and trends or data shared from other regulatory authorities.

The FDA's implementation of an enterprise risk management system will be the best measure of this recommendation. The FDA's allocation of resources in a way that reflects decisions grounded in enterprise risk management will also be a measure of this recommendation. The FDA will also have to select what statistics best measure the impact of its inspections, trainings, and surveillance efforts. Choosing what metrics to monitor most closely will be part of the assessment. The timetable on which the FDA collects this data is up to the agency's management, but it should be frequent, perhaps every quarter, but at least every 6 months.

Should the results of an enterprise risk management analysis suggest full reorganization of the FDA, such a process would take time. In order to work towards this change promptly, the

---

[1] Enterprise risk management is a discipline by which an organization "assesses, controls, exploits, finances, and monitors risks from all sources for the purpose of increasing the organization's short- and long-term value to its stakeholders" (Casualty Actuarial Society-Enterprise Risk Management Committee, 2003, p.8).

FDA needs conduct enterprise-wide risk assessment, analysis, and evaluation. If its results suggest an inefficient or unscientific allocation of resources in the agency's current operations, as one expects they will, FDA will need, at that time, to lobby Congress for permission to revise their operations.

The agency has more freedom in running their capacity building programs. Therefore, an enterprise risk management assessment, analysis, and evaluation can take be used to reorganize international programs in the next 3 to 5 years.

Enterprise-wide Risk Management

Multinational food and medical product companies have been using enterprise risk management for some time (see Box 6-1). Even the most profitable business cannot afford to monitor every transaction on its supply chain with the same diligence. Instead, multinational companies develop a hierarchy of risk and devote resources into the highest risks in the hierarchy. These companies may have a broader data set to inform their estimates than the FDA would have. Nevertheless, the FDA has to work with the data available. Over time the agency may develop data sharing relationships with its counterpart agencies abroad. FDA may also want to collaborate to develop its own risk assessment tool.

A number of organizations have supported a risk-based approach to food and medical product regulatory strategy. The Pew Health Group encouraged using risk to guide inspections (Pew Health Group, 2011), as have industry spokespeople (Vijay, 2011). The committee's recommendation is also consistent with the 2010 Institute of Medicine report *Enhancing Food Safety* that argued for consistency in applying a risk based food safety system (IOM, 2010).

BOX 6-1
Enterprise Risk Management

Risk is the potential any action or inaction has to result in an undesirable outcome. The concept of enterprise risk management comes from the financial services industry, but has been adapted for use in a variety of businesses, as well as in running governments and universities. The Committee of Sponsoring Organizations of the Treadway Commission defined Enterprise Risk Management as, "a process, effected by an entity's board of directors, management and other personnel, applied in strategy setting and across the enterprise, designed to identify potential events that may affect the entity, and manage risk to be within its risk appetite, to provide reasonable assurance regarding the achievement of entity objectives" (COSO, 2004, p.2).

The principles of enterprise risk management allow any type of organization to assess areas where it has exposure to harm and evaluate the extent of the danger. Assessing mitigation strategies is an important part of enterprise risk management, as financial and administrative planning against the organization's risk profile. The advantage of an enterprise-wide risk management assessment (as opposed to a functional or discipline based assessment) is that the organization's management gains a framework that presents the connected relationships between decisions and the allows them to integrate their responses to multiple threats (COSO, 2004). The use of enterprise risk management can guide staffing and training decisions. Over time, the use of enterprise risk management can help the organization transition from a culture of responding to crises when they happen to predicting and preventing them (Protiviti Inc., 2006).

In understanding the committee's emphasis on enterprise risk management it is important to consider that this is a way to manage the agency's *enterprise*. That is to say, a way to manage everything the agency does. Enterprise risk management is a strategic perspective to set priorities for the agency, not a tactical perspective applied to any sub-function of the enterprise, such as food safety or medical device safety. Many of the systematic steps in risk management at the enterprise level and at the subordinate levels can be described in similar terms. At the level of the organization's leadership, concerns over specific product lines or countries need to be reconciled with the entire risk and opportunity profile the FDA needs to address. Food, drug, vaccine, and medical device safety must be reconciled with each other and with other FDA responsibilities. Enterprise risk management can reconcile an array of risks at the agency level. The goal is for the FDA to optimally balance its limited resources with the full array of risks the agency needs to control.

This committee recommends an enterprise-wide risk assessment be used to inform FDA's capacity building projects and all its routine work. An enterprise-wide assessment will help the FDA allocate its staffing, trainings, and operations to the highest risk, highest priority activities, not just the inspections. The FDA has, for some time, been working to base inspections on a risk assessment paradigm. In 2007 the FDA was already using a risk-based process to rank foreign manufactures according to the urgency of the need for inspection (GAO, 2007). In a speech to the Partnership for Safe Medicines, the FDA commissioner explained that the agency has systematically ranked more than 1,000 active pharmaceutical ingredients according to respective risk of economically–motivated adulteration (Hamburg, 2010). Clearly, the FDA has a strong foundation on which to build its enterprise risk management system. Its use of risk to guide foreign inspections is exemplary. The challenge to the agency now is to persuade others that it can better protect consumers if it allocates more of its resources, not just inspections, based on modern risk management.

The use of enterprise risk management will be especially valuable to the FDA given poor economy and fiscal austerity. The agency has been underfunded for years. The fiscal year 2010 budget was relatively generous to FDA. This, combined with modest increases in fiscal years 2008 and 2009, brought the agency's budget back to 1994 levels (see Figure 6-1) (McCain, 2011). At the same time, the agency's responsibilities have increased dramatically. The increasing number of foreign food facility inspections demanded by the Food Safety Modernization Act (about 19,200 by 2016) cannot be reasonably managed by an agency that, according to a 2007 GAO report, operates on about one-seventh of its required budget (GAO, 2007; McCain, 2011). The committee believes that enterprise risk management will help the FDA triage its funding which, especially during the 2012 election cycle will likely be, "hijacked and delayed by political maneuvering" (Semeniuk, 2011).

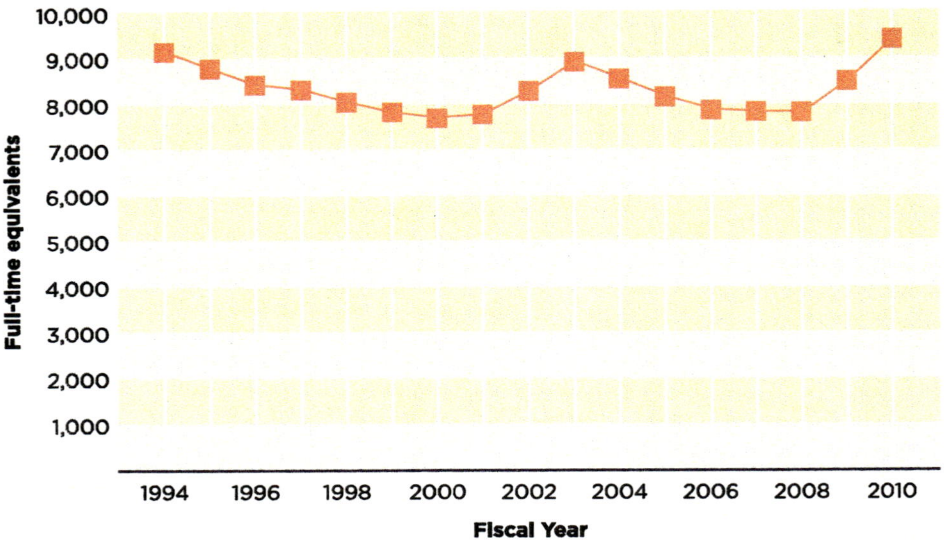

FIGURE 6-1 Full-time equivalents supported by congressional appropriations, from fiscal year 1994 to fiscal year 2010.
SOURCE: McCain, 2011.

Implementing Enterprise Risk Management at the FDA

The committee recognizes that implementing an enterprise-wide risk management program is challenging for any large organization. Fortunately, the International Organization of Standardization and other enterprise risk management experts publish guidance on implementing enterprise risk management strategies (COSO, 2004; ISO, 2009; Protiviti Inc., 2006). These sources all emphasize that the risk management framework is different for every organization. The committee agrees; this report does not dictate what the FDA's strategy will be. Such a level of prescription would be inappropriate and impossible: it would require analysis of the agency's internal data and consideration of internal contextual factors that expert committees have no knowledge of. Instead of dictating the agency's plan, the committee recommends that the FDA undertake an enterprise-wide risk assessment in keeping with the agency's objectives, and the Department of Health and Human Services' (HHS') goals as explained in their *Global Health Strategy* (HHS, 2011). The *Global Health Strategy* provides a framework in which to evaluate all the FDA's activities and consider their risks. The department's goals are protecting the health of Americans through global health action; advancing American interests in diplomacy, development and security though global health action; and leading in science, policy, and programs that advance global health (HHS, 2011). The FDA's enterprise risk assessment will need to consider these goals, and identify where the agency's biggest risks are in relation to meeting them.

The FDA's risk management framework will define the processes, staffing, timelines and budgeting the agency needs to apply to manage its risks. First, the agency will undertake a thorough risk assessment. This will include identifying the risks the agency faces and evaluating its response options. In this phase the agency will need to define how risks will be measured and when, and also how it will determine the level of the risks identified (ISO, 2009). Input from all stakeholders will be important to this process, especially as the agency tries to determine if there are likely combinations of risk (ISO, 2009). The framework will mandate the schedule on which the agency revisits its priorities to keep pace with changing risks.

The next step will be a risk analysis that accounts for the sources and causes of risk as well as their consequences and likelihood of reoccurring. The risk analysis step may include analyzing internal data and running simulations of different crises. The last step is risk evaluation which analyzes the identified risks against pre-determined criteria to guide decisions. In risk evaluation, the FDA will consider the costs, effort, and benefits of all actions. A well-executed risk evaluation will provide the FDA's leaders with the information they need to develop their capacity-building priorities.

Implementation in the Short-Term Should Focus on FDA Activities Outside the United States

There are many restrictions on the FDA's authority to allocate its resources domestically. Therefore, especially in the next three to five years, the committee sees promise in using enterprise-wide risk management to organize the FDA's foreign operations.

Enterprise risk management depends on ongoing assessment of current and potential future risks. The FDA can use its data and, when confidentiality agreements allow, reliable data from its counterpart agencies abroad to inform its understanding of product risks. These risks are always changing; the product lines and suppliers considered highest risk a decade ago are different from those that are highest risk today. The FDA is best positioned to know which countries are increasing their exports to the United States. It should better define which countries are increasing their high-risk exports or which product lines are increasing in risk. Once it has identified these trends, it can allocate its resources accordingly. The FDA should also target its capacity building efforts to the countries and regions that export the highest risk products. The committee recommends that the FDA focus its resources on high-risk suppliers abroad for the next 3 to 5 years.

Enterprise risk management assessments should inform the FDA's decisions on where to put its overseas staff, which overseas offices to scale up, and the best use of its overseas staff's time. FDA should devote the most energy to training people in countries that are exporting high-risk products. For example, holding workshops on food safety for regulators in the Middle East and North Africa, as the FDA did in 2010, does not appear to be a decision grounded in risk management (FDA, 2011a). Arab countries export little food to the United States or anywhere else; they are net food importers (World Bank, 2009). The implementation of a risk management system to all FDA work might better empower the staff of the Office of Technical Cooperation and Capacity Building to choose more useful topics and audiences for capacity building programs.

Implementation in the Longer-Term Should Be FDA Activities in Both Domestic and International Markets

The results of these assessments should also inform the FDA's inspections in the United States. There are some firms in the United States that have never failed inspection, yet Congress demands that FDA revisit the sites every 2 years. The FDA is surely better aware than anyone that this is not an efficient use of its inspectors' time, yet they bound by dated laws. An enterprise risk management system would allow the FDA to reallocate its resources to give more attention to inspections abroad.

The committee recognizes that the FDA will need to work with Congress to change the laws governing it if it is to fully revise its domestic work based on risk. It is important to remember that the existing laws were designed for a time when most foods and medical products were produced domestically. Nowadays, much of the food and pharmaceutical supply comes from abroad. This shift demands a complimentary shift in the allocation of fixed resources to ensure product safety.

The Food Safety Modernization Act requires the FDA to inspect at least 600 foreign facilities in 2011 and double those inspections every year until 2016.[2] The FDA will struggle to meet these requirements, especially if Congress does not increase its funding (Stewart and Gostin, 2011). If the agency were able to reallocate its domestic staffing, it could give more attention to needs overseas. This does not mean that the FDA should neglect inspection and product safety responsibilities in the United States. The *Salmonella*-tainted egg crisis of 2010 and persistent quality control problems at Johnson & Johnson are a reminder that American companies can also prove to be high risk (Un oeuf is enough, 2010; Kavilanz, 2010; Silverman, 2011).

USING INFORMATION TECHNOLOGY

The modern systemic risk management system the committee recommends that FDA use depends on upgrades to its information technology system. A series of recent GAO reports have highlighted inaccuracies in the FDA's foreign supplier database and problems with its data management system (GAO, 2008, 2010a, 2010b, 2011). The FDA science review committee recommended in 2007 that the agency, "enhance the program to monitor performance metrics and put the appropriate [information technology] infrastructure in place to track the evolution of those metrics" (FDA Subcommittee on Science and Technology, 2007, p.42). The committee sees efficient use of modern information technology as indispensible to a risk-based regulatory system. The proper use of such a system could improve cooperation and communication among regulatory agencies. Information technology holds great promise to enhance surveillance. The results drawn from reliable data management systems will give the public and legislators a better understanding of product safety threats.

Recommendation 6-2: FDA should develop an information and informatics strategy that will allow it to do risk-based analysis, monitor performance metrics, and move towards paperless systems. In the next 3 to 5 years, the FDA should propose, in all its international harmonization activities a standardized vocabulary, a minimum dataset to be collected, and the frequency of data collection.

This recommendation can be measured when the FDA releases a standardized vocabulary for data collection, a codebook of the minimum data required from all points on the supply chain, and a timetable explaining how often this data should be collected.

As with the implementation of enterprise risk management, there are aspects of this recommendation that will take a decade to execute. A full overhaul of the FDA informatics and information strategy will take at least 10 years. However, in the next 3 to 5 years, the FDA can work out a standardized vocabulary and data collection protocols to propose for international use.

[2] 21 USC 350(j)(a)(2)(D)

Information and Informatics Strategies

For the purposes of this report, *information strategies* are ways to ensure that all data about food and medical products are accurately collected, well-annotated, recorded in permanent electronic media, and securely shared with authorized personnel for better information management. The committee uses the term *informatics strategies*, to describe how the data are cleaned of errors, transformed to proper formats, analyzed, and shared promptly with regulatory agents for better decision-making.

Modern information management uses networked computing infrastructure across national borders. Information management lays the foundation for computer-assisted automated information extraction. Without such data, risk modeling would be impossible. The strategy outlined in this report also emphasizes the need to share information across international borders. The committee feels that the FDA should promote the development of secure and open protocols for electronic data capture, computerized data management, electronic data sharing, and decentralized data exchange. It is suitable that the FDA provide leadership in this international endeavor.

A good architecture for storing, collecting, and exchanging information is key to reliable, modern food and medical product regulation, although the importance of such a system, especially in developing countries, is not always obvious. A regulatory agency has to access data and information about drug registration, facility inspections, and surveillance from disparate data sources and in varying formats on an ongoing basis. In developing countries much of this data is still stored as paper documents. This severely decreases the productivity of the already thinly-staffed regulatory agencies. A functional informatics system thus has the ability to enhance the productivity of regulatory agencies in developing countries. Well-defined data architecture and topologies can allow the multiple agencies regulating food and medical products to coordinate their work and reduce redundancy. In addition to sharing across different agencies within a country, common data architectures and good systems for information sharing can also facilitate better international harmonization. For example, the use of a reliable information system can allow the FDA to share inspection reports with its counterpart agencies in developing countries and vice versa.

Collecting data in common formats can also lay the groundwork for developing tools that will make regulatory agencies more productive. Pharmacovigilance and post-market surveillance are two areas that could greatly improve with informatics tools that allow for simpler data collection and analysis. The path to having modern informatics tools in developing country regulatory agencies depends on the FDA leading in the definition of common standards which will enable data collection, sharing, and (at some time in the more distant future) advanced decision support. The committee believes that moderate investments in informatics and information technology will yield significant long-term benefits in the quality of food and drug regulation.

Challenges in Implementation

The committee recognizes that implementing an information and informatics strategy will be difficult, especially in developing countries. First of all, the data sharing that it recommends requires collecting information from many sources at different agencies. For example, border rejection data, public safety breakout events, regulated product safety recall records, assessment report of export and import companies, and product ingredient tracking information, all need to be collected and linked. There is also room for misunderstanding when many people are responsible for data collection. Field staff may have different interpretations of questions that can lead to inconsistencies in the data. Attempts to work with the EU border rejection data, described in Appendix G, made it clear that worker inconsistency is a threat to data quality. Also all large data analysis projects must deal with missing data and attempt to control for human error as much as possible.

International survey and data collection experts in academia have expertise in standardizing data collection across many different languages. Standardizing questions and response categories are challenging, but not impossible, especially for people who have worked on similar problems before. Programmers can easily adapt decision making algorithms to tablet computers and mobile phones, tools that would be accessible to field staff. Using such an algorithm, even minimally educated staff could be trained to collect and transmit standard data.

The FDA's informatics strategy should aim to produce reports that will be compatible with reports produced by its counterpart agencies abroad. As Chapter 2 explains, the committee sees collaboration with FDA's counterpart agencies abroad as fundamental to ensuring product safety. In a report on drug safety the GAO also encouraged such collaborations. The FDA should ensure that its information strategy uses the same measurement conventions, or has an accurate way to adjust for different conventions.

Most of all the FDA's information and informatics strategy will need to protect confidential information. The committee understands that willingness to share data may be minimal at first, especially in developing countries with a history of deficits in this area. De-identified or aggregated data can still be useful, however.

Models for Implementation

The biomedical research and financial services industries use modern information sharing, and the FDA might do well to study the lessons learned from these industries. All of them define a minimal set of XML-based files for information sharing. The data elements, semantics, and structure of such data sharing reports can be jointly determined in international standard setting committees. These committees would do well to draw on expertise at the World Wide Web Consortium and Institute of Electrical and Electronics Engineers. Participating countries should agree to minimal data reporting elements. Experts need to identify the key minimal data set that will allow for the best communication among regulators, and the best product safety assurances. Information management tools such as Protégé are based on ontologies, explicit definitions categories and sub-categories of information and the relationships between them (Noy and Mcguinness, 2000). The use of Protégé and systems like it promotes a common understanding of the concepts and data being captured among different organizations. Over time a shared ontology can facilitate adherence to basic standards and improve standards (Pisanelli et al., 1999).

The committee proposes that the FDA encourage its counterparts in developed countries to develop similar information sharing and informatics strategies. Ideally, all agencies can agree on standardized data collection and information sharing practices from the start. Eventually, developed country regulatory authorities can expand the system to include developing country regulatory authorities (GAO, 2011). The FDA should demonstrate how information and informatics strategies can improve its logistics and risk management in both domestic and export markets.

FDA has made a good start at modernizing its informatics strategy by implementing the PREDICT system, a dynamic, integrated, risk-based evaluation method. FDA uses PREDICT to target their inspections. The system aims to expedite entry of products that meet American market standards, while vigilantly screening products likely to be adulterated or misbranded (FDA, 2011c).

The PREDICT system uses web-based technology to prevent dangerous products from passing through customs. At the port, inspectors check each product for a code which links to an FDA database on the product manufacturer, country of origin, history of recalls, and import alerts. Inspectors scrutinize the products that the system flags as possible threats. This makes the most of a limited number of inspectors. PREDICT uses automated data mining and pattern recognition algorithms to identify patterns that humans would miss, such as ratings of inherent product risk, results of field exams, and analyses from facility inspections (FDA, 2011c). This committee believes systems like PREDICT are a step in the right direction. Collecting data from more sources and using a standard data format would improve PREDICT and allow inspectors to cross-reference disparate databases.

BRIDGIING TRAINING GAPS AT HOME AND ABROAD

Training deficits are at the root of many product safety problems in emerging economies. Chapter 3 describes the consequences of poor training in some detail. The committee sees training regulators abroad as an invaluable piece of the strategy to build capacity for food and medical product regulation in emerging economies.

Recommendation 6-3: The FDA should facilitate training for regulators in developing countries. The purpose is workforce training and professional development through an ongoing, standing regulatory science and policy curriculum. In the next 3 to 5 years, the FDA should broaden the scope of FDA University to educate FDA staffers on international compliance with its regulations. In the long term, the FDA should consider the options the committee puts forth in this chapter.

The first measure of this recommendation is revisions in the curriculum at the FDA staff college, and the creation of an international curriculum. The number of countries participating in the international trainings, the number of people trained, and the number passing certification tests will also be useful indicators. A more capable workforce and a credentialing system can help improve morale at regulatory agencies. Therefore, the percentage of staff staying in government service after 5 years, 5 years, etc. will be long-term indicators of the training success.

The training that the committee recommends should take three forms: the training of regulators from abroad, the training of trainers, and the training of FDA staff. The following justification explains these options in more detail.

As with the earlier recommendations in this chapter, some aspects of this recommendation will take 10 years to achieve. The committee understands that training regulators at an international regulatory college and developing an apprenticeship program akin to the Centers for Disease Control and Prevention's (CDC's) EIS program will take about a decade. However, revising the FDA staff college curriculum for a more international focus should happen in the next three to five years.

Training of FDA Staff

First of all, the committee recommends that the FDA staff college include more emphasis on the application of FDA regulations abroad. Domestic FDA staffers should be more aware of the international compliance with their regulations and the challenges of adherence to standards, enforcement and quality assurance in developing countries. Learning about international compliance with the FDA's regulations would also guarantee the same kind of international focus in the training for American regulators that the committee recommends for those in low- and middle-income countries.

FDA also faces challenges in employing scientists who speak foreign languages. The committee recommends that FDA consider incentive programs to encourage learning foreign languages among their technical staff or hire scientists already fluent in foreign languages.

More importantly, the FDA needs to encourage an institutional shift, whereby taking an overseas posting for two to five years is not seen as a way to de-rail a career. The committee believes that FDA should reward personnel who complete foreign rotations. FDA could consider an advancement system used at the United Nations Children's Fund, for example, whereby serving at a field mission accelerates an employee's promotions.

The FDA could revise the curriculum at its staff college in the next three to five years. Changing the institutional culture to reward service in foreign offices will take much longer, probably about a decade. Nevertheless, the committee believes that with an attitudinal shift from senior leadership, the effect of FDA's new global outlook could be begin to be realized in five years.

Training Foreign Regulators

The committee sees some training gaps as particularly problematic. First, regulators abroad are desperate for better training in risk assessment. As Chapter 4 explains, meeting this need is in the best interest of the FDA as much as it is to the benefit of their counterparts abroad. A full curriculum in risk assessment can include training in risk management and risk communication. Mid-career professionals may also be rusty on the mathematics and basic science that underlie risk assessment or food hygiene. There is also a need for training in laboratory science and protocols, probabilities, and other fundamentals. The committee also saw a need for general training in food safety concepts and procedures, the training that would qualify a food safety inspector, for example. Regulators in all sectors need a formal credentialing system that complements a clear career progression at their agencies. Respected credentialing could also do much to improve the professionalism and *esprit de corps* of the regulatory workforce.

In-service training is core to staffing a modern regulatory agency, and the committee sees the FDA's staff college as a gold-standard training institution in the emerging field of regulatory science and policy. The committee also recognizes that an international fixed curriculum of regulatory procedures and regulatory science cannot and should not be the purview of the FDA or any one country's regulatory authority. First of all, the FDA, like its counterpart agencies around the world, is charged with protecting health and product safety among its country's citizens. Regulatory agencies are not primarily training or international development agencies. The committee is also sensitive to the fact that FDA's mandate already far exceeds its modest budget. The Food Safety Modernization Act of 2011 and the road map outlined in the agency's *Pathway to Global Product Safety and Quality* will also require expensive changes to the status quo (FDA, 2011b).

There was consensus from all the foreign guests at the study meetings that having FDA lead an international training institution would not be wise anyway. Perceptions of imperialism, political tensions, and the Cold War era's lingering resentments could sabotage the U.S. government's best intentions to train on regulatory science. This is why the committee believes that FDA should use its diplomatic staff abroad and their gravity in international forums to *facilitate* training for foreign regulators, not necessarily to host it, and to expand the concept of the regulatory staff college to an international forum. The FDA would also do well to work with existing training networks such as the Asia Pacific Economic Cooperation Partnership Training Institute Network (APEC PTIN) to expand its trainings and make them standing.

Models for Training

A hodge-podge of inconsistent donor trainings is part of the problem, after all. The development banks, the World Health Organization (WHO) and the Food and Agriculture Organization of the United Nations, donor organizations, and NGOs are all willing to host the occasional training on rational drug use or post-harvest storage. These trainings are a useful service, but, as Chapter 3 explains, developing country regulators cannot rely these trainings or plan their professional development around them. Sometimes the European Medicines Agency or the FDA hosts one-time trainings on good manufacturing practices or good clinical practices, but they do not revisit the same topic again on any schedule; their budgets and mandates would not allow them to do so. The training institution needed is one that offers a predictable, standing curriculum. This would also help ensure that training meets the proper audience. As mentioned in Chapter 3, the participants in donor trainings are too often senior staff who are close to retirement. This is understandable as long as trainings are seen as a diversion and a chance to collect per diem payments. It would be difficult to maintain such misconceptions about a formal college where students work through a credentialing program.

A Standing Regulatory Science College

The committee recommends that FDA use its authority to facilitate the creation of a standing international regulatory science college. Ideally, the costs of this college will be shared among many donor countries, foundations, and development banks. The center would not necessarily have to be a brick-and-mortar college, although that is a possibility, but it should rely on adjunct faculty to teach a standing, predictable curriculum of regulatory science. Students should complete credentialing examinations and earn universally accepted certifications in regulatory science.

Training of Trainers

It will take over a decade to implement the type of college the committee envisions. However, in the next 3 to 5 years the FDA can facilitate the training of trainers. Training trainers is both cost-effective and conducive to building a technical infrastructure in developing countries. Trainers can learn the regulatory science material in English or Spanish or another major world language, but return to their home countries and train others in local languages.

The committee recommends that the FDA partner with existing training networks for training of trainers. The APEC-PTIN would be an excellent organization for the FDA to work with on training trainers, as would the U.S. Agency for International Development (USAID). Trainings in the United States offer students from emerging economies a chance to observe the practices of a robust regulatory system at close range. The committee believes that information on the regulatory requirements of the American regulatory system and other stringent regulatory authorities will be an important piece of the curriculum in all trainings.

Another advantage of training trainers through existing networks is that the training remains relevant and avoids the pitfalls described in Chapter 3 of introducing scientists to equipment and protocols that they will never have access to at home.

An Apprenticeship Program

Another different, but complementary approach, would be establishing a training pilot project based on the Epidemic Intelligence Service (EIS) at the U.S. Centers for Disease Control and Prevention (Bollyky, 2010). The pilot project could put mid-career FDA officials into developing country national regulatory authorities or the WHO on 1- or 2-year rotations. In these rotations the FDA staff would work closely with their counterparts in foreign agencies to identify product safety problems before they affect consumers.

The FDA should consider basing this training program off the Foreign Epidemiology Training Program, another international capacity building program inspired by the EIS program. This program began in 2000 as part of the Hurricane Mitch and Hurricane Georges Reconstruction with funding from USAID and input from the American Association of Public Health Laboratories, the Pan American Health Organization, and ministries of health throughout Central American and the Caribbean (López and Cáceres, 2008). Initially the CDC ran the program as a two-year master's degree-accredited, in-service training for epidemiologists, but eventually the program expanded to include credentialing at the basic and intermediate levels as well (López and Cáceres, 2008). At each level, the training emphasizes field work over classroom work, and relies on mentors to train students in an apprentice-like method (López and Cáceres, 2008). In the beginning of the program CDC staff were the mentors, and the University of North Carolina designed much of the curriculum (Figure 6-2). Over time, Central American and Caribbean universities have taken over the classroom training. Graduates of this program have gone on to reorganize their counties' national epidemiology offices (López and Cáceres, 2008).

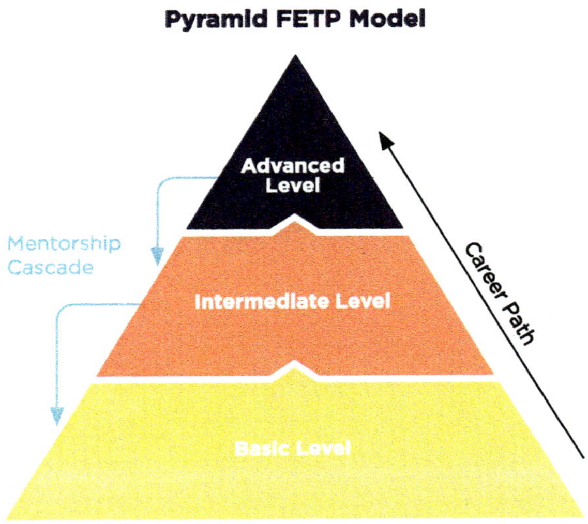

FIGURE 6-2 Conceptual model of the pyramid training approach used in the FETP.
SOURCE: López and Cáceres, 2008.

The committee recommends that the FDA study the Field Epidemiology Training Program and use it as a model for training foreign food and medical products regulators. The program should begin with a 1-month intensive training program for FDA regulators in regulatory science, the role of international institutions in supporting food and drug safety regulation, and the role of food and drug safety in global health, international trade, and development. This training program should be followed by field deployment. The focus of the program, as in the Field Epidemiology Training Program, should be learning by doing and public service. The alumni of the program could form the foundation of a more globally oriented FDA. If successful, this program could expand to include mid-career professionals from foreign regulatory authorities. Program alumni could eventually establish a global training program as in the EIS alumni program model (Pendergrast, 2010).

The committee realizes that FDA and other regulatory agencies may be reluctant to allow foreign nationals to work in their agency even on a brief rotation. There is precedent, however, for such international collaborations. The U.S. military routinely trains foreign officers at their staff colleges, for example. The Joint Forces Staff College in Norfolk has trained 171 officers from 46 countries (Joint Forces Staff College, 2011). The Army's Command and General Staff

College recently inducted four of its foreign graduates into the school's hall of fame (The Associated Press, 2011). Foreign students are active at the War College in Carlisle and the Industrial College of the Armed Forces in Washington, DC. Holding seats for foreign students in its staff colleges benefits the U.S. military as much as it does the foreign officers they train. These schools enroll officers from countries were the military controls the government and expose them to a system where civilians control the military.

A Role for Academic Partnerships

Because of its limited budget, the FDA should also partner with academic programs that train foreign regulators. The University of Maryland's Joint Institute for Food Safety and Applied Nutrition has experience training regulators from abroad. Their U.S.-China SPS Leadership Development Program is an example of an excellent training program. The U.S. Department of Agriculture (USDA), FDA, CDC, Environmental Protection Agency, HHS, and the Executive Office of the President all participated in the program; the U.S. Meat Export Federation and the USA Poultry and Egg Export Council funded it (Final agenda: 2007 U.S.-China SPS leadership development program, 2007). This program was a two-month immersion for Chinese regulators, exposing them to how the American system works, how Congress passes laws, how the different agencies involved in regulation work together, and how the American government works with industry and academia (Final agenda: 2007 U.S.-China SPS leadership development program, 2007).

Another noteworthy training program is Purdue University and Kilimanjaro School of Pharmacy's Sustainable Medicine Program in Tanzania. The program trains manufacturing scientists in an effort to alleviate Tanzania's dependence on other countries for life saving medicines, especially drugs for pediatric HIV, malaria, tuberculosis, and parasitic disease. Students are trained in good manufacturing practices and pharmaceutical science and at the program's laboratory and factory. The laboratory, operated by Howard University and Purdue University graduate students, allows trainees to receive hands-on experience in pharmaceutical good manufacturing practices. With German government funds, the program is building a pharmaceutical factory that will meet international manufacturing standards, only the second such facility in sub-Saharan Africa (Purdue University, 2011, 2012). This program and the University of Maryland's U.S.-China SPS Leadership Development Program are exemplary programs, and ones that the FDA and other government agencies should consider as models.

Involvement of Industry and Academia

In developed countries, product safety depends on the regulatory authority, industry, and academia. In the weakest developing country regulatory systems, the regulatory authority works in isolation. They have no means to communicate with regulated industry, and no input from academia. Especially in India and China, academics maintain a distance from both government service and private sector consulting. An international regulatory science college would enlist academic and industry experts from around the world to contribute. This could help drive an attitudinal change long overdue in low- and middle-income countries.

Industry and academia are indispensible to food and medical product safety. Government regulators in many parts of the world need to acknowledge the expertise of their colleagues in other sectors. Similarly, non-governmental stakeholders should be willing to contribute their expertise to training. Especially among academics in developing countries, there needs to be a cultural shift to encourage occasional consulting for private-sector firms, product research, or time spent in government service. Teaching through an international regulatory science college would provide many academics with a venue to serve. The college would expose faculty and students alike to a variety of different ideas, and allow everyone to see the roles academia and industry play in robust regulatory systems. Academics would come to see this service not as a departure from the academic career track, but a necessary building of professional creditability.

Encouraging a collaborative yet independent relationship between industry and academia can also advance the economies of low- and middle-income countries. Research and development into new technologies is missing even in emerging manufacturing powerhouses. A robust research sector can create the new technologies that fuel economic development, and industry funding of research can lead to better facilities at universities (Jones-Evans et al., 1999).

LEADERSHIP IN ADOPTING STANDARDS

There are many ways to build a stronger workforce in developing countries. The committee sees value in a training and credentialing system, but training is not the only answer. As Chapter 3 describes, regulators and industry staff in developing country often fail to observe international safety standards. Sometimes the regulatory authority would welcome better adherence to standards, but the overall political will for such changes is tepid. The FDA has the scientific expertise and the international authority to solve these problems, leading by example in the development and adoption of international standards.

Recommendation 6-4: U.S. policy makers should integrate food and medical product safety objectives into their international economic development, trade, harmonization, and public health work. To this end, the FDA should lead in the development and adoption of international and harmonized standards for food and medical products.

This recommendation can be measured by how many international standards the U.S. adopts and the number of initiatives that FDA and other agencies undertake to work with low- and middle-income countries technical assistance to adopt those standards.

The integration of trade, development, and health should be judged by the initiatives U.S. government agencies and intergovernmental institutions launch to achieve food and drug regulatory objectives in developing countries. Another measure of the recommendation is the degree to which FDA participates in and supports these initiatives.

This recommendation has a long time horizon. In the next three to five years, the FDA can begin adopting harmonized international standards, but the full realization of integrating product safety into the larger U.S. international policy agenda will take a decade.

Using Trade as a Tool to Promote Product Safety

The United States alone cannot ensure the safety of food and medical products produced across the globe. The United States needs partners in this endeavor, including national regulators in emerging economies. The United States must use the broader global health and trade agenda to advance food and medical product safety. By supporting developing country exporters' economic interests, the United States can gain their cooperation on food and drug safety. The consistent use of harmonized standards is in everyone's best interest.

Food and drug safety is a matter of domestic consumer protection, but it is also a tool for improving global health, trade facilitation, economic development, and poverty alleviation. Chapter 4 describes how these functions reinforce each other. The sale of high-value agricultural products is a lifeline to many in the world's poorest nations (IFAD, 2008). Manufacturing jobs are a way out of poverty for millions, especially in Asia (Islam, 2001). The emerging middle classes of Asia, Latin America, and Africa spend more on health care and nutritious foods than the poor do. Healthy workers are productive workers, who are able to fuel their countries' economic advancement.

The United States should take advantage of the relationships between product safety, health, trade, and development. There are many organizations already working on international health; there are systems and funding infrastructure in place for health and development. The United States can work with the organizations already active, and use their systems whenever possible. This approach is more practical than creating a new global food and medical product regulatory architecture. The agenda for these partnerships should be standard setting, information sharing, training for low- and middle-income countries, and improved regulatory cooperation.

A good first step would be for U.S. policymakers to better integrate global food and medical product safety objectives into its own global health, trade, and development policies. The mandate for that integration already exists. Since the passage of the Food and Drug Administration Modernization and Accountability Act of 1997, one of three mandates for the FDA is reducing regulatory burdens and advancing international harmonization.[3] International and U.S. bilateral trade agreements are designed to encourage the transparent adoption of international science-based standards, developing country capacity building, and to consider the development implications (i.e. the technical and economic feasibility) of standards and regulation.[4] [5] [6] The 2009 U.S. Trade Policy Agenda indicated the intention to pursue product safety as a trade facilitation measure in trade talks (USTR, 2009). USAID has long supported drug quality assurance programs (PSM, 2011), and the USDA's Foreign Agricultural Service, "links U.S. agriculture to the world to enhance export opportunities and global food security" (USDA, 2011).

Food security and nutrition programs are important to the Obama administration (The Whitehouse). The Feed the Future program invests in food security and agriculture to improve nutritional status and reduce poverty (Feed the Future). Through the Feed the Future activities, U.S. policy makers can promote food safety and incorporate it into their programs. USAID's recent $12 million investment in aflatoxin reduction in Africa is a commendable example of applied nutrition and agriculture programming that promotes food safety (USAID, 2011).

There is precedent for coordinated action as well. In May 2011, the FDA, in collaboration with the Office of the U.S. Trade Representative, signed a memorandum of understanding with the Asia Pacific Economic Cooperation's food safety forum and the World Bank to collaborate on food safety training programs (USTR, 2011). This project aims to enhance food safety and to facilitate trade throughout the Asia Pacific region (USTR, 2011). The FDA has also long worked with other U.S. agencies and WHO on international drug safety (Carpenter, 2010). U.S. trade officials routinely collaborate with the Department of Labor and

---

[3] 21 USC 393(b)

[4] Agreement on the Application of Sanitary and Phytosanitary Measures, Apr. 15, 1994, Marrakesh Agreement Establishing the World Trade Organization, Annex 1B, THE LEGAL TEXTS: THE RESULTS OF THE URUGUAY ROUND OF MULTILATERAL TRADE NEGOTIATIONS 59 (1999), 1867 U.N.T.S. 493 (1994), art. 3, 5, 9.

[5] Agreement on Technical Barriers to Trade, Apr. 15, 1994, Marrakesh Agreement Establishing the World Trade Organization, Annex 1B, THE LEGAL TEXTS: THE RESULTS OF THE URUGUAY ROUND OF MULTILATERAL TRADE NEGOTIATIONS 121 (1999), 1868 U.N.T.S. 120 (1994), art. 2.4, 11.

[6] 19 USC 3802

the Environmental Protection Agency to encourage the adoption of international environmental and labor regulations through trade negotiations (USTR; USTR). Many of USAID's greatest successes: oral rehydration therapy, smallpox eradication, and vaccination campaigns, have funded the infrastructure needed to adapt existing technology and ensure its safe distribution in poor countries (Christenson, 2011; HaRP).

An increasing number of international initiatives are seeking to better integrate trade, development, and regulatory objectives as well. The Organisation on Economic Co-operation and Development (OECD) and the World Bank have adopted the cause of regulatory reform, citing its benefits for trade and development, rule of law, and the achievement of societal objectives (IFC, 2006, 2011; OECD, 2002, 2005, 2011). The World Trade Organization (WTO) has increasingly recognized effective implementation of good regulatory practices as an important means of avoiding and minimizing unnecessary barriers of trade. The most recent triennial review of the WTO Technical Barriers to Trade (TBT) Committee has added regulatory policy coordination to its agenda and stressed the need for more coordination between national regulators, international standard setting bodies, and trade officials (WTO, 2009). Association of Southeast Asian Nations (ASEAN) countries have established a Consultative Committee on Standards and Quality (ACCSQ) and adopted a Framework Agreement on Mutual Recognition Arrangements in order to promote an ambitious agenda on regional cooperation on standards, technical regulations, and conformity assessment (Steger, 2011). Asia Pacific Economic Cooperation (APEC) countries and OECD have launched a cooperative effort to integrate objectives on regulatory quality and market openness (APEC and OECD, 2005).

But more needs to be done. International or harmonized standards and certification regimes provide predictability for exporters and investors. They also simplify compliance with product safety rules, and permit economies of scale (Henson and Jaffee, 2008). Intergovernmental institutions, such as Codex Alimentarius, can generate international risk-based standards for foods. These intergovernmental institutions able garner support better than bilateral negotiations or memoranda of understanding. USAID, working with other bilateral donors and development banks, should help provide the resources and technical assistance that developing countries require to meaningfully participate in Codex and other international standard setting organizations.

FDA and U.S. trade officials, including, but not limited to, those at the U.S. Trade Representative (USTR), the Department of Treasury, and USDA, should work in closer collaboration where U.S. trade and regulatory goals overlap. The committee acknowledges that trade and regulatory objectives will not always overlap, but the goal of better product safety will advance the cause of free trade. For example, complex production chains involving food and drug components from multiple suppliers and sourced from different countries are difficult for the FDA to oversee, leading to redundant inspections and conformity assessments. The unbundled supply chain is a logistical and regulatory problem for FDA, it is also a failure from the trade perspective because lack of cooperation hinders free trade. Promoting regulatory cooperation and convergence in this context can help advance both U.S. trade and regulatory objectives.

U.S. bilateral and regional trade agreements can establish the structures and incentives necessary to develop and adopt common standards, policies, and assessment procedures for emerging or persistent food and drug regulatory challenges. The WTO SPS and TBT Committees convene officials from 157 member countries to discuss regulations, standards, testing and certification procedures in connection with food and drugs. The mandates of these committees include information sharing, promoting the adoption of international standards, and providing technical assistance to developing country members.[7] [8] These Committees provide potentially useful venues for building consensus for common regulatory approaches on difficult food and drug safety challenges.

The FDA should work harder to make the adoption of international food and drug safety standards a priority in the United States. The consistent use of standards in the American market could motivate trading partners to do the same (Roberts and Josling, 2011). Even where FDA cannot adopt an international food safety standard, it should work with other industrialized countries to streamline the means by which low- and middle-income countries can demonstrate conformity or comparability (Horton and Wright, 2008). The USTR should work with FDA to use trade negotiations and forums such as the WTO TBT and SPS Committees to promote the adoption of international, risk-based, commodity-specific, performance standards food and medical products.

EXPANDING ONE-UP, ONE-BACK TRACK AND TRACE

Counterterrorism requires that food companies be able to identify the immediate previous and immediate subsequent recipient of all the products in their supply chains (Gessner et al., 2007). This is called one-up, one-back traceability. The committee recognizes that expanding the one-up, one-back requirements to medical products would be costly and complicated, but is nevertheless something the FDA needs to consider. Not only do one-up, one-back requirements protect American consumers, but they help producers abroad build stronger supply chains.

Recommendation 6-5: FDA, which currently requires one-up, one-back track and trace requirements for food, should, in the next year, hold a multi-sector, international, public workshop on applying it to medicines, biologics, and (when appropriate) to devices.

This recommendation can be measured simply by observing whether or not the FDA holds a public consultation on expanding one-up, one-back. The proceedings of this consultation and all the stakeholder input will be useful to FDA and to foreign regulators and producers who struggle with traceability in their supply chains. The immediate goal of this recommendation is to articulate how the FDA can extend one-up, one-back traceability to medical products. For this recommendation, the committee values the *process* as much as the outcomes. It is not possible for the committee to foresee the outcomes of this meeting, but bringing together all stakeholders to discuss it will be a marked step in the right direction. While implementing this one-up, one-back traceability requirements for medical products would take at least 5 years, the process and dialogue about it can begin, with a workshop within the next year.

[7] Agreement on the Application of Sanitary and Phytosanitary Measures, Apr. 15, 1994, Marrakesh Agreement Establishing the World Trade Organization, Annex 1B, THE LEGAL TEXTS: THE RESULTS OF THE URUGUAY ROUND OF MULTILATERAL TRADE NEGOTIATIONS 121 (1999), 1867 U.N.T.S. 493 (1994), art. 3, 5, 9.

[8] Agreement on Technical Barriers to Trade, Apr. 15, 1994, Marrakesh Agreement Establishing the World Trade Organization, Annex 1B, THE LEGAL TEXTS: THE RESULTS OF THE URUGUAY ROUND OF MULTILATERAL TRADE NEGOTIATIONS 59 (1999), 1868 U.N.T.S. 120 (1994), art. 5.4, 12.7-.8, 13.1.

Planning for Recalls

The ability to intervene quickly in an emergency is the essence of response to a product safety emergency. The faster the regulatory authority and companies move to remove an unsafe product from the market, the fewer the consumers harmed. Product recalls are used to this end, both voluntary recalls from industry and mandatory ones from the FDA. Identifying the source of the contamination is usually the rate limiting step in response to a product safety crisis. The last twenty years have seen substantial efforts to increase the speed at which outbreak investigations and product trace-back or trace-forward investigations take place. Several collaborative programs have received worldwide attention. The PulseNet program described in Chapter 3 is an example of such a program. PulseNet was established during the 1990s; it has a worldwide network of participating laboratories that provide genetic fingerprints of pathogen microorganisms from patients and foods (CDC, 2011).

A number of national and international foodborne outbreaks have stimulated the search for more efficient tracing systems. Regulatory requirements for food and medical products also increasingly emphasize the importance of traceability. In the United States, the Bioterrorism Act of 2002 required the FDA to register all food manufacturers, producers, and warehouses whose products are on the U.S. market.[9] It also requires that food producers, excluding farmers and restaurateurs, have information on immediate previous sources of foods (one-up) and the immediate subsequent recipients (one-back).[10] These records need to be available in the event that "FDA has a reasonable belief that an article of food is adulterated and presents a threat of serious adverse consequences or death to humans or animals."[11] The Food Safety Modernization Act of 2011further strengthened traceability by requiring FDA to develop and implement enhanced tracking systems for high risk foods.[12] Congress has established certain recordkeeping requirements:

- "they must relate only to information that is reasonably available and appropriate;
- they must be science-based;
- they may not prescribe specific technologies to maintain records;
- the public health benefits must outweigh the cost of complying with the requirements;
- they must be practical for facilities of varying sizes and capabilities;
- to the extent practical, they may not require a facility to change business systems to comply;
- they must allow for the maintenance of records at a reasonably accessible location, provided that the records can be made available to FDA within 24 hours of a request; and
- they may not require a full pedigree, or a record of the complete previous distribution history of the food from the point of origin" (FDA, 2011d).

Traceability is a common requirement among developed countries though the specifics of different traceability programs can vary substantially. Tracing back the sources of imported products is a common problem, particularly if the exporting country has no traceability requirement. Increasingly U.S. importers are requiring enhanced traceability in their contracts as

[9] 21 USC 350(d)
[10] 21 USC 350(c)
[11] 21 USC 350(c)
[12] 21 USC 2223

a way to manage risk and to comply with the law. While there is still room for improvement, traceability requirements have been credited with decreasing the response times to food safety emergencies (Agriculture and Agri-Food Canada, 2012; Food Standards Agency, 2002). They also improve inventory management, and can allow for more targeted (and therefore less wasteful) recalls (Mejia et al., 2010).

Medical product traceability lags behind food traceability. The requirements appear to be largely limited to finished product lot or unit identification or both, particularly for medical devices (GS1, 2009; ISO, 2003). While the FDA has articulated a need for enhanced programs, particularly in relation to counterfeit drugs, traceability has not risen to the point of a regulatory requirement. Tracing the supply chain is no less essential in the production of medical products than food, however. Counterfeit drugs are a growing problem, especially in developing countries.

By demanding traceability in the medical products market, the FDA could improve supply chain management in developing countries. If all producers are required to maintain one-up, one-back traceability for their export products, economies of scale will make it attractive to extend the same standards to products for the domestic market. Such requirements would be evidence of a commitment from the FDA to tighten the drug supply chain around the world. This would be most valuable in the poorest countries, the ones most devastated by fake drugs.

RESEARCHING INEXPENSIVE TECHNOLOGY

The human capital, research infrastructure, and creativity at American and foreign universities needs to better harnessed for global food and medical product safety. Groundbreaking research can also come from government labs and from industry. The committee's concern is that the U.S. government should be encouraging research into frugal technologies that would be useful in low- and middle-income countries. The committee values a collaborative research model that would build the private sector and academia in developing countries and involve them in the regulatory system. Cooperative Research and Development Agreements (CRADA) are especially useful tools for technology transfers; the committee encourages the FDA and USDA to enter into these useful partnerships.

Recommendation 6-6: Starting in the next two years, the FDA and USDA should implement Cooperative Research and Development Agreements and other programs to encourage businesses and academia to research and develop innovations for low-cost, appropriate fraud prevention, intervention, tracking, and verification technologies along the supply chain.

The number of requests for proposals that the FDA and USDA issue will be the main measure of this recommendation. Eventually the number of patents issued and publications about low-cost appropriate technologies will also reflect the impact of this recommendation.

The time frame on this recommendation is fluid: the first CARDAs can be made in the next 2 years, and renewed over time, becoming an ongoing piece of the FDA and USDA's capacity building operations. The agencies should also explore other programs to involve industry and academia in research that benefits producers in developing countries. This too should begin in the next 3 to 5 years and continue.

Determinants of Research Investments

There are three key determinants of agricultural research investments by for profit companies. The first is the size of the potential market for new technology. Second is the ease of improving the technology relative to the research investment. Last is the ability of a firm to capture the returns on its investments and protect intellectual property (Pray and Fuglie, 2008). Since the mid-19th century, much agricultural research has been carried out by the public sector because the knowledge produced from agricultural research has the non-rivalness and non-excludability characteristics of a public good. Without public sector investment research would suffer.

It can be argued that food safety research is an impure public good because it has benefits that are both private (i.e., product liability) and public (i.e., health). The appropriability of benefits of new technology and the costs associated with a recall may affect a firm's decision to invest in food safety research. However, some technology developed through applied research will not be appropriable and thus not covered by the private sector. To date, much of the food safety research has been directed at supply-side questions, such as technologies to ensure proper detection of pathogens. The public sector has done more of the basic research, the original investigation that advances the science but has no immediate, commercial value. The private sector has focused on applied market research where they find justifiable economic returns.

Research for the Small-scale Producer

For the most part, the focus of research on pathogen reducing technologies has been on the needs of the big players on the supply chain. The technologies developed exhibit economies of scale on a per unit basis. In the case of beef, for example, following the 1993 *E.coli* O157:H7 outbreak associated with Jack-in-the-Box hamburgers, Frigoscandia Equipment developed a steam pasteurization technology that reduced 90-99 percent of the pathogen loads on beef carcasses (Corantin et al., 2005; Golan et al., 2004) . The cost of steam pasteurization varies from $0.28-.46 per cattle head for large slaughterhouses to $3.58-7.05 for small slaughterhouses. Clearly, steam pasteurization is not cost-effective for most small slaughterhouses, even in the United States, unless a smaller-scale version requiring less throughput is produced (Malcolm et al., 2004). Technologies appropriate for small-scale and medium-scale producers for the most part have not been addressed. Currently there is a need to either adapt this technology so that it is cost-effective for small-scale slaughterhouses or find an equally effective cheaper technology. Similar examples abound in hazard reducing food technologies. To date there has been little incentive for the private sector to put research and development efforts towards tackling problems for small- and medium-scale producers.

A substantial portion of food and medical products production in developing countries is done by small scale producers, either acting alone or by providing larger companies with key components and ingredients. There is therefore a need to give incentives to private sector actors to develop hazard-reduction technologies for small- and medium-scale producers. The food industry in developed countries increasingly requires suppliers to implement hazard-reduction measures with limited knowledge of whether these standards are more effective than the control measure given the size of the producer. Though the private sector is increasingly implementing traceability schemes, this does not solve the problem of finding appropriate and cost-effective solutions to ensure an acceptable level of risk. Research efforts need to be directed at finding appropriate cost-effective technologies for reducing risk for small- and medium-scale producers in both developed and developing countries, rather than looking at prescriptive solutions which may not be scaled neutrally. Based on the experience gained in the United States and other developed countries, small- and medium-sized companies have less money to invest in research or use to buy expensive equipment. Targeted funding of size-appropriate technologies would allow such companies to address product safety concerns.

The public sector has difficulty testing their research outside of the laboratory setting. They also struggle to bring their innovations to market quickly. Therefore, it might not be efficient to rely on the public sector for the research that would help ensure safety from small- and medium-scale producers. Rather, the FDA and USDA, in conjunction with research funding agencies, should advance research and development programs that would encourage small- and medium-sized companies in developing countries to meet product safety goals. The USDA and FDA should encourage private sector participation in this research.

In recent years, the financial crisis has constrained public sector research, leading to greater collaboration in agricultural and food safety research under the CRADA system. A CRADA is a written agreement between a private company and a government agency to work together on project development (USGS, 2009). Such agreements optimize resources and share research costs. They also improve technology transfer, providing incentives to the private sector to aid in the commercialization of federally developed technology (USGS, 2009).

The committee recommends similar collaborations with developing countries. This would also enhance the academic infrastructure in developing countries. The technologies developed by these collaborations would also help the small- and medium-sized companies in the United States. The FDA should also facilitate research collaborations by providing guidance to new technology providers in developing countries about the requirements for pre-market approval. FDA should also consider funding the advancement of promising technologies.

GIVING MARKET INCENTIVES FOR SUPPLY CHAIN MANGEMENT

The FDA's charge to protect the American consumer can also work to the advantage of consumers in emerging economies. Chapter 4 describes how market incentives can help importers and exporters, of American and foreign consumers. Market incentives are a useful means to encourage adherence to standards and help control supply chains in developing countries. Economic incentives could also do much to increase political will for product safety in developing countries. The proper incentives would eliminate the false dichotomy that pits product safety against economic development.

Recommendation 6-7: FDA should ensure an adequate mix of incentives to importers of food and medical products that are confirmed to meet U.S. regulatory standards. One such promising initiative is the 2-year FDA Secure Supply Chain pilot program. The FDA should evaluate this program immediately after its pilot phase (scheduled to end in 2014). The program should be expanded, if successful, to include a greater number of importers and food.

The number of incentive programs FDA proposes and the volume of imports going through these programs will be a simple measure of this recommendation's effectiveness.

The evaluation of the Secure Supply Chain program should take place immediately after the program is finished. As of February 2012, the FDA is working out the logistics of the program start-up, so the evaluation should happen in the spring of 2014. The scale-up of the program is contingent on the results of this evaluation, and should begin in the next 3 to 5 years.

A View of the Entire Supply Chain

Food, pharmaceuticals, vaccines, biologics, and medical devices move through a complex supply chain before entering the United States. The FDA does not have regulatory authority over all of the upstream activities in this supply chain. It is difficult to re-create this chain even for domestically manufactured products. Safety risks in manufacturing of both food and medical products are not just limited to the final manufacturing stage, or to the active ingredient manufacturing stage. Problems may arise anywhere in the supply chain, from inadequate raw material to user errors. While strengthening food and drug regulatory authorities in developing countries would help in better regulation of upstream supply chain in the medium to long term, currently many of the developing country regulatory authorities regulate only the final stages of the food and medical product production.

Furthermore, private sector food and medical product manufacturers have a great deal of freedom in choosing their suppliers. Developing country firms are often attractive suppliers because of their lower prices. In developing countries' domestic markets there are limited price premiums on better quality products, and usually no widely-used certification process. The regulatory authority can encourage upstream quality controls by offering speedy market access to those suppliers that implement quality controls in their suppliers.

Sharing information from nodes along the entire supply chain could greatly reduce the risks of unsafe or falsified products entering the supply chain. Therefore, the FDA should put mechanisms in place to better see the upstream actors on the supply chain for food and medical products entering the United States. Foreign manufacturers should be rewarded for giving detailed information about their sources. These incentives can take various forms such as faster product clearance for import and quicker distribution in the U.S. market. Box 6-2 describes the USDA's Animal, Plant, and Health Inspection Service, which works to the benefit of U.S. regulators and their counterparts abroad to facilitate trade in safe foods.

There are flaws in the Food Safety Modernization Act in that its mandates, however well-meaning, are largely unfunded (Ozersky, 2010). Congress should ensure that the FDA has sufficient funding to develop and establish importer incentive programs both food and medical products. The committee commends the FDA for the Secure Supply Chain pilot program that aims to do just this (FDA, 2009a). The FDA had a public hearing on this two-year pilot program in January 2009 (Federal Registrar, 2009). As of February 2012 the FDA is still resolving the logistical details of the program, assuming that the pilot starts in 2012, FDA should promptly evaluate the program in 2014. This evaluation should be focused on scaling-up to include more producers and food producers.

End-to-end supply chain visibility for food and medical products is the best insurance against safety lapses. The committee recommends that FDA evaluate the results from the Secure Supply Chain pilot for the technical and operational feasibility of scaling. A full-scale program should then be instituted in which all interested manufacturers are enthusiastically encouraged to participate. In order to reduce the risk of non-compliance of these incentives programs with WTO law, FDA should develop these food and drug importer incentive programs in close consultation with U.S. trade officials and ensure participation is voluntary and pursuant to objective criteria that do not favor applicants of any one country over those of another.

BOX 6-2
The Animal Plant and Health Inspection Service

The Animal Plant and Health Inspection Service, is a USDA agency which was established in 1972 to consolidate the USDA's roles in protecting animal and plant health. Since its founding, APHIS has continued to develop its mission of safeguarding American agriculture (USDA, 2007b). APHIS creates regulations, forms agreements, and implements emergency protocols that maintain the safety standards for food imports into the United States (USDA, 2007a).

Funding for APHIS' programs comes from a variety of sources including the agency's user fees. These are charges for APHIS' programs such as the export certification services and agricultural quarantine and inspection service (USDA, 2010b). USDA also collects user fees for APHIS services that directly benefit the recipient or are necessary to protect the American public (USDA, 2010c).

The success of APHIS' mission involves agreements and partnerships with other organizations such as the World Organization for Animal Health and the International Plant Protection Convention, which set standards to guide animal and plant trade. Additionally, APHIS works with the North American Plant Protection Organization, which provides a Phytosanitary Alert System that notifies the authorities of any emerging diseases or pests. These organizations work together to promote the development of practical, risk based approaches that can reduce and manage the pest and disease risks in agricultural trade (USDA, 2006). APHIS also collaborates with and assists their foreign partners in building their animal and plant health infrastructures. This support reduces the probability that a threat could enter the country undetected and destroy American agriculture (USDA, 2010a).

There are also several programs within APHIS that are effective in helping to reduce the spread of disease and foreign pests to the United States. Preclearance measures, which include thorough offshore inspections and trade facilitation, ensure the safety of food imports (USDA, 2007c). APHIS also has a Plant Protection and Quarantine program that entails the inspection and screening of passenger baggage, mail, and cargo for prohibited agricultural products that may bring unwanted pests into the United States (USDA, 2002).

APHIS' procedures encourage cooperation not only with other organizations, but also with individual countries. In South America, APHIS partners with countries through bilateral commissions and field programs, in addition to their preclearance processes, as a method to control the pests (U.S. Department of State). A recent example of this partnership is between APHIS and Uruguay's agriculture department. Uruguay requested market access to export fresh blueberries to the United States. The Uruguayan department submitted a risk assessment in accordance with APHIS preclearance requirements (USDA-APHIS, 2007). Preclearance and surveillance programs like that in Uruguay are conducted in countries throughout South America, as well as other regions of the world.

Promising Initiatives

Globalization has dramatically altered where food and medical products come from. The FDA cannot inspect all of the import lines to the United States, or all foreign manufacturers exporting to the United States (GAO, 2008). Even if it could, the GAO pointed out that, "relying solely on inspections is insufficient to secure the drug supply chain" (GAO, 2010a, p.29). The same is true of relying exclusively on end product testing and food safety inspections to ensure food safety (Young, 2011). There need to be other ways to ensure the safety of import lines.

Market incentives drive food safety in the United States (Thomsen and McKenzie, 2001). The Food Safety Modernization Act requires the traceability of food supply chain and holds suppliers accountable for ensuring HACCP compliance. The ability to assess the safety of ingredients from produced overseas, in places the FDA has no authority, is a challenge (FDA, 2009a). By expanding incentives programs the FDA could help encourage foreign producers to adhere to international standards and work to produce higher quality products. The Food Safety Inspection Service has a program in place to ensure the quality of imported meat. This is not an incentives program, but it is a good example of bilateral coordination to facilitate trade (Box 6-3).

BOX 6-3
The Food Safety Inspection Service

The Food Safety and Inspection Service (FSIS) is the office within the USDA "responsible for ensuring that domestic and imported meat, poultry, and egg products are safe, wholesome, and accurately labeled" (FSIS, 2009). Meat imported into the United States must meet the same safety, quality, and labeling standards required of domestically produced meat. In order to assure this, FSIS only allows importation of meat that has gone through its rigorous approval protocol that covers the entire import process (FSIS, 2009).

Any country that wants to export meat to the United States must undergo an FSIS inspection and certification process called an *equivalence determination process*. This certification evaluates the meat inspection processes of the exporting country. If the export inspection protocol in place is deemed equivalent to U.S. domestic inspection protocol, the country may be granted eligibility. By setting the standard at equivalence, FSIS ensures products of equal quality without requiring that exporting countries conform to exact U.S. inspection procedures. Within a country, each producer wishing to export meat to the United States must undergo a similar certification. The evaluation process includes both offsite assessment of written protocols and procedures and an onsite inspection by an FSIS team. Both elements stress five primary categories of risk assessment as established by FSIS: animal disease controls, sanitation controls, residue controls, slaughter and processing controls, and controls for enforcement. Countries and sites are periodically reevaluated to ensure ongoing safety and equivalence. Countries and specific producers may lose eligibility, often temporarily, due to an outbreak of a disease affecting livestock or other adverse health conditions (FSIS, 2009, 2011).

After the appropriate export country inspection paperwork has been filed, meat is re-inspected by an FSIS inspector before it is allowed past the port of entry. Products that are approved during this second inspection are allowed into the United States for sale and are treated no differently than domestically produced products from that point forward (FSIS, 2009).

Equivalent inspection practices, rather than identical ones, must be accepted by importing countries under the guidelines set forth by the WTO, specifically the Sanitary and Phytosanitary Measures Agreement (SPS). The SPS agreement concerns the international trade in food, animal, and plant products. As with all WTO agreements, the SPS seeks to limit barriers to international trade, in part by ensuring that developing countries, often using less technologically advanced equipment, are not unfairly discriminated against. Regardless of the exact measures in place, if exports are of a suitable standard they must be treated as such (WTO, 2012).

The Secure Supply Chain program promotes drug safety. In this program, foreign firms voluntarily provide the same information FDA requires of American firms (FDA, 2009b). The pilot program includes 100 firms; each firm can include up to five drugs. To be eligible firms must be able to trace their products from manufacture through entry to the United States. They also need a plan for recalling the drug or active ingredient. Qualifying firms receive expedited entry of select products through customs (FDA, 2009b). FDA currently is working out the details of how this will work with the U.S. Customs and Border Protection agency for using the Customs-Trade Partnership Against Terrorism program, which offers priority processing for products from companies with secure supply chains. The Secure Supply Chain pilot aims to enable FDA to determine the practicality of using a secure supply chain program to prevent importing sub-standard drugs (FDA, 2009b). The committee suggests that this program be evaluated immediately after its pilot phase, implemented and expanded, if successful, to include a greater number of importers and to food.

INCREASING CIVIL LIABILITY

Appendix B describes how the civil liability system, so essential to product safety in the United States, is flawed in low- and middle income countries, and so does not deter faulty manufacturing.

Recommendation 6-8: Over the next 10 years, U.S. government agencies should work to strengthen the ability of those harmed by unsafe food and medical products to hold foreign producers and importers liable in civil lawsuits.

The establishment of mechanisms that increase liability will measure this recommendation. This process will be slow, and it will require major revisions to the status quo that involved multiple government agencies. It is unlikely these changes could be made in less than 10 years.

Product Liability in Developed Countries

The United States legal system has two ways to ensure food and medical product safety. The first way is the regulatory framework built around the Federal Food, Drug, and Cosmetic Act; regulatory framework is the primary focus of the current report. Recent legislation has provided the FDA with a variety of new tools with which to enforce this regulatory framework for both foods and medical products. If there is a sufficient likelihood that food is adulterated or misbranded, the FDA may administratively detain products or mandate a recall if there is reasonable probability that food will cause "serious adverse health consequences or death to humans or animals".[13] Food production facilities must register with the FDA in order to introduce their products into U.S. interstate commerce; the FDA can suspend that registration if there is reasonable probability that the food from that facility will harm humans or animals.[14] The Food & Drug Administration Amendments Act of 2007 also expanded the legal tools FDA uses to ensure drug and vaccine safety. The FDA may withdraw approval from a marketed drug or biologic,[15] order labeling changes or the inclusion of package inserts about new safety

[13] 21 USC 350(l)
[14] 21 U.S.C. 350(d)(a)
[15] 21 USC 355(e)

information and recommendations,[16] mandate post-market observational studies or clinical trials to assess risks,[17] and require sponsors to have strategies to ensure that the benefits of a drug will outweigh its risks.[18] In general, most violations of the Federal Food, Drug, and Cosmetic Act are also subject to criminal enforcement, but few are subject to civil enforcement (Hutt et al., 2007).

The second way that the U.S. legal system ensures food and medical product safety in the United States is product liability. Entities involved in the manufacture, distribution, and marketing of a food or drug product to the public are obligated under U.S. common law and, in some cases, U.S. federal and state statutes to ensure the safety of that product. Individuals that suffer harm from that food or drug product in the United States may bring a civil lawsuit against the manufacturers, importers, distributors, and marketers of that product. Any entity with significant contacts with the United States is potentially subject to the jurisdiction of U.S. courts. Redress is typically monetary compensation to cover the damages incurred by the injured party, but it may also involve punitive damages.

Product liability plays an essential role in ensuring food and drug safety in the United States. The volume of commerce in FDA-regulated food and medical products far exceeds the resources and legal authority that FDA has to monitor and enforce the safety of those products. The threat of product liability suits, high litigation costs, and reputational damage help fill the gap by providing a significant economic incentive to companies to maintain and improve the safety of their products. Ultimately, it is retailers and manufacturers that are in the best able to ensure the safety of their products.

There are limits to the role of product liability in imports. First of all, the FDA does not have jurisdiction in foreign markets, and even when its staff is permitted to inspect foreign establishments there are practical challenges to working in a new country and in a different language. Furthermore, U.S. plaintiffs have limited ability to litigate and enforce judgments against foreign firms with few U.S. contacts or assets. It is difficult for Americans to bring lawsuits against foreign firms in foreign country courts for injuries that occurred in the United States (Appendix B). U.S.-based importers and distributors may be able to avoid product liability when there is doubt that they knew or should have known about their suppliers' actions (Bamberger and Guzman, 2008). It may be difficult for consumers to establish accountability for unsafe products when the supply chain is so complicated (Bamberger and Guzman, 2008). With the possibility of more limited liability, manufacturers and distributors of imported products may not have the same market incentives as their U.S. counterparts for continual improvement in consumer safety.

Congress and U.S. government agencies (including, but not limited to, the Department of Justice, the Department of the Treasury, and the U.S. Trade Representative) should consider measures to strengthen the ability of those harmed by unsafe food and medical products to hold foreign producers, exporters to the United States, and U.S. importers of foreign products liable. Congress could increase appropriations for criminal enforcement of the Food, Drug, and Cosmetic Act or amend it to make violations subject to civil penalties. The FDA could issue more stringent guidance for high-risk drugs and foods, such as requiring importers to maintain a staff person at each foreign production facility for high-risk products (Bollyky, 2009). Scholars have made other thoughtful proposals to increase liability. The issuing of bonded warranties would oblige sellers to pay statutory damages to people injured by unsafe products (Baker and

[16] 21 USC 355 (o) and 21 USC 355(r)
[17] 21 USC 355 (k)(3)
[18] 21 USC 355-1

Moss, 2009). Another option would be using discriminatory strict liability with damages based on the risk posed by the product and by the importer's history (Bamberger and Guzman, 2008). Finally, developing country governments seeking to improve the safety of their food and drug production should consider measures to facilitate the ability of domestic consumers to hold firms accountable in civil suits for the harms caused by unsafe products (Appendix B).

CONCLUSION

During its meetings, the committee heard from FDA staff about the agency's current work in capacity building and the challenges it faces in protecting the American food and medical products supply. The committee commends FDA on its work, but sees some areas where it might improve its operations. First, it should use an enterprise risk management system to identify its most important priorities. That is, it should use risk to inform all its staffing and training decisions, not just its inspections. In the next three to five years, the FDA should use enterprise risk management to inform its work abroad, but eventually the committee recommends that it use this tool to plan its domestic work as well. The committee recognizes that Congress might need to revise the laws governing FDA for this to happen.

The agency's use of risk will depend on reliable data collection. A modern information and informatics strategy will allow the agency to collect and analyze data promptly. FDA's PREDICT system is a step in the right direction. The committee believes that in the next ten years the agency should work toward a paperless system in its own operations and in its dealings with its counterpart agencies abroad. The first step towards this system would be the development of a standard data format and vocabulary and could be developed in three to five years.

Regulators around the world need training on how to respond to the challenges of globalization. FDA has the technical depth and international presence to contribute to an ongoing, standing regulatory science and policy college, but developing this college will take a decade. In the meantime, the agency can work with universities and through existing training networks to make better training opportunities available. The FDA's staff college is an exemplary training center that should be a model for an international regulatory science and policy college. In the next three to five years, FDA could require their staff to take courses on the international implementation of and compliance with American regulations. In the longer term, that is, in the next decade, FDA could work to develop a training program like the CDC's Field Epidemiology Training Program. Involving industry and academia in these efforts will also set a valuable example.

The United States could also lead by example in their consistent use of international product standards. Harmonized standards make the market more predictable for foreign investors and exporters. USAID and other agencies can demonstrate American commitment to harmonized standards but empowering scientists in low- and middle-income countries participate actively in standard setting meetings. Over the next decade, product safety objectives should be fully integrated into U.S. foreign policy.

The United States could also set a powerful example for industry and government around the world by expanding the one-up, one-back track and trace requirements for food to medical products. The committee realizes that this would be complicated, but believes that the FDA could make progress by holding a public workshop on expanding one-up, one-back, in the next year. This workshop should include international stakeholders from government, industry, and academia.

There is great potential for innovation in American universities. The government should, starting in the next two years, encourage research into simple and elegant technology that will help small-scale producers prevent fraud and control their supply chains. Similarly, the government can improve supply chain management by giving market incentives that reward supply chain management. The committee is especially impressed by the FDA's Secure Supply Chain pilot program. The 2014 evaluation for this pilot should consider how to best expand this program to include a greater number of producers.

Market incentives can do much to improve the safety of the food and medical products used around the world. The committee also sees value to increasing civil liabilities on foreign importers over the next 10 years.

REFERENCES

Agriculture and Agri-Food Canada. 2012. *Canadian traceability*. http://www.ats-sea.agr.gc.ca/trac/trac-eng.htm (accessed March 29, 2012).

APEC, and OECD. 2005. *APEC-OECD integrated checklist on regulatory reform.*

Baker, T., and D. Moss. 2009. Government as a risk manager. In *New perspectives on regulation*, edited by D. Moss and J. Cisterno. Cambridge, MA: The Tobin Project.

Bamberger, K. A., and A. T. Guzman. 2008. Keeping imports safe: A proposal for discriminatory regulation of international trade. *California Law Review* 96(6):1405-1447.

Bollyky, T. J. 2009. Global health interventions for U.S. Food and drug safety: CSIS Global Health Policy Center.

———. 2010. *Bridging the gaps: Fda's role in improving the development pathway for neglected disease therapies, testimony for the U.S. Senate appropriations subcommittee on agriculture, rural development, the Food and Drug Administration, and related agencies.*

Carpenter, D. 2010. *Reputation and power: Organizational image and pharmaceutical regulation at the FDA*. Princeton, NJ: Princeton University Press.

Casualty Actuarial Society-Enterprise Risk Management Committee. 2003. *Overview of enterprise risk management.* Fairfax, VA: Casualty Actuarial Society.

CDC. 2011. *What is PulseNet?* http://www.cdc.gov/pulsenet/whatis.htm#developed (accessed November 21, 2011).

Christenson, K. 2011. *USAID celebrates 50 years of saving lives across the globe.* http://blog.usaid.gov/2011/11/usaid-celebrates-50-years-of-saving-lives-across-the-globe/#more-8963 (accessed November 21, 2011).

Corantin, H., S. Quessy, M. L. Gaucher, L. Lessard, D. Leblanc, and A. Houde. 2005. Effectiveness of steam pasteurization in controlling microbiological hazards of cull cow carcasses in a commercial plant. *Canadian Journal of Veterinary Research* 69(3):200-207.

COSO. 2004. *Enterprise risk management — integrated framework.*

FDA. 2009a. *FDA's approach to medical product supply chain safety.* Washington, DC.

———. 2009b. *FDA launches pilot program to improve the safety of drugs and active drug ingredients produced outside the United States.* http://www.fda.gov/NewsEvents/Newsroom/PressAnnouncements/ucm109064.htm (accessed November 21, 2011).

———. 2011a. *Food safety conference.* http://www.fda.gov/InternationalPrograms/WorkshopsandConferences/ucm240912.htm (accessed November 21, 2011).

———. 2011b. *Pathway to global product safety and quality.* Washington, DC: U.S. Food and Drug Administration.

———. 2011c. *PREDICT: Briefing slides for importers and entry filers.* FDA Office of Regulatory Affairs and Office of Regulatory Management.

———. 2011d. *Product tracing: Information available related to product tracing under the Food Safety Modernization Act (FSMA).* http://www.fda.gov/Food/FoodSafety/FSMA/ucm270851.htm (accessed November 18, 2011).

FDA Subcommittee on Science and Technology. 2007. *FDA science and mission at risk: Report of the subcommittee on science and technology.* US Food and Drug Administration.
Federal Registrar. 2009. *Secure supply chain pilot program; notice of pilot program.*
Feed the Future. *About.* http://www.feedthefuture.gov/about (accessed January 23, 2012).
Final agenda: 2007 U.S.-China SPS leadership development program. 2007. Paper read at Third Leadership Development Program in the United States for the People's Republic of China on U.S. Systems and Approaches for Implementation of the World Trade Organization Agreement on the Application of Sanitary and Phytosanitary Measures June 4 - July 24, 2007, College Park, MD.
Food Standards Agency. 2002. *Traceability in the food chain: A preliminary study.* Food Chain Strategy Division.
FSIS. 2009. *Fact sheets: FSIS import procedures for meat, poultry & egg products.* http://www.fsis.usda.gov/Fact_Sheets/FSIS_Import_Procedures/index.asp (accessed January 25, 2012).
———. 2011. *Regulations and policies: Checklist for importing meat, poultry and processed egg products.* http://www.fsis.usda.gov/regulations_&_policies/Import_Checklist/index.asp (accessed January 25, 2012).
GAO. 2007. *Drug safety: Preliminary findings suggest weaknesses in FDA's inspection program for inspecting foreign drug manufacturers.* GAO-08-224T.
———. 2008. *Drug safety: Better data management and more inspections are needed to strengthen FDA's foreign drug inspection program* GAO-08-970.
———. 2010a. *Drug safety: FDA has conducted more foreign inspections and began to improve its information on foreign establishments but more progess is needed.* GAO-10-961.
———. 2010b. *Food and Drug Administration: Response to heparin contamination helped protect public health; controls that were needed for working with external entities were recently added.* GAO-11-95.
———. 2011. *Drug safety: FDA faces challenges overseeing the foreign drug manufacturing supply chain.* GAO-11-936T.
Gessner, G. H., L. Volonino, and L. A. Fish. 2007. One-up, one-back ERM in the food supply chain. *Information Systems Management* 24(3):213-222.
Golan, E., T. Roberts, E. Salay, J. Caswell, M. Ollinger, and D. Moore. 2004. *Food safety innovation in the United States: Evidence from the meat industry.* Washington, DC: U.S. Department of Agriculture.
GS1. 2009. *GS1 Global Traceability Standard for Healthcare (GTSH): Implementation guide.*
Hamburg, M. A. 2010. Remarks. *Partnership for Safe Medicines Interchange 2010.*
HaRP. *Child Health Research (CHR) project achievements* http://www.harpnet.org/chr/chr_achievments.html (accessed November 21, 2011).
Henson, S., and S. Jaffee. 2008. Understanding developing country strategic responses to the enhancement of food safety standards. *World Economy* 31(4):548-568.
HHS. 2011. *The global health strategy of the U.S. Department of Health and Human Services.* Washington, DC.
Horton, L. R., and E. Wright. 2008. *Reconciling food safety with import faciliation objectives: Helping developing country producers meet U.S. And EU food requirements through transatlantic cooperation.* Washington, D.C.: International Food and Agricultural Trade Policy Council.

Hutt, P. B., R. A. Merrill, and L. A. Grossman. 2007. *Food and drug law, cases and materials*. 3rd ed, *University casebook series*: Foundation Press.

IFAD. 2008. *The role of high-value crops in rural poverty reduction in the Near East and North Africa.* Rome, Italy.

IFC. 2006. *Simplification of business regulations at the sub-national level: A reform implementation toolkit for project teams.* Washington, DC: The World Bank.

———. 2011. *About Doing Business: Measuring for impact.* Washington, DC: The World Bank.

IOM. 2010. *Enhancing food safety: The role of the Food and Drug Administration*. Washington, DC: The National Academies Press.

Islam, R. 2001 February 5-9. *Poverty alleviation, employment, and the labor market: Lessons from the asian experience*. Paper presented at Asia and Pacific forum on poverty: Reforming Policies and Institutions for Poverty Reduction, Asian Development Bank, Manila, Philippines.

ISO. 2003. *ISO 13485:2003- abstract.*

———. 2009. *ISO 31000: Risk management-- principles and guidelines.*

Joint Forces Staff College. 2011. *Overview* http://www.jfsc.ndu.edu/schools_programs/if/overview.asp (accessed November 30, 2011).

Jones-Evans, D., M. Klofsten, E. Andersson, and D. Pandya. 1999. Creating a bridge between university and industry in small European countries: The role of the industrial liaison office. *R&D Management* 29(1):47-56.

Kavilanz, P. 2010. *Tylenol plant still plagued by FDA violations* http://money.cnn.com/2010/12/01/news/companies/tylenol_plant_new_problems/index.htm (accessed December 20, 2011).

López, A., and V. M. Cáceres. 2008. Central America field epidemiology training program (CA FETP): A pathway to sustainable public health capacity development. *Human Resources for Health* 6(27).

Malcolm, S. A., C. A. Narrod, T. Roberts, and M. Ollinger. 2004. Evaluating the economic effectiveness of pathogen reduction technologies in cattle slaughter plants. *Agribusiness* 20(1):109-123.

McCain, J. 2011. Doing more with less? Past and present challenges for the FDA. *Pharmacy and Therapeutics* 36(3):145-155.

Mejia, C., J. McEntire, K. Keener, M. Muth, W. Nganje, S. Stinson, and H. Jensen. 2010. Traceability (product tracing) in food systems: An IFT report submitted to the FDA, volume 2: Cost considerations and implications. *Comprehensive Reviews in Food Science and Food Safety* 9(1):159-175.

Noy, N. F., and D. L. Mcguinness. 2000. *Ontology development 101: A guide to creating your first ontology.*

OECD. 2002. *Regulatory policies in OECD countries: From inverventionism to regulatory governance.* Paris, France.

———. 2005. *OECD guiding principles for regulatory quality and performance.*

———. 2011. *Regulatory policy and governance: Supporting economic growth and serving the public interest.*

Ozersky, J. 2010. The food-safety bill: Flawed, and needed. *TIME.*

Pendergrast, M. 2010. *Inside the outbreaks: The elite medical detectives of the epidemic intelligence service*. New York, NY: Houghton Mifflin Harcourt Publishing Company.

Pew Health Group. 2011. *After heparin: Protecting consumers from the risks of substandard and counterfeit drugs.* Washington, DC: Pew Health Group.

Pisanelli, D. M., A. Gangemi, and G. Steve. 1999. Toward a standard for guideline representation: An ontological approach. *Proceedings of the AMIA Symposium*:906-910.

Pray, C. E., and K. O. Fuglie. 2008. The private sector and international technology transfer in agriculture. In *Public-private collaboration in agricultural research*, edited by K. O. Fuglie and D. E. Schimmelpfennig: Iowa State University Press. Pp. 269-299.

Protiviti Inc. 2006. *Guide to enterprise risk management: Frequently asked questions.*

PSM. 2011. *USAID fights fake drugs and helps countries find the fakes.* http://www.safemedicines.org/2011/01/usaid-fights-fake-drugs-and-helps-countries-find-the-fakes-126.html (accessed November 21, 2011).

Purdue University. 2011. *Making medicine in Sub-Saharan Africa.* West Lafayette, IN: Purdue University.

———. 2012. *Sustainable medicine program in Tanzania (east & west Africa).* http://www.ipph.purdue.edu/sustain/ (accessed January 30, 2012).

Roberts, D., and T. Josling. 2011. *Tracking the implementation of internationally agreed standards in food and agricultural production.* International Food and Agricultural Trade Policy Council.

Semeniuk, I. 2011. US science agencies dodge deep cuts. *Nature* 479:455-456.

Silverman, E. 2011. *Which drugmaker fails most FDA inspections.* http://www.pharmalot.com/2011/03/which-drugmaker-fails-most-fda-inspections/ (accessed November 20, 2011).

Steger, D. 2011. The importance of institutions for regulatory cooperation in comprehensive economic and trade agreements: The Canada-EU CETA. *Legal Issues of Economic Integration* 39(1).

Stewart, K., and L. Gostin. 2011. Food and Drug Administration regulation of food safety. *Journal of the American Medical Association* 306(1):88-89.

The Associated Press. 2011. *Foreign officers chosen for hall of fame.* http://cjonline.com/news/2011-10-04/foreign-officers-chosen-hall-fame (accessed Novemeber 30, 2011).

The Whitehouse. *President obama's global development policy and global food security.* http://www.whitehouse.gov/sites/default/files/Food_Security_Fact_Sheet.pdf (accessed January 23, 2012).

Thomsen, M. R., and A. M. McKenzie. 2001. Market incentives for safe foods: An examination of shareholder losses from meat and poultry recalls. *American Journal of Agricultural Economics* 82(3):526-538.

U.S. Department of State. *Embassy of the United States, Montevideo, Uruguay: Animal and Plant Health Inspection Service (APHIS).* http://uruguay.usembassy.gov/aboutus-offices-aphis.html (accessed April 2, 2012).

Un oeuf is enough. 2010. *The Economist*, September 2.

USAID. 2011. *Press release: U.S. Announces support for the Africa-led partnership for aflatoxin control in Africa.*

USDA-APHIS. 2007. *Importation of fresh blueberry fruit from Uruguay and South Africa into the continental United States (draft).* United States Department of Agriculture.

USDA. 2002. *APHIS factsheet: Safeguarding America's bounty.*

———. 2006. *International services: International standards setting activities.* http://www.aphis.usda.gov/international_safeguarding/international_stand_setting_activities.shtml (accessed September 1, 2011).
———. 2007a. *About APHIS.* http://www.aphis.usda.gov/about_aphis/ (accessed September 1, 2011).
———. 2007b. *History of APHIS.* http://www.aphis.usda.gov/about_aphis/history.shtml (accessed September 1, 2011).
———. 2007c. *Pant import: Preclearance activities.* http://www.aphis.usda.gov/import_export/plants/plant_imports/preclearance_activities.shtml (accessed September 2, 2011).
———. 2010a. *International services.* http://www.aphis.usda.gov/international_safeguarding/index.shtml (accessed September 2, 2011).
———. 2010b. *What happens to the money that APHIS collects through user fees?* http://www.aphis.usda.gov/userfees/what_happens.shtml (accessed Septmeber 2, 2011).
———. 2010c. *What is a user fee.* http://www.aphis.usda.gov/userfees/what_is.shtml (accessed September 1, 2011).
———. 2011. *About the Foreign Agricultural Service.* http://www.fas.usda.gov/aboutfas.asp (accessed November 18, 2011).
USGS. 2009. *Cooperative research and development agreement (crada).* http://www.usgs.gov/tech-transfer/what-crada.html (accessed December 22, 2011).
USTR. *Bilateral and regional trade agreements.* http://www.ustr.gov/trade-topics/environment/bilateral-and-regional-trade-agreements (accessed November 18, 2011).
———. *Cooperative programs.* http://www.ustr.gov/trade-topics/labor/cooperative-programs (accessed November 21, 2011).
———. 2009. *2009 trade policy agenda and 2008 Annual Report.* Washington, DC.
———. 2011. *USTR and FDA welcome collaboration by APEC and the World Bank to enhance food safety and faciliatate food trade.* http://www.ustr.gov/about-us/press-office/press-releases/2011/may/ustr-and-fda-welcome-collaboration-apec-and-world-bank (accessed November 18, 2011).
Vijay, N. 2011. *Pharma industry needs risk-based approach for plant inspections: Micro labs ed.* http://www.pharmabiz.com/ArticleDetails.aspx?aid=65772&sid=1 (accessed October 31, 2011).
World Bank. 2009. *Improving food safety in Arab countries.* Washington, DC: The World Bank, FAO, and the International Fund for Agricultural Development.
WTO. 2009. *Fifth triennial review of the operation and implementation of the Agreement of Technical Barriers to Trade under Article 15.4.*
———. 2012. *Understanding the WTO: Agreements: Standards and safety.* http://www.wto.org/english/news_e/news01_e/sps_oct2001_e.htm (accessed January 26, 2012).
Young, P. B. 2011. Safety first. *NGF: Next Generation Food*, January 14, 78.

7

Conclusions and Priorities

This report is the product of the Institute of Medicine's *Committee on Strengthening Core Elements of Regulatory Systems in Developing Countries'* deliberations. One task of this study was to identify the core elements of a functional regulatory system. The committee described these elements and also what it sees as the minimal elements of a functional system, in Chapter 2. The core elements of regulatory systems relate to specific responsibilities that a regulatory authority takes to ensure product safety; the minimal elements include processes that are necessary to allow government to function.

From March to December 2011 the committee visited key emerging economies, spoke to representatives of the U.S. and various foreign governments, multinational and national food and medical product companies, donor organizations, development banks, and universities. These meetings informed the committee's analysis of the main gaps in developing country regulatory and product safety systems. A literature review complemented this analysis. Table 4-1 describes how the committee used the problems identified in Chapter 3 as its targets in forming its recommendations.

Chapters 5 and 6 describe the actions the committee believes would protect the safety of the food and medical product supply and build the capacity for reliable regulation in developing countries. As the study's statement of task (Box 1-1) points out, developing nations are a diverse group of 150 low- and middle-income countries. In its analysis the committee gave more attention to those countries that trade substantially with the United States, especially India, China, Thailand, South Africa, Mexico, and Brazil. An interest in equity led it to give some attention to the problems of the poorest countries as well.

The committee's recommendations are informed by a perspective that shares much with the Department of Health and Human Services' *Global Health Strategy.* The committee's strategy had four main points: the primacy of a global public health, the importance of risk-based investments, the usefulness of market incentives, and the necessity of international coordination. It recommended ways the FDA can use limited resources for maximum effect. The committee was not asked to project the cost of these investments, nor did it have the proper data or suitable expertise to do so, but it recommended a path for FDA to make the most of its limited resources, and suggested other duties for other government agencies, international organizations, industry, and universities.

ENTERPRISE RISK MANAGEMENT AS A TOOL TO SET PRIORITIES

The value of enterprise risk management is central to the committee's recommendations and to its strategy for strengthening the capacity of regulatory systems abroad. In order to set its priorities as an agency, the FDA needs to undertake an agency-wide risk assessment, risk analysis, and risk evaluation. This includes its capacity building work. The committee recommends that the FDA choose which foreign offices to scale up, what topics to cover in trainings, and how to assign its staff using a scientific risk analysis.

Some aspects of the FDA's governing plan seem informed by modern risk management. The agency has, for example, responded to globalization by putting offices in India, China, Chile, and Mexico. Other agency decisions, such as opening offices in Europe and the Middle East, seem on the surface less grounded in scientific risk analysis. Ultimately, the committee does not have access to the data that would inform the FDA's risk assessment, risk analysis, and risk evaluation framework. The FDA is in the best position to undertake this project. The committee believes that the results of a risk analysis could help Congress to increase appropriations to FDA and give the agency latitude to shift its attention more to places outside of the United States where much of the world's food and medical products are produced.

The committee is sensitive to the constraints the FDA's limited budget puts on its work. Given the current climate in Congress and the international economic downturn it is unlikely that the agency's appropriations will increase dramatically in the near future. Because of its limited budget the FDA should consider working though existing networks such and partnering with universities on training programs, and should use enterprise risk management to make the most of its modest budget.

A THREE TO FIVE YEAR STRATEGY FOR THE FDA

The committee realizes that only FDA has all the information necessary to rank its priorities, and it can best do this though enterprise risk management, dependent on quality data collected using modern information systems. Recommendations 6-1 and 6-2 address these needs. A full overhaul of the FDA informatics and information strategies will probably take a decade; reorganizing the agency would also take a long time. However, the committee outlined steps toward these goals that can be met in the next 3 to 5 years. First among these is the use of enterprise risk management to allocate funding and staffing to the FDA's foreign programs. Only over time, after Congressional approval, could the agency make similar adjustment to align its domestic actions with risk management principles. Similarly, the paperless information system envisioned in recommendation 6-2 is probably at least 8 years away. But in the next 3 to 5 years, the FDA can identify a standardized vocabulary and data collection method to use in its international activities.

In general, building strong regulatory systems abroad will be a long process, and success will be incremental. However there are some steps of the recommendations to FDA put forth in Chapters 5 and 6 that can be met in the next 3 to 5 years. The committee sees these recommendations as practical steps the FDA can take to improve product safety worldwide. Therefore, in the next three to five years the FDA should:

1. Join the regulatory authorities of the European Union, Canada, Japan, Norway, Iceland, Switzerland, Australia, and New Zealand in a working group on sharing inspections, making a plan for a system of mutual recognition of inspections to eliminate the wasteful duplication of work among similarly rigorous regulatory agencies (Recommendation 5-3).
2. Work (as one of several U.S. government agencies charged in Recommendation 5-5) to strengthen pharmacovigilance and foodborne diseases surveillance systems in developing countries. The agency has technical depth in surveillance that it can channel to developing countries both directly and thorough WHO and FAO.

3. Use enterprise risk management to focus its international programs, trainings, and offices (Recommendation 6-1).
4. Develop an informatics strategy that will eventually allow the FDA to move to paperless system, and articulates a standard data format and vocabulary (Recommendation 6-2).
5. Revise the curriculum of the FDA staff college to better educate its employees on the international ramifications of compliance with U.S. regulations, while working through universities and existing networks to train regulators abroad (Recommendation 6-3).
6. Lead in the development and adoption of international standards for food and medical products. The committee acknowledges the leadership the United States shows in developing international standards, but believes American adoption of harmonized standards leaves something to be desired (Recommendation 6-4).
7. Give serious, public consideration to expanding the one-up, one-back food traceability requirements to medical products (Recommendation 6-5).
8. Issue Cooperative Research and Development Agreements and other tools to encourage research into frugal technologies for fraud prevention, supply chain management, tracking, and verification that would be useful in developing counties (Recommendation 6-6).
9. Evaluate the Secure Supply Chain Pilot program in 2014 with a plan to scale the program up (Recommendation 6-7).

POLITICAL WILL TO IMPLEMENT THE COMMITTEE'S RECOMMENDATIONS

In their public statements over the last two years, the Department of Health and Human Services (HHS) and its subordinate agencies, especially the FDA, have shown a commitment to responding to the challenges brought on by globalization. The department's *Global Health Strategy* reflects political will for the changes the committee recommends. The strategy's first objective is to enhance global surveillance for disease and health concerns (HHS, 2011). This is consistent with the committee's recommendation that FDA, CDC, USDA, and USAID should provide technical training in pharmacovigilance and foodborne disease surveillance.

The *Global Health Strategy* also gives some attention to improving the safety of the global supply chain for food and medical products (HHS, 2011). The committee believes that there are market incentives that can strengthen the global supply chain and that access to hard-currency markets such as the United States can be that incentive. The Secure Supply Chain program, that promises speedy entry into the U.S. market to foreign producers whose products meet U.S. regulatory requirements, is an example of such a program. The elegance of the one-up, one-back traceability requirements is also a compelling example of supply chain management. One-up, one-back was initially met with low enthusiasm by food producers, and there is every reason to expect that many medical product producers will resist the committee's recommendation 6-5. Nevertheless, this is a necessary step to improve the global supply chain. Despite the FDA's budget constraints, it can advance a serious dialogue about the medical products supply chain by immediately holding a public hearing on expanding the one-up, one-back requirement. Its Secure Supply Chain pilot program is also promising and should be evaluated, with the intent of large scale expansion, in 2014.

The HHS *Global Health Strategy*'s fifth objective is to strengthen and implement science-based international health and safety standards and support multilateral efforts to improve them (HHS, 2011). Recommendation 6-4 on FDA leadership in adopting standards contains steps towards achieving this objective. Aside from being good health policy, a harmonized set of standards would do much to facilitate trade and, indirectly, to improve the economic development of low- and middle-income countries that trade with the United States. Recommendation 6-3 also supports the strengthening of international health and safety standards. The international, standing regulatory science training the committee recommends would do much to empower regulators from the poorest countries to better represent their nations at Codex and other standard setting meetings. Standards developed with wider input would better reflect the needs of all stakeholders.

Facilitating an international regulatory science college would also help advance the *Global Health Strategy* objective of strengthening health systems (HHS, 2011). Training a stronger regulatory workforce to oversee food and medical product regulatory systems is an international health and development goal. Educating students from developing countries in the new field of regulatory science would improve the technical knowledge of the regulatory workforce. A more knowledgeable, credentialed workforce would be expected to have better morale. This will take more than ten years to realize, but the investments in training that the FDA could contribute both alone and through existing networks, could improve product safety and strengthen the health system in developing countries.

CONCLUSIONS

This report presents the work of the IOM *Committee on Strengthening Core Elements of Regulatory Systems in Developing Countries* in answer to the task given by the FDA and shown in Box 1-1. In response to this task, it outlined in Chapter 2 the core elements of regulatory systems. Chapter 3 responds to Item B on the statement of task. In Chapter 3 the committee identifies the main needs in developing country regulatory and product safety systems. Item C in the statement of task asks for areas where progress might be made in the next 3-5 years; the committee outlines this in Table 4-1, and in this chapter, Chapter 7, as well as in the explanation of its recommendations in Chapters 5 and 6. In response to the statement of task Items D the committee refers readers to Chapter 7. Statement of task Item E, on contributions of universities, donors, and international organizations, is answered briefly in Table 4-1 and in more detail in Chapter 5. Parts of Chapter 6 particularly Recommendations 6-3 and 6-6 also suggest contributions for industry and academia. Chapters 5 and 6 also address Item F in the statement of task by describing how the FDA can work in partnership with other stakeholders.

The committee relied on the specific questions outlined in the statement of task to guide its deliberations. Table 7-1 lists the sections of the report that respond to each question.

In accordance with the Statement of Task's last paragraph, the committee gave the most attention to the problems of the emerging manufacturing nations that do the most trade with the United States. The committee's concern with equity also motivated it to consider the problems of the poorest countries as well.

This report identifies the main common problems in food and medical product safety across a range of countries and product lines. The committee concluded that developing countries have consistent problems with adherence to international standards, controlling supply chains, infrastructure deficits, laws, their workforce, institutional fragmentation, surveillance, communication, and political will.

The 13 recommendations put forth in this report represent the committee's consensus view of how to best bridge the gaps in food and medical product regulatory systems in low- and middle-income countries. These are multi-sectoral recommendations that have scope for implementation by a variety of actors. The committee believes that the changes it suggests could greatly improve the safety of food and medical products around the world.

The thirteen recommendations put forth in this report represent the committee's consensus view of how to best bridge the gaps in food and medical product regulatory systems in low- and middle-income countries. These are multi-sectoral recommendations that have scope for implementation by a variety of actors. The committee believes that the changes it suggests could greatly improve the safety of food and medical products around the world.

TABLE 7-1 A Guide to the Statement of Task Questions and Their Answers in This Report

Question	Addressed in Report
1. What critical issues do developing country regulatory authorities face and how are they prioritized?	Chapter 3
2. In what ways do they participate in standard-setting processes, organizations and harmonization efforts?	Chapter 3
3. What issues do they face in utilizing/implementing standards in a sustainable way?	Chapter 3
4. What are the core elements of their regulatory systems and are there others that should be considered?	Chapter 2
5. What are the major gaps in systems, institutional structures, workforce and competencies?	Chapter 3
6. In what ways could those gaps be addressed?	Chapters 4, 5, 6
7. In what ways could the U.S. FDA help address those gaps?	Chapters 5, 6, 7
8. In what ways could others (as delineated above) help meet those gaps?	Chapters 5, 6
9. In what ways could FDA partner with others to help meet those gaps?	Chapters 4, 5, 6
10. What recommendations have already been put forward to strengthen regulatory systems?	Chapter 3
11. What obstacles exist to implement those recommendations?	Chapter 3
12. What steps could be taken to remove those obstacles?	Chapter 4

REFERENCE

HHS. 2011. *The global health strategy of the U.S. Department of Health and Human Services.* Washington, DC.

Appendix A

Glossary

Active pharmaceutical ingredient (API): Any substance or mixture of substances intended to be used in the manufacture of a drug (medicinal) product and that when used in the production of a drug becomes an active ingredient of the drug product. Such substances are intended to furnish pharmacological activity or other direct effect in the diagnosis, cure, mitigation, treatment or prevention of disease or to effect the structure and function of the body (Active Pharmaceutical Ingredient Committee, 1999).

Aflatoxins: Toxins produced by mold that grows in nuts, seeds and legumes.

Agreement on Sanitary and Phytosanitary Measures (SPS Agreement): Agreement concerning the application of food safety and animal and plant health regulations as established by the World Trade Organization in 1995. Under these agreements, countries can set their own standards for safety as long as they are based on science.

Agrifood: The business of producing food agriculturally, as opposed to hunting and fishing.

Audit: a systematic examination to determine whether what is actually happening complies with documented procedures.

Biologics/biological products: A wide range of products including vaccines, blood and blood components, allergenics, somatic cells, gene therapy, tissues, and recombinant therapeutic proteins. These products are regulated by the U.S. Food and Drug Administration (FDA).

Codex Alimentarius Commission: The Codex Alimentarius Commission is a subsidiary body of the Food and Agriculture Organization of the United Nations and the World Health Organization. The Commission is entrusted with the elaboration of international standards of food to protect the health of consumers and to ensure fair practices in the food trade.

Codex committees: These subsidiary bodies of the Codex Alimentarius Commission include 9 general subject committees, 15 specific commodity committees, 6 regional coordinating committees and time-limited ad-hoc Intergovernmental Task Forces on specific subjects.

Critical control point: A step at which control is essential to prevent or eliminate a food safety hazard or reduce it to an acceptable level.

Discriminatory strict liability: Holds those who import and sell foreign products in the United States legally liable for regulatory violations pertaining to goods. It mandates more severe penalties for violations related to imports than domestically produced goods. Under this form of liability importers and sellers may be found liable for issues with products even if they took appropriate safety precautions and were unaware that the product is unsafe (Bamberger and Guzman, 2008).

Drug regulation: Encompasses a variety of functions, such as licensing, inspection of manufacturing facilities and distribution channels, import and export controls, product assessment and registration, pharmacovigilance, quality control, control of drug promotion and advertising and control of drug clinical trials.

Economies of scale: Factors that cause the average cost of producing a product to fall as the volume of its output increases.

Enterprise risk management: Enterprise risk management is a discipline, by which an organization in any industry assesses, controls, exploits, finances, and monitors risks from all sources for the purpose of increasing the organization's short- and long-term value to its stakeholders. (Casualty Actuarial Society-Enterprise Risk Management Committee, 2003).

Epidemiology: The study of occurrence, distribution, and determining factors associated with the health and diseases of a population; the study of how often health events or diseases occur in different groups and why.

Equivalence: The process of recognition that enables the sanitary and phytosanitary measures employed in one country to be deemed equivalent to those of a second country, trading in the same product, although different control measures are being practiced.

Excipient: A pharmacologically inactive substance used as a carrier for the active ingredients of a medication.

Farm-to-Table: Includes all steps involved in the production, storage, handling, distribution, and preparation of a food product.

Food contaminant: Any biological or chemical agent, foreign matter, or other substance not intentionally added to food which may compromise food safety or suitability.

Food control: A mandatory regulatory activity of enforcement by national or local authorities to provide consumer protection and ensure that all foods during production, handling, storage, processing and distribution are safe, wholesome and fit for human consumption; conform to quality and safety requirements; and are honestly and accurately labeled as prescribed by law.

Food hygiene: All conditions and measures necessary to ensure the safety and suitability of food at all stages of the food chain.

Food inspection: The examination, by an agency empowered to perform regulatory and/or enforcement functions, of food products or systems for the control of raw materials, processing, and distribution. This includes in-process and finished product testing to verify that they conform to regulatory requirements.

Food Safety Modernization Act: Signed into law by President Obama on January 4, 2011. The Act aims to ensure the U.S. food supply is safe by shifting the focus of federal regulators from responding to contamination to preventing it.

Food surveillance: The continuous monitoring of the food supply to ensure consumers are not exposed to components in foods, such as chemical contaminants or biological hazards, which pose a risk to health.

Food safety risk: The likelihood of harm to health resulting from exposure to hazardous agents in the food supply.

Foodborne illness: An illness, usually either infectious or toxic in nature, caused by an agent that enters the body through the ingestion of food.

Good Agricultural Practices (GAP): Practices of primary food producers (such as farmers and fishermen) that are necessary to produce safe and wholesome agricultural food products conforming to food laws and regulations.

Good Manufacturing Practices (GMP): Conformance with codes of practice, industry standards, regulations and laws concerning production, processing, handling, labeling and sale of foods decreed by industry, local, state, national and international bodies with the intention of protecting the public from illness, product adulteration and fraud.

Hard currency markets: Refers to globally traded currencies that are expected to serve as a reliable and stable store of value. Factors contributing to a currency's hard status might include the long-term stability of its purchasing power, the associated country's political and fiscal condition and outlook, and the policy posture of the issuing central bank.

Hazard: A biological, chemical or physical agent in, or condition of, food with the potential to cause harm.

Hazard analysis: The process of collecting and interpreting information on hazards and conditions leading to their presence to decide which are significant for food safety and therefore should be addressed in the HACCP plan.

Hazard analysis critical control point (HACCP) plan: A document prepared in accordance with the principles of HACCP to ensure control of hazards which are significant for food safety in the segment of the food chain under consideration.

Hazard analysis critical control point (HACCP) system: The hazard analysis critical control point system (HACCP) is a scientific and systematic way of enhancing the safety of foods from primary production to final consumption through the identification and evaluation of specific hazards and measures for their control to ensure the safety of food. HACCP is a tool to assess hazards and establish control systems that focus on prevention rather than relying mainly on end-product testing.

High value agriculture: Agricultural goods with a high economic value per kilogram, per hectare, or per calorie, including fruits, vegetables, meat, eggs, milk, and fish (Gulati et al., 2005).

Import lines: Finance facilities for importers covering documentary credits, bills receivables, and import loans.

Lot release of vaccines: The process of evaluating each individual lot of a licensed product before giving approval for its release the market. This process is carried out for vaccines and other biologicals in most countries. A general practice of release involves the review of manufacturer's production data and quality control test results (product summary protocol) by national regulatory authorities and national control laboratories. This may or may not be supplemented by laboratory testing by the national control laboratory, or by an agency or contracted laboratory performing tests for the national regulatory authority.

Medical devices: Medical instruments, apparatus or materials used on patients for surgery, treatment, or diagnosis (Mori et al., 2011).

Medical products: A wide range of products that include pharmaceutical drugs and medical devices.

Melamine: A synthetic chemical with a variety of industrial uses, including the production of resins and foams, cleaning products, fertilizers, and pesticides. If ingested in sufficient amounts, melamine can result in kidney failure and death.

Monitoring: In a HACCP plan, the act of conducting a planned sequence of observations or measurements of control parameters to assess whether a critical control point is under control.

One Health Initiative: A global strategy for expanding interdisciplinary collaborations and communications in all aspects of health care for humans, animals and the environment. Its goal is to advance health care by accelerating biomedical research discoveries, enhancing public health efficacy, expanding scientific knowledge, and improving medical education and clinical care.

One-up, one-back: In the food arena, activities performed to determine the distribution (one-up) and origin (one-back) of a product, usually to identify contaminated food. The activities are conducted jointly with local health departments and appropriate federal agencies. They entail the review and analysis of records such as harvesting dates, specific field and product locations, number of packages within a lot, and packaging and shipping dates.

Ontology: The structural frameworks for organizing information. It represents knowledge as a set of concepts within a domain, and the relationships between those concepts.

Product safety: The reduction in the probability that use of a product will result in illness, injury, death or negative consequences to people, property or equipment. Use of a product refers to its consumption, physical implantation into the body, or placement into physical use (Marucheck et al., 2011).

Product security: The delivery of a product that is uncompromised by intentional contamination, damage, or diversion within the supply chain (Marucheck et al., 2011).

PulseNet: A national network of federal, state, and local laboratories coordinated by CDC that uses standardized collection and sharing of pulsed-field gel electrophoresis (PFGE) molecular subtyping data to link isolates obtained from diverse sources. PulseNet allows scientists at public health laboratories throughout the country to rapidly compare the PFGE patterns of bacteria isolated from ill persons and determine whether those bacteria are similar.

Regulations: Establish government agencies, such as the U.S. Consumer Products Safety Commission (CPSC) and the Food and Drug Administration (FDA) with the responsibility for performing critical duties, such as approving products as safe and effective prior to entering the market, inspecting manufacturing facilities, and pursuing recalls. These agencies assure that firms meet basic rules for safety, and they also possess the authority to impose sanctions or fines when they discover violations or non-compliance (Marucheck et al., 2011).

Regulatory science: The science of developing new tools, standards, and approaches to assess the safety, efficacy, quality, and performance of all regulated products. It involves training in basic sciences that relate to the regulatory system; the development and validation of regulatory tests; screening and compliance testing; investigation of test results; and submission of dossiers for government or in-house review (FDA; Irwin et al., 1997).

Risk: The possibility or probability of loss, injury, disadvantage, or destruction.

Risk analysis: A process consisting of three components: risk assessment, risk management and risk communication.

Risk assessment: A transparent means by which to link the nature and extent of public health protection (risk reduction) achieved as a result of different risk management actions (or interventions). Risk analysis is composed of three activities (1) risk assessment, (2) risk management, and (3) risk communication.

Risk characterization: The qualitative and/or quantitative estimation, including attendant uncertainties, of the probability of occurrence and severity of known or potential adverse health effects in a given population based on hazard identification, hazard characterization and exposure assessment.

Risk communication: The interactive exchange of information and opinions concerning risks among risk assessors, risk managers, consumers and other interested parties.

Risk management: The process of weighing policy alternatives in the light of results of risk assessment, and, if required, selecting and implementing appropriate control options, including regulatory measures.

Standard setting: The establishment of a standard through the formulation of written rules and procedures.

Standards: Established norms or codified requirements for a product, such as material specifications or technical standards for performance. Standards may be developed by regulatory agencies, public organizations or industry associations (Marucheck et al., 2011).

Stringent regulatory authority: A national drug regulatory authority participating in the International Conference on Harmonization of Technical Requirements for Registration of Pharmaceuticals for Human Use or the Pharmaceutical Inspection Co-operation Scheme. Countries with stringent regulatory agencies include the United States, European Union member states and Japan, but for their purposes the committee also included Australia, New Zealand, Norway, Iceland, Switzerland, and Canada in this group.

Supply chain: A system of organizations, people, technology, activities, information and resources involved in moving a product or service from supplier to customer. Supply chain activities transform natural resources, raw materials and components into a finished product that is delivered to the end customer.

Surveillance: A key component of epidemiology, it can be defined as the ongoing collection, analysis, interpretation, and dissemination of health-related data. Surveillance is one of a number of methods used by epidemiologists to gather information on a disease.

Surveillance system: A group of integrated and quality-assured, cost-effective, and legally and professionally acceptable processes, designed for the purpose of identifying in an ongoing, flexible, standardized, timely, simple, sensitive, and predictive manner the emergence of meaningful epidemiologic phenomena and their specific associations. These processes include human, laboratory, and informatics activities to skillfully manage information derived from an entire defined community (or subgroup thereof that is sufficiently representative and large) and to disseminate that information in a timely and useful manner to those able to implement appropriate public health interventions.

Third party certification: An independent assessment declaring that specified requirements pertaining to a product, person, process or management system have been met.

Trace: The ability to know the historical locations, the time spent at each location, record of ownership, packaging configurations and environmental storage conditions for a particular drug (Koh et al., 2003).

Track: Involves knowing the physical location of a particular drug within the supply chain at all times (Koh et al., 2003).

Track and trace: The foundation for improved patient safety by giving manufacturers, distributors and pharmacies a systemic method to detect and control counterfeiting, drug diversions and mishandling (Koh et al., 2003).

Verification: In HACCP, the use of methods, procedures, or tests in addition to those used in monitoring to determine compliance with the HACCP plan, and/or whether the HACCP plan needs modification in order to enhance food safety.

REFERENCES

Active Pharmaceutical Ingredient Committee. 1999. *Good manufacturing practices in active pharmaceutical ingredients development.* Brussels, Belgium: APIC.

Bamberger, K. A., and A. T. Guzman. 2008. Keeping imports safe: A proposal for discriminatory regulation of international trade. *California Law Review* 96(6):1405-1447.

Casualty Actuarial Society-Enterprise Risk Management Committee. 2003. *Overview of enterprise risk management.* Fairfax, VA: Casualty Actuarial Society.

FDA. *The promise of regulatory science.* http://www.fda.gov/ScienceResearch/SpecialTopics/RegulatoryScience/ucm228206.htm (accessed January 24, 2012).

Gulati, A., N. Minot, C. Delgado, and S. Bora. 2005. Growth in high-value agriculture in Asia and the emergence of vertical links with farmers. Paper read at Workshop on Linking Small-Scale Producers to Markets: Old and New Challenges, December 15, 2005.

Irwin, A., H. Rothstein, S. Yearley, and E. McCarthy. 1997. Regulatory science - towards a sociological framework. *Futures* 29(1):17-31.

Koh, R., E. W. Schuster, I. Chackrabarti, and A. Bellman. 2003. *White paper: Securing the pharmaceutical supply chain.* Cambrdige, MA: Auto-ID Center, Massachusetts Institute of Technology.

Marucheck, A., N. Greis, C. Mena, and L. Cai. 2011. Product safety and security in the global supply chain: Issues, challenges and research opportunities. *Journal of Operations Management* 29(7-8):707-720.

Mori, M., R. Ravinetto, and J. Jacobs. 2011. Quality of medical devices and in vitro diagnostics in resource-limited settings. *Tropical Medicine and International Health* 16(11):1439-1449.

Appendix B

A Review of Tort Liability's Role in Food and Medical Product Regulation

Philip Chen
O'Neill Institute for Global and National Health Law
Georgetown University Law Center

I. Introduction

Public administrative systems and private tort liability[1] both play important roles in product regulation in the United States and elsewhere in the world. Administrative systems are driven mainly by government agencies that police the market through standard setting and enforcement. Tort liability is privately driven, and occurs after injuries arise from product use and failure. Its impact is primarily felt through the monetary judgments that courts impose on industry actors deemed liable under the law.

This paper provides an overview of (1) the role that tort (primarily product) liability plays in food and medical product regulation; (2) the key factors that affect the capacity of the tort liability system to function; and (3) the state of this system in countries of interest to the Committee's work.

With respect to these three considerations, this review maintains the following: Tort liability historically preceded and then played an overlapping role with modern administrative systems. Today, tort liability's role in food and medical product regulation can be analyzed by considering its impact on four objectives: safety, compensation, product availability, and product innovation. The extent of the tort system's impact on those objectives is a product of the liability rules that are laid down (for example, strict liability versus negligence); the extent of access to the legal process by plaintiffs; and the quality of civil justice institutions, such as the judiciary. Each country of interest to the Committee faces different challenges in its own product liability system and civil justice institutions, as well as in its regulatory agencies.

This review provides a general historical and conceptual introduction, primarily from the perspective of the U.S. and European experience. Because legal systems are rooted in particular historical and cultural contexts, the determination of the appropriate scope of tort and administrative responsibility with respect to food and medical products in a specific country depends on a detailed examination of the social context there. The key variables identified in this discussion may serve as a starting point for such a detailed examination.

II. Historical Perspectives on Tort Liability and Regulatory Systems for Food and Medical Products

Food and medicines have been regulated since ancient times through criminal and civil mandates.[2] In the Western world, Roman law prescribed quality and other requirements for food and drink, enforceable by the state. It also provided for civil

---

[1] Although this paper refers to tort liability (the common law term), it intends to include the similar concept of delict in civil law systems.

[2] Peter Barton Hutt and Peter Barton Hutt II, *A History of Government Regulation of Adulteration and Misbranding of Food*, 39 FOOD DRUG & COSM. L.J. 2 (1984). The following historical discussion is drawn from the authors' discussion at pages 1-26.

liability, which could be pursued through private legal action in some instances. Early English history also reflected public and private enforcement of food standards. Under old English law, the Crown established basic quality systems such as uniform weights and measures, bread and grain standards, and officials to ensure compliance. At the same time, the common law permitted a buyer to sue a seller of substandard food for damages.[3] Owners of restaurants were subject to strict liability for sales of food and drink.[4] Nevertheless, before industrialization, at least in common law countries, tort suits based on product quality were few, perhaps in part because the costs of litigation outweighed the benefits.[5]

Beginning in the mid-19th century, the development of mass production, industrialization, science, and national markets led to changes in both how the state oversaw food and medical products. In the United States, the rise of the modern regulatory agency in the first half of the 20th century also coincided with expansion of the scope of product liability. Today's U.S. Food and Drug Administration itself grew from its niche in the Bureau of Chemistry within the Department of Agriculture into the Food and Drug Administration and took on broader regulatory powers.[6]

Tort law also evolved in the US under pressure from the growing number of consumer claims and lawsuits.[7] For food products, consumers traditionally could not sue manufacturers directly in tort unless the latter had a contractual relationship with the former.[8] In essence, the legal relationships characterizing the supply chain became an obstacle interposed between the injured and the producer. However, by mid-century, those barriers had severely eroded. Lawyers for industry told their clients: "[W]ith minor, if any, exceptions, a manufacturer, canner, packer, or processor is presently held to be liable to a consumer for lack of care in the preparation or inspection of his product, where such lack of care proximately results in injury to the consumer."[9] At the same time, the pressure from litigation was also at work: some well-known manufacturers made greater efforts to institute product safety measures in response to the concern of potential exposure to lawsuits.[10]

Tort liability for goods developed into a specialized area of product liability law, with its own plethora of detailed rules and doctrines. Foremost among these was the

---

[3] *Id.*, at 22.

[4] James M. Guiher & Stanley C. Morris, *Handling Food Products Liability Cases*, 1 FOOD DRUG COSM. L.Q. 115 (1946).

[5] JANE STAPLETON, PRODUCT LIABILITY 10 (1994).

[6] DANIEL CARPENTER, REPUTATION AND POWER 75-112 (2010) (describing the history of FDA's regulatory powers from the 1920s through the passage of the Food, Drug and Cosmetic Act).

[7] The American Canners' Association data showed 151 claims and 5 lawsuits in 1923, and 2174 claims and 259 lawsuits by 1939. *See* Guiher and Morris, at 110; *see also* Bradshaw Mintener, *Food Products Liability Law*, 1 FOOD DRUG COSM. L.Q. 96, 99 (1946).

[8] This legal concept is known as privity. *See* Rollin Perkins, *Unwholesome Food As A Source of Liability*, 5 IOWA L. REV. 86, 87 (1919). However, the consumer could sue the retailer, who could, in turn, sue the distributor, and so on up the chain. However, such an approach might be "inadequate [because] [t]he dealer may be financially unable to respond to the extent of the injury." *Id.*

[9] Guiher and Morris, at 113.

[10] REED DICKERSON, PRODUCTS LIABILITY AND THE FOOD CONSUMER 253 (1951) ("The same story was told: a rising claim-consciousness since World War I, resulting in the adoption of all known feasible precautions in an attempt to make food products as claim-proof as possible."). Coca-Cola instituted a fully automated washing and disinfection system to reduce claims caused by contaminants or impurities in its drinks. DICKERSON, at 254-255.

concept of *strict liability*. Under strict liability, the plaintiff need only show that the product was defective and caused the injury, he or she need not prove that the manufacturer was *at fault* or had breached a duty owed to the plaintiff. Over the course of the 1960s and 1970s, both judges and scholars emphasized that such rules would result in safer products because manufacturers would be incentivized to take greater precautions to reduce their tort liability costs.[11]

From the late 1970s through 1990s, growing criticism of this tort framework arose because of a "litigation explosion" of product liability suits and the rise of costs of goods and services perceived to be the result of these cases.[12] Historically, the majority of cases brought under product liability were premised on defects in production and manufacturing. More recently, cases against medical products producers are largely brought on grounds of inadequate warning and defective design and questions increasingly grew over whether such suits improved safety or thwarted the development of beneficial products.[13]

Today, the debate over the appropriate role of product liability continues in the United States and other developed countries, as competing demands of social objectives together with the costs and benefits of the tort system are balanced. In the next section, this review considers these objectives and the factors that influence the effectiveness of the product liability system.

III. Analysis of the Relationship between Administrative Systems for FDA-Regulated Products and Product Liability

Modern administrative systems and tort liability systems today have different purposes and methods to achieve their goals. An administrative regulatory system for food, drugs, and medical devices is primarily designed to oversee safety and effectiveness of the products in the marketplace. It accomplishes this by setting standards that industry must meet, and by enforcing those standards throughout the design, production, and marketing process using a variety of tools, including registration, pre-marketing approval, guidance, recall, detention, and seizure. Regulators and other law enforcement officials also have access to more coercive tools such as civil and criminal penalties.

The modern tort liability system has a hybrid purpose, particularly in the United States.[14] On the one hand, it provides compensation and redress for injuries to an individual caused by another party.[15] In addition, tort systems, especially through the

---

[11] *See generally* RICHARD A. EPSTEIN, TORTS 389-92 (1999). For an example of influential scholarly work on this point, see GUIDO CALABRESI, THE COSTS OF ACCIDENTS: A LEGAL AND ECONOMIC ANALYSIS (1970).

[12] JANE STAPLETON, PRODUCT LIABILITY 31-33 (1994).

[13] *See* STEVEN GARBER, PRODUCT LIABILITY AND THE ECONOMICS OF PHARMACEUTICALS AND MEDICAL DEVICES 40 (1993). A product is defective due to an inadequate warning "when the foreseeable risks of harm posed . . . could have been reduced or avoided by the provision of reasonable instructions or warnings by the seller or [relevant parties], and the omission of [these warnings] renders the product not reasonably safe." A defective design is one in which "the foreseeable risks of harm posed by the product could have been reduced or avoided by the adoption of a reasonable alternative design by the seller or [relevant other parties], and the omission of the alternative design renders the product not reasonably safe." RESTATEMENT OF TORTS (3D): PRODUCT LIABILITY at sec. 2.

[14] KENNETH S. ABRAHAM, THE LIABILITY CENTURY 8-9 (2008) ("[T]ort is in practice a system of mixed goals.").

[15] *See generally* JULES L. COLEMAN, RISKS AND WRONGS (1992).

vehicle of product liability, clearly have market effects when large monetary judgments are entered against producers. (Settlements may have similar effects.) The fear of such potential damages, the media and public scrutiny they bring, can foster greater care and discipline on the part of producers. This, in turn, may have other intended or unintended consequences, such as price increases that could be passed on to consumers.

This section proceeds in three parts. First, it will briefly suggest some key goals that society seeks to meet in dealing with the development and use of FDA-regulated products and the tort system's relationship to them. Second, it identifies access rules and the quality of civil justice institutions as additional factors that must be considered when examining a tort system's effectiveness. Third, it discusses ways in which other significant product liability systems, namely the European and New Zealand models, vary from the U.S. model. The purpose of this third discussion is to show the significant variation within product liability practices, and to emphasize that the legal system's own procedural internal rules and institutions must also be considered when making any general conclusion about tort and administration.

A. Societal Goals

This section relies upon Steven Garber's framework for identifying the goals associated with the regulation of food and medical products.[16] Broadly speaking, society has four major objectives with respect to these products: safety, compensation, availability, and innovation. The tort system affects each of these objectives in a range of ways.

1. Safety

By imposing monetary damages on tortfeasors, the tort law increases the costs to them of their activities. In the case of a defectively manufactured FDA-regulated product, the tort law penalizes the producer (or potentially others along the supply chain), and thus incentivizes companies to take greater precautions to prevent future production of defective goods.[17] The rules that determine when liability attaches will affect the likelihood that damages will result. For example, as discussed earlier, as a general matter, a rule establishing strict liability for product defects will shift costs to the producer, while a negligence rule may reduce the burden.

2. Compensation

One of the key distinctions between administrative and tort systems is that tort systems require legally responsible private parties to compensate the injured. In fact, this compensating of the plaintiff by the legally responsible defendant is at the core of tort liability. The definition of compensation, including the scope and calculation of costs, such as pain and suffering, are different from jurisdiction to jurisdiction.

Administrative systems typically do not provide compensation to injured parties,[18] and any fines or penalties assessed as a result of regulatory enforcement action inure to

---

[16] Steven Garber identifies four "outcomes of interest": product availability, pricing, safety and effectiveness, and innovation. This paper presents a variation of this framework and adds the goal of compensation. *See* GARBER, at xxvi-xxix.

[17] Tomas J. Philipson and Eric Sun, *Is the Food and Drug Administration Safe and Effective*?, 22 J. ECON. PERSP. 85, 92 (2008).

[18] One historical exception to this is state-administered worker compensation. In the FDA-regulated products arena, a number of countries have compensation funds administered and financed by the state (or by private industry) for particular FDA-regulated product categories. *See, e.g.*, FONDAZAIONE ROSSELLI, ANALYSIS OF THE ECONOMIC IMPACT OF THE DEVELOPMENT RISK CLAUSE AS PROVIDED BY DIRECTIVE

the treasury. Regulatory bodies can set up compensation funds and administer them, although in the US context, this has not been the common practice.[19] Private health, disability, or other forms of insurance may also cover compensation for personal injuries.[20] The availability and extent of these systems will vary from country to country.

3. Availability

The increased cost to manufacturers as a result of product liability lawsuits can also impact the availability of FDA-regulated products by making it no longer economically feasible to continue selling the product. This may produce a social benefit by driving out substandard products. The Dalkon Shield case is often described in this way.[21] In other instances, actual or potential tort liability may cause producers in key industries to consider exiting the market or to raise prices significantly, which may result in greater social harm. For FDA-regulated products in the United States, one of the more visible examples of this phenomenon was product litigation over childhood vaccines, which resulted in shortages of key medicines until the government intervened to reduce the scope of liability for vaccine-makers.[22]

4. Innovation

Related to the issue of availability is that of innovation. Increasing the cost to producers of certain FDA-regulated products may impact innovation by driving companies to abandon projects that may be too risky. This point is made most frequently in the debate over the "development risk clause" in the European Union's Product Liability Directive. The "development risk clause" is a defense to liability when the manufacturer can show "that the state of scientific and technical knowledge at the time when he put the product into circulation was not such as to enable the existence of the defect to be discovered."[23] This clause was introduced precisely to ensure that innovation was not inhibited by product liability.[24]

5. Empirical Studies

It is worth noting that in considering the practical effect of the tort system on issues such as safety, availability, and innovation, no empirical studies provide definitive conclusions (particularly across national jurisdictions). Experts all acknowledge the problems in obtaining and interpreting the pertinent data.[25] For example, in the case of

---

85/374/EEC ON LIABILITY FOR DEFECTIVE PRODUCTS 93-99 (2004)(Denmark, UK, Austria, Germany (public funds for certain products); Sweden, Finland, Germany (manufacturer funded).

[19] In the United States in the FDA-regulated product area, the National Vaccine Injury Compensation Program is an exception. *See* n.22 *infra*.

[20] A. Mitchell Polinsky and Steven Shavell, *The Uneasy Case for Product Liability*, 123 HARV. L. REV. 1437, 1462 (2010).

[21] GARBER, at 83-84.

[22] Supply concerns were central to the passage of the National Childhood Vaccine Injury Act of 1986. *See* H.R. Rep. No. 99-908, at 1986 U.S.C.C.A.N. 6344, at 6347-6348. To address this issue, the Act modified tort liability for vaccine manufacturers. It eliminated the ability of plaintiffs to claim that a vaccine was defectively designed, while creating a simplified compensation process for claimants. However, it allowed suits against manufacturers on the ground that the vaccine was defectively manufactured, or if manufacturers engaged in fraudulent and other similar activity. *See* Bruesewitz v. Wyeth, 131 S. Ct. 1068, 1072-1074 (2011).

[23] Council Directive 85/374 art. 7(e), 1985 OJ (L 210) (EEC) (on the approximation of the laws, regulations and administrative provisions of the Member States concerning liability for defective products).

[24] STAPLETON, at 225-229.

[25] *See, e.g.*, GARBER, at vi; Jean C. Buzby, et al., *Jury Decisions and Awards in Personal Injury Lawsuits Involving Foodborne Pathogens*, 36 J. CONSUMER AFF. 220, 235-37 (2002).

the European development risk clause and its relationship to innovation, a recent study commissioned by the European Union acknowledged that "[i]t is very difficult to collect sound empirical evidence on the effect the [clause] has on a company's innovative effort."[26] Multiple variables may enter into the calculation of a potential innovator to continue or abandon research during the course of product creation. With respect to foodborne illness litigation, experts that reviewed jury verdicts noted the difficulty in determining "exactly how firms are affected by such legal action because the actual decision making on food safety issues by firms is generally kept confidential."[27]

Even if such data were fully available in the U.S. context, it is not clear how any legal or policy conclusions that are drawn would be directly applicable to other countries, since results in other countries depend on the structure of legal institutions, rules of access, social and political attitudes towards litigation, among others.[28] These issues are discussed below.

B. Factors Influencing Results and Effectiveness of the Tort Liability System

The way in which the tort system affects regulatory outcomes such as safety for food and medical products is largely affected by three main factors: (1) substantive rules governing liability; (2) the ability of injured parties to access the tort system; and (3) the quality of the civil justice institutions that govern the tort system.[29] With respect to (1), the key policy and legal concerns were discussed above in Part III.A. This subsection discusses access and institutional concerns.

1. Access

The civil liability system in most countries is based in the judicial system. The primary method of access is through the injured parties' filing of a lawsuit in a court. Many practical factors influence the relative ease of plaintiffs to use the courts for redress: the principal elements include the cost of litigation and fact-finding.[30] For example, one study of consumer food-borne illness litigation in the US concluded that a key factor in determining the success of such a lawsuit was the ability to identify the

---

[26] FONDAZAIONE ROSSELLI, at 3.

[27] Buzby, at 236. Buzby concludes that "[t]here is also reason to suspect that the strongest incentive for food firms to improve food safety is the threat of large outbreaks of foodborne illness resulting in widespread litigation and uninsured economic losses." *Id.* at 237.

[28] Matthew Reimann, *Liability for Defective Products at the Beginning of the Twenty-First Century: Emergence of a Worldwide Standard?*, 51 AM. J. COMP. L. 751, 812 (2003). Jane Stapleton, an expert on U.S. and European product liability systems makes this exact point about comparability: "In the absence of Rand-type [empirical] studies, such 'arguments' [over the effect of product liability on the economy] reduce to speculation and rhetoric. The internal complexity of market dynamics would make any such future studies very difficult to do and their conclusions would probably carry little weight when applied to another legal and economic system where, for example, claims rates are much lower, tax policy is different, and public provision in areas such as health care is much more generous." STAPLETON, at 35.

[29] *See* Christopher Hodges, *Approaches to product liability in the EU and Member States*, *in* PRODUCT LIABILITY IN COMPARATIVE PERSPECTIVE (2005). Hodges identifies a number of these factors in considering product liability: "substantive law on liability"; "mechanisms for funding lawyers and court costs, and the extent and proportionality of the financial risk to claimant and defendant"; "rules of procedure"; "law on damages"; "sometimes, conflict/jurisdictional issues such as proper law, jurisdiction and enforcement of judgments." *See id.* at 192.

[30] RICHARD A. NAGAREDA, MASS TORTS IN A WORLD OF SETTLEMENT 8 (2007) ("Improved capitalization gave plaintiffs' law firms the financial wherewithal to undertake the kinds of lengthy, expensive discovery campaigns permitted . . . and essential as a strategic matter in litigation against large-scale corporate defendants.").

pathogen that caused injury.[31] This likely requires "supporting medical information [and] microbiological testing on any suspect food," which could be costly.[32]

Tort systems have sought to reduce the burden of such lawsuits on individual plaintiffs, particularly with respect to product liability, through a number of mechanisms. The most well known is the class action. This vehicle allows plaintiffs to combine their lawsuits, which contain the same nucleus of law and fact, thus saving the need to litigate individually across many courts.[33] In the United States, the expansion of class action mechanisms facilitated a wide number of lawsuits concerning FDA-regulated products.[34] A second well-known method of cost-reduction for the plaintiff is the contingent fee, in which clients agree to allow attorneys to take a percentage of a successful judgment in return for the attorneys' covering the costs of the litigation up front.[35] Other mechanisms can include state-funded legal aid. The importance of access is reflected in a recently commissioned study by the European Union in which "greater access to legal assistance" was most frequently mentioned as a "major factor" in "contributing to the success of product liability claims in European jurisdictions."[36]

2. Civil Justice Institutions

The other essential component of an effective tort system is the quality of civil justice institutions. Some of the principal elements of a functioning judicial system include: independence of courts from the executive branches, impartiality of judges, adequacy of resources, and the ability of the courts to enforce judgments.[37] These attributes are described as "the cornerstone of the rule of law." Improving the baseline legal institutions such as the judiciary is now considered to be a fundamental part of economic development by multilateral institutions such as the World Bank. Without a functioning set of judicial institutions, substantive tort law rules are not meaningful.

C. Contextualized Determinations

Although tort and administrative systems have different goals, they overlap and influence safety outcomes for FDA-regulated products. Precisely how and to what extent is a combination of the specific institutional design of the tort and the administrative system, the substantive rules governing them, as well as their available resources. The United States itself has a contoured approach that has precluded lawsuits for some types

---

[31] Buzby, at 235-36.
[32] *Id.*, at 236.
[33] *Fed.* R. Civ. P. 23. (listing requirements for class certification).
[34] See Deborah Hensler et al., Class Action Dilemmas 23-31 (2000) (discussing the historical development of class action mechanisms in the United States and noting that "mass personal injury class actions seemed to be growing in number and scope" and listing litigation over HIV-contaminated blood products, asbestos, and silicone breast implants).
[35] *See* Herbert M. Kritzer, Risks, Reputations, and Rewards: Contingency Fee Legal Practice in the United States 254 (2004) (noting that "contingency fees can provide a means of access to justice" but also noting that other mechanisms exist such as "legal aid, legal expense insurance . . . [and] fee shifting"). He concludes that the system "encourage[s] lawyers to pursue . . . highly risky and costly cases" but that some of those cases are ones in which "in the absence of legal attack, dangerous products and practices would have gone unabated." *Id.* at 267.
[36] Lovells, Product Liability in the European Union: A report for the European Commission 36 (2003) (findings based on a survey of product liability attorneys, regulators, industry, and consumers).
[37] James H. Anderson, et al., Judicial Systems in Transition Economies, 57-61 (2005) (World Bank report on legal and judicial reform, focusing on Europe and Central Asia).

of product liability claims with respect to particular pharmaceutical and medical device products.[38]

Traditionally, the approach of European states and the United States diverged in terms of the reliance and availability of product liability. The European Union moved towards a greater acceptance of product liability when it adopted regional legislation.[39] Momentum to adopt a regional product liability rule was deeply influenced by the injuries suffered across Europe due to widespread birth defects caused by the drug thalidomide.[40] The European rule adopts similar strict liability approaches, however, it differed in some respects in how it allocated burdens of proof.[41] One early difference was that it permitted agricultural products to be exempted from the strict liability system; however, because of the subsequent Bovine Spongiform Encephalopathy (BSE) crisis, the European Union amended the law to require each country to apply strict liability for those products.[42]

European and U.S. systems also approach the issue of class actions and litigation costs in different ways. The U.S. view seeks "to overcome the problem that small recoveries do not provide the incentive for any individual to bring a solo action prosecuting his or her rights. A class action solves this problem by aggregating the relatively paltry potential recoveries into something worth someones . . . labor."[43] As a result, the U.S. approach seeks to deputize the private bar to achieve public policy goals such as market safety. While European jurisdictions have begun to permit class action-styled, group lawsuits, they differ in significant ways, reflecting a desire to control the growth of such litigation.[44] On the cost side, the two also diverge: European jurisdictions tend to require the loser to pay winner's legal fees, which may tend to discourage risk taking by plaintiffs.[45]

---

[38] For example, the medical products realm in the US currently evinces a complicated patchwork of liability rules. Product liability suits against medical device manufacturers can no longer be brought if the claim is based on standards "different from" or "in addition to" FDA requirements. Accordingly, plaintiffs cannot bring cases under theories of design defect or inadequate warning defects under state tort law for medical devices that have undergone pre-market authorization. *See* Riegel v. Medtronic, Inc., 552 U.S. 312 (2008). If the device was in violation of FDA standards (for example, in manufacturing), then the suit could be maintained. However, if the medical device was marketed pursuant to the 510(k) process, the manufacturer could be fully subject to product liability. *See* Medtronic, Inc., v. Lohr, 518 U.S. 470 (1996). For NDA innovator pharmaceuticals, lawsuits can continue to be brought under the inadequate warning defects theory. *See* Wyeth v. Levine, 555 U.S. 555 (2009). However, suits against generic pharmaceutical manufacturers filed under the same grounds must be dismissed. *See* PLIVA, Inc. v. Mensing, 131 S.Ct. 2567 (2011). Claims against vaccine manufacturers must proceed in a special tribunal under the National Childhood Vaccine Injury Act. *See* Bruesewitz v. Wyeth, 131 S. Ct. 1068 (2011).

[39] Council Directive 85/374 art. 7(e), 1985 OJ (L 210) (EEC) (on the approximation of the laws, regulations and administrative provisions of the Member States concerning liability for defective products).

[40] STAPLETON, at 45.

[41] *Id.*, at 66.

[42] European Union, Defective products: liability, at http://europa.eu/legislation_summaries/consumers/consumer_safety/l32012_en.htm (last visited Nov. 7, 2011).

[43] Amchem Products, Inc. v. Windsor, 521 U.S. 591, 617 (1997).

[44] Richard A. Nagareda, *Aggregate Litigation Across the Atlantic and the Future of American Exceptionalism*, 62 VAND. L. REV. 1, 28-30 (2009).

[45] *Id.*, at 30.

Some countries with well-developed regulatory systems have made deliberate public policy choices to emphasize one end of the tort-regulatory spectrum. For example, New Zealand significantly curtailed its tort law and replaced substantial portions with a government-administered "no-fault" system in 1974.[46] Under the New Zealand system, personal injury lawsuits are replaced with application to a state-run compensation fund. As a general matter, lawsuits for accidental injuries caused by FDA-regulated products cannot be brought under tort.[47] Instead, the injured party applies to a government agency, the Accident Compensation Commission (ACC) for redress. The ACC system reduces substantially the ability of the traditional tort system to deter actions of product manufacturers. It arguably places a larger burden on the administrative agency to provide adequate oversight and to ensure compliance.

What constitutes the optimal mix of administrative regulation and product liability may depend not only on the state of the civil justice system, but also on the quality of the public agencies charged with overseeing the safety of FDA-regulated products. As a general matter, administrative systems are largely affected by (1) resource constraints and (2) regulatory independence. Without adequate financial, technical, and human resources, agencies cannot meet existing or expanding responsibilities.[48] Regulatory effectiveness also depends on the agency given an appropriate scope of authority and capacity to resist any inappropriate influence on the part of vested interests. For example, when an agency is unduly dependent upon industry, its policies may reflect those viewpoints in a manner that compromises its mission.[49] This risk may be higher in countries in which regulatory capacities are still developing. Because FDA-regulated products, particularly pharmaceuticals and medical devices, require substantial scientific expertise to develop and to evaluate, a developing country may have a smaller pool of domestic scientific expertise. Those individuals may be highly sought after by both regulators and industry, increasing the risk of inappropriate conflicts of interest.[50]

---

[46] Legal reform was led by a government commission, which produced the Woodhouse Report, detailing the costs and inefficiencies of the tort liability system. See Peter H. Schuck, *Tort Reform, Kiwi-Style*, 27 YALE L. & POL'Y REV. 187, 188 (2008).

[47] One exception may be for food-borne illnesses, because the ACA does not cover personal injuries arising from accidents that are the result of ingesting "a virus, bacterium, or protozoan." See Accident Compensation Act, Section 25(1)(ba); Bill Marler, My View of Food Poisoning Law in Australia and New Zealand, at http://www.marlerblog.com/case-news/my-view-of-food-poisoning-law-in-australia-and-new-zealand/

[48] One current domestic example of this situation: U.S. FDA recognized early on that its expanding responsibilities due to technological change and globalization placed an even greater strain on its ability to accomplish its mission. *See, e.g.*, FDA SCIENCE BOARD SUBCOMMITTEE ON SCIENCE AND TECHNOLOGY, FDA SCIENCE AND MISSION AT RISK (2007) at http://www.fda.gov/ohrms/dockets/ac/07/briefing/2007-4329b_02_01_FDA%20Report%20on%20Science%20and%20Technology.pdf (finding that the agency cannot fulfill its mandate because "its scientific workforce does not have sufficient capacity and capability").

[49] See George Stigler, *The Theory of Economic Regulation*, 2 BELL J. ECON. & MGMT. SCI. 3 (1971) (articulating concept of agency capture).

[50] This risk is not confined only to developing countries. In the US context, the pool of scientific expertise in FDA-regulated products is often highly specialized, and commonly resides in industry and in academic settings. The US FDA has established a conflict-of-interest and disclosure system but concerns rose over the number of waivers granted for persons with identified conflicts. *See, e.g.*, FDA Advisory Committees Process for Recruiting Members and Evaluating Potential Conflicts of Interest

IV. A Brief Review of Product Liability Practices in Selected Foreign Jurisdictions

This section briefly addresses product liability systems in four countries that are critical to this Committee's review: Brazil, India, China, and South Africa. Each country has a unique legal system and culture, with its own institutional structure and challenges. This brief review is not exhaustive, but is meant to introduce the central legal doctrines and institutions that bear on the matter of product liability, particularly for food and medical products.

A. Brazil

Brazil's current product liability system is primarily founded on the Consumer Protection Code, which it adopted in 1990.[51] The code was the result of a constitutional amendment, and sought to widen consumer access to courts. It did so through a number of key mechanisms. First, liability for defective products is strict, and does not depend on a finding of negligence.[52] Second, the law introduced a more liberal class action procedure that permits non-governmental associations to bring lawsuits on behalf of injured consumers.[53] Third, it reduced class plaintiffs' burden of litigation costs. Under traditional practice, legal costs were borne by the loser. This rule tends to discourage product litigation because it places substantial financial risk on the plaintiff. The consumer protection code alters the calculus by only shifting costs to the class plaintiff if the suit itself is deemed to be frivolous.[54] The code also places a legal obligation on manufacturers to recall products if they have knowledge of the dangerousness of the product. If the product is not recalled, that fact is deemed as satisfying a finding of negligence on the part of the manufacturer, which can impose further potential liabilities.[55]

Although the consumer protection code has increased the capacity of parties to sue under product liability in doctrine, a number of factors constrain the expansion of such suits. For example, unlike in the United States, there is little use of contingency fee arrangements, and plaintiffs have only limited discovery rights.[56] The product liability bar is small and access to scientific expertise necessary to prosecute significant actions is limited.[57] One practitioner observes that consumer claims against pharmaceutical products rarely succeed unless "the product is severely defective, and causes a significant side effect to the consumer" and "only those cases that receive media attention make it to litigation."[58]

---

http://www.gao.gov/new.items/d08640.pdf and Guidance for the Public, FDA Advisory Committee Members, and FDA Staff on Procedures for Determining Conflict of Interest and Eligibility for Participation in FDA Advisory Committees at http://www.fda.gov/downloads/RegulatoryInformation/Guidances/UCM125646.pdf.

[51] Consumer Protection Law (No. 8,078 of September 11, 1990).

[52] Alejandro Hernandez Maestroni, *Part I: Introduction: Overview of the Study Undertaken by the National Law Center for Inter-American Free Trade*, 20 ARIZ. J. INT'L & COMP. L. 1, 7 (2003). Brazil recognizes manufacturing, design, and failure-to-warn defects. Although Brazil codifies liability as strict, there is debate over whether manufacturers can claim a "development risk" defense. *Id.* at 25 and 30-31.

[53] Antonio Gidi, *Class Actions in Brazil*, 51 AM. J. COMP. L. 311, 363-69 (2003) (discussing Art. 82).

[54] *Id.*, at 340.

[55] Julio Cesar Bueno, Brazil, in the International Comparative Legal Guide to Product Liability 2011 at sec. 1.4.

[56] Gidi, at 320.

[57] *Id.* at 333.

[58] Otto Banho Licks, Life Sciences: Brazil (2010), at www.practicallaw.com/lifescienceshandbook.

The larger legal framework is also facing challenges in the midst of significant institutional reforms. After the end of military rule, the new constitution established a separate and independent judiciary. The courts crafted their own tenure, pay, and disciplinary systems, with little oversight by other branches of government.[59] Serious cases of judicial corruption and waste continued, however, severely undermining the credibility of the courts and resulted in a constitutional amendment that now seeks to rein in the judiciary.[60] From a case management perspective, today, the judiciary continues to face a high backlog of civil cases.[61] Different localities face severe institutional challenges: in Sao Paolo, each judge has an average of 8,000 to 10,000 cases.[62] In sum, while the rules governing product liability liberalized, the practical difficulties that plaintiffs face in accessing the courts, together with the state of the civil justice system, indicate that the tort system is likely to play a constrained role in product regulation.

B. India

India's modern legal system is grounded in the common law tradition. However, as a result of rising concerns over consumer rights, it substantially reformed its approach to civil liability in 1986 by enacting the Consumer Protection Act. Under the Act, a consumer can recover for injuries suffered but must establish that the manufacturer was negligent.[63]

The law establishes special consumer commissions and forums, with authority similar to the regular civil courts, to enforce rules and adjudicate claims under the consumer law, including cases of product liability. These special bodies were meant to ease access by making the legal process "less formal, cheaper, and faster."[64] Under the Act, court fees are low, and the initial pleading requirements are minimal. Complainants can litigate with or without a lawyer. Moreover, the law includes consumer-friendly provisions allowing consumer associations or similar public interest groups to sue on behalf of injured parties. Cases have been brought for food adulteration, and plaintiffs in one case obtained a judgment for $12,000 for contaminated canola oil.[65] Yet despite the changes in the law, it appears that product liability suits are only a small fraction of Consumer Protection Act cases.[66]

In the alternative, plaintiffs still can proceed under the traditional common law tort system. In that forum, the ability of plaintiffs to obtain discovery is greater than in non-common law systems. Plaintiffs can also file class actions, but such actions have

---

[59] Mariana Mota Prado, *The Paradox of Rule of Law Reforms*, 60 U. TORONTO L.J. 555, 559-560 (2010) (discussing Brazilian judicial reform).

[60] Prado, at 561. According to one study, corruption generally costs Brazil the equivalent of 0.5% of its GDP or approximately US$5 billion per year. *See* DAVID FLEISCHER, COUNTRIES AT THE CROSSROADS: FREEDOM HOUSE 2010 REPORT ON BRAZIL, at 15 (http://freedomhouse.org/template.cfm?page=140&edition=9&ccrpage=43&ccrcountry=178).

[61] According to an earlier study, there were 17.3 million cases in the system, 1 for every 10 persons. *See* U.N. Special Rapporteur, Report of the UN Special Rapporteur on the Independence of Judges and Lawyers, ¶21, U.N. Doc E/CN.4/2005/60/Add.3. (Feb. 22, 2005).

[62] *Id.* at ¶23.

[63] Consumer Protection Act of 1986 at Art. 14(1)(d).

[64] Reimann, at 804.

[65] AVTAR SINGH, LAW OF CONSUMER PROTECTION 223-224 (2005) (the judgment figure is in the equivalent of 2011 US dollars).

[66] Reimann, at 804.

been rare in mass tort lawsuits.[67] Access is also hindered because attorneys cannot take cases on a contingent fee basis.

As an institution, India's courts also face the problem of corruption, which is reportedly quite severe at lower levels of the system.[68] It is estimated that use of the regular civil courts in India is "among the lowest in the world."[69] This may be the result of the massive backlog of cases in the courts: estimated to be 20 million in the lower courts.[70]

The administrative system for FDA-regulated products has similarly undergone significant change and reorganization. The food safety regulatory system was reformed under the Food Safety and Standards Act of 2006. A notable feature of this legislation is the empowerment of Adjudicating Officers and a special Tribunal to summarily handle cases of food safety arising under the law, and regulators can seek civil compensation for victims in that forum in addition to fines and penalties.[71] The officers have exclusive jurisdiction of cases arising under the Act, placing it outside the authority of the regular civil courts.[72]

Although the substantive rules for liability do not appear as friendly as under U.S. law, India has taken significant recent steps towards increasing the access of plaintiffs to legal remedies under the product liability system through its consumer legislation. However, institutional problems caused by docket congestion and corruption plague the effectiveness of the civil justice system, and place in question its ability to serve as a backstop for product safety.

C. China

China's legal and regulatory system is a product of civil law, Soviet law, and common law influences. China's approach to FDA-product regulation is primarily state-centered. It relies heavily upon government agencies to conduct inspections and to penalize violations, either through fines or criminal prosecution. Usually, these are organized as periodic crackdowns, and in recent years, such campaigns have been waged on identified products of public concern, such as dairy and cooking oil.[73]

With respect to the substantive law, China formally adopted a tort law in 2009 that re-codified and provided greater detail on the scope of tort liability in various

---

[67] INTERNATIONAL COMMISSION OF JURISTS, ACCESS TO JUSTICE: HUMAN RIGHTS ABUSES INVOLVING CORPORATIONS 58-9 (2011).

[68] *See* IMMIGRATION AND REFUGEE BOARD OF CANADA, INDIA: INDEPENDENCE OF AND CORRUPTION WITHIN THE JUDICIAL SYSTEM (2007-April 2009); INTERNATIONAL COMMISSION OF JURISTS, ACCESS TO JUSTICE: HUMAN RIGHTS ABUSES INVOLVING CORPORATIONS 53 (2011).

[69] Marc Galanter & Jayanth K. Krishnan, *"Bread for the Poor": Access to Justice and the Rights of the Needy in India*, 55 HASTINGS L.J. 789-90 n.1 & n.2 (2004) (discussing empirical data in India and also finding that "reliable data [on the court system] are scarce.")

[70] MAJA B. MICEVSKA, ARNAB K. HAZRA, PROBLEM OF COURT CONGESTION: EVIDENCE FROM INDIAN LOWER COURTS (2004) at http://www.zef.de/fileadmin/webfiles/downloads/zef_dp/zef_dp88.pdf.

[71] Food Safety and Standards Act, 2006, No. 34, secs. 65, 68, 70 (compensation provisions and powers of Adjudicating Officer and Appellate Tribunal).

[72] Food Safety and Standards Act, 2006, No. 34, sec. 72.

[73] *See, e.g., Zhang Yan and Cao Yin, 32 held in 'gutter oil' crackdown*, CHINA DAILY, Sept. 14, 2011, at http://europe.chinadaily.com.cn/china/2011-09/14/content_13682763.htm (last visited Nov. 7, 2011).

specific areas. It provides for strict liability for defective products.[74] A defect is an "unreasonable danger existing in a product" that "endangers the safety of human life" or is not compliant with relevant safety standards.[75] It appears that Chinese law also includes a development risk clause similar to the European one.[76] In its new Food Safety law, China also provided for damages equivalent to ten times the cost of the product if manufacturers produce unqualified food or sellers knowingly sell unqualified food.[77]

In terms of the civil justice system and access of plaintiffs to courts, large-scale product liability actions are not prevalent. Court institutions are not formally independent, and accordingly are subject to directives from various political authorities, which have tended to discourage such lawsuits.[78] Accordingly, successful tort lawsuits against manufacturers for mass torts in the FDA-regulated sphere are few, particularly when they are perceived to lead to potential social instability.[79] Aggregated, class lawsuits are permitted under the Civil Procedure Law,[80] however, recent national bar association rules concerning the formation and prosecution of class actions require that any case with ten or more plaintiffs should receive the approval of three or more partners

---

[74] Tort Law (promulgated by Standing Committee of the National People's Congress, Dec. 26, 2009, effective July 1, 2010), art. 41, *translated in* World Intellectual Property Organization http://www.wipo.int/wipolex/en/text.jsp?file_id=182630 (last visited Nov. 7, 2011) (P.R.C.).

[75] Product Quality Law, (promulgated by Standing Committee of the National People's Congress, Feb. 22, 1993, amended and effective July 8, 2000), art. 46, *translation at* the Ministry of Science and Technology of China, http://www.most.gov.cn/eng/policies/regulations/200501/t20050105_18422.htm (last visited Nov. 7, 2011) (P.R.C.).

[76] Product Quality Law, art. 41(3).

[77] Food Safety Law, (promulgated by Standing Committee of the National People's Congress, Feb. 8, 2009, effective June 1, 2009), art. 96, *translation at* United States Department of Agriculture, http://www.fas.usda.gov/gainfiles/200903/146327461.pdf (P.R.C.).

[78] Article 3 of China's Constitution states that judicial authorities are "created by the people's congresses to which they are responsible and under whose supervision they operate." Article 128 notes that "The Supreme People's Court is responsible to the National People's Congress and its Standing Committee. Local people's courts at different levels are responsible to the organs of state power which created them." More recently, the guiding doctrine of the judiciary (the "Three Supremes") was enunciated by President Hu Jintao and reiterated by the head of the Supreme Peoples' Court. The three key principles were 1) supremacy of the Party; 2) supremacy of the people; and 3) supremacy of the law. *See Wang Shengjun: "Three Supremes" shall always be the guiding thought of the courts*, XINHUA NET, June 23, 2008, at http://news.xinhuanet.com/legal/2008-06/23/content_8420938.htm (crediting original source as Legal Daily) (site last visited November 2, 2011). The doctrine was widely interpreted in China as highlighting the importance of political and Party factors over that of law.

[79] For example, although product liability lawsuits were filed in connection with the deaths and injuries arising out of the 2008 contamination of milk and milk powder, these cases were ultimately not resolved in the courts. According to various media reports, courts did not accept case filings until a significant number of victims agreed to a settlement mechanism developed by the state. *See* Andrew Jacobs, *Parents Reject China Milk Settlement*, N.Y. TIMES, Jan. 13, 2009 at http://www.nytimes.com/2009/01/14/world/asia/14china.html?ref=melamine; Edward Wong, *Milk Scandal in China Yields Cash for Parents*, N.Y. TIMES, Jan. 16, 2009 at http://www.nytimes.com/2009/01/17/world/asia/17milk.html?ref=melamine; Michael Wines, *Local Court Is China's First to Accept a Tainted-Milk Suit*, N.Y. TIMES, Mar. 25, 2009 at http://www.nytimes.com/2009/03/26/world/asia/26milk.html?ref=melamine.

[80] Civil Procedure Law, (promulgated by the National People's Congress, Apr. 9, 1991, effective Apr. 9, 1991), arts. 53-55, *translation at* China.org.cn, the authorized government website at http://www.china.org.cn/english/government/207339.htm (site last vested Nov. 7, 2011) (P.R.C.).

in the law firm and be reported to the local bar association upon receiving the case.[81] Such restrictions, together with the state's general aversion to large-scale litigation because of its effect on political stability, tend to reduce the role that product liability plays in these matters.

D. South Africa

South Africa's product liability system did not contemporaneously follow the changes in doctrine that occurred in North America and in Europe.[82] From a doctrinal standpoint, until recently, South Africa followed traditional tort principles, and required the plaintiff to show that the manufacturer's behavior was negligent before a court would make a finding of liability.[83] Much of this started to change as early as 2004, when South Africa's Department of Trade and Industry put forth a policy proposal to draft comprehensive consumer protection legislation. The agency recognized the country's consumer laws as "outdated, fragmented and predicated on principles contrary to the democratic system."[84] This effort culminated in the country's Consumer Protection Act in 2008.

Under the new law, producers are strictly liable to consumers for producing goods that are unsafe, defective, or hazardous, regardless of whether the producer was negligent.[85] There is no liability, however, if the harm caused is "wholly attributable" to compliance with existing regulatory standards.[86] One can infer from this language that producers of FDA-regulated products that comply with South Africa's regulatory standards may be shielded from liability but only as long as it can be shown that the harm was completely caused by compliance with the relevant rules. Although the text of the law suggests every type of product defect is subject to strict liability, this approach is a significant departure from its own past practice and in some ways different from comparative practice.[87] Since the law was not in effect until April 2011, it may be premature to draw final conclusions on its overall effect on product liability and safety.

Despite these changes in the substantive law, access-to-justice issues in South Africa remain a significant barrier. A study notes that a one hour legal consultation would cost an average household approximately 1 weeks' worth of wages.[88] Although

---

[81] All China Lawyers' Association, Guiding Opinion on Attorney Handling of "Mass Cases", Mar. 20, 2006, at Secs 1.1, 3.1, 3.2 at http://www.dffy.com/faguixiazai/ssf/200606/20060620110110.htm (in Chinese)(last visited Nov. 7, 2011). It also notes that lawyers should be particularly cognizant of such rules when "sensitive cases" arise. *See id.* at Sec. 5. One report suggests that the All China Lawyers' Association is considering revisions to the rule. *See All China Lawyers' Association will revise "Guiding Opinion on Attorney Handling of Sensitive Mass Cases,"* Feb. 5, 2010, at XINHUA NET http://news.xinhuanet.com/legal/2010-02/05/content_12936276.htm (site last visited Nov. 3, 2011).

[82] J. NEETHLING, LAW OF DELICT 317 (2010) ("In this regard [product liability law] it must, however, be pointed out that South African law is still in its infancy.").

[83] *Id.* at 317-18.

[84] Department of Trade & Industry, Draft Green Paper on the Consumer Policy Framework 09/04, Gazette No. 26774, at 6.

[85] Consumer Protection Act 68 of 2008 s. 61(1) (South Africa).

[86] Consumer Protection Act 68 of 2008 s. 61(4)(a) (South Africa).

[87] For example, under pre-existing South African law of delict, such a claim would have been subject to a finding of negligence. Moreover, U.S. and European practice do not apply principles of strict liability in those instances.

[88] AFRIMAP AND OPEN SOCIETY FOUNDATION FOR SOUTH AFRICA, SOUTH AFRICA: JUSTICE SECTOR AND THE RULE OF LAW 29 (2005) (discussion paper).

contingency fees were permitted in 1997, the losing party still bears all costs of the lawsuit.[89] The new legislation allows registered consumer groups to conduct litigation on behalf of consumers. This type of representative litigation may also ease access-to-justice problems.[90]

Approaching the system from an institutional perspective, the new law reaffirms that consumers have access not only to the regular courts, but also special courts such as the Consumer Tribunal and provincial and lower consumer courts.[91] It is anticipated that the system of consumer courts will expand as the law is implemented.[92] As a general matter, the courts are functionally independent and funding appears adequate, although there are significant disparities between urban and rural areas.[93] Although significant practical obstacles exist for plaintiffs in pursuing product liability suits in South Africa, revisions to the tort system and passage of consumer protection seem to have created momentum for potential advances.

V. Conclusion

Assessing the role that the tort system has in the regulation of food and medical products in developing countries requires a highly factual and context-dependent understanding of the potential capacity of both the civil justice and administrative regulatory systems. As this committee recognizes, "developing countries" for the purposes of this study may encompass "a heterogeneous group of 150 or more low- and middle-income countries." In countries where administrative agencies are under-resourced or challenged by lack of independence, efforts to support the civil justice system, particularly in the area of tort liability may help support the regulation of food and medical products.

---

[89] Christopher Roederer, *The Transformation of South African Private Law After Ten Years of Democracy*, 37 COLUM. HUM. RTS. L. REV. 447, 494 (2006).
[90] Consumer Protection Act 68 of 2008, s.78 (South Africa).
[91] Consumer Protection Act 68 of 2008, s.69 (South Africa).
[92] *SA Consumers' Rights in Spotlight*, Feb. 7, 2011, at http://www.imc.org.za/news/657-sa-consumers-rights-in-spotlight.html (quoting Department of Trade and Industry spokesperson).
[93] AFRIMAP AND OPEN SOCIETY FOUNDATION FOR SOUTH AFRICA, SOUTH AFRICA JUSTICE SECTOR AND THE RULE OF LAW at 1-2, and chs. 3 & 4 (2005) (full report).

Appendix C
Food and Medical Product Regulatory Systems of South Africa, Brazil, India, and China

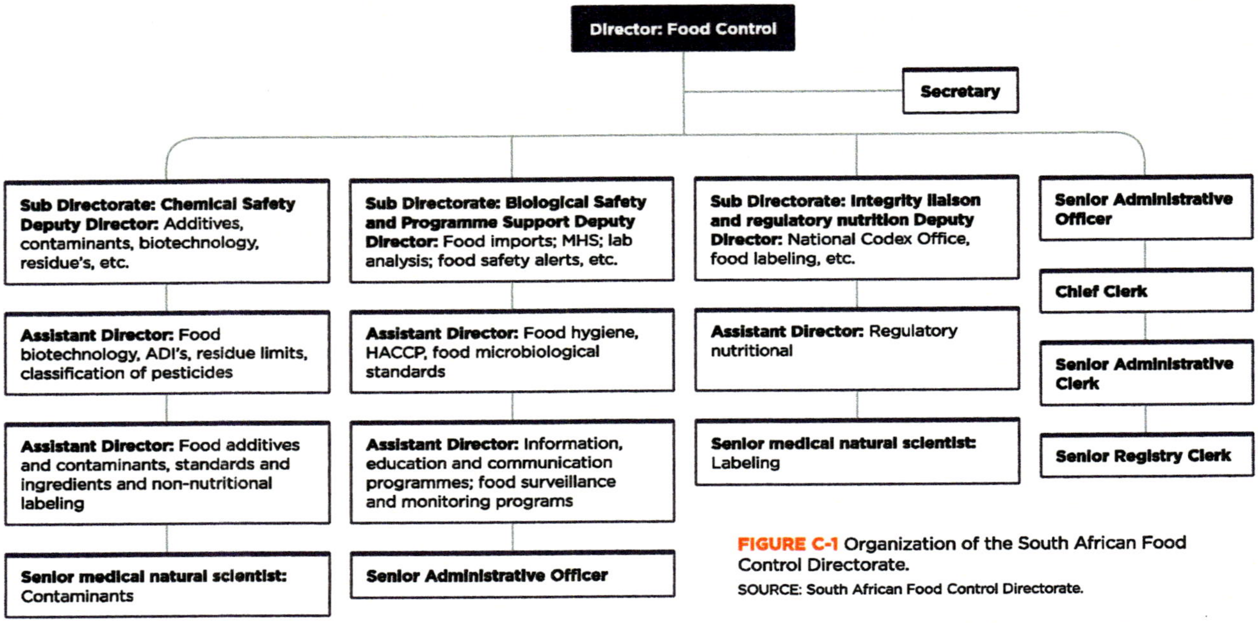

FIGURE C-1 Organization of the South African Food Control Directorate.
SOURCE: South African Food Control Directorate.

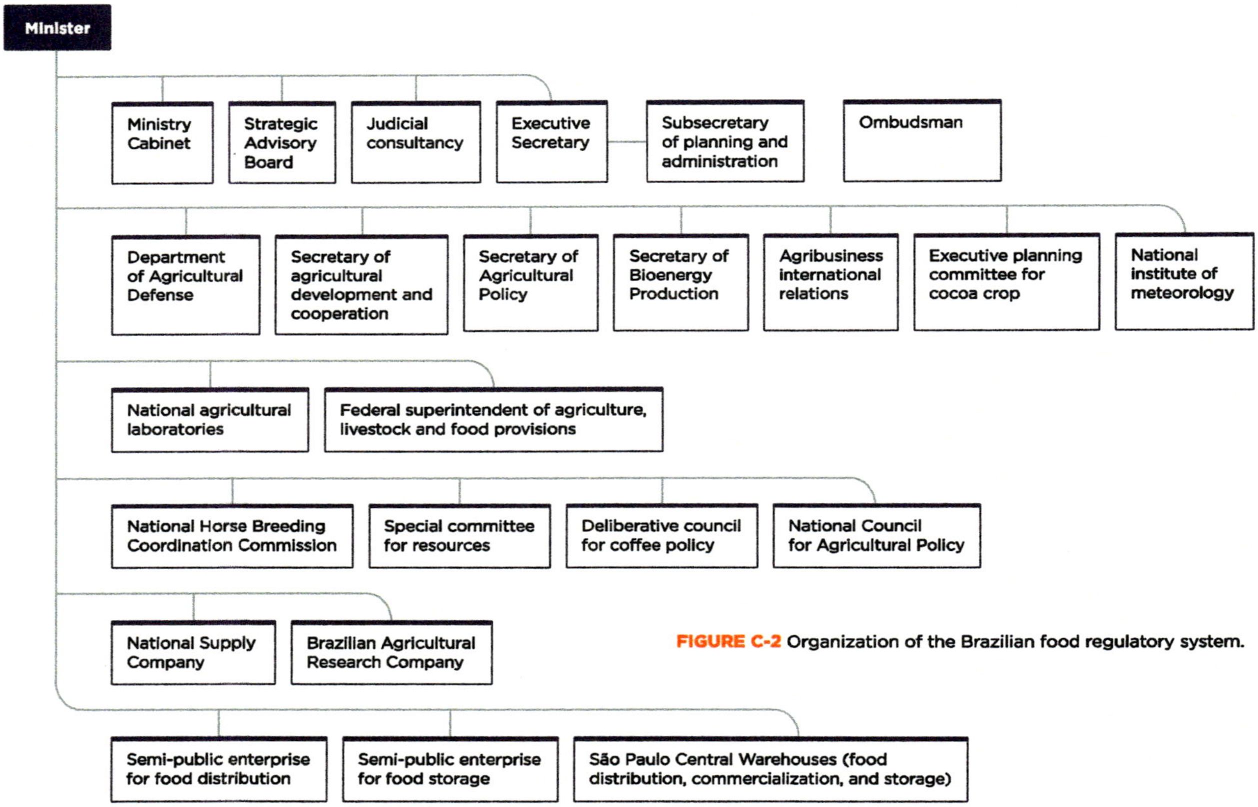

FIGURE C-2 Organization of the Brazilian food regulatory system.

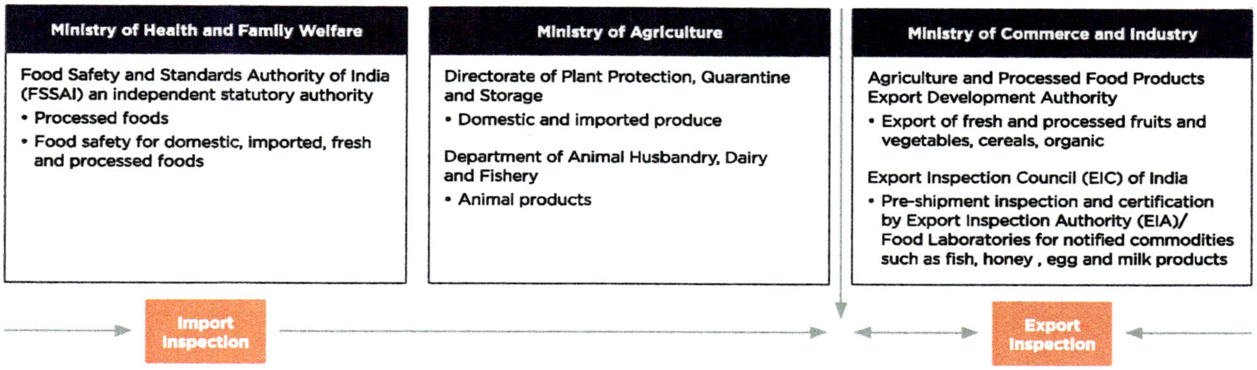

FIGURE C-3 Organization of Indian food regulation.
SOURCE: USDA.

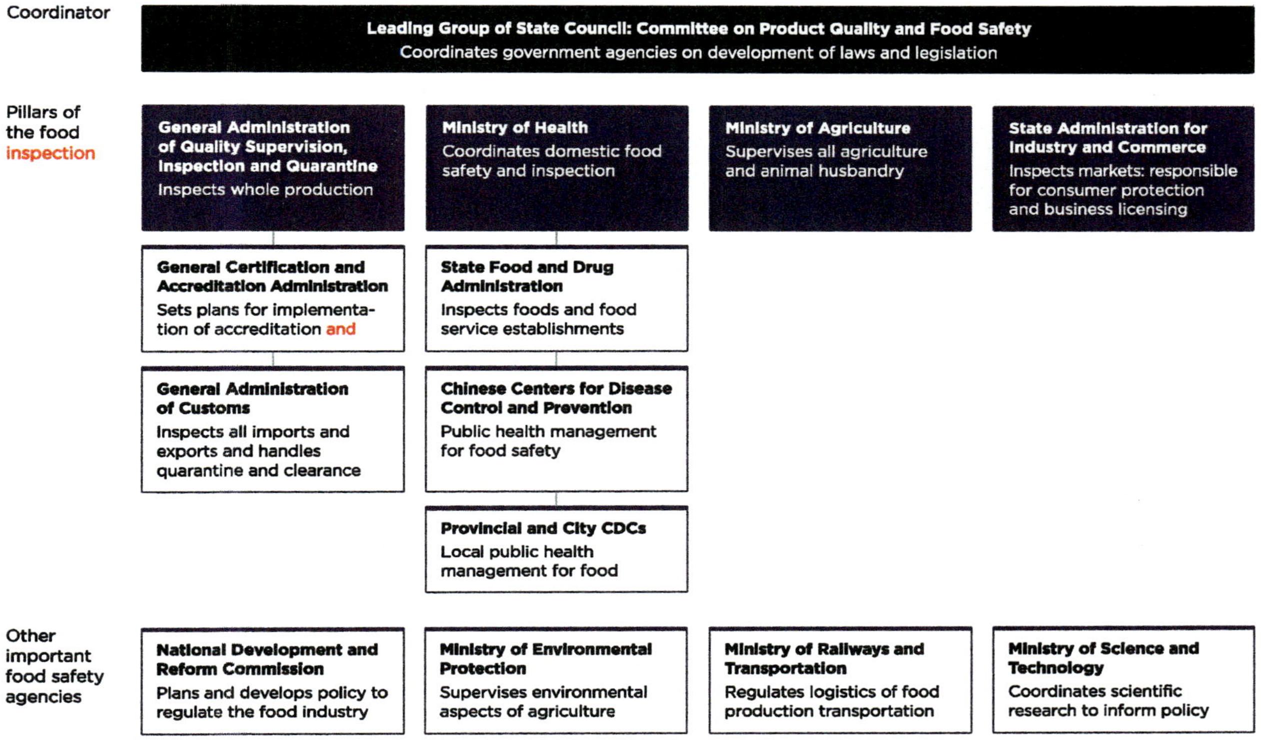

FIGURE C-4 Organization of Chinese food regulatory system.
SOURCE: Broughton and Walker, 2010.

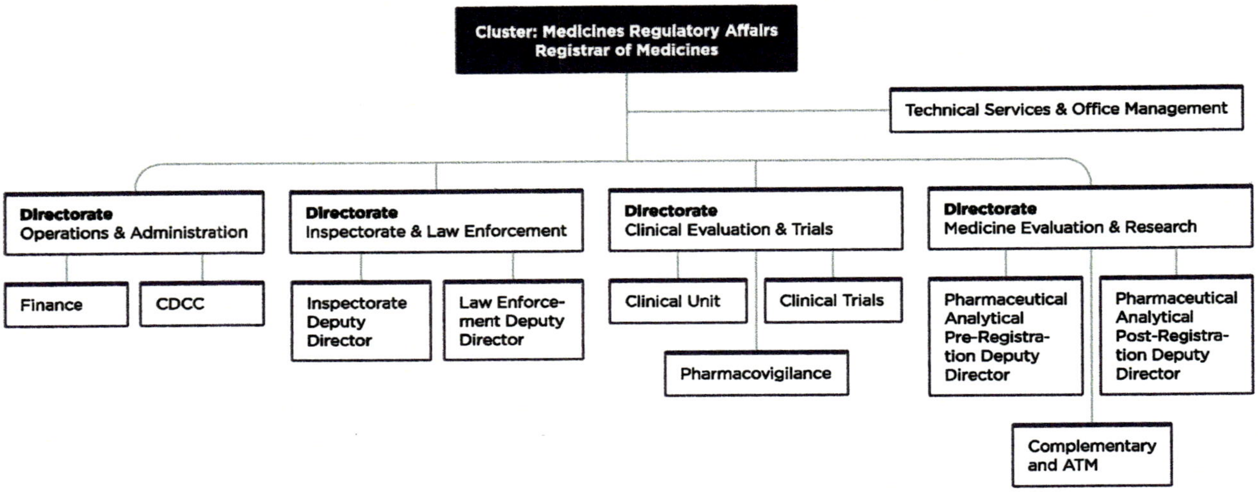

FIGURE C-5 Organization of South African medical product regulatory system.
SOURCE: Government of South Africa.

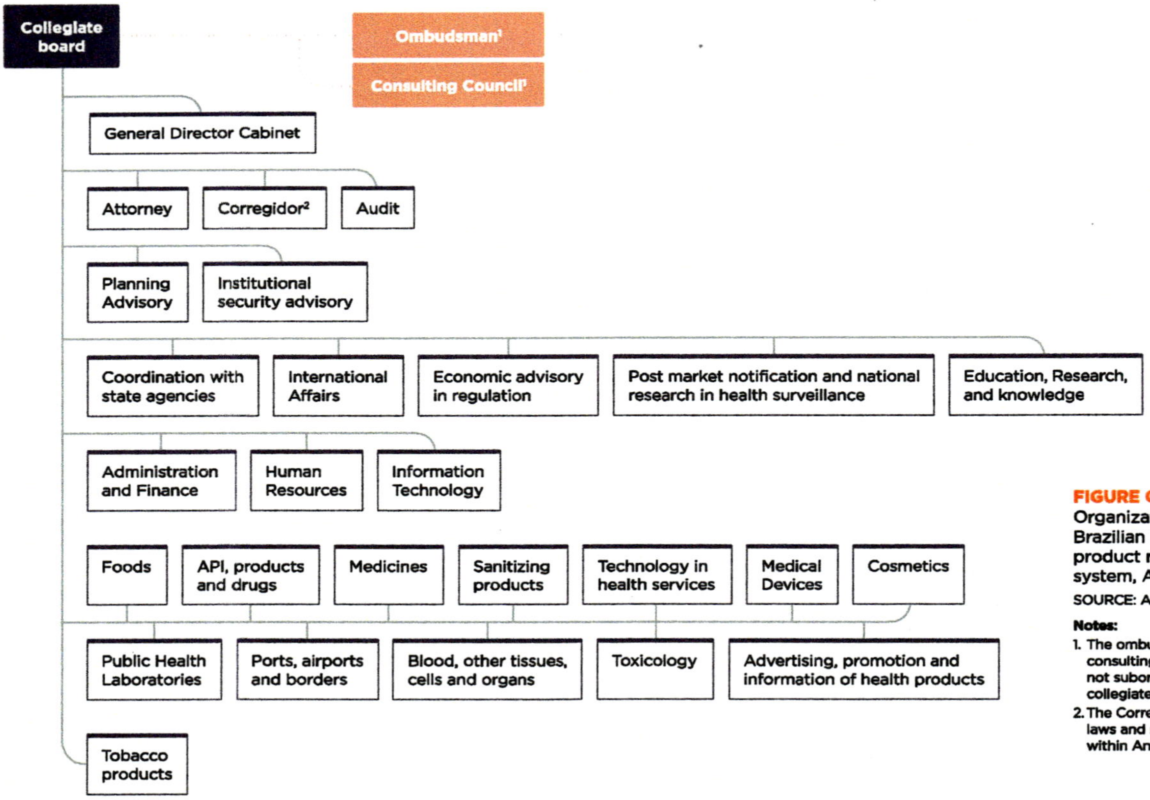

FIGURE C-6 Organization of the Brazilian medical product regulatory system, ANVISA
SOURCE: ANVISA

Notes:
1. The ombudsman and consulting council are not subordinate to the collegiate board.
2. The Corregidor enforces laws and regulations within Anvisa.

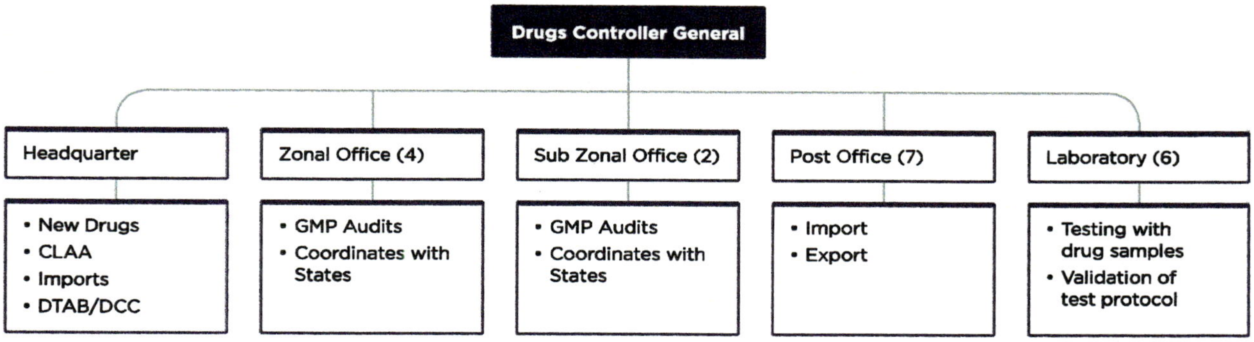

FIGURE C-7 Organization of the Indian Drug Controller General.
SOURCE: Government of India.

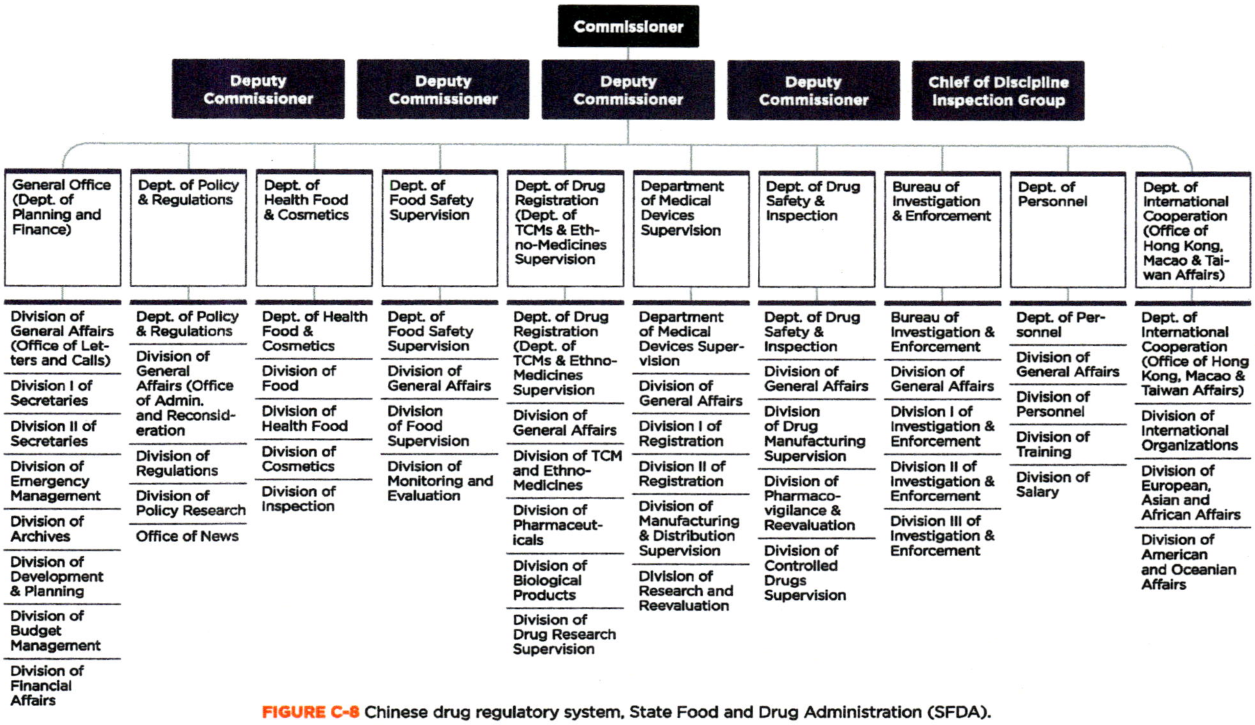

FIGURE C-8 Chinese drug regulatory system, State Food and Drug Administration (SFDA).
SOURCE: SFDA, 2011.

APPENDIX D Chinese Food Regulatory System

Authority	Person(s) Responsible	Internal Departments	Functions
The Food Safety Committee of the State Council	Director Deputy Director Committee Members: 21 department managers		• Analyze food safety situation, study, deploy, arrange and guide food safety work; • Put forward major policies and measures on the supervision of food safety; • Supervise the implementation of food safety supervision obligations; • Analyze food safety situation, study, deploy, arrange and guide food safety work;
The Food Safety Committee Office of the State Council	Director: Deputy Director 12 department & bureau leaders	Department of General Affairs, Department of Coordination & Guidance, Department of Supervision & Inspection, Department of Emergency Management	• Organize the implementation of the State Council's policies on food safety work, organize the launching of the investigation and study on important food safety problems, and put forward policy suggestions • Organize the drafting of the national food safety plan, and coordinate and prompt its implementation • Undertake the comprehensive coordination tasks as designated by the Food Safety Commission of the State Council, prompt the perfection of the coordination linkage mechanism, improve the comprehensive supervision mechanism, and direct local comprehensive food safety coordination institutes in implementing related works • Urge the examination of the implementation conditions of food safety laws and regulations and the decisions and deployments of the Food Safety Commission of State Council; • Urge the examination of related departments of the State Council and the provincial level of the People's Government's fulfillment of food safety supervision obligations, and be responsible for assessment and evaluation • Direct the improvement of the inspection and governance mechanism for potential hazards in food safety, and organize the implementation of food safety regulations, governance and joint inspection actions • Prompt the development of food safety emergency systems and capabilities, organize the drafting of national food safety accident emergency pre-planning, and supervise, direct and coordinate the major food safety accident handling and accountability investigation and handling work • Regulate and direct food safety information work, organize and coordinate food safety publicity and training work, launch international communications and cooperation in terms of food safety • Undertake meetings, messages, and other daily tasks of the Food Safety Commission of the State Council; undertake other tasks as designated by the Food Safety Commission of the State Council.

Authority	Person(s) Responsible	Internal Departments	Functions
Ministry of Health	Minister: Party Leadership Group Secretary: Zhang Mao Vice Minister Chief of Disciplinary Inspection Group	General Office, Department of Human Resources, Department of Planning and Finance, Department of Health Policy and Regulation, Emergency Office, Disease Prevention and Control Bureau, Department of Rural Health Management, Department of Maternal and Child Health Care & Community Health, Department of Medical Administration, Health Supervision Bureau, Department of Drug Administration, Department of Science, Technology & Education, Department of International Cooperation, Bureau of Health Care, Party Membership Committee, Department of Retired Cadres, Supervision Bureau	• Undertake comprehensive food safety coordination, and organize the investigation and handling of major food safety accidents; • Organize the formulation of food safety standards; • Responsible for the assessment and notification tasks of food and related product safety risks; • Establish the conditions and inspection regulations as certified by the food safety inspection institute; and • Release important food safety information in a unified manner.
Comprehensive Coordination and Health Supervision Authority on Food Safety	General Director Deputy General Director Deputy Inspector	Division of General Affairs, Division of Legal Affairs and Audit, Division of Food Safety Policy & Information, Division of Food Safety Standard, Division of Food Safety Evaluation & Warning; Division of Major Food Safety Accident Inspection, Division of Occupational Health Supervision & Management, Division of Radiological Health Supervision & Management, Division of Environmental Health Supervision & Management, Division of Communicable Disease Prevention, Control & Supervision and School Health Supervision & Management, Division of Medical Treatment Enforcement Supervision	• Organize the drafting of food safety standards; • Undertake, organize, investigate and handle major food safety accidents; • Organize the implementation of food safety monitoring, risk assessment, and notification work; • Draft the conditions and inspection regulations as certified by the food safety inspection institute; • Issue important food safety information; and • Responsible for health monitoring and management of public areas and drinking water.
Health Supervision Center of the Ministry of Health	Director Party Committee Secretary Deputy Director	Party Committee Office, Disciplinary Inspection & Supervision Office, General Administrative Office, Division of Human Resources, Division of Financial Assets, Division of Comprehensive Investigation Assistance Guidance, Division of Health Supervision Information, Division of Health Supervision Training Guidance, Division of Health Standard, Division of Health Inspection Technology Regulation, Division I of Health License Acceptance, Division II of Health License Acceptance, Division I of Health License Review, Division II of Health License Review	• Undertake 6 administrative licensing works as directly examined and approved by the Ministry of Health, including - Acceptance and review of new foods - Acceptance and review of imported foods from countries with no national food safety standards - Acceptance and review of disinfectants and disinfection apparatus - Acceptance and review of products related to drinking water safety - Acceptance and review of the certification of chemical product toxicity, radioactive protection facilities and radioactive product detection appraisal institute - Acceptance of new types of food additives

APPENDIX D *Continued*

Authority	Person(s) Responsible	Internal Departments	Functions
China National Center for Food Safety Risk Assessment	Director	The business technology departments include risk assessment, risk monitoring, risk communication, risk notification, food safety standard, residual lab, data/information analysis unit, etc; Secretariat of the National Food Safety Risk Assessment Expert Committee, and Secretariat of the National Food Safety Standard Assessment Committee	• Carry out basic work on food safety risk assessment, collect, process and analyze the scientific data, technological information and inspection results related to food safety risk assessment, submit the risk assessment and analysis results to the National Food Safety Risk Assessment Expert Committee, and once approved, create the assessment report and report to the Ministry of Health, which will be responsible for releasing it to society in accordance with laws in a unified manner. In cases of major food safety risks, the assessment results is reported to the National Food Safety Risk Assessment Expert Committee after being submitted to the council for deliberation. • Undertake the technical work related to risk monitoring, participate in studies to draft the monitoring plan, and summarize and analyze monitoring information. • Study and analyze food safety risk trends and principles, and put forward risk notification suggestions to related departments. • Create publicity for food safety knowledge and maintain good communications and relationships with the media and the public. • Conduct scientific research related to food safety risk monitoring, assessment and notification, and organize the implementation of training sessions related to nationwide food safety risk monitoring, assessment and notification. • Establish a working relationship with the Chinese Center for Disease Control and Prevention, and provide technical guidance on food safety accident emergency response. • Provide business guidance to branch centers and provide technical guidance to local risk assessment technology support institutes. • Undertake the daily tasks of the Secretariat of the National Food Safety Risk Assessment Expert Committee, and the Secretariat of the National Food Safety Standard Assessment Committee.

Authority	Person(s) Responsible	Internal Departments	Functions
Institute for Nutrition and Food Safety, Chinese Center for Disease Control and Prevention	Director Deputy Director	9 national level detection, monitoring and assessment centers and major labs; 4 international organization cooperation centers, branches or reference labs; and the 11 secretariats or professional committees of the 7 academic societies	• Provide technical support and services for the government's establishment of laws, regulations, and standards in terms of nutrition and food safety as well as administration in accordance with law, and conduct studies on prevention and control strategies and control measures • Carry out comprehensive analysis against each factor in food which influence health (nutrition, safety, and function, etc.), and put forward assessment suggestions • Establish and perfect food-borne illness and food contamination monitoring system, carry out food-borne illness and food contamination monitoring and early warning, and provide technical support for emergency response for food-borne illness and food contamination • Undertake and implement the China National Nutrition and Health Survey, establish and perfect local food ingredients, national nutrition, and national health monitoring system, and launch the monitoring and control of nutrition and related diseases • Organize and undertake the formation and modification of national nutrition and food health standards, inspection methods and related technical regulations • Establish and perfect nutrition and food safety control technology, and carry out promotion and implementation • Check and assess relevant products such as general food, health food, new food sources (including genetically modified foods, etc.), special diets, food additives, food packaging materials, food containers, tools and equipments, decontaminants, etc., as well as raw materials, carry out nutrition, safety and functional assessment and technical arbitration work, and provide certification services to the government and society • Establish and perfect the lab quality control system for nutrition and food, and undertake the quality control work of relevant national labs • Provide business guidance in the nationwide nutrition and food safety efforts as well as training for professionals • Establish a national nutrition and food information system, enhance information communication, and accelerate information resource sharing • Carry out applied research on nutrition and food, and accelerate the achievement of results • Carry out international cooperation and communication in terms of nutrition and food health

APPENDIX D *Continued*

Authority	Person(s) Responsible	Internal Departments	Functions
Food Safety National Standard Review Committee	Chairman of Committee	Secretariat Professional Working Team for Pollutants Professional Working Team for Microbes Professional Working Team for Food Additives Professional Working Team for Nutrition & Special Diets Professional Working Team for Food Products Professional Working Team for Production & Operation Regulations Professional Working Team for Food Container Packaging Materials Professional Working Team for Sampling and Analysis Methods	• Review national food safety standards; • Put forward suggestions on the implementation of national food safety standards; • Provide consultations on the major problems related to national food safety standards; and • Undertake other tasks related to national food safety standards.
State Food and Drug Administration	Commissioner Deputy Commissioner Chief of Disciplinary Inspection Group	General Office (Department of Planning & Finance), Department of Policy & Regulation, Department of Health Food & Cosmetic Supervision, Department of Food Safety Supervision, Department of Drug Registration (Department of TCMs & Ethno-Medicines Supervision), Department of Medical Device Supervision, Department of Drug Safety & Inspection, Bureau of Investigation & Enforcement, Department of Personnel, Department of International Cooperation (Office of Hong Kong, Macao & Taiwan Affairs), Party Membership Committee, Disciplinary Inspection & Supervision Bureau, Department of Retired Cadres	• Establish policies and plans on food safety supervision and management in consumption and supervise their implementation, and participate in the drafting of relevant laws and regulations as well as department rules • Responsible for the monitoring and management of the food health license and food safety in consumption • Establish food safety management regulations in consumption and supervise their implementation, carry out the national food safety investigation and monitoring work in consumption, and release information related to food safety monitoring and supervision in consumption • Organize, check and handle food safety problems in consumption • Direct the supervision and management, emergency, audit, and information building tasks of related local authorities on food and drugs • Carry out international communications and cooperation related to food and drug supervision and management.
Department of Health Food & Cosmetic Supervision, State Food and Drug Administration	Director-General Deputy Director-General	Division of General Affairs Division I of License Division II of License Division of Production & Operation Supervision	• Undertake health food license management work • Undertake health food approval work • Draft health food license technical codes and supervise their implementation • Draft health food production, operation, and management codes and supervise their implementation

Authority	Person(s) Responsible	Internal Departments	Functions
Department of Food Safety Supervision, State Food and Drug Administration	Director-General Deputy Director-General	Division of General Affairs Division of Food Supervision Division of Monitoring & Evaluation Division of Food Auditing	• Undertake food safety supervision work in catering services • Undertake catering service license management work • Draft catering service license management system and supervise its implementation • Draft catering service food safety management codes and supervise their implementation • Undertake the investigation, monitoring, and assessment of food safety in catering services • Release information related to food safety supervision in catering services • Draft food safety supervision, management and audit system for catering services and supervise its implementation; • Direct food safety inspection and detection work in catering services • Direct all work related to food safety accident handling in local catering services
General Administration of Quality Supervision, Inspection and Quarantine of the People's Republic of China	General Director & Party Leadership Group Secretary Deputy General Director & Deputy Party Leadership Group Secretary Deputy General Director & Party Leadership Group Member Deputy General Director & Party Leadership Group Member & CNCA Director Chief of Disciplinary Inspection Group & Party Leadership Group Member Party Leadership Group Member & Standardization Administration Director Party Leadership Group Member & Department of Human Resources Director-General Chief Docimaster Chief Engineer	General Office, Department of Legislation, Department of Quality Administration, Department of Computation, Department of Clearance Business, Department of Health Quarantine Supervision, Department of Animal and Plant Quarantine Supervision, Department of Inspection Supervision, Bureau of Import and Export Food Safety, Bureau of Safety Supervision of Special Equipment, Department of Production Quality Supervision, Department of Food Production Supervision, Department of Law Enforcement Supervision (Anti-counterfeit Office of AQSIQ), Department of International Cooperation (WTO Office), Department of Science and Technology, Department of Human Resources, Department of Finance, Party Membership Committee, Department of Retired Cadres	• Organize the drafting of the laws and regulations related to quality supervision, inspection and quarantine, study and draft policies on quality supervision, inspection and quarantine work, establish and release related regulations and systems; organize the implementation of the laws and regulations on quality supervision, inspection and quarantine, direct and supervise administrative law enforcement work on quality supervision, inspection and quarantine, and take responsibility for the national technical laws and regulations related to quality supervision, inspection and quarantine • Organize the implementation of immigration health quarantine and health supervision work • Organize the implementation of safety, health, and quality supervision inspection and supervision management on imported and exported food and cosmetics; and manage the production of imported and exported food and cosmetics, processing unit health registration, and the external health registration of export enterprise • Organize the preliminary supervision and subsequent management of imported and exported commodity inspection and quarantine; manage immigration inspection and quarantine symbols (marks), import safety quality license, and export quality license, and take responsibility for supervision and management • Manage product quality supervision work; manage and direct quality supervision and inspection; responsible for implementing product quality monitoring and mandatory inspection for domestic production enterprises; manage industrial product production license work; organize the checking and handling of illegal activities which violate standardization, metering and quality laws and regulations; and launch forged and fake commodity crack down activities • Manage the national authentication and approval supervision and management committee as well as the national standardization management committee.

APPENDIX D *Continued*

Authority	Person(s) Responsible	Internal Departments	Functions
Department of Food Production Supervision, General Administration of Quality Supervision, Inspection and Quarantine of the People's Republic of China	Director-General Deputy Director-Generals	Division of General Affairs Division of Animal-derived Food Supervision Division of Plant-derived Food Supervision Division of Food-related Product Supervision Division of Food Safety Risk Supervision Division of Cosmetic Production Supervision	• Draft the quality safety supervision and management work system of the production and processing links of domestic food and food-related products • Undertake quality safety supervision, risk monitoring and market access work of the food and food-related products at the production and processing phases • Organize the investigation and handling of relevant quality safety accidents under the specified authorities
Bureau of Import and Export Food Safety, General Administration of Quality Supervision, Inspection and Quarantine of the People's Republic of China	Director-General Deputy Director-General	Division of General Affairs Division I of Food Safety Division II of Food Safety Division III of Food Safety Division IV of Food Safety Division of Risk Warning	• Draft the safety, quality supervision and inspection and quarantine work system of imported and exported food and cosmetics; • Undertake the inspection and quarantine, supervision and management, risk assessment, and emergency precaution measures of imported and exported food and cosmetics; • Undertake the investigation and handling work against major imported and exported food and cosmetic quality safety accidents.
State Administration for Industry & Commerce of the People's Republic of China	Party Leadership Group Secretary & General-Director Deputy Party Leadership Group Secretary & Deputy General-Director Party Leadership Group Member & Deputy General-Director Deputy General-Director Chief of Disciplinary Inspection Group & Party Leadership Group Member	General Office, Department of Law, Anti-Monopoly and Anti-Unfair Competition Bureau, Direct Selling Regulation Bureau, Consumer Protection Bureau, Department of Market Regulation, Regulation Department for Market Circulation of Food, Enterprise Registration Bureau, Registration Bureau of Foreign-invested Enterprise, Department of Advertising Regulation and Management, Department for Regulation and Management of Private Economy, Department of Personnel, Department of Foreign Affairs (Office of Hong Kong, Macao & Taiwan Affairs), Party Membership Committee, Department of Retired Cadres, Trademark Office, Trademark Appeal Board, Disciplinary Inspection Group, Supervision Bureau	• Responsible for all tasks related to market supervision and management and administrative law enforcement, draft relevant laws and regulations, and establish industrial and commercial administrative rules and policies • Undertake the obligations of regulating and maintaining market operations in accordance with laws • Undertake the obligations of supervising commodity quality and food safety in distribution, organize the launching of the consumer rights protection work in related services, investigate and handle illegal activities in the production of forged and fake commodities, guide consumer inquiries, complaints, report acceptance, handling, and network system building, and protect the legitimate rights and interests of operators and consumers • Responsible for trademark registration and management, protect the exclusive right to use the trademark and investigate and handle trademark infringement actions in accordance with laws, settle trademark disputes, enhance confirmation and protection work against famous trademarks, and take responsibility for the registration, filing and protection of special symbols and official symbols • Lead the national industrial and commercial administration work.

APPENDIX D *Continued*

Authority	Person(s) Responsible	Internal Departments	Functions
Regulation Department for Market Circulation of Food, State Administration for Industry & Commerce of the People's Republic of China	Director-General	Division of General Affairs, Division of Specification Guidance, Division of Monitoring & Inspection	• Responsible for food safety supervision and management in distribution, and draft specific measures and methods for food safety supervision and management in distribution • Organize the implementation of food safety supervision and inspection and quality monitoring in distribution, as well as the relevant market access system • Handle and settle major food safety emergencies in distribution, and investigate and handle major food safety cases
Ministry of Commerce	Minister International Trade Negotiation Representative (Minister level) & Vice Minister Chief of Disciplinary Inspection Group Deputy International Trade Negotiation Representative (Vice Minister level) Assistant Minister	General Office (Bureau of Negotiation Representative Secretary), Department of Human Resources, Policy Research Department, Comprehensive Department, Department of Treaty and Law, Department of Finance, Department of Market Supervision, Department of Market System Development, Department of Circulation & Development, Department of Market Operation Regulation (State Cocoon & Silk Office), Anti-monopoly Bureau (Anti-monopoly Office of State Council), Department of Foreign Trade, Department of Trade in Services, Department of Mechanic, Electronic and High-Tech Industry (State Mechanic and Electronic Office), Department of Foreign Investment Administration, Department of Foreign Aid, Department of Foreign Investment & Economic Cooperation, Bureau of Fair Trade for Imports and Exports, Bureau of Industry Injury Investigation, Department of International Trade and Economic Affairs, Department of WTO Affairs (Consultation Bureau), Department of Asian Affairs, Department of Western Asian and African Affairs, Department of European Affairs, Department of American and Oceanian Affairs, Department of Taiwan, Hong Kong and Macao Affairs, Department of Electronic Commercial Affairs, Department of Foreign Affairs, MOFCOM Committee of Communist Party of China, Department of Retired Cadres	• Organize the implementation of important consumer market regulations and controls and major production and distribution management, take responsibility for establishing and perfecting the necessities of market supply emergency management mechanisms, monitor and analyze market operations and commodity supply and demand situations, investigate and analyze commodity price information, carry out early warning and forecast guidance, take responsibility for backlog control and market regulation and control work of major consumer goods under work divisions, and supervise and manage the distribution of finished oil as specified • Responsible for establishing imported and exported commodities and processing trade management methods as well as import and export commodity management and technology catalogue, draft policies and measures to accelerate the transformation of foreign trade growth, organize the implementation of import and export quotas of major industrial products, raw materials, and important agricultural products, coordinate bulk import and export commodities among relevant departments, direct the establishment of trade promotion and foreign trade promotion system • Carry out antitrust audit against the concentration of business operators in accordance with laws, guide enterprises in coping with overseas antitrust indictment response, and carry out multilateral and bilateral competitive policy communication and cooperation.

APPENDIX D *Continued*

Authority	Person(s) Responsible	Internal Departments	Functions
Ministry of Agriculture	Party Leadership Group Secretary & Minister Deputy Party Leadership Group Secretary & Vice Minister Vice Minister Party Leadership Group Member of Ministry of Agriculture & Vice Minister Central Commission for Disciplinary Inspection at the Ministry of Agriculture Disciplinary Inspection Group Leader & Party Leadership Group Member of Ministry of Agriculture Party Leadership Group Member of Ministry of Agriculture & Department of Human Resources Director-General Party Leadership Group Member of Ministry of Agriculture Chief Economist & General Office Director State Chief Veterinarian Chief Economist	General Office, Department of Human Resources, Department of Industry Policy and Law, Department of Rural Economy & Management Administration, Department of Market and Economic Information, Department of Development and Planning, Department of Finance, Department of International Cooperation, Department of Science, Technology & Education, Department of Crop Farming Administration, Department of Agriculture Mechanization Administration, Department of Animal Husbandry, Veterinary Bureau, Agricultural Reclamation Bureau, Bureau of Rural and Township Enterprises, Fishery Bureau, Supervision Bureau, Party Membership Committee, Department of Retired Cadres	• Study and put forward key agricultural product import and export suggestions • Organize the implementation of quality supervision and certification of each agricultural product and green food as well as the protection of new varieties of agricultural plants.

APPENDIX D *Continued*

Authority	Person(s) Responsible	Internal Departments	Functions
Ministry of Industry and Information Technology	Party Leadership Group Member Chief Engineer Chief Economist	General Office, Polices & Regulations Department, Department of Planning, Department of Finance, Department of Industrial Policies, Department of Science & Technology, Performance Inspection & Coordination Bureau, Department of Medium & Small Enterprises, Department of Energy Conservation and Resources Utilization, Department of Work Safety, Department of Raw Material Industry, Department of Equipment Industry, Department of Consumer Goods Industry, Department of Civil-Military Integration Promotion, Department of Telecommunication, Department of Software Service Industry, Department of Communications Development, Bureau of Telecommunication Administration, Bureau of Communications Security, Bureau of Radio, Department of Informatisation Promotion, Department of Information Security Coordination, International Cooperation Department, Human Resources & Education Department, Party Membership Committee, Supervision Bureau, Department of Retired Cadres, Department of Services	• Undertake food industry management work • Responsible for the creation of the food industry honesty system • Organize the drafting of industrial technology codes and standards, direct industrial quality management work, and organize the implementation of basic industrial technology
Department of Consumer Goods Industry, Ministry of Industry and Information Technology	Director General Deputy Director General Deputy Inspector	Division of General Affairs Division of Textiles Division I of Light Industry Division II of Light Industry Division of Foods Division of Medicines	• Undertake the management of such industries as light industry, textile, food, medicine, and home appliances, etc • Draft production plans for cigarette, salt and saccharin • Undertake the administrative management of the salt industry and national salt reserves

APPENDIX D *Continued*

Authority	Person(s) Responsible	Internal Departments	Functions
China National Food Industry Association	Chairman Deputy Managing Director Secretary-General Deputy Secretary-General	General Office, Department of Leading Enterprise Development, Department of Statistical Information, Department of Science & Technology, Department of Market Development, Department of General Businesses, Food Safety Newspaper Office, Magazine Office, and 13 professional committees	• Investigate and study the industry structure, organizational structure, production and operation of the food industry, and put forward suggestions in terms of domestic food industry development planning, policies, industrial policies, laws and regulations, etc. • Investigate, study and analyze basic domestic food safety situations, put forward opinions and suggestions in terms of improving general food safety levels to the government and relevant departments, assist the legislative and administrative departments in establishing and perfecting food safety policies, laws and regulations, technical standards, and law enforcement measures, publicize and actively implement the Food Safety Law and relevant laws and regulations, and summarize and bring about advanced management systems, scientific methods and application technologies in safeguarding food safety and improving food quality • Maintain the legitimate rights and interests of members, coordinate member relationships, present the opinions and requirements of members to the government • Carry out industrial statistical surveys under the authorization of relevant national departments, establish a statistical investigation system, collect statistical data, release industry information, sort and analyze statistical investigation data and conditions, submit statistical reports to relevant departments of the State Council, and deliver relevant statistical statements • Conduct report meetings, seminars, experience exchange meetings, etc, to promote research communications and help enterprises improve operation management and develop enterprise culture, thus improving the overall quality of enterprises • Organize talent, technology and occupational skill trainings, cultivate talents for the industry, and improve employee quality gradually • Organize product exhibitions, shows, and sales exhibitions under the authorization of the government or as demanded by the market and industry development, and participate in the development of the food market • Participate in or organize the formation of food industry related standards under the authorization of relevant national departments, and organize publicity and implementation • Assist relevant government departments in carrying out work, and carry out preliminary demonstration of major industrial technology transformation, technology importation, investment and developed projects under the authorization and trust of government departments • Participate in the issuance and qualification examination of industrial production and operation licenses under the authorization of relevant national departments • Run the newspaper, magazine, news report, and yearbook as sponsored by China National Food Industry Association

APPENDIX D *Continued*

Authority	Person(s) Responsible	Internal Departments	Functions
Chinese Institute of Food Science and Technology	President Secretary General	Office, Academic Department, Consultation Department, International Department, Journal of Chinese Institutes of Food Science and Technology Editorial Department, Department of Organization Communication, under which 18 branches and 2 working committees are established	• Organize the food industry science and technology workers in studying and discussing development strategies and technical and economic policies of the food industry, and provide scientific basis for the decisionmaking of relevant government departments • Carry out academic communications activities • Edit and publish academic and scientific food publications in accordance with relevant specifications, and organize the communication of food technology information and market information • Carry out continuing education and organize the training of food technology personnel • Carry out food technology consultation services • Find excellent academic treatises, scientific and technological achievements and scientific promotion through academic activities • Commend excellent academic treatises, scientific and technological achievements, scientific promotion and outstanding science and technology talents with the approval of relevant government departments • Undertake scientific and technological projects and engineering project demonstrations, technical post qualification appraisals, scientific and technological achievement demonstrations, scientific and technological literature compilations and audits, standard revisions, etc, as entrusted by relevant units.
China Food Addi-tives & Ingredients Association	President Deputy President Yazheng Secretary General	Division of Information, Division of General Businesses, Editorial Department, Financial Department, 12 professional committees	• Hold food additives and ingredients exhibition • Organize Chinese enterprises to go abroad to participate in exhibitions • Edit and publish the magazine *China Food Additives* • Organize the formation of standards, and draft industrial plans, laws, regulations, and policies • Reflect member requirements and maintain industry benefits

APPENDIX D *Continued*

Authority	Person(s) Responsible	Internal Departments	Functions
China Dairy Industry Association	Chairman: Song Kungang Secretary General: Liu Meiju		• Promote the relevant policies of the Party and the State on the dairy industry • Reflect industry requirements and existing problems to relevant government departments, and put forward reasonable suggestions • Organize the promotion and application of new technologies, new processes, new equipments and new products within the industry, and carry out engineering technology consultation services • Organize communications and training activities on the economy, technology and management of domestic and overseas dairy industry • Organize the collection of domestic and overseas economic and technological information in the dairy industry, and excel in relevant technological and information journals • Appraise and select top industry personnel and advanced enterprises • Participate in international organizations and relevant meetings on behalf of the dairy industry • Establish industry rules and agreements on behalf of the member units.
China Fermentation Industry Association	President Deputy President & Secretary General	Office, Scientific and Technologic Innovation Office, Fermentation Industry Editorial Department, China Fermentation Industry Association Website, Consultation Department	• Bring about new products, new processes, new technologies, new materials, and new equipments • Organize domestic and overseas technology communications and investigation trips abroad, and receive overseas visitors • Explore the technology market, carry out technical consultation services, and organize the import and export of biotech fermentation products • Coordinate the product pricing, technology and experience exchange among enterprises • Establish quality supervision and inspection and quality standards under the trust of the government, and put forward suggestions on the policies related to development planning
Local Government		Food Safety Office, Health Supervision Bureau, Food & Drug Supervision & Management Bureau, Industrial and Commercial Bureau, Quality & Technology Supervision Bureau	• The local People's government above county level determines the food safety supervision and management obligations of the health administration, agriculture administration, quality supervision, industrial and commercial administration management, and food and drug supervision and management departments of corresponding levels in accordance with the *Food Safety Law* and the regulations of the State Council. The relevant departments are responsible for the food safety supervision and management work within their administrative regions under their scope of responsibility. • The health administration, agriculture administration, quality supervision, industrial and commercial administration management, and food and drug supervision and management departments above the county level should enhance communications and cooperation, exercise their functions and powers, and undertake their respective obligations in accordance with laws.

Appendix E

Meeting Agendas

MARCH 2-3, 2011

MEETING 1 - AGENDA

Keck Building
500 Fifth Street NW
Washington, DC 20001

Day 1 Goals:
1) Introduce the National Academies' study process
2) Discuss bias and conflict-of-interest
3) Fully understand this study's statement of task
4) Learn about the capacity and priorities of the FDA

DAY ONE: WEDNESDAY, MARCH 2, 2011
Keck Building, Room 109

8:30 Breakfast Available

9:00-11:00 **SESSION 1 - CLOSED**
IOM COMMITTEE PROCESS AND CHARGE TO COMMITTEE

Objectives: To review the National Academies' study process that includes a bias and conflict-of-interest discussion; to discuss the role of the committee in addressing the statement of task; and to ensure the committee understands their statement of task.

11:00-11:10 Break

SESSION 2 - OPEN
QUESTIONS ON STATEMENT OF TASK

11:10-11:30 Project Timeline and Statement of Task
Sponsor Representative Introductions
Jim Riviere, Committee Chair

11:30-12:15 Questions to Sponsor
Mary Lou Valdez, Associate Commissioner for International Programs, FDA
Kate Bond, Associate Director for Technical Cooperation/Capacity-Building, FDA

12:15 Lunch

SESSION 3 - OPEN
THE FDA PERSPECTIVE

Objective: To learn about the FDA's current capacity and its international work.

12:45	Welcome the Public and Introduce Commissioner Hamburg **Jim Riviere,** Committee Chair
12:45-1:05	Keynote Address: Why is this study important to the FDA? **Margaret Hamburg,** Commissioner, FDA
1:05-1:25	**Questions**
1:25-2:30	What is the capacity of the FDA Centers? What are the key issues they face in international work? **Deb Autor,** Director, FDA Center for Drug Evaluation and Research **Karen Midthun,** Director, FDA Center for Biologics Evaluation and Research **Lillian Gill,** Senior Associate Director, FDA Center for Devices and Radiological Health **Don Kraemer,** Acting Deputy Director for Operations, FDA Center for Food Safety and Applied Nutrition
2:30-2:50	How is the FDA already working to build regulatory systems abroad? **Mac Lumpkin,** FDA Deputy Commissioner for International Programs
2:50-3:20	Panel discussion with presenters **Jane Henney,** Moderator
3:20-3:35	Break

SESSION 4 - OPEN
CORE ELEMENTS OF REGULATORY SYSTEMS

Objective: To identify the core elements of regulatory systems in developing countries and what gaps exist in these systems.

3:35-4:00	Core Elements of Medical Device Regulatory Systems in Developing Countries **Michael Gropp,** Vice President, Global Regulatory Strategy, Medtronic **Greg Kalbaugh,** Director and Counsel, US Chamber of Commerce, US-India Business Council
4:00-4:25	Core Elements of Food Regulatory Systems in Developing Countries **Ernesto Enriquez,** Ministry of Health, Mexico **Paul B. Young,** Director, Chemical Analysis Operations, Waters Corporation
4:25-4:55 Countries	Core Elements of Drug and Biologics Regulatory Systems in Developing **Jose Luis Di Fabio,** Area Manager, PAHO **Ekopimo Okon Ibia,** Director and US Regulatory Policy Lead, Global Regulatory Strategy, Policy, and Safety, Merck & Co., Inc.
4:55-5:45	What are the gaps in the systems? A panel discussion with presenters **Martha Brumfield,** Moderator
5:45	**Adjourn**

DAY TWO: THURSDAY, MARCH 3, 2011
Keck Building, Room 110

Day 2 Goals:

1) Learn about existing recommendations and the obstacles to implementing them
2) Make a strategy for how to tackle the statement of task
3) Discuss how to structure the final report
4) Begin considering possible recommendation topics

8:00	Breakfast Available

SESSION 5 - CLOSED
REACTIONS TO PRESENTATIONS AND PLANNING TRAVEL

Objective: To discuss the presentations and plan the travel meetings.

SESSION 6 - OPEN
EXISTING RECOMMENDATIONS AND OBSTACLES TO IMPLEMENTATION

Objective: To learn what recommendations have already been made to strengthen regulatory systems and what obstacles exist to implementing these recommendations.

10:10-10:30	The Global Harmonization Task Force **Michael Gropp,** Vice President, Global Regulatory Strategy, Medtronic
10:30-10:50	Promoting the Quality of Medicines **Patrick Lukulay,** Director, Promoting the Quality of Medicines Program, US Pharmacopeia
10:50-11:10	Capacity Building and the Partnership Training Institute Network **Paul B. Young,** Director, Chemical Analysis Operations, Waters Corporation
11:10-11:30	The Global Food Safety Initiative **Mike Robach,** Vice President Corporate Food Safety and Regulatory Affairs, Cargill
11:30-11:50	The International Medical Products Anti-Counterfeiting Taskforce **Howard Zucker,** Senior Advisor, Division of Global Health & Human Rights, Massachusetts General Hospital
11:50-12:30	Lunch
12:30-1:15	What prevents implementing recommendations? A panel discussion with presenters **Tom Bollyky,** Moderator

SESSION 7 – CLOSED
DISCUSSION AND STRATEGY FOR THE WAY FORWARD

Objective: To review the previous session, begin discussing recommendations, and give feedback on the meeting.

TRAVEL MEETING 1 - AGENDA

DAY ONE: WEDNESDAY MAY 11, 2011
CHINESE ACADEMY OF ENGINEERING, BEIJING

SESSION ONE
ORIENTATION

Objective: To explain the study and the purpose of our visit, to exchange introductions with representatives of the Chinese government, and to explain the IOM study process.

9:00-9:15	Welcome **Jim Riviere,** *Committee Chair*
9:15-9:30	Introductions
9:30-9:50	Institute of Medicine Process **Patrick Kelley,** *Board Director*

SESSION TWO
FDA'S CHINA PRESENCE

Objective: To learn about the FDA's work in China.

9:50-10:10	The FDA in China **Christopher Hickey,** Country Director , FDA
10:10-10:25	Questions

SESSION THREE
REGULATOR PANEL

Objective: To how Chinese regulators work and the key issues they face.

10:25-12:00	Panel Discussion, **Junshi Chen,** *Moderator* **Yinglian Hu,** *Professor,* National Academy of Governance **Ma Yong,** *Secretary General*, China National Food Industry Association **Geng Xiao,** *Director*, Columbia Global Center **Chen Rui,** *Deputy Director General*, MOH **Gao Fang,** *Deputy Director General*, Ministry of Agriculture
12:00-1:00	Lunch

SESSION FOUR
REGULATED INDUSTRY PANEL

Objective: To learn how regulated industry works with national, regional and foreign regulators, how they manage their supply chains, how able they are to comply with standards and harmonization efforts.

1:00-2:30 Panel Discussion, **Martha Brumfield,** *Moderator*

Wen Chang, *Vice Chairwoman*, China Pharmaceutical Quality Association

Sun Wei, *Director of Scientific and Regulatory Affairs,* Coca-Cola China

Steve Yang, *VP, Head of R&D, Asia and Emerging Markets*, AstraZeneca

Li Yu, *Scientific and Regulatory Affairs*, MARS China

Penggui Zai, *Food Regulatory Affairs Manager*, Wahaha Group

Libin Zhao, *Department of International Regulatory Affairs*, Tianjin Tasly Institute

2:30-2:40 Discussion Response

Philip Chen, *Director,* China Health Law Initiative

2:40-2:50 Break

SESSION FOUR
DONOR AND INTERNATIONAL ORGANIZATION PANEL

Objective: To explore how international organizations are working on health systems and infrastructure building, and to understand the role of a strong regulatory framework for health, agriculture and economic development.

3:00-4:30 Panel discussion, **Jake Chen,** *Moderator*

Gerd Fleischer, *Food Safety,* GIZ

Zuo Shuyan, *Expanded Program on Immunization,* WHO

Peter Karim Ben Embarek, *Team Leader Food Safety and Nutrition,* WHO

Jiankang Zhang, *Country Program Leader*, PATH

4:30-4:40 Discussion Response

Geng Xiao, *Director,* Columbia Global Center

DAY TWO: THURSDAY, MAY 12, 2011
CHINESE ACADEMY OF ENGINEERING, BEIJING

7:30-8:15 Working breakfast for committee and staff at Intercontinental Hotel

8:30	9:00	9:30	10:0	10:30	11:00	11:30	12:00	12:30	1:00	1:30	2:00	2:30	3:00	3:30	4:00	4:30	5:00	5:30
Rx at CAE Martha Brumfield Jake Chen Patrick Kelley Steve Yang, AZ Wen Chang, BMS		Note taking	Travel		**GIZ at GIZ** Martha Brumfield Jake Chen Kelley, Ginivan Chris Hickey		Note taking	Lunch	Travel		**SFDA at SFSDA** Martha Brumfield Jake Chen Kelley, Ginivan Translator		Note taking					
Food Cos at CAE Corrie Brown Meg Ginivan Qiang Zheng Penggui Zhai Translator		Note taking											Note taking	Travel				Note taking
	Travel		**AQSIQ at AQSIQ**		Note taking	Lunch			Travel		**WHO at WHO**		Note taking	Travel		**FDA at Intercon**		Note taking

DAY THREE: FRIDAY MAY 13, 2011
CHINA HOTEL, GUANGZHOU

SESSION ONE
ORIENTATION

8:30-8:45	Welcome and introductions **Jim Riviere**, *Committee Chair*
8:45-9:00	Institute of Medicine Process **Patrick Kelley**, *Board Director*

SESSION TWO A
FOOD AND DRUG REGULATION

9:00-10:00	Panel Discussion, **Jake Chen**, *Moderator* **Benny Liu,** *Director Fresh Development,* Wal-Mart China **Ke Ding,** *Deputy Director Drug Discovery,* Guangzhou Institute of Biomedicine and Health, Chinese Academy of Sciences **Qian Cheng**, *Deputy Director,* South China Center for Innovative Pharmaceuticals

SESSION TWO B
GUANGDONG FDA

9:40-10:00	Travel to Guangdong FDA
10:00-12:30	Discussion **Chris Hickey,** *Country Director*, FDA **Guangdong Provincial Regulators**

SESSION THREE
WRIGLEY FACTORY: SUPPLY CHAIN CASE STUDY

10:10-11:00	Travel to Wrigley Factory
11:00-12:00	Factory tour
12:00-1:00	Lunch
1:00-2:00	Closing remarks, **Thanh Nguyen,** *Regional Quality Director Asia-Pacific Supply Chain,* Wrigley

SESSION THREE
THE FDA PERSPECTIVE
CHINA HOTEL, GUANGZHOU

3:30-5:00	Panel Discussion, **Corrie Brown,** *Moderator* **Dennis Doupnik,** *Investigator,* FDA **Dennis Hudson,** *Consumer Safety Officer,* FDA **WeiHua Evid Liu,** FDA

TRAVEL MEETING 2 – AGENDA

DAY ONE: MONDAY, JUNE 20, 2011
UNIVERSITY OF SÃO PAULO, SCHOOL OF PUBLIC HEALTH, PROFESSOR EDMUNDO JUAREZ ROOM
AVENIDA DOUTOR ARNALDO, 715, SÃO PAULO

SESSION ONE
ORIENTATION

Objective: To explain the study and the purpose of our visit to the participants and to explain the IOM study process.

9:00-9:05	Welcome **Helena Ribeiro,** *Director,* University of São Paulo School of Public Health
9:05-9:15	Study Overview **Jim Riviere,** Committee Chair
9:15- 9:25	IOM Process **Gillian Buckley,** Study Director

SESSION TWO
FDA'S LATIN AMERICA PRESENCE

Objective: To learn about the FDA's work in Latin America.

9:25-9:45	The FDA in Latin America **Ana Maria Osorio,** *Assistant Regional Director - Latin America,* US FDA
9:45-10:00	Questions
10:05- 10:20	Break

SESSION THREE
REGULATORS' ROUNDTABLE

Objective: To gain a better understanding of how Latin American regulators work and the key issues they face.

10:20-11:20	Roundtable Discussion, **Carlos Morel,** *Moderator* **Renato Spindel,** *Director,* Scult Health Planning and Consultancy Ltda. **Amelia Villar,** *Consultant in Essential Medicine and Biologicals,* PAHO
11:20-11:30	Discussion Response **Terezinha de Jesus Andreolli Pinto,** *Professor,* University of São Paulo School of Pharmaceutical Sciences
11:30-12:40	Roundtable Discussion, **Andy Stergachis,** *Moderator* **Adriana Valenzuela,** *Head of International Affairs,* Division of Livestock Service, Chile Ministry of Agriculture

Marta H. Taniwaki, *Science Researcher*, State Food Technology Institute
Claudio Poblete, *Professor of Livestock Legislation*, Universidad Mayor School of Veterinary Medicine
Hector Lazaneo, *Division Director*, Ministry of Livestock, Agriculture and Fisheries, Uruguay

12:40-1:40 Lunch

SESSION FOUR
REGULATED INDUSTRY ROUNDTABLE

Objective: To learn how regulated industry works with national, regional and foreign regulators, how they manage their supply chains, how able they are to comply with standards and harmonization efforts, and what incentives could help them comply with standards and harmonization efforts.

1:40-2:45 Roundtable Discussion, **Clare Narrod,** *Moderator*
Rosane Cuber Guimarães, *Good Practices Manager,* Department of Quality Assurance, Bio-Manguinhos/Fiocruz
Lauro Moretto, *Executive Vice-President*, Association of the Pharmaceutical Industry in the State of Sao Paulo
Carlos Alberto Goulart, *Executive President*, Brazilian Association for Importers of Medical Equipment, Products and Supplies
Débora Germano, *Associate Director of Regulatory Affairs,* Pfizer Brazil

2:45-3:05 Discussion Response
Silvia Storpirtis, *Associate Professor,* University of São Paulo School of Pharmaceutical Sciences
Marco Antonio Stephano, *Professor,* University of São Paulo School of Pharmaceutical Sciences

3:05-3:20 Break

SESSION FIVE
INTERNATIONAL AND DONOR ORGANIZATION ROUNDTABLE

Objective: To explore how international organizations are working on health systems and infrastructure building, and to understand the role of a strong regulatory framework for health, agriculture, and economic development.

3:20-4:30 Roundtable Discussion, **Tom Bollyky,** *Moderator*
Raymond Dugas, *Regional Food Safety Advisor*, PAHO
Sergio Nishioka, *Scientist,* WHO, Department of Immunization, Vaccines and Biologicals
Ana Marisa Cordero Peña, *Agricultural Health and Food Safety Specialist* Inter-American Institute for Cooperation on Agriculture

5:00 Adjourn

6:30-8:00 Working dinner for committee members and staff

TRAVEL MEETING 3 – AGENDA

THURSDAY, JUNE 23, 2011
ACADEMY OF SCIENCE OF SOUTH AFRICA
FIRST FLOOR, BLOCK A, THE WOODS, 41 DEHAVILLAND CRESCENT, PERSEQUOR PARK, PRETORIA

SESSION ONE
ORIENTATION

Objective: To explain the study and the purpose of our visit to the participants and to explain the IOM study process.

9:00-9:05 Welcome
Nthabiseng Toale, *Program Manager*, Academy of Science of South Africa

9:05-9:15 Study Overview
Jim Riviere, IOM Committee Chair

9:15-9:25 IOM Process
Patricia Cuff, IOM Senior Program Officer

9:25-9:35 Questions

SESSION TWO
FDA'S AFRICA PRESENCE

Objective: To learn about the U.S. FDA's work in Africa.

9:35-9:45 The FDA in Africa
Beverly Corey, Senior Regional Advisor for Africa, US FDA

9:45-9:55 Questions

SESSION THREE
REGULATORS' ROUNDTABLE

Objective: To understand how African regulators work and the key issues they face.

9:55-11:10 Roundtable Discussion, **Andy Stergachis,** *Moderator*
- **Margareth Ndomondo-Sigonda,** *Pharmaceutical Coordinator*, New Partnership for Africa's Development, African Union
- **Derek Litthauer,** *Director*, National Control Laboratory for Biological Products, University of the Free State
- **Robert Crookes,** *Acting Medical Director,* South African National Blood Service
- **Worasuda Yoongthong,** *Assistant Head Policy & System Development, Head of National Drug Policy,* Office of Food and Drug Administration, Thailand

11:10-11:20 Discussion Response
Nicholas Crisp, *Managing Director*, Benguela Health Pty Ltd.

11:20-11:35 Break

11:35-12:35 Roundtable Discussion, **Clare Narrod,** *Moderator*
Malose Daniel Matlala, *Deputy Director Food Control*, Department of Health
Pieter Truter, *Technical Specialist,* National Regulator for Compulsory Specifications
Raymond Wigenge, *Director of Food Safety,* Tanzania Food and Drugs Authority
Sarah Olembo, *Technical Expert Sanitary and Phytosanitary Issues and Food Safety*, African Union Commission

12:35-12:45 Discussion Response
Nick Starke, *Chairman,* International Life Sciences Institute

12:45-1:45 Lunch

SESSION FOUR
REGULATED INDUSTRY ROUNDTABLE

Objective: To learn how regulated industry works with national, regional and foreign regulators, how they manage their supply chains, how able they are to comply with standards and harmonization efforts, and what incentives could help them comply with standards and harmonization efforts.

1:45-3:00 Roundtable Discussion, **Tom Bollyky,** *Moderator*
Elaine Alexander, *Executive Director,* South Africa Table Grape Industry
Maeve Magner, *Chief Executive*, RTT
Skhumbuzo Ngozwana, *President*, South African Generic Manufacturers' Association
Kirti Narsai, *Head of Scientific and Regulatory Affairs*, Pharmaceutical Industry Association of South Africa
Raymonde de Vries, *Corporate Quality Assurance*, Unilever Foods

3:00-3:15 Break

SESSION FIVE
INTERNATIONAL AND DONOR ORGANIZATIONS ROUNDTABLE

Objective: To explore how international organizations are working on health systems and infrastructure building, and to understand the role of a strong regulatory framework for health, agriculture and economic development.

3:15-4:30 Roundtable Discussion, **Jim Riviere**, *Moderator*
Gavin Steel, *Senior Program Associate*, Strengthening Pharmaceutical Systems, Management Sciences for Health
Celestine Kumire, *Programme Manager*, Southern African Regional Programme on Access to Medicines & Diagnostics, John Snow Inc.

Henry Leng, *Senior Researcher*, Accessing Medicines in Africa and South Asia
Nick Starke, *Chairman,* International Life Sciences Institute
Sarah Simons, *Executive Director,* Center for Agriculture and Bioscience International

4:40-4:50 Discussion Response
Sarah Olembo, *Technical Expert SPS and Food Safety*, African Union Commission

5:00 Adjourn

FRIDAY, JUNE 24, 2011
ACADEMY OF SCIENCE OF SOUTH AFRICA

7:45-8:30 Working breakfast for committee members and staff at Illyria Hotel

9:00–10:00	10:30	11:00–12:00	12:30	1:00–1:30	2:00–3:30
Biol. Regulators Jim Riviere Clare Narrod Kenisha Peters Crookes, Bird Litthauer, Pepper	Note taking	**Food Regulators** Jim Riviere Clare Narrod Kenisha Peters Olembo Wigenge	Note taking	Lunch	Closed Meeting Illyria Hotel Next Steps
Med. Regulators Andy Stergachis Gillian Buckley Yoongthong Crisp Ndomomdo-Sigonda	Note taking	**Health System** Andy Stergachis Gillian Buckley Leng Banoo Steel, Kumire	Note taking		
Medical Products Tom Bollyky Patricia Cuff Ngozwana Narsai Vogt	Note taking	**Food Industry** Tom Bollyky Patricia Cuff de Vries Magner	Note taking		

MEETING 2 - AGENDA

JULY 27-28, 2011

DAY ONE: WEDNESDAY, JULY 27, 2011

The Keck Building, Room 201

8:30	Breakfast available

SESSION 1 – OPEN
THE GLOBAL SYSTEM AND SUPPLY CHAIN

Objectives: To understand the depth and breadth of the publically available enforcement data, and the use of information technology for international surveillance, operations and supply chain management.

9:00-9:15	Welcome and orientation **Jim Riviere,** Committee Chair
9:20-9:50	Systems Mapping with EU and FDA Enforcement Data **Ying Zhang,** PhD Candidate, *Georgetown University* **Jake Chen,** Committee Member
9:50-10:10	Questions
10:10-10:40	Global Information Technology Management **Noel Greis,** Director, Kenan Institute of Private Enterprise, University of North Carolina at Chapel Hill
10:40-11:00	Questions
11:00-11:15	Break

SESSION 2-CLOSED
REPORT OUTLINE

Objective: To approve an outline for the final report, to assign sections.

SESSION 3- CLOSED
TRAVEL MEETING DEBRIEF

Objective: To review the themes that emerged in China, South Africa and Brazil focusing on statement of task questions 1-5.

DAY TWO: THURSDAY, JULY 28, 2011

The Keck Building, Room 109

8:30	Breakfast available

SESSION 1 - CLOSED
BIAS AND CONFLICT OF INTEREST REVIEW

Objective: To approve an outline for the final report.

SESSION 2 - CLOSED
CORE ELEMENTS OF REGULATORY SYSTEMS

Objective: To draft recommendations on statement of task item A and questions 4, 5.

SESSION 3 - CLOSED
BRIDGING THE GAPS IN REGULATORY SYSTEMS

Objective: To draft recommendations on statement of task item C and questions 6-9.

SESSION 4 - OPEN
TELECONFERENCE WITH ANVISA

Objective: To learn about the Brazilian regulatory system

1:00-2:00 **Dirceu Barbano,** Director, ANVISA (teleconference)
Carlos Morel, Discussion Leader

SESSION 5 - CLOSED
A PLAN FOR THE FDA

Objective: To draft recommendations on statement of task items B, D, and F.

SESSION 6 - CLOSED
PARTNERSHIPS

Objective: To draft recommendations on statement of task item E and questions 10-13.

TRAVEL MEETING 3 - AGENDA
August 31-September 2, 2011

DAY ONE: WEDNESDAY, AUGUST 31, 2011
PUBLIC HEALTH FOUNDATION OF INDIA, VASANT KUNJ, NEW DELHI

7:45-8:30 Working breakfast for committee members and staff at the Crowne Plaza Hotel

9:00	9:30	10:00	10:30	11:00	11:30	12:00	12:30	1:00	1:30	2:00	2:30	3:00	3:30	4:00	4:30	5:00
International Orgs. Jim Riviere Bob Buchanan Gillian Buckley Kenisha Peters Bejon Misra Abhay Kadam			**Pharmaceuticals** Jim Riviere Bob Buchanan Gillian Buckley Kenisha Peters Dilip Shah			Lunch			**Vaccines** Jim Riviere Bob Buchanan Gillian Buckley Kenisha Peters Sunil Bahl Pramod Kumar			Note taking	**Medical Products** Jim Riviere Bob Buchanan Gillian Buckley Kenisha Peters Jagdish Dore Ajay Pitre Jasvir Singh			Note taking

DAY TWO: THURSDAY, SEPTEMBER 1, 2011
TRAVELLING MEETINGS

7:15-8:00 Working breakfast for committee members and staff at the Crowne Plaza Hotel

8:30 / 9:00 / 9:30	10:00 / 10:30	11:00 / 11:30 / 12:00	12:30	1:00 / 1:30 / 2:00	2:30 / 3:00	3:30 / 4:00 / 4:30	5:00
Pharma @ PHFI Kenisha Peters Prashant Yadav Bob Buchanan Neeraj Mohan Anil Pareek Sana Mostaghim	Travel to APEDA	**APEDA @ APEDA** Kenisha Peters Bob Buchanan S. Dave Asit Tripathy Devendra Prasad	Travel to Quality Council	**Working Lunch @ Quality Council** Gillian Buckley Jim Riviere Kenisha Peters Prashant Yadav Bob Buchanan Anil Jauhri Vani Bhambri Arora	Travel to Export Council	**Export Council @ Export Council** Kenisha Peters Prashant Yadav Bob Buchanan S.K. Saxena Rajeev Raizada R.M. Mandlik C.B. Kotak Arvind Patil Pramod Swaich	Note taking
Indian Pharmacopeia @ PHFI Jim Riviere Gillian Buckley G.N. Singh	**ICMR @ PHFI** Jim Riviere Gillian Buckley Prashant Yadav Mukesh Kumar (by phone)		Travel to Quality Council		Travel to FICCI	**Chamber of Commerce @ FICCI** Jim Riviere Gillian Buckley Sameer Barde	Note taking

DAY THREE: FRIDAY SEPTEMBER 2. 2011
TRAVELLING MEETINGS

7:15-8:00 Working breakfast for committee members and staff at the Crowne Plaza Hotel

Regulators @ PHFI Jim Riviere Kenisha Peters Prashant Yadav Gillian Buckley Bob Buchanan W. Yoongthong Moazzem Hossain	Note taking	Travel to PATH	**PATH @ PATH** Jim Riviere Kenisha Peters Prashant Yadav Gillian Buckley Bob Buchanan Tarun Vij + staff	Lunch	**Min. of Chem. @ BHEL** Jim Riviere Kenisha Peters Prashant Yadav Arun Jha	Travel to AYUSH	**AYUSH @ AYUSH** Jim Riviere Kenisha Peters Prashant Yadav Ghazala Javed Janardhan Pandey D.C. Katoch M. Mitra	Note taking	
				Lunch	**USDA @ Embassy** Gillian Buckley Bob Buchanan David Leishman Ritambhara Singh	**FDA @ Embassy** Gillian Buckley Bob Buchanan Bruce Ross		**USAID @ Embassy** Gillian Buckley Bob Buchanan James Browder	

Appendix F

Committee Member Biographies

Jim E. Riviere, DVM, PhD, DSc (Chair) is the Burroughs Wellcome Fund Distinguished Professor of Pharmacology and Alumni Distinguished Graduate Professor and director of the Center for Chemical Toxicology Research and Pharmacokinetics at the College of Veterinary Medicine, North Carolina State University (NCSU). In the summer of 2012, Dr. Riviere will be the University Distinguished Professor and McDonald Chair of Veterinary Medicine at Kansas State University. Dr. Riviere received his BS (summa cum laude) and MS degrees from Boston College, his DVM and PhD in pharmacology as well as a DSc (*hon*) from Purdue University. He is an elected member of the Institute of Medicine of the National Academies, serves on its Food and Nutrition Board and is a fellow of the Academy of Toxicological Sciences. He is a member of Phi Beta Kappa, Phi Zeta and Sigma Xi, and has served on the Science Board of the Food and Drug Administration. His honors include the 1999 O. Max Gardner Award from the Consolidated University of North Carolina, the 1991 Ebert Prize from the American Pharmaceutical Association, the Harvey W. Wiley Medal and FDA Commissioner's Special Citation, and the Lifetime Achievement Award from the European Association of Veterinary Pharmacology and Toxicology. He is the Editor of the *Journal of Veterinary Pharmacology and Therapeutics*, co-founder and co-director of the USDA Food Animal Residue Avoidance Databank (FARAD) program, and was formerly the director of the Biomathematics Program in the College of Physical and Mathematical Sciences at NCSU. He has served as an officer in various Specialty Sections of the Society of Toxicology, and has served on the editorial boards of various toxicology, pharmacology and veterinary journals. He has published over 490 full-length research papers and chapters, holds 6 U.S. patents, has authored/edited 10 books in pharmacokinetics, toxicology and food safety, and received over 18 million dollars as principal investigator on extramural research grants. His current research interests relate to the development of animal models; applying biomathematics to problems in toxicology, including the risk assessment of chemical mixtures, pharmacokinetics, nanomaterials, absorption of drugs and chemicals across skin; and the food safety and pharmacokinetics of tissue residues in food producing animals.

Thomas Bollyky, JD is senior fellow for global health, economics, and development at the Council on Foreign Relations (CFR). He is also an adjunct professor of law at Georgetown University and consultant to the Bill and Melinda Gates Foundation. Prior to coming to CFR, Mr. Bollyky was a fellow at the Center for Global Development and director of intellectual property and pharmaceutical policy at the Office of the U.S. Trade Representative (USTR), where he led the negotiations for pharmaceuticals, biotechnology, and medical technologies in the U.S.-Republic of Korea Free Trade Agreement and represented USTR in the negotiations with China on the safety of food and drug imports. He was also a Fulbright Scholar in South Africa where he worked as a staff attorney at the AIDS Law Project on treatment access issues related to HIV/AIDS and a senior attorney at Debevoise & Plimpton LLP where he represented Mexico before the International Court of Justice in Avena and other Mexican Nationals (Mexico v.

United States of America) and José Ernesto Medellín before the United States Supreme Court in Medellin v. Dretke. Mr. Bollyky is a former law clerk to Chief Judge Edward R. Korman, an International Affairs Fellow at the Council on Foreign Relations, an Eesti and Eurasian Public Service Fellow at the Estonian Ministry of Education and a health policy analyst, through the Outstanding Scholar Program, at the U.S. Department of Health and Human Services. He received his BA in Biology and History at Columbia University and his JD at Stanford Law School, where he was the President of the Stanford Law & Policy Review. Mr. Bollyky is a term member of the Council on Foreign Relations and a member of the New York and U.S. Supreme Court bars and the American Society of International Law.

Corrie Brown, DVM, PhD is a professor in the Department of Pathology at the University of Georgia, College of Veterinary Medicine. Her research interests include the pathogenesis of disease in food-producing animals, emerging diseases and animal health infrastructure in developing nations. She teaches courses in general pathology, systemic pathology and international veterinary medicine. She is currently associate editor of *Emerging Infectious Disease* and serves on the editorial boards of *Transboundary and Emerging Diseases*, *Zoonoses and Public Health* and *Veterinary Pathology*. She received a DVM from the University of Guelph and a PhD from the University of California, Davis. Dr. Brown has served on three National Academies committees: the Committee on Genomics Databases for Bioterrorism Threat Agents: Striking a Balance for Information Sharing (2003-2004); the Committee on Assessing the Nation's Framework for Addressing Animal Diseases (2003-2004); and the Committee on Achieving Sustainable Global Capacity for Surveillance and Response to Emerging Diseases of Zoonotic Origin (2008).

Martha Brumfield, PhD has a consulting practice focusing on concordance in global regulatory requirements and providing educational workshops toward that goal. Other areas of focus include excellence in clinical trial conduct; facilitation of scientific consortia and programs supporting patient access to medicines.

At present she is engaged with the non-profit Critical Path Institute as a consultant to guide international program development and to provide regulatory guidance to consortia. She is also engaged with other non-profits, Regulatory Harmonization Institute and GlobalMD, to deliver educational workshops on regulatory and clinical trial topics in Asia.

Most recently, Dr. Brumfield was Senior Vice President, Worldwide Regulatory Affairs and Quality Assurance at Pfizer, Inc. She led a global team that supported lifecycle pharmaceutical research, development and commercialization through creation and implementation of regulatory strategies and quality assurance oversight. Dr. Brumfield also played a key role in managing the broader company relationships with global regulators, trade associations, academics and others on regulatory policy issues. Dr. Brumfield has been active in several external organizations including PhRMA, CMR, and APEC LSIF and has worked extensively with the PhRMA Simultaneous Global Development program. During 20 years at Pfizer, Dr. Brumfield held a variety of leadership positions in which she led regulatory teams responsible for the United States, Europe, and emerging markets. Dr. Brumfield also served as the company's head of drug safety surveillance and reporting, and managed global adverse event reporting requirements and the integration of Pharmacia's related safety operations. Dr. Brumfield earned a BS and MS in Chemistry from Virginia Commonwealth University, a PhD in Organic Chemistry from the University of Maryland, and served as a post-doctoral fellow at the Rockefeller University.

Robert Buchanan, MS, MPhil, PhD is director of the University of Maryland's AGNR Center for Food Safety and Security Systems, received his BS, MS, MPhil, and PhD degrees in food science from Rutgers University, and post-doctoral training in mycotoxicology at the University of Georgia. He has 35 years of experience teaching, conducting research in food safety, and working at the interface between science and public health policy, first in academia, then in government service in both USDA and FDA and most recently at the University of Maryland. His scientific interests are diverse and include extensive experience in predictive microbiology, quantitative microbial risk assessment, microbial physiology, mycotoxicology and food safety systems. He has published extensively on a wide range of subjects related to food safety and is one of the co-developers of the widely used USDA Pathogen Modeling Program. Dr. Buchanan has served on numerous national and international advisory bodies including serving as a member of the International Commission on Microbiological Specification for Foods for 20 years, a six-term member of the National Advisory Committee for Microbiological Criteria for Foods, the U.S. Delegate to the Codex Alimentarius Committee on Food Hygiene for 10 years, and a participant on multiple expert consultations for WHO and FAO.

Jake Yue Chen, MS, PhD is an associate professor with tenure at Indiana University School of Informatics and Purdue University Department of Computer and Information Science in Indianapolis (IUPUI). He is the founding director of the Indiana Center for Systems Biology and Personalized Medicine, a member of the Indiana University Simon Cancer Center, and a member of the Center for Computational Biology and Bioinformatics at Indiana University School of Medicine. He is also an ACM senior member, IEEE senior member, and chair of the IEEE Engineering in Biology and Medicine Society Central Indiana Chapter. He currently serves on the editorial boards of several international bioinformatics journals including *BMC Systems Biology*, organized over 100 academic meetings in informatics and computer science, and he has served on many grant review panels for NIH, NSF, DOD, and DOE. He is the recipient of the Canary Foundation 2008 Bioinformatics Dissemination Award, a Translational Research into Practice (TRIP) scholar at Indiana University, and a 2010 Cambridge Health Institute's Translational Medicine Conference Distinguished Faculty. He holds masters and doctoral degrees in computer science & engineering from the University of Minnesota and a bachelor's degree in Biochemistry & Molecular Biology from Peking University of China.

His research expertise spans over biological data management, biological data mining, bioinformatics, systems biology, and clinical applications of genomics in predictive and personalized medicine, with more than 100 research publications—including two edited books, *Biological Database Modeling* and *Biological Data Mining*—and more than 100 invited talks worldwide.

He also has considerable experience in leading informatics R&D projects in the biopharmaceutical industry. Prior to joining academia in 2004, he helped design commercial GeneChip microarray products for humans, mice, and rats at Affymetrix, Inc. in San Jose, California and led a team to data mine the world's first comprehensive human protein interactome collected at Myriad Proteomics, Inc. in Salt Lake City, Utah. In Indiana, he co-founded the non-profit Indiana Biomedical Entrepreneur's Network to promote biotechnology commercialization efforts and two biotech startup businesses to promote predictive and personalized medicine practices.

Junshi Chen, MD graduated from the Beijing Medical College in 1956 and has been engaged in nutrition and food safety research for more than 50 years at the Institute of Nutrition and Food Safety, Chinese Center for Disease Control and Prevention (the former Chinese Academy of Preventive Medicine). He has conducted large epidemiologic studies on diet, nutrition and chronic diseases, in collaboration with Dr. T. Colin Campbell of Cornell University and Professor Richard Peto from the University of Oxford since 1983. In the late 1980's, he conducted a series of studies on the protective effects of tea on cancer, including laboratory studies and human intervention trials. He is the member of the expert panel that authored the WCRF/AICR report "Food, Nutrition and the Prevention of Cancer: a Global Perspective" (1997). Recently, he was appointed as the chair of the Chinese National Expert Committee for Food Safety Risk Assessment and the vice-chair of the National Food Safety Standard Reviewing Committee.

Internationally, he serves as the Chairperson of the Codex Committee on Food Additives, a member of the WHO Food Safety Expert Panel and director of the International Life Sciences Institute Focal Point in China. Dr. Chen has published more than 140 articles in peer reviewed journals.

Jane Henney, MD has served in a series of senior health policy leadership positions in the public sector for nearly 30 years. Beginning in 1980, she served for 5 years as the deputy director of the National Cancer Institute. Subsequently, she joined the University of Kansas Medical Center as vice chancellor of health programs, and, for 18 months, interim dean of the School of Medicine. She then served as deputy commissioner for operations of the Food and Drug Administration, where she stayed until assuming the position as the first vice president for health sciences at the University of New Mexico.

In 1998 she was nominated by President Bill Clinton and confirmed by the U.S. Senate as the commissioner of the U.S. Food and Drug Administration. She served in this capacity until January 2001. After leaving the FDA, she was appointed senior scholar in residence at the Association of Academic Health Centers. From July 2003 until the beginning of 2008 Dr. Henney served as Senior Vice President and Provost for Health Affairs at the University of Cincinnati. In addition to her current academic responsibilities at the University, she also serves on the boards of the Commonwealth Fund in New York, the China Medical Board in Boston and the Association of Academic Health Centers in Washington, DC. She is a member of the Board of Directors of AmerisourceBergen Corporation and CIGNA in Philadelphia and AstraZeneca PLC in London. In addition, she serves on a wide range of foundations, associations and governmental advisory committees.

Dr. Henney has received many honors and awards in her field, including election to the Institute of Medicine of the National Academies, the Society of Medical Administrators and honorary membership in the American College of Health Care Executives. She is a recipient of the Excellence in Women's Health Award from the Jacobs Institute, the Public Health Leadership Award from the National Organization of Rare Disorders, the HHS Secretary's Recognition Award and, on two separate occasions, the PHS Commendation Medal. She has received honorary degrees from North Carolina State University, Manchester College and the University of Rochester.

A native of Indiana, Dr. Henney received her undergraduate degree from Manchester College, her medical degree from Indiana University, and completed her subspecialty training in medical oncology at the M.D. Anderson Hospital and Tumor Institute and the National Cancer Institute.

Carlos M. Morel, MD, PhD is a member of the Brazilian Academy of Science, a physician and a doctor of science. He studied at the Faculty of Medicine at the Federal University of Pernambuco and at the Carlos Chagas Filho Biophysics Institute of the Federal University of Rio de Janeiro (UFRJ). He has a PhD from UFRJ based on work done at the Swiss Institute for Experimental Cancer Research in Lausanne. Dr. Morel was a professor at the Faculty of Medicine and the Institute of Biological Science at the Federal University of Brasilia. His scientific production includes 79 original papers published in indexed journals, 15 book chapters and a book *Genes and Antigens of Parasites* acknowledged by *Nature*.

He is a researcher at the Oswaldo Cruz Foundation (Fiocruz) where he created the Department of Biochemical and Molecular Biology, gathering an internationally renowned team in molecular parasitology and biotechnology. He served as director of the Oswaldo Cruz Institute from 1985 to 1989 and as president of Fiocruz from 1993-1997. From 1998-2004, Dr. Morel was the director of a special program of UNICEF, UNDP, the World Bank and WHO for research and training in tropical diseases. He contributed actively to the conception of several international programs for research and development on neglected diseases: Global Forum for Health Research; Medicines for Malaria Venture; Global Alliance for Tuberculosis Drug Development; the Drugs for Neglected Diseases Initiative; and the Foundation for Innovative New Diagnostics. He is currently the Fiocruz representative on the Board of Directors of the Drugs for Neglected Diseases Initiative. He was the first president of the Board of Directors of the Global Alliance for TB Drug Development and served on this board until 2007. Since 2004 he has coordinated the establishment of the Fiocruz Center for Technological Development in Health (CDTS).

His current research and teaching activities are in technological development, scientific and technological networks and innovation management, with a focus on health and neglected diseases. He is a professor of the post-graduate program in Public Politics, Strategies and Development at the UFRJ Institute of Economy. He has recently published in *Science, Nature* and the electronic journal *Innovation Strategy Today.*

Clare Narrod, PhD is a research scientist and risk analysis program manager at the University of Maryland's Joint Institute for Food Safety and Applied Nutrition (JIFSAN) since January 2012. Before joining JIFSAN, Dr. Narrod was a senior research fellow in the Markets Trade and Institutions Division of the International Food Policy Research Institute (IFPRI). Dr. Narrod worked at the United States Department of Agriculture (USDA), Office of the Chief Economist, as a risk assessor and regulatory economist where she reviewed food safety and animal and plant health rules for departmental clearance. She also has worked at the Food and Agriculture Organization (FAO) where she led a number of livestock projects that focused on understanding the policy, technology and environmental determinants and implications of scaling up livestock production. From 1998-2000 Clare served as an American Association for the Advancement of Science (AAAS) Risk Fellow at USDA. In the past she has held consultant positions at the World Bank and at the Inter-American Institute for Cooperate in Agriculture. She has conducted field work in Brazil, China, Ethiopia, Ghana, India, Indonesia, Kenya, Mali, Mexico, Nigeria, the Philippines, Thailand, United States, Vietnam, and Zambia. She received her PhD in Energy Management and Environmental Policy and her master's degree in International Development and Appropriate Technology both from the University of Pennsylvania.

Andy Stergachis, PhD, MS, BPHARM focuses on pharmacoepidemiology, global medicines safety, pharmaceutical outcomes research, and public health systems research. He directs the Global Medicines Program in Department of Global Health at the University of Washington. He is currently the principal investigator of the University of Washington components of two projects funded by the Bill & Melinda Gates Foundation, including the pharmacovigilance component of a multi-center global clinical trials program of alternative antimalarial case management and prevention strategies in pregnancy. He is the principal investigator of the UW component of a USAID-funded cooperative agreement with Management Sciences for Health on strengthening pharmaceutical systems in developing countries. Through his affiliation with the Northwest Center for Public Health Practice, he also works on workforce development and public health systems research in emergency preparedness with the public health community. He is also affiliated with the UW's Pharmaceutical Outcomes Research and Policy program. He is author of over 100 peer reviewed publications, including an assessment of pharmacovigilance activities in low- and middle-income countries. He has earned numerous awards for his work in pharmacy, medication safety and public health, including the American Pharmaceutical Association Foundation 2002 Pinnacle Award for his career commitment to improving the quality of the medication use process. He is a Fellow of the International Society for Pharmacoepidemiology. He has served on Institute of Medicine committees, including the Committee on Poison Prevention and Control System, and the Committee on Assessment of the U.S. Drug Safety System. His international responsibilities include the Virtual Advisory Group to Global Alert and Response for the World Health Organization. Locally, he is a member of the Public Health Reserve Corps.

Prashant Yadav, MBA, PhD is the director of a research initiative focused on healthcare supply chains in the developing world at the William Davidson Institute at the University of Michigan. He also holds faculty appointments at the Ross School of Business and the School of Public Health at the University of Michigan.

Dr. Yadav's research explores the functioning of healthcare supply chains using a combination of empirical, analytical and qualitative approaches. He serves as an advisor in the area of pharmaceutical supply chains to the Bill and Melinda Gates Foundation, World Bank, World Health Organization, UNITAID, UK Department for International Development, and many other global health organizations. He is the author of many scientific publications and his work has been featured in prominent print and broadcast media including The Economist, The Financial Times, Nature, and BBC. He serves on the advisory boards of several public private partnerships and currently serves as co-chair of the Procurement and Supply Chain Working Group of the Roll Back Malaria Partnership.

Prior to coming to the William Davidson Institute at the University of Michigan, Dr. Yadav was a Professor of Supply Chain Management at the MIT-Zaragoza International Logistics Program and a Research Affiliate at the MIT Center for Transportation and Logistics where he led the creation of a high impact research initiative focused on pharmaceutical supply chains in developing countries. From 2008-2010 he was also a visiting scholar at the INSEAD Social Innovation Center.

Dr. Yadav obtained his bachelor of chemical engineering from the Indian Institute of Technology, his MBA from the FORE School of Management and his PhD from the University of Alabama. Before academia, he worked for many years in the area of pharmaceutical strategy, analytics and supply chain consulting.

Appendix G

Analyzing Food Safety Alerts in European Union Rapid Alerts Systems for Food and Feed

Ying Zhang, Elizabeth Wells, and Jake Chen

This paper presents an overview of the types of problems different countries have in meeting import requirements of one of the biggest global importers: the European Union (EU). This paper uses publically available data to identify patterns in the types of problems different countries have in meeting import requirements; to understand where in the supply chains the product safety failures occur; to explain the types of threats border inspectors commonly identify; and to evaluate the types of data that are most needed for tracing safety trends.

Many countries collect and make public data on their food regulatory authority's border rejections, but there is no single international federated database combining these records. This study uses tracking data from the European Union Rapid Alert Systems for Food and Feed.

Data and Methods

Data Sources

This paper uses official food safety information from the European Union Rapid Alert Systems for Food and Feed (EURASFF). EURASEF is an information sharing framework managed by the European Free Trade Association in coordination with the European Food Safety Authority (EFSA) and the European Commission. Foods and animal feeds that pose risk to human health requiring official action, "such as withholding, recalling, seizure or rejection of the products concerned" (Europa, 2011), are reported to EURASFF under article 50 of Regulation (EC) No. 178/2002.[1] Table G-1 presents the inclusion criteria for records included in this paper's analysis.

TABLE G-1 Inclusion and Exclusion Criteria for Data Collection

EURASFF
Inclusion criteria
1. Notified between January 1st 2006 and June 2nd 2011
2. Search type is limited to food only
3. Reported by any EU member country
Exclusion Criteria
Food produced in EU member countries

[1] *Laying down the general principles and requirements of food law, establishing the European Food Safety Authority and laying down procedures in matters of food safety.* Regulation (EC) No. 178/2002, art. 50. The European Parliament and the Council of Europe (28 January 2002).

The EURSAFF database presents the number of recalls and safety notifications recorded at their ports. This paper attempts to put these raw numbers in a context that accounts for the amount of trade the exporting country does with the EU. Therefore, we have retrieved trade data from Eurostat external trade statistics for food (European Commission, 2011), which classifies traded products using the WTO's Harmonized System Codes. Table G-2 presents the criteria used to draw data from Eurostat, and lists the Harmonized System Codes we included.

TABLE G-2 Inclusion Criteria Trade Statistics

Inclusion criteria
1. Reporter countries are limited to EU 27 members
2. Trade partners are limited to the 60 countries from which more than ten food safety alert had been generated between 2006 and 2010
3. Product types are limited to HTS code 1-23

Coding Metrics

Each safety alert in the database contains a short description of the product, origin countries, transit countries and the reason for the notification. This study used a coding system to categorize the type of threat reported and the place on the supply chain where it might have occurred. Briefly, the risk code refers to the reason that the product was rejected. This suspected risk can be microbial, chemical, physical, mycotoxins, or problems in processing, labeling. There is also another category that was used for rejections that resisted classification, or unclear records. Table G-3 describes the risk codes, labeled A-Y.

The supply chain categorizes the point at which the product became unsuitable for human consumption. This may have occurred at any point between the farm and the port. In most cases it is not explicit where on the supply chain contamination occurred, these entries are coded as 0. Table G-4 shows how the coder combined risk codes and supply chain codes.

Limitations

The quality of the publically available data is one major limitation of this study. Also, the reasons for the safety alert and recall are recorded in free text; there is no standard language used for reporting in these databases. Some notes are ambiguous or confusing. For example, "unauthorized usage" of certain ingredients in food production can be interpreted as an administrative issue when a novel food ingredient was introduced without approval. It might also be a violation of using prohibited chemicals as food additives or dyes. The coding matrix also has limitations. Some cases can be given more than one code. For instance, "bad preservation state" or "bad hygienic state" can be interpreted as a processing problem (code F) when the food product is not stored or transported properly; it could also be coded as a physical defect (code E).

This analysis was also held back by the lack of a comprehensive up-to-date master list for chemicals prohibited in food and food packaging, especially food dyes and additives. It is not always clear if a consignment was problematic because the chemicals detected were illegal (code C) or in violation of threshold levels (code D). Therefore, when analyzing the coding results, we do not over-interpret codes that might overlap.

TABLE G-3 Risk/Content Code

Risk/Content	Code	Description	Example
Microbial Contamination	A	Microbial pathogen identified in the product	Escherichia coli (940 CFU/100g) in clams (Tapes decussatus) from Tunisia
Mycotoxin Contamination	B	Mycotoxin (a toxin produced by pathogenic microbes) identified in the product	Aflatoxins (B1 < 0.1; Tot. < 0.1 / B1 < 0.1; Tot. < 0.1 / B1 = 10.0; Tot. = 10.9 μg/kg - ppb) in peanuts in shell from China
Chemical Contamination (Absolutely Prohibited)	C	Chemical prohibited in the reporting country or region identified in a product	prohibited substance metronidazole (0.2 μg/kg - ppb) in honey from China
Chemical Contamination (Over Threshold)	D	Chemical over the maximum residue level of the reporting country or region standards identified in a product	zinc (14.5 mg/l) in cane vinegar from Senegal
Physical Contamination	E	Contamination that can be identified through organoleptic inspection.	dried peas from Ukraine infested with insects (Bruchus Pisorum)
Processing	F	Inadequate or inappropriate processing	bad temperature control - rupture of the cold chain - of frozen poultry meat from Brazil
Labeling	G	Ingredients not labeled or labeled incorrectly	absence of labeling on linoleic acid soft capsules from China

Administrative Reason	H	Absent, improper, fraudulent or expired documents according to the reporting country standards	absence of health certificate(s) for corned beef from Brazil
Other	X	risk not clearly defined	suffocation risk as a result of the consumption of mini cup jelly from Taiwan
Issues not interested	Y	Issues that are not of concerns for the United States (e.g. genetically modified food, irradiation, etc.)	unauthorised genetically modified (presence of GM rice BT 63) rice spaghetti from China

TABLE G-4 Coding metrics combining risk/content codes with supply chain codes

		Supply Chain					
		Raw Material	Manufacturing	Packaging	Transportation	Market	Others
Risk/content		1	2	3	4	5	0
Microbes	A	A1	A2	A3	A4	A5	A0
Mycotoxin	B	B1	B2	B3	B4	B5	B0
Chemical (Absolutely prohibited)	C	C1	C2	C3	C4	C5	C0
Chemical (Over threshold)	D	D1	D2	D3	D4	D5	D0
Physical	E	E1	E2	E3	E4	E5	E0
Processing	F	F1	F2	F3	F4	F5	F0
Labeling	G	G1	G2	G3	G4	G5	G0
Administrative Reason	H	H1	H2	H3	H4	H5	H0
Others	X	X1	X2	X3	X4	X5	X0
Issues not interested	Y	Y1	Y2	Y3	Y4	Y5	Y0

Findings

As the world biggest food importer and exporter (European Commission, 2010), the EU has a well-developed and rigorous food safety alert reporting and information sharing system. EURASFF 2010 records identified 2,878 risky food products in 2010, half of them coming from outside the EU.

Figure G-1 shows the fifteen countries whose food exports to the EU that triggered the official action. between 2006 and 2010 However, when the cumulative number of safety alerts is divided by the cumulative food import volume, only seven countries – India, Morocco, Pakistan, Turkey, Egypt, the United States and Iran – still ranks in the top 15 (Figure G-2).

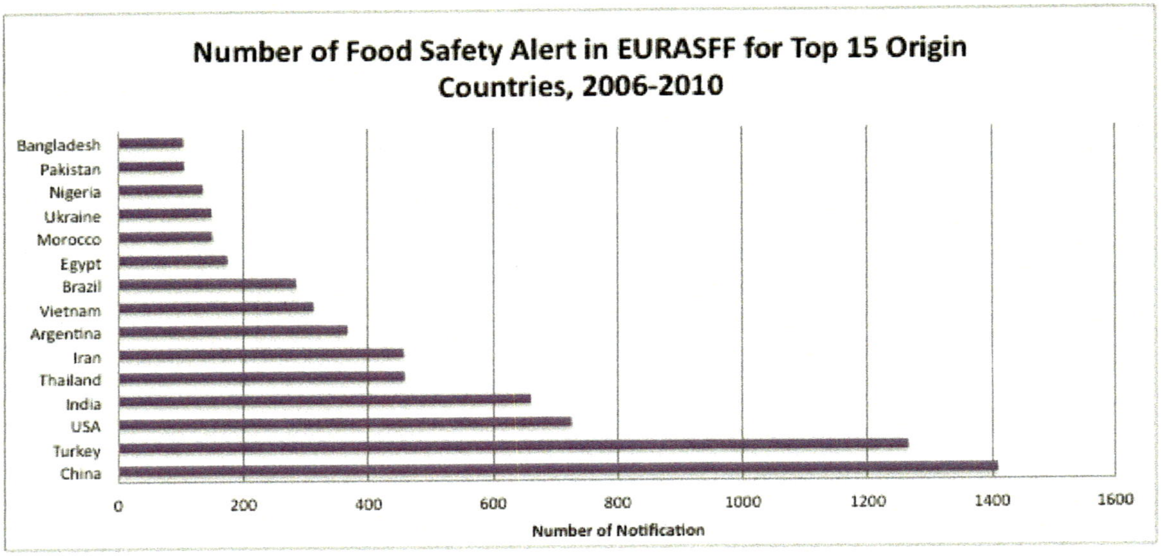

FIGURE G-1
Number of food safety alert in EURASFF for top 15 origin countries, 2006-2010

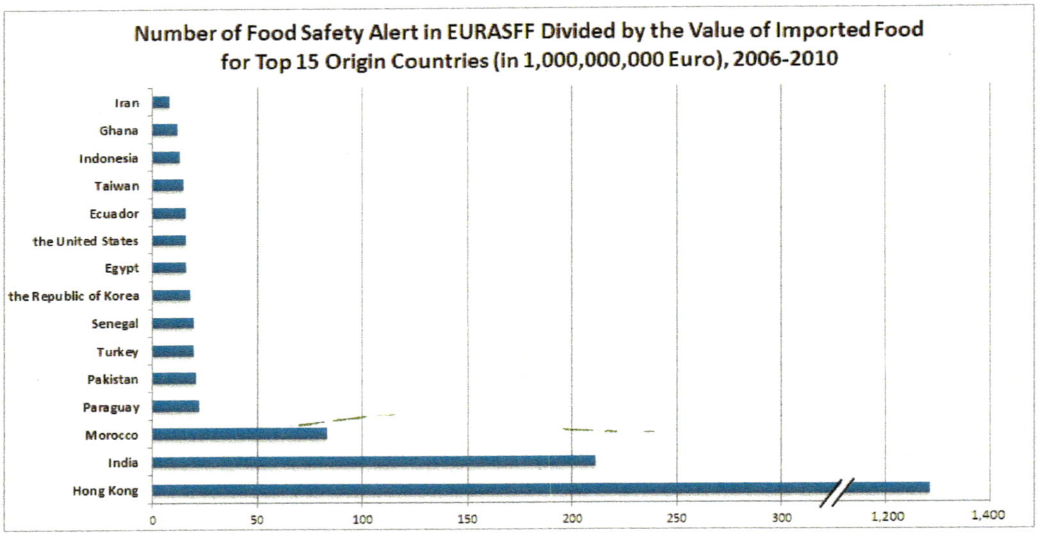

FIGURE G-2
Number of food safety alert in EURASFF divided by the value of imported food for top 15 origin countries (in billions of euros), 2006-2010.

Figures G-3 and G-4 attempt to illustrate the relationship between the number of safety alerts associated with a country's exports to the EU, the amount of trade the country does with the EU, and the country's wealth. In these graphs the x-axis shows the number of safety alerts, the y-axis shows food import volume in billions of euros, and the radius represents the country's gross domestic product (GDP) in U.S. dollars according the World Bank (World Bank, 2010), with the exception of the GDP of Taiwan, which is from the International Monetary Fund (IMF, 2010).

Figure G-3 shows that China is the subject of many safety alerts and also does a great deal of trade with the EU. The United States is the subject of many food safety alerts, most of them because of novel food ingredients, unauthorized irradiation, and genetically modified organisms. This is a function of different food standards between the United States and Europe.

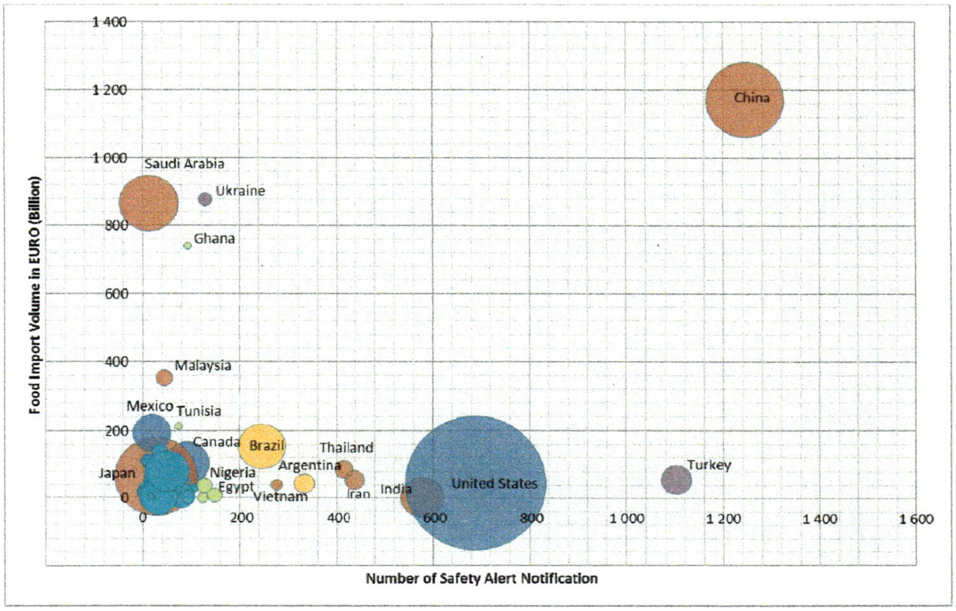

FIGURE G-3 Number of safety alert notifications, food import volume and GDP of EU food importers.

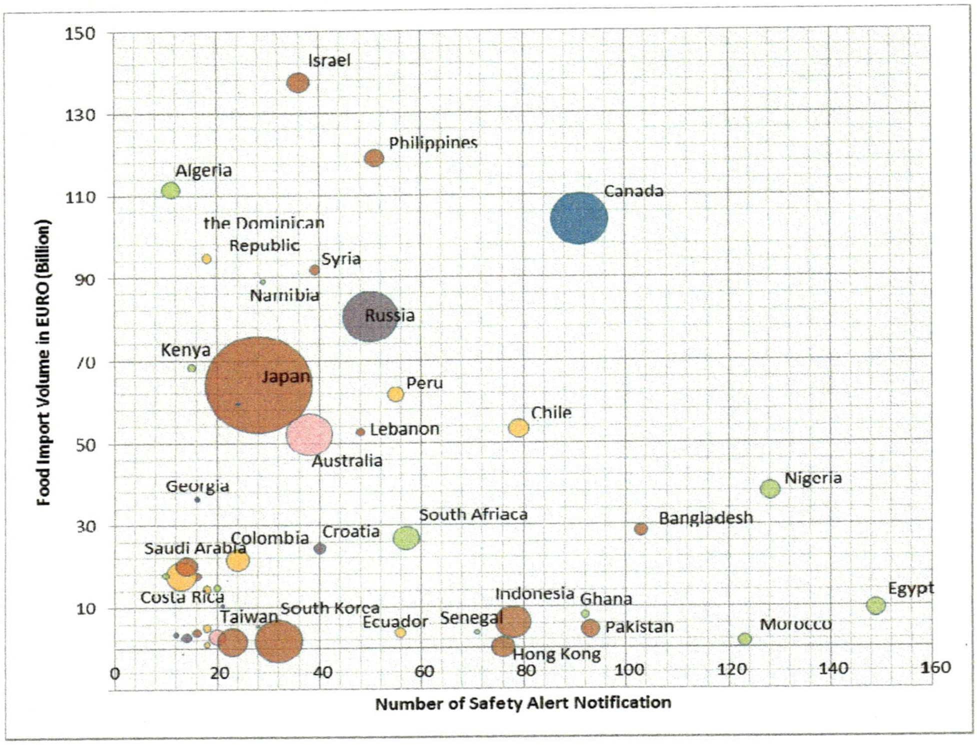

FIGURE G-4 Number of safety alert notification, food import volume and GDP of EU food importers. (enlarged version of lower left part of Figure 2A)
(Legend: Red: Asia; Pink: Oceania; Orange: Central and South America; Blue: North America; Purple: Europe; Green: Africa; Radius: Average GDP in US dollars from 2006 to 2010)

About two-thirds of food safety alerts come from nuts and seeds, fish and seafood products, and fruits and vegetables.

FIGURE G-5 Number of food safety alert notification in EURASFF by food categories 2006-2010.

Mycotoxin, mainly aflatoxin, contamination is responsible for the majority of safety alerts among nuts and seed products from India, Argentina, the United States, Iran, and China (Figure G-6A). For other food categories, the nature of the risk is more diverse, but certain patterns can still be observed from some countries. For instance, while fish and seafood from Vietnam and China show relatively even distribution in microbial contamination, chemical contamination, and physical contamination, those from Bangladesh and India are mostly rejected because of prohibited chemicals (Figure G-6B). In most cases the prohibited chemicals mentioned were restricted antibiotics, nitrofurans, and cadmium. Among fruits and vegetables, more than 300 records of aflatoxin contamination on dried figs accounts for nearly half of all the alerts on Turkish fruits and vegetables, this pattern does not hold for the other countries with problems exporting fruits and vegetables (Figure G-6C). India, one of the biggest exporters of herbs and spices, seems to have aflatoxin contamination as their biggest food safety issue, while most of the records for Thailand report microbial contamination, mainly salmonella (Figure G-7D).

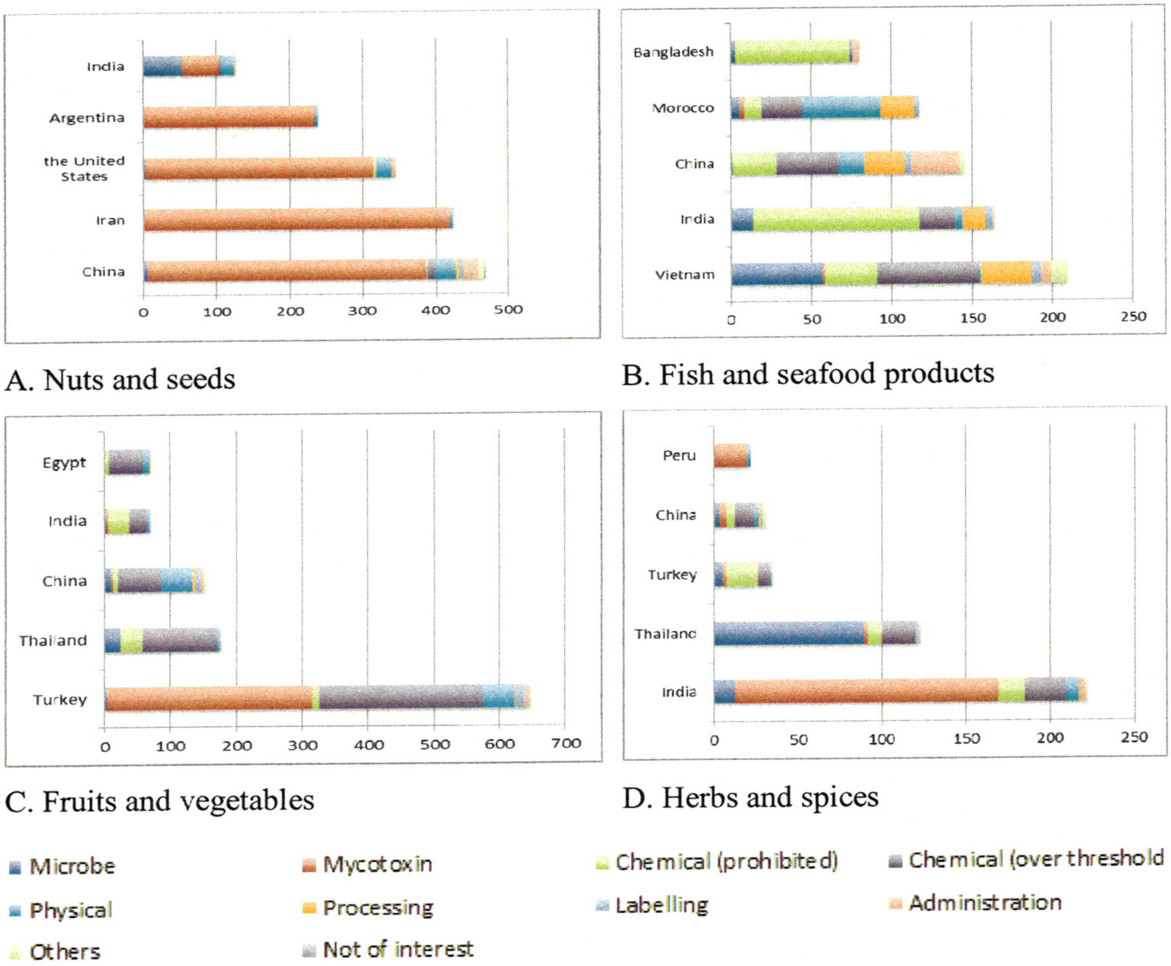

FIGURE G-6A, G-6B, G-6C, and G-6D The composition of health risks of the top four food categories in EURASFF, 2006-2010.

In Figures G-7A and G-7B, a two-dimension contour plot shows the interaction between risk and supply chain codes for Morocco and Hong Kong. The color coding indicates the number of food safety alerts which illustrates the unique patterns of food export problems both countries.

Data for rejections of consignments from Hong Kong shows problems with chemical contamination introduced in packing. Mostly, this was from chemicals from the packaging migrating onto the food.

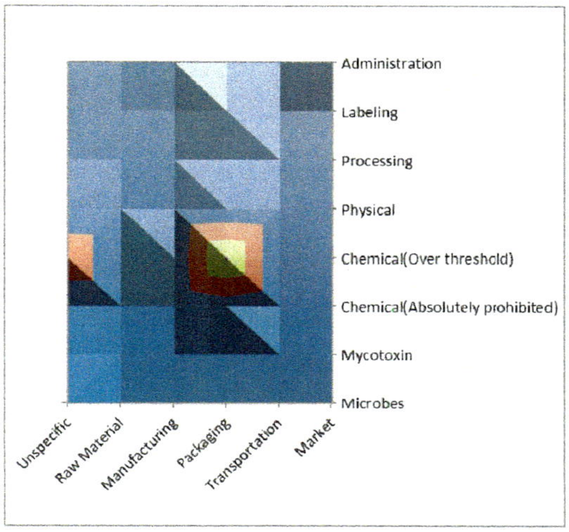

A. Hong Kong

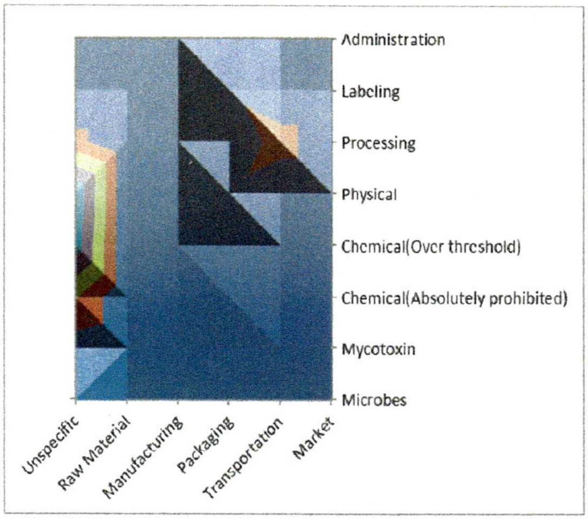

B. Morocco

0-10 10-20 20-30 30-40 40-50

Number of SafetyAlert Notification

FIGURE G-7A and G-7B EURASFF food safety alert records for all food categories coded by risk/content and supply chain stage, 2006-2010

Summary of the key findings from EURASFF data analysis:

1. Countries named in the most food safety alert reports do not show the highest incidence after adjusting for trade volume;
2. Three categories of food products (nuts and seed products, fish and seafood products, fruits and vegetables) cause over two thirds of all the food safety reports.
3. Mycotoxin, mainly aflatoxin, contamination is the most commonly reported problem. It is an issue for both developed and developing countries.

Discussion

The EURASFF system is operating under the provision of Regulation (EC) No. 178/2002, in which Article 50 lays down the requirement for RASFF notification, defining when a notification should be triggered, and how timely the information should be reported to the EU. Indeed, the RASFF has a standardized format for reporting, a real-time sharing and communication platform for all the member states, and a wide variety of data incorporating border rejections, internal communication and public safety alerts (Europa, 2009). In today's global supply chains, foods pass through dozens of countries during production. It is not always clear what the origin country is. EURASFF does document where the raw materials come from, and where the product is in transit before entering the EU, but the data is not consistent.

It is also important to consider the trade volume in assessing trends in product safety failures. Countries whose products trigger the most safety alerts do not necessarily have the most problems after adjusting for trade volume. Therefore different strategies might be taken to reduce rejections from based on the overall amount of trade countries do. The trends identified in this paper require further analysis, however. The EURASFF database has 24 categories for food products, and these categories do not align with the WTO Harmonized Codes. It would help if regulatory agencies reported Harmonized International Commodity Codes for the products they reject.

Understanding the shared and unique patterns each country faces in exporting food may be useful in planning trainings or other capacity building projects for these countries. For instance, aflatoxin is an almost universal problem, and might be best solved through global control and prevention.

More importantly, the enhanced coordination between the EU, US and other developed countries could improve food safety worldwide. The EU has just launched a system-wide re-evaluation on all approved food additives, colors and sweeteners[2], which will potentially have great impact on international trade of food products. It would be helpful for American and European regulators to cooperate on developing common standards for food additives.

---

[2] Commission Regulation (EU) No 257/2010 of 25 March 2010 setting up a programme for the re-evaluation of approved food additives in accordance with Regulation (EC) No 1333/2008 of the European Parliament and of the Council on food additives Text with EEA relevance. *Official Journal L 08*, 26/03/2010 P. 0019 – 0027. [http://eur-lex.europa.eu/LexUriServ/LexUriServ.do?uri=OJ:L:2010:080:0019:01:EN:HTML], retrieved on December 8th, 2011.

REFERENCES

Europa. 2009. *Scope of the RASFF* http://ec.europa.eu/food/food/rapidalert/rasff_scope_en.htm (accessed December 8, 2011).

———. 2011. *Questions and answers on the role and achievements of the rapid alert system for food and feed.* http://europa.eu/rapid/pressReleasesAction.do?reference=MEMO/11/729 (accessed December 8, 2011).

European Commission. 2010. *Food safety -from the farm to the fork.* http://ec.europa.eu/food/international/trade/index_en.htm (accessed December, 2011).

———. 2011. *Eurostat data navigation tree: EU27 trade since 1988 by HS2-HS4 (DS_016894).* http://epp.eurostat.ec.europa.eu/portal/page/portal/statistics/search_database# (accessed December 8, 2011).

IMF. 2010. *Report for selected countries and subjects: Taiwan.* http://www.imf.org/external/pubs/ft/weo/2010/01/weodata/weorept.aspx?sy=2000&ey=2010&scsm=1&ssd=1&sort=country&ds=.&br=1&c=528&s=NGDP_R%2CNGDP_RPCH%2CNGDP&grp=0&a=&pr.x=64&pr.y=5 (accessed December 8, 2011).

World Bank. 2010. *GDP.* http://search.worldbank.org/quickview?name=%3Cem%3EGDP%3C%2Fem%3E+%28current+US%24%29&id=NY.GDP.MKTP.CD&type=Indicators&cube_no=2&qterm=gdp (accessed December 8, 2011).

Appendix H

Strengthening Core Elements of Regulatory Systems in Developing Countries: Identifying Priorities and an Appropriate Role for the U.S. Food and Drug Administration

SECTION B: BACKGROUND AND OBJECTIVE

There is increasing recognition within the U.S. Food and Drug Administration (FDA) of the need to engage more strategically in the arena of global regulatory technical assistant and to harness more effectively the potential for multiple, cascading benefits of FDA's and others' investments in this domain. Strengthening regulatory capacity is immensely important to the FDA's ability to better monitor and ensure the safety of the supply chain for food, feed, medical products and cosmetics that enter the United States and is part of the FDA's regulatory remit to assure the quality and safety of these products at home.

The FDA is responsible for tens of millions of shipments of such commodities every year, as exemplified by the 40 percent of fresh fruit and produce in the United States that comes from other countries and the approximately 80 percent of active pharmaceutical ingredients in drugs consumed in the United States that come from outside our borders. A very large percentage of source countries represent developing economies with varying levels of regulatory oversight. Thus, we have a strong national interest in making sure that the countries of origin of these products have regulatory systems that apply, utilize and enforce standards that support product safety comparable to that in the United States. The FDA is in a position to help lead efforts with its well-recognized strength as one of the global regulatory "gold standards," and FDA's advice and collaboration is generally welcomed.

In the case of food safety, around the globe, the 20th century paradigm of a focus on food safety intervention at ports-of-entry is shifting to a focus on accountability of those involved in the food enterprise from farm to table, and accompanying national authorities' regulatory capacity and systems to set standards and to help assure that accountability. This global shift suggests that the FDA's leadership in developing risk-based approaches and preventive controls in support of food safety could contribute to new, normative global standards to be adopted through a multitude of networks, partnerships, and information-sharing venues.

In the case of medical products, drug falsification is growing in complexity, scale, geographic scope, and negative public health impact. Data limitations prevent public health policy makers from addressing adequately the issues surrounding falsified medicines in a comprehensive, systematic, and sustainable way. Increasing international trade of pharmaceuticals and sales via the internet has further facilitated the entry of falsified products into the normal supply chain. Combating falsified medicines requires collaboration at national, regional, and international levels, involving a diverse range of stakeholders.

Equally important, strengthening regulatory capacity in the developing world will reap tremendous benefits for the health and quality of life of individuals and communities in those countries. Stronger regulatory systems in other countries can help to bolster current U.S. Government (USG) investments being made in public health and development, e.g., through the President's Global Health Initiative and USG Agencies, as well as U.S. contributions through multilateral organizations, and the broader global health and development community. These efforts increasingly embrace the principles of health systems strengthening, government ownership and universal coverage. Regulatory frameworks, authorities and institutions need to be seen as central to these efforts in assuring the safety and quality of food and medical products, and in securing the full benefits of those investments; and networks of regulators need to be linked to the broader global health community. Good regulation that assures the quality and safety of food and medical products is as fundamental to the success of a health system as is the quality of any other components of a health system.

There is also much opportunity and need for greater efficiency and sustainable impact in complementing what has traditionally been a commodity based approach with a systems-approach to FDA's global engagement and what has been a traditionally ad hoc approach with what should be a sustainable, strategic approach. We need to explore the benefits and challenges of strengthening regulatory systems through dialogue and carefully delineated strategies that align well with the FDA's mission and that allow us to partner with others, both in the regulatory arena and in the broader global health arena.

SECTION C: DESCRIPTION/SPECIFICATION/WORK STATEMENT

FDA has requested that the Institute of Medicine convene a Consensus Study to assist FDA in (1) identifying the core elements of needed regulatory systems development in developing countries; and (2) prioritizing these needs and recommending a strategic approach to FDA's moving forward to address regulatory capacity needs in the context of globalization. In addition to identifying the core elements of regulatory systems development, the Consensus study would also identify potential areas in which progress could be made in a 3-5 year time frame; priorities for FDA engagement; and areas to which others (bilateral donors, development banks, foundations, academia, industry and non-governmental organizations) are best suited to contribute and how FDA might best "partner" with these other institutions to bring to their efforts that expertise that FDA has in an effort to leave a more sustainable "footprint" from both their and our resource commitments.

Questions to be explored by the Consensus Study Committee shall at least include

1. What critical issues do developing country regulatory authorities face? How are they prioritized?
2. In what ways do they participate in standard-setting processes, organizations and harmonization efforts?
3. What issues do they face in utilizing/implementing standards in a sustainable way?
4. What are the core elements of their regulatory systems and are there others that should be considered?
5. What are the major gaps in systems, institutional structures, workforce and competencies?
6. In what ways could those gaps be addressed?

7. In what ways could the U.S. FDA help address those gaps?
8. In what ways could others (as delineated above) help meet those gaps?
9. In what ways could FDA partner with other to help meet those gaps?
10. What recommendations have already been put forward to strengthen regulatory systems?
11. What obstacles exist to implement those recommendations?
12. What steps could be taken to remove those obstacles?
13. What incentives and controls would be needed to support efforts?

WORK PLAN

Committee on Regulatory Systems Capacity in Developing Countries

A multi-disciplinary committee of members comprised of global health thought leaders with expertise in regulatory affairs and health systems and representing developed and developing country regulatory authorities shall be assembled. The committee shall meet a number of times to conduct its work.

The Committee shall meet once for presentation of the charge and discussion with the sponsors (in open session) and to develop a work plan (in closed, deliberative session). Preliminary input into critical issues, gaps and priorities for developing country regulatory authorities will be given. (Questions 1-3)

The second meeting shall focus on questions 4-6, defining the core elements of regulatory systems; gaps in systems, institutional structures, workforce and competencies.

The third meeting shall include a public session with invited speakers to initiate discussions related to questions 7, 8, and 9 (ways the FDA could address those gaps and the roles of others in meeting needs).

The Committee shall then meet two additional times in closed session to develop a consensus report with recommendations on strengthening regulatory systems, identifying barriers and obstacles, ways to address those obstacles, and incentives and controls (Questions 10-13).

Product and Dissemination Plan

One consensus report shall be produced, with the potential for derivative publications in peer-reviewed journals.

Staffing

The core staff for the project shall include a senior program officer who will be the lead study director for the committee (100%); an associate program officer who will assist in all committee activities (100%); and a senior program assistant (100%) who will provide project administrative support (100%). The core team will be supplemented by a financial associate (5%); board administrative assistant (5%). The director of the Board on Global Health will provide general guidance and oversight and technical support at 15%.

Time Frame

The time frame for the Consensus Study would be 15 months, from September 2010 to December 2011.